CRITIC...

THE ...

"Those of us who are Christians need to know what those outside of our tradition are saying about love. This book provides a variety of insights to that end. In its pages, you will discover dimensions of love that are often ignored by traditional Christian teachings. Some of what is written will disturb us, but most of it will inspire us to find, in living out love around the world, that we Christians need partners. This book will help us to do that."
– **Tony Campolo, Ph.D.**, Professor Emeritus of Sociology at Eastern University, founder of the Evangelical Association for the Promotion of Education, and author of over 35 books, including *Red Letter Christians* and *The God of Intimacy and Action*

"Love pervades all of creation and has manifested itself in all the stages of human history. But we are now at a moment of our earthly life that love must be present across religious boundaries. This kind of love has in fact become a necessity for our survival, as has love and care for God's other creatures. The spiritual paradigm based on love therefore addresses our human condition in a most timely manner."
– **Seyyed Hossein Nasr, Ph.D.**, Professor of Islamic Studies at George Washington University and author of *The Heart of Islam* and *The Garden of Truth*

"This book is literally a self-contained library on the subject of love. If you are seeking information, insight, or seed thought for your own explorations, you will have it all in this amazing compilation which encourages the remembrance of who we are and why we are here – to be love."
– **Gloria D. Karpinski**, author of *Where Two Worlds Touch*

"When we read the words of those who have come before us as well of those who walk with us today, we pass on the dream that someday we will once again live our humanity. Reading the words of this book can be a reflection of what we can bring to the circle of life. I endorse all works which lead us to find our individual humanity."
– **Carlo Hawk Walker**, Elder of the Western Cherokee of Missouri, Pipe Carrier, Lakota Sundancer, co-author of the *World Peace Treaty*, and author of the *Medicines of The Heart* CD

"So many words for love! This book is full of stories and insights on love, allowing the reader to sense beyond what we normally think about love, which has been so commercialized and sexualized in our culture. Love is what can truly guide our hearts and minds, so the more we can understand this simple and yet complex aspect of being sentient, the more we can fully be alive in this changing world."
– **Kris Steinnes**, founder of the Women of Wisdom Foundation and author of the award winning *Women of Wisdom: Empowering the Dreams and Spirit of Women*

THE PENTACLE

The Oracle Institute chose the Pentacle as a symbol for its humanitarian work after researching, designing, and considering dozens of potential logos. We selected the Pentacle because of its noble history and the fact that the Truth about this ancient symbol – like all Truth – needs to be revealed.

The oldest known use of the Pentacle dates to 3,000 B.C.E., when it was used by the Sumerians and Babylonians to depict angles and provide directional orientation. Scholars believe that these civilizations also used the Pentacle for astrological purposes, assigning the five points to the planets: Mercury, Mars, Jupiter, Saturn, and Venus.

The great Greek mathematician Pythagoras was fascinated by the Pentacle. He recognized in its geometry a division of lines which resulted in the "golden ratio," an emblem of perfection that was incorporated into Greek art and architecture. Pythagoras was the first person to refer to the harmony and balance of the Cosmos, and his followers embraced the mystical concept of the soul's eternal existence through the process of transmigration. His followers also ascribed the points of the Pentacle to the five classical elements: earth, air, fire, water, and ideas.

Later, Roman Emperor Constantine used the symbol as a seal and an amulet. When the Roman Catholic Church was formed, some Christians adopted the Pentacle as a representation of the five wounds of Jesus Christ, which pierced: his two hands, his two feet, and his side. Other Christians associated the Pentacle with the five senses: touch, taste, smell, hearing, and sight.

In medieval times, the Pentacle was associated with the legends of King Arthur and the Knights of the Round Table, who were said to possess five virtues: friendship, generosity, chastity, courtesy, and piety. During the Renaissance, Leonardo da Vinci revived the Pentacle when he illustrated that the proportions of the human body symmetrically align within this sublime shape.

Today, at the close of the Fourth Spiritual Paradigm, it is fair to say that the Pentacle represents the five primary religions: Hinduism, Judaism, Christianity, Buddhism, and Islam. May these now ancient religions update their teachings and unify their wisdom traditions in order to guide humanity toward the utopian state described by their prophets as "heaven on earth."

And at the dawn of the prophesied Fifth Spiritual Paradigm, may we recall the most glorious and enduring use of the Pentacle – as a symbol for Venus, the goddess of Love. We, at The Oracle Institute, believe that it is this very aspect of the Supreme Being and of our own Divine nature which will inspire each of us to seek the perennial promise of the Pentacle:

Spiritual Enlightenment

THE L☉VE:
Of the Fifth Spiritual Paradigm

Book II of a Foundational Trilogy

Written in Association with:
The Oracle Institute

Narrated by:
Laurel
(pen name of Laura M. George, J.D.)

Edited by:
Dave & the Pats

Book I of the Trilogy:
The Truth: About the Five Primary Religions

Book III of the Trilogy:
The Light: And the New Human

The Oracle Institute Press, LLC

Published by:
The Oracle Institute Press, LLC

A Division of:
The Oracle Institute

P.O. Box 368
Hamilton, VA 20159
www.TheOralceInstitute.org

Publisher's Cataloging-in-Publication Data

   The love : of the fifth spiritual paradigm / written in
      association with the Oracle Institute ; narrated by
      Laurel ; edited by Dave & The Pats.
         p. cm.
         Includes bibliographical references.
         LCCN: 2009923785
         ISBN-13: 978-0-9773929-2-6
         ISBN-10: 0-9773929-2-9

         1. Love--Religious aspects. 2. Religion.
      3. Religions. 4. Spiritual life.   I. Laurel, 1961-
      II. Oracle Institute.

      BL626.4.L68 2010   205'.677
                                    QBI09-600012

Printed and bound in the United States

Cover & Interior Design by:
Kate, Ink – www.KateInk.com

Fine Art by:
Brian Bartunek

TABLE OF CONTENTS

INTRODUCTION

The Nature of Love During the Fourth Spiritual Paradigm

Oh Child of God:

If you can see without using your eyes,
If you can hear without using your ears,
If you can feel without using your hands, and
If you can know without using your mind,
Then you are bound to teach those who have yet to understand.

Such is the nature of Love.

Recently, the chasm has grown between those who are embracing Love and those who are not. Some refer to this phenomenon as spiritual polarization. Others opine that the forces of "Light" and "Dark" are preparing for battle. And still others pretend that nothing is happening at all.

Nevertheless, a few brave souls recognize that our current problems stem from spiritual confusion and stagnation ... from a lack of Love. We wish to honor these advanced souls, some of whom have contributed to this anthology. And we applaud all the other bearers of light who are working tirelessly to lessen the divide created by outdated belief systems – such as those propagated by the five primary religions.

Sadly, religion has become the new racism. Sectarian strife has now replaced skin tone, economic disparity, and national boundaries to constitute the greatest barrier facing humanity. Yet, the problem is so easily solved and our future so readily secured, we must not lose heart. Time is of the essence, as depicted by the hourglass on this book cover. But we have the ability to attain the glorious utopian future intended by our Creator.

In order to achieve this goal, however, we must first accept the fact that our fate lies in our own hands. Quite simply, we are responsible for each other and for our planet. Additionally, we must choose better leaders if we wish to end the current chaos and pass into the prophesied New Millennium. Thus, it is incumbent upon all those who have passed into unconditional Love to help us through this period of turmoil. Current teachers are bound to this sacred task just as their predecessors were obligated before them. Abraham, Buddha, Jesus, and Muhammad – these were the masters of the Fourth Spiritual Paradigm. They were the messengers of old, who sacrificed all in order to guide us toward God.

Unfortunately, though, the prophets' prescription of Truth, Love, and Light has not taken root because men of power purposely twisted their Divine messages. Indeed, rather than promote all the prophets' hallowed instructions and build a spiritual Tower of Truth, the leaders of the five primary religions created mythological mayhem – a Tower of Babel – the direct result of focusing on just *one* prophet or just *one* holy book as the source of Divine guidance.

God knew that we would one day invent modes of mass travel and mass communication. God also knew that we would one day have the ability to study the divergent belief systems represented by the five primary religions. Ultimately, then, God intended for us to analyze these disparate paths, note the similarities, accept the universal themes, and discard the rest – the outdated dogma that no longer makes sense in a more sophisticated 21st Century world. Thus, it was preordained that humanity would undertake the arduous process of assimilating the Divine messages of all the faiths. The Oracle Institute is dedicated to this difficult mission.

So today, we face the Herculean task of synthesizing the entire collection of sacred works deposited on Earth. Inevitably, these questions arise: Whose job is it to read and interpret the ancient scriptures? Moreover, who can be trusted with such an important task? If we ask our local minister, rabbi, priest, or imam for assistance, will they be impartial or do they have a vested interest in promoting their own religion? Exactly who is qualified to judge the merits of these now ancient belief systems?

I would argue that each one us – in our own way, using our own abilities – has this sacred duty of inquiry. I also would argue that this duty cannot be delegated. Only you can decide for yourself what "feels" like spiritual truth inspired by God, and what "feels" like man-made doctrine produced by fallible human beings. For if you do the research yourself, you will be able to discern for yourself what constitutes Truth, Love, and Light.

In this regard, perhaps, we are in "End Times." Perhaps humanity finally is ready to end the monopoly of the five primary religions. Are you ready to start trusting yourself with the care of your soul? Have you begun a personal journey of faith – the only path to spiritual enlightenment and reunion with God?

Once you embark on a quest for spiritual truth, you will be amazed at all there is to learn and digest. In fact, once you start searching you may never stop. I was so enraptured by my own quest that I eventually read enough material to write a book of my own! It was the first book of The Oracle Institute trilogy: *The Truth: About the Five Primary Religions*. In

The Truth, I summarized what I uncovered about orthodox religion, and I explained why none of these religions felt like "home." To this day, I am searching for my spiritual tribe.

But that's okay ... I am at peace. I accept that I am a truth seeker, and I accept that others may need a more defined spiritual base. For me, though, the quest itself is my religion. As I continue to search, I think of myself as a spiritual sponge, soaking up as much material as I can, squeezing out what doesn't make sense, and retaining all the good stuff – the knowledge and experience that gets me a little closer to enlightenment. I call this the *Saddha* process of soul growth. Simply put, *Saddha* is a Buddhist word that means faith based on firsthand experience and trustful confidence. It is the opposite of blind faith – which is what most religions teach.

Once you start processing religious history for yourself, you may discover some startling truths (and some outright horrors). First, each prophet came with a new message from God. Second, each message was a little more sophisticated than the last. Third, there was a common theme to the messages ... can you guess what it is? *Love*.

Let me give you a concrete example. The Jewish prophet Moses, who lived around 1,250 B.C.E., delivered the Ten Commandments, most of which were prohibitions against immoral acts. Then, Jesus was born around 4 B.C.E., and he added what I call the Eleventh Commandment – Love thy neighbor – which requires affirmative moral action. When Muhammad arrived around 570 C.E., he brought an even more advanced message. Muhammad taught that all the Abrahamic faiths should join in brotherly Love (whereas, Jesus only approached other Jews with his message). Thus, God's plan for us became more and more clear: **We should extend Love to everyone.**

It also is fascinating to consider the larger context of the history of religion. Prior to the Big Bang, which scientists estimate took place approximately fourteen billion years ago, there was a period of perfect union. Everything – both ethereal and material – resided together in unity. This was the **First Spiritual Paradigm**, when God was all that existed, and humans were either part of God or, at a minimum, an unmanifested thought form within the Divine consciousness.

Thereafter, the Big Bang occurred and with it, separation. In a manner yet to be fully understood, God splintered and expanded with thunderous thermodynamic force. It was the beginning of life, but also disunity. In *The Holy Bible*, this cosmic event is described as the "fall of mankind." Indeed, our separation from God was so painful that early man struggled to adopt a meaningful belief system. Eventually, Goddess religions emerged, and for twenty thousand years humanity worshipped Divine feminine energy as the life-giving force. This was the **Second Spiritual Paradigm.**

Then, around 5000 B.C.E., humanity split the Godhead and the era of polytheism began. It was at this juncture that we invented the Sumerian, Egyptian, Greek, Roman, and Hindu pantheon of gods and goddesses. This was the **Third Spiritual Paradigm.**

Later, a Hebrew tribe rediscovered monotheism, recognizing the truth that God must be a singular entity. However, rather than imagining God as one source comprised of both masculine and feminine energies, the religions of Abraham made a critical error – they attached a gender to God. In so doing, Judaism, Christianity, and Islam ignited a new theological era approximately two thousand years ago. This was and remains the **Fourth Spiritual Paradigm.**

The Fourth Spiritual Paradigm has been marked by impressive cultural, economic, and technological growth. Indeed, because most of this planet has been worshipping a male God, masculine energy has been tapped to fuel all sorts of intellectual endeavors, resulting in the Industrial Age, the Information Age, and now an unprecedented era that has yet to be defined. This is the upside of the masculine half of God – what sages call "creative" energy.

Yet, we also have experienced the downside of masculine energy, including the development of dangerous industrial chemicals, manufacturing waste, immoral biotechnology, and terrifying military weapons that now threaten our very survival. In sum, the negative trickle-down effect of our perceiving God as a male force (with a male heir, in the case of Christianity), has been the suppression of the feminine half of God – what mystics call "wisdom" energy.

Thus, the Fourth Spiritual Paradigm has been a period of unfettered progress in terms of intellectual invention and concrete application, but it also has been a period of social disorder marked by ethical inconsistency and spiritual confusion. That's because, as a whole, the world has prized the pursuit of knowledge and innovation at the expense of philosophical purity and moral virtue. The net result is that our intellect now overshadows our wisdom, as evidenced by the fact that our technology now exceeds our capacity to comprehend or contain its raw power.

It would be incorrect, however, to equate feminine energy with Love. Rather, both masculine and feminine energy are needed to produce (or reproduce) Love – the most powerful force in the Universe. This is why many people in the New Age movement think of God as pure Love. This is an overly simplistic view of Deity, but one that is much closer to the truth.

In the esoteric traditions, masters describe the masculine half of God as the creative force in the Universe, and the feminine half of God as the wisdom force. They are correct – based on our dualistic perception of reality – that both energies exist and that both energies must be brought into balance if we are to attain spiritual equilibrium. And what, exactly, will happen once we collectively reach this state of equipoise? When the Sacred Feminine fully reemerges? We will reach the **Fifth Spiritual Paradigm.**

As foreshadowed in our holy books, the Fifth Spiritual Paradigm will be an era of compassion such as the world has never seen – a paradigm based on the Golden Rule, on Love. It is humanity's destiny to reach this prophesied paradise while still on Earth. Contrary to the teachings of most religions, we need not die or go to "heaven" to attain this utopian state.

However, we control how and when this new spiritual paradigm arrives. God is not sending a Messiah to save the righteous, or a Mahdi to destroy the sinners ... which are many. The truth is that we are responsible for what takes place on this planet. Always remember that free will was our primary gift from the Creator. Consequently, we hold the power to save ourselves and we also hold the power to destroy ourselves, whether through volitional stupidity or through continuing apathy. In sum, if we ignore the complexities of our time much longer, future generations may lose the ability to birth the New Millennium. One of the worst scenarios, of course, is that we bomb ourselves back to the Stone Age. A do-over. Atlantis all over again.

Or we can build the New Atlantis, the New Jerusalem, the New World – whatever you wish to call it. We now have that power because God, through the prophets and the other masters (scientists, philosophers, and ethicists), has given us all the information we need to manifest the Fifth Spiritual Paradigm.

We've had plenty of time to explore our world and learn our lessons during the Second, Third, and Fourth Paradigms. We've tried various modes of conflict resolution, yet war is still our preferred method. We've seen what happens when financial power is placed in the hands of the few, yet we are surprised by greed and corruption. And we've witnessed the consequences when political leaders roll back freedoms and religious leaders proclaim dominion over our souls – apathy, fear, and self-loathing abound.

Hence, after thousands of years of practical experience, we should know how to preserve this planet, how to protect the wildlife, and how to Love each other. Moreover, after thousands of years of preaching spiritual unity, orthodox religion should have brought some measure of calm to the planet. Instead, we may rightly conclude that religion has done a much better job at promoting division, bloodshed, and tears. For true believers with fair minds and pure hearts, there can be no doubt: The five primary religions were created by men of power – not the prophets, and not God. *Surely, if God created a religion, we would be living in harmony by now.*

In their defense, the five man-made religions were created during earlier phases of our collective spiritual evolution – when humanity was uneducated and prone to superstitious thinking. For instance, Christianity was born of a mythological medley comprised of Egyptian legends, Greek gods, and Roman holidays. Thus, the Virgin Mary needed to rival the Egyptian goddess Isis, who magically conceived her son too. The Greek god Hades blended into Satan, the *New Testament* lord of the underworld. Like numerous caesars before him, Jesus was elevated to "son of God" status by the Roman Empire. And Christ's birthday was substituted for the festival to the Roman god Mithras.

In the 21st Century, we no longer need bind ourselves to the cosmology or mythology of our ancestors. We currently possess the scientific knowledge and advanced moral code to reject these outdated and often ridiculous belief systems. On the other hand, we apparently lack the wisdom to craft a more sophisticated religion, as no unifying theosophy has been presented to or accepted by the masses. The result is a spiritual vacuum, in which some people desperately cling to the old religions for comfort, while others struggle to synthesize primordial mysteries with the latest discoveries. Clearly, the world is suffering on a spiritual level. We are writhing in pain, like a young mother who is about to give birth …

Not surprisingly, astrologers report that we *are* birthing a new age – we are leaving the Age of Pisces and entering the Age of Aquarius. It takes approximately 2100 years for a millennial change, with the sum total of the twelve astrological ages adding up to the roughly 26,000 years it takes for our planet to complete its precessional orbit around the Sun. Our current precession ends on December 21, 2012 – a date that is looming in the minds of many people around the world due to the ending of the Mayan Calendar, the many End Times prophecies contained in the holy books, and the oral teachings of various indigenous cultures.

The stage in between each astrological millennium is often referred to as a "Great Cusp." Currently, we are experiencing a Great Cusp – the period of turbulence that always precedes a major paradigm shift. The last time we experienced a Great Cusp was when Jesus was crucified. That event and the social unrest that followed birthed Christianity – the religion which has come to define the Fourth Spiritual Paradigm. The Roman Empire faced many crises during the last Great Cusp. Indeed, that empire eventually fell as a result of the social, economic, philosophical, and spiritual challenges presented at the dawn of the Piscean Age. As more closely examined in some of the essays which follow, we face even greater challenges at the dawn of the Age of Aquarius.

Given the present spiritual chaos, The Oracle Institute believes it would be a huge step forward if the world would simply admit that "the emperor is wearing no clothes" ... that orthodox religion does not have the answers we seek. Additionally, we believe that each of us must prepare to discern spiritual truth for ourselves. Such honesty and courage is called for if we are to address the unprecedented challenges of the New Millennium. To do otherwise is to risk making the wrong decisions (or making no decisions at all), in which case we may not survive the Great Cusp. Without overstating the matter, life now is being threatened on a global scale. The only way to reach the Fifth Spiritual Paradigm is to accept that massive change is upon us.

As part of our preparation, let us reinstall the Sacred Feminine to her rightful seat beside the male half of the Godhead. Let us ask for wisdom – a Divine power which will balance us, help us to survive the Great Cusp, and manifest the Fifth Spiritual Paradigm.

So rest a while with this book. Catch your breath. And realize that at this critical juncture, there is only one spiritual concept upon which we need agree:

Love is the Way

We hope you enjoy the following collection of Love poems, articles, and essays. These works have been generously contributed by lightworkers who are doing their best to preach and practice the way of Love.

We thank them for guiding us into the Fifth Spiritual Paradigm.

May this book inspire everyone who reads it, and
May this book energize the Fifth Spiritual Paradigm.
For the good of All and according to the free will of All.

So it mote be.

'ERETS HAQODESH

All roads lead up to Palestine, but none from it. ...
To be buried in Palestine is to be buried under an altar. ...
Further, the atmosphere of the Holy Land makes wise.
They expressed their Love of the land as follows:
He who walks four yards in the land is assured of happiness
in the world to come ....

Is it not the gate of heaven? All nations agree on this point.
Christians believe that the souls are gathered there and
then lifted up to heaven.
Islam teaches that it is the place of the ascent ...
and the place of gathering on the day of resurrection.
Everybody turns to it in prayer and visits it in pilgrimage. ...

This sacred place serves to remind men and
to stimulate them to Love God.

Rabbi Judah Halevi (1075–1141), *The Kuzari*

While all life forms instinctively seek a safe and healthy environment, surely mankind is the most territorial species on the Earth.
To prove this point, one need only admit how willing we are to
kill each other over a patch of ground and how reluctant we are to share
our home with others.

Consequently, whether we prefer the view of a pristine natural vortex or
of a man-made sectarian "holy land" – *'erets haqodesh* in Hebrew – we now
must accept as fact that this planet belongs to us all. Man-made borders are
not ordained; they are the result of historical preferences and prejudices that
the world community should no longer honor or suffer. Furthermore, the survival of our planet, one of the most precious gifts given to us by our Creator,
now is in jeopardy. Thus, the time has come for us to practice ecological Love
and view the entire Earth as sacred ground.

PRAYER FOR MOTHER EARTH

By Joyce Pace Byrd, L.P.C.

Mother, may I speak of your heart?
As one of your many daughters,
may I join my voice to the great song?

You have brought us forth on this bejeweled planet
from the marrow of your being,
nourished and sustained us,
enfolded us in the communion of Love,
enabled us to participate in the great symphony of creation.

What joy you offer this family of life –
to greet mornings with the brilliant hibiscus and sun-bright finches,
or scores of the diligent earthworms who silently aerate your soils.
What delight to come upon bold fans of fungi
springing up from the forest floor in the dance of renewal,
or to watch soaring bats and feathery moths
as they leap and pirouette through an evening ballet.

What joy to feel your gentle breath ruffling the ferns and grasses,
or the pounding of the mighty wind-streams
that bring the rains and clean the air;
to be enchanted by giants of the sea as they breach and dive,
while tiny corals remind us there are worlds within worlds,
like the unseen currents undulating in sky and stone,
nourishing your precious body.

Had I all of eternity I could make only brief note
of the miracles you bring forth each day.
So seldom have I told you,
so seldom given thanks,
so seldom been attuned to the great gift of incarnation:
the precious opportunity to hold consciousness in a body
upheld and sustained in the pulsing of your heart.

Only now, dear Mother, do we begin to understand
that we have taken all from you,
never realizing that you – like every other being –
need care, regeneration, and Love.
Only now do we glimpse your intricate complexity
and grasp that we have the power
to surround you with discord or harmony.

Though I am small and unpracticed, it is my privilege to serve you.
In wonder and gratitude, I join my voice in unceasing hymns of praise.
I lend all of my energies to your purpose
and send what strength I have directly to your heart.

———≈◆≈———

Dear One: You and I have embarked upon an adventure of the soul … a
walk up Lovers' Lane. Why up? Because in the next four hundred pages or so,
we will explore the many forms of Love expressed by human beings, starting
with our Love for this planet and culminating with true Love of God.

It is therefore fitting that we began with a prayer – thank you, Joyce! She
and the other authors in this anthology have come together to challenge,
guide, confuse, and inspire you … but mostly to Love you. At the end of each
selection, please send the author your Love in return. And then say a prayer for
our entire world. It is good practice for the Fifth Spiritual Paradigm – sending
your Love to strangers.

Today, I watched the inauguration of our 44th President, Barack Obama.
I purposely waited to begin writing my interior comments, hoping that he
would say something about Love. Clearly, President Obama is a change agent.
Surely, he knows that we are in a Great Cusp. But does he know that Love is
the key to the paradigm shift – the key to the change about which he so often
speaks?

"What if the mightiest word is Love?" asked his friend Elizabeth
Alexander in her inaugural poem. There … she said it … she knows! But of
course she knows – she is a poet. Can a politician speak of Love? He can if
he's here to help birth the Fifth Spiritual Paradigm! We shall see …

For now, for us, onward and upward – starting with our Love of Earth and
then moving steadily, fearlessly, and warmly Godward.

SOPHIA AND SUSTAINABILITY

By Bernice H. Hill, Ph.D.

Today we face a major challenge: *Our relationship to Earth is in extreme jeopardy.* Addressing this challenge requires a basic and swift evolution of our collective consciousness. Pollution and global warming are occurring at much faster rates than scientists had predicted. We, as a species, have ignored the renewal needs of our planet, treating it like a combined convenience store and garbage dump. At this point, depletion and spoilage are evident and undeniable.

Sustainability of the Earth may be considered in a variety of ways. There is the practical: China is reported to be investing $165 billion to reduce pollution. There is the daring: A well-known scientist has proposed firing rockets to release sulfur into the atmosphere to slow the warming. And there is the religious: Recently, the Christian community formed "Creation Care," a program of prayer and social action.

A Jungian perspective, however, looks at the underlying issues of a matter. Such an analysis would be long term and more subtle in approach. Jungians would consider the archetypes, the worldviews, and the processes in the natural psyche that apply to our attitudes toward the Earth and our growing environmental problems. A Jungian approach would search for a principle of psychological and spiritual transcendence – an awareness that we require a higher level of integration and that it is now time for us to become "citizens of the world."

Archetypes are those primordial, universal energy patterns that form our behaviors, attitudes, and values, both individually and collectively. They carry the full range of possibilities – positive and negative – for a particular theme. They are found in our myths, symbols, dreams, visions, and cultural stories. A prime example is Joseph Campbell's exploration in *The Hero with a Thousand Faces.*

In considering our relationship to the Earth, the archetype of "Sophia" rises to prominence. Jung has written that Sophia is the archetype of greatest universality. She is found throughout all cultures and all times. She carries great wisdom and an all-embracing erotic vision of life that is closely tied to the Earth. She is not just an abstract principle, but a path, encoded in our fundamental processes, that moves us toward a goal. If we have a deeper understanding of Sophia's principles, we will see she requires us – on many levels – to look at the quality of our living experience.

Early Sophia: The First and Second Spiritual Paradigms

The earliest forms of Sophia emphasized her power and influence on Earth and the human psyche. In the ancient text *Hypostasis of the Archons* found at Nag Hammadi, it is written that Sophia pre-existed God and gave birth to the male godhead. When God says there are "no other gods before me," Sophia chastises his arrogance. She also claims her spiritual authority over the ethereal First Spiritual Paradigm by saying, "You are wrong, Samuel" (meaning Lord of the blind).

Sophia then stretches forth her finger to send light into matter and follows the light down into the region of "Chaos." This power of Sophia within the Earth realm was described in numerous early recordings:

> *I am nature, the universal Mother, mistress of all the elements,*
> *primordial child of time, sovereign of all things spiritual, queen of the*
> *dead, queen of the immortals. My nod governs the shining heights of*
> *heaven, the wholesome sea breezes, the lamentable silences of the world*
> *below. I know the cycles of growth and decay.*

Lucius Apuleius Platonicus, Metamorphoses

Certainly, from the beginning of time Sophia has been represented by the Great Mother from whom all life arises and is sustained. She was worshipped during the Second Spiritual Paradigm from 25,000 to 5000 B.C.E., an immense period of time in human history. Her fecundity is honored in the corpulent statue of *Venus of Willendorf.*

Themes which reveal the intertwining of nature and spirit and the paradox of life and death are everywhere in images of the Sacred Feminine. In ancient Mesopotamia, she was depicted as Ishtar, a goddess with a winged headdress who held the ring of divine authority. She was sculpted with owls at her feet, which represent the secrets of the underworld and death.

Venus of Willendorf

In pre-dynastic Egypt, Sophia was often shown as a bird goddess with her arms uplifted, again like wings. Another frequent association was with the lion – a fire symbol. This theme was evident in the statues of the Egyptian goddess Sekhmet. It was said that Sekhmet, carrying the paradox of fierce feminine power, would return in times of epoch change. At the temple in Luxor, there are 17 statues of Sekhmet.

The uniting of paradox is even more evident in Isis, the great goddess of the two lands of light and dark in Egypt. She was the agent for the resurrection of her consort, Osiris, who was dismembered and killed by his brother Set. With the resurrected Osiris, Isis conceives her son Horus, and thereby brings forth another basic symbol of transformation: *The triumph of life over death*.

Sophia in the Pantheon: The Third Spiritual Paradigm

For millennia, Sophia's preeminence was evident. In the city states of Greece and Rome, her qualities were expressed through the ancient goddess Cybele, who also was shown with lions – thought to represent the fiery and ecstatic state associated with her worship. However, Cybele began to fade from Roman culture around 200 B.C.E., as did the goddesses worshipped elsewhere in the ancient world: Isis in Egypt, Artemis in Ephesus, and Demeter in Greece. For example, Athena, the Greek goddess of wisdom, was redefined as the daughter of Zeus and demoted to the goddess of civilization. Occasionally, she still was portrayed with a reminder of her heritage – an owl in her hand – but insult was added to injury when Athena was reduced to the inventor of the bridle to tame horses.

The final stages of Greek culture marked an even greater decline in the power of Sophia. In particular, when Aristotle stressed the world of ideas and rationality, logic or *logos* – which had been Sophia's domain – became defined as masculine. Indeed, the modern definition of "sophism" means a specious or even deceitful argument – a further denigration of her memory.

Thereafter, Buddhism, Christianity, and Islam (*circa* 550 B.C.E., 50 C.E., and 600 C.E., respectively), all make mention of Sophia; yet, each tradition adapts her to their own cosmology. Simultaneously, these traditions become increasingly critical of nature. The goal of all these religions is to rise above the Earth and achieve nirvana, heaven, or paradise.

The strongest belief in Sophia was retained by the Gnostic Christians (2nd and 3rd Centuries C.E.). While some Gnostic sects saw Sophia as

God's playmate, existing before the manifest world and responsible for helping man journey back to Source, dualistic Gnostics blamed her curiosity for the fall of the soul into matter. This was deemed a tragedy, for the material world was seen as unworthy. As a result, dualistic Gnostics condemned sexuality, viewed women as the cause of humanity's problems, and adopted the patriarchal style of the times. And so Sophia became split: Her more negative aspect was called the "Whore of Babylon" and Earth was lost as a valued expression of creation.

Sophia Veiled: The Fourth Spiritual Paradigm

Sophia, in her orthodox Christian form, surfaced as the Virgin Mary, mother of Jesus. According to Caitlin Mathews in her book, Sophia: the Goddess of Wisdom, the Catholic Church began to incorporate Mary into Christian art around 400 C.E., by depicting her as a vessel of rebirth and higher transformation. And in 680 C.E., the Catholic Church pronounced the doctrine of Mary's "Immaculate Conception." Later, during the Renaissance, Mary was usually seen as a divine protector, a figure that mankind could appeal to in times of trouble. Over time, she became increasingly elevated, and in 1950 the Catholic Church declared the "Assumption of Mary" into heaven. Jung wrote that while it was good that the church finally recognized the importance of the Sacred Feminine, it had exalted Mary in the masculine sense, and this would be injurious to the feminine principle of wholeness.

Yet, underground Christian sects managed to retain Sophia's connection to nature through the Black Madonna. The Black Madonna was sometimes called the "Lady of the Caves," where her statues were often hidden. The blackness may have related to the fact that, if found, the church burned the statues as pagan. Her darkness, however, may have reflected earlier times, for Isis and Cybele were black of skin. There also is ample evidence that the Black Madonna may have represented Mary Magdalene in those sects which believed that she was Jesus' wife. Today, the Black Madonna is the Mary of indigenous people, and she is found in Poland, Spain, and Mexico.

While the Catholic Church essentially ignored nature or viewed it as sinful, it is important to recognize that some Christian mystics retained the integration of nature and spirit: Saint Hildegard of Bingen (1098–1179 C.E.), Saint Francis of Assisi (1181–1286 C.E.), and Jacob Boehme (1575–1624 C.E.) all spoke of their Love for the natural world as an expression of God. They believed our spirit's journey was vitally intertwined with the Earth. And many writers believe that the Sophian message included the essential teachings of Jesus. As Jung explained in *Answer to Job*, Sophia softened Yahweh of the *Old Testament* and helped him to remember principles of compassion.

The fundamental identification of Sophia as an archetype for humanity's relationship to nature resurfaced recently in newly discovered ancient texts. Of particular note is the *Gospel of Mary*, written in the 2nd Century but not found until 1896 C.E. (with fragments finally published in the Western world in 1996). In this *Gnostic Gospel*, Mary Magdalene is described as an intimate of Christ who is mentored by him, and she is recognized as a leader of the early church who supported and taught the apostles. Tapestries of this period also illustrate the prominence of the relationship between Jesus and Mary Magdalene.

The Gospel of Mary further records new teachings of Jesus, such as, "All that is born, all that is created and all the elements of nature are interwoven and united with each other." Jesus goes on to say, "All that is composed will be decomposed." This is the fundamental Sophian challenge: *to view ourselves as a process unfolding within nature*. Such a view places us beyond religious dogma and opens us to the ongoing process of creation.

For us to mature as a species, we must open to the deeper capacity of our psyches and come to reflect on its foundational aspects. Sophia, as an inclusive archetype, understands "the dark." The wholeness she encompasses includes nature as our container and our destroyer, and we need to grapple with that truth to comprehend its wisdom. Theologian Henri Corbin wrote, "It is not the incarnate Sophia's role to bind or connect us to the earth, but to help us recognize that our understanding of ourselves as separate from the earth is a delusion."

Few paintings illustrate the integrative power of the Sacred Feminine more beautifully than this painting by Alex Grey entitled *Sophia*. Here we see the themes of descent and the balancing of opposites – the basic principles of soul work. It is evident in the

Sophia by Alex Grey

two lower circles: one containing Demeter, who is the nurturer or She who brings forth new life; and the other encircling Kali, who is the transformer or She who demands the sacrifice that leads to truth. The themes are underscored in the serpentine caduceus – the active equilibrium of opposing forces coming together in such a way as to create a higher form. And the theme is driven home by the flower held in Sophia's hand, the child pulled close to her heart, and in the symbols of the *Kabbalah*, whose purpose is to connect the finite world with the infinite.

Post-Modern Sophia: The Fifth Spiritual Paradigm

Sophia is emerging in this time of immense change to challenge us once again with her wisdom. She instructs us through her basic principles: the creative tension of opposites; descent journeys; and transcendence to a new form. Repetitive experience with each of these principles changes the nature of our ego, our reality, and our relationship to the "other." These principles demonstrate the dynamism embedded in an energy matrix of nature and the direction of our soul's evolution. Awakening to these vital underlying patterns raises intense questions about our relationship to nature – questions that now need to be confronted.

First, we must acknowledge that our culture is unconsciously imbued with a masculine God. Philosophers have pointed out that humanity's image of itself will necessarily be translated into its image of the Divine (and vice versa). This means that human beings create the kinds of gods they are prepared to receive at a given historical period of time. Thus, for twenty thousand years humanity conceived a matriarchal deity, for about four thousand years we worshipped both male and female deities, and for the past two thousand years we have promoted a patriarchal deity. Sadly, wars are now being fought over rival definitions of this male God.

Second, we need to accept that Jesus taught during a patriarchal era (as did Muhammad). Thereafter, some of Jesus' teachings were adopted by the Catholic Church – an invention of the Roman Empire – which framed God around a masculine preference and then projected a patriarchal model on all institutions. Today, the continued denigration of the Sacred Feminine and of the material world is a direct result of a Christian worldview which lacks an awareness of Sophia as an equal component of the godhead and the Earth as a living entity.

In contrast to this patriarchal view, consider the following quote:

> *Source is omnipresent, omnipotent and omniscient. There is a force – a Source of consciousness, in which we all reside (even the bad guys) and of which we are composed. The True God is beyond form. No being can ever be separate from God because all things in form manifestation take place within the Source. Some parts have forgotten their Divine identity – have no memory of the wholeness of which they are a part. They compete for power with others, and they neither acknowledge, nor comprehend the endless supply of Living Power, energy, and Love that eternally circulates between Source and all living things which are manifest.*

Ashayana Deane, Voyagers

This is the integral perspective: *Earth is a natural part of an immense living dynamic process, which, like us, arises from Source.*

Another reason for our polarization is that in America, we keep death hidden. It is very un-American to die. It's a failure because America is a warrior culture and we should never lose a battle. This fear and denial of death gets translated into a fear of nature, a denial of matter itself, and a devaluing of the Earth. Jung wrote that death becomes the most important issue to examine after mid-life. It is a question we must wrestle with, for death draws the material and ethereal worlds together and Sophia represents a bridge in-between.

The Challenge: Individual Responsibility and Mother Earth

Sophia is a revitalizing archetype because she has faith in the living processes. Her presence balances the male godhead, reconciles dark and light, blends nature and spirit, and thereby generates a wider understanding of the human condition while on Earth. Sophia also asks us to be more philosophical (i.e., *philo … sophia*), about our own life and death experience. In this regard, she offers us a living Universe that is much more immense and complex than that encompassed within our present patriarchal view.

For example, Sophian philosophy relates to the sustainability of the Earth as opposed to the "Rapture," an apocalyptic myth that Christian fundamentalists believe will be fulfilled when the Earth is destroyed and they are transported to heaven. Such a belief system is based on fear and represents the improper use of will – a quick fix when spiritual paradigms are shifting, as they are now. In other words, many evangelicals welcome the demise of Earth because they think it will hasten their entry into heaven.

Jung pointed to a healthy function of detachment from the fear of death when he wrote about the process of individuation, which he described as the way to increase self-knowledge. The very principles of Jungian work – the creative tension of opposites, descent journeys, and the transcendent function – are all born on the wave of the Sophia archetype. These principles move us through the density of matter and ultimately bring us a sense of lightness and a taste of union with Source, which transcends all notions of a gendered Supreme Being. Thus, appropriate detachment helps us to comprehend the apparent duality between the seen and the unseen worlds and to view the Earth as sacred while we await the mystery of the afterlife.

In order to make it through the present environmental crisis, we need to spiritually mature and free ourselves from a patriarchal paradigm that is based on gender duality and fear of the life-death-life cycle. We will not become "citizens of the world" until we Love Earth as much as we claim to Love heaven.

Jung famously wrote, "My work has proved empirically that the pattern of God exists in every man … not only the meaning of his life, but his renewal and the renewal of his institutions depend on his conscious relationship with this pattern." Addressing the Earth's issues requires a profound renewal of our spiritual beliefs and the resulting institutions. Let us, therefore, expand our perception of the soul's journey, which is inexorably intertwined with nature Herself. This is Sophian wisdom.

I have a female mannequin in my bedroom, my sacred space. When I first came upon her, she had no arms or legs. She was chipped in several places and needed a fresh coat of paint in others. But her torso was the right size, and I liked that her eyebrows and few remaining eyelashes were dark like mine. A pile of limbs rested nearby. I plugged legs into her hip sockets and then worked on her arms. When done, I looked at her slender naked body and thought: *From this graveyard, I have resurrected a queen.*

I restored the mannequin to display a vintage gown that I had dyed purple and hand painted. It may sound ghastly what I did to that dress, but the result was truly stunning. I didn't merely Love the dress for its beauty, though. In 1961 my mother wore it to a dance with my father, and in 1979 I wore it to my senior prom. Back then it was sky blue.

When I got her home, I pulled the dress over her head and slipped shoes on her tiny feet. I placed a wig on her head – dark curls fell to her waist. I stepped back to admire her. And through the tears her name came to me: *Sophia.* A name, an archetype that Bernice has used to help us grasp the Sacred Feminine.

LOOK OUT

By Wendell Berry

Come to the window, look out, and see
the valley turning green in remembrance
of all springs past and to come, the woods
perfecting with immortal patience
the leaves that are the work of all of time,
the sycamore whose white limbs shed
the history of a man's life with their old bark,
the river under the morning's breath quivering
like the touched skin of a horse, and you will see
also the shadow cast upon it by fire, the war
that lights its way by burning the earth.

Come to your windows, people of the world,
look out at whatever you see wherever you are,
and you will see dancing upon it that shadow.
You will see that your place, wherever it is,
your house, your garden, your shop, your forest, your farm,
bears the shadow of its destruction by war
which is the economy of greed which is plunder
which is the economy of wrath which is fire.
The Lords of War sell the earth to buy fire,
they sell the water and air of life to buy fire.
They are little men grown great by willingness
to drive whatever exists into its perfect absence.
Their intention to destroy any place is solidly founded
upon their willingness to destroy every place.

Every household of the world is at their mercy,
the households of the farmer and the otter and the owl
are at their mercy. They have no mercy.
Having hate, they can have no mercy.
Their greed is the hatred of mercy.
Their pockets jingle with the small change of the poor.
Their power is their willingness to destroy
everything for knowledge which is money
which is power which is victory
which is ashes sown by the wind.

CHAPTER 1: LOVE OF EARTH

Leave your windows and go out, people of the world,
go into the streets, go into the fields, go into the woods
and along the streams. Go together, go alone.
Say no to the Lords of War which is Money
which is Fire. Say no by saying yes
to the air, to the earth, to the trees,
yes to the grasses, to the rivers, to the birds
and the animals and every living thing, yes
to the small houses, yes to the children. Yes.

The two cardinal sins are greed and pride. Unbridled greed leads to an obsession with money and material possessions. Undaunted pride leads to an obsession with power and world domination. That is what I wrote a few years ago in *The Truth: About the Five Primary Religions*, and I stand by these words. Of course, the thought is not original to me:

> *Sin is both in the mind and in the act. ... Bodily cruelty springs from greed, which not only refuses to share what is one's own but takes what belongs to others, robbing the poor, playing the overlord, cheating, defrauding, putting up one's neighbor's goods – and often their very persons – for ransom. ...*
>
> *And who is hurt by the offspring of pride? Only your neighbors. For you harm them when your exalted opinion of yourself leads you to consider yourself superior and therefore to despise them. And if pride is in a position of authority, it gives birth to injustice and cruelty and becomes a dealer in human flesh. ...*
>
> *Every scandal, hatred, cruelty, and everything unbecoming springs from this root of selfish Love. It has poisoned the whole world ... and the universal body of Christianity.*

Saint Catherine of Sienna, *The Dialogue*

Wendell reminds us that our abuse of this planet is the direct result of greed and pride. Sure, there is some ignorance involved as well. But primarily, it is the industrial giants who are despoiling nature, encouraged by those nations – like the United States – that have an imperial view toward the rest of the world. It must stop.

As God is the steward of the heavenly realms, the unseen dimensions, so we are the stewards of this earthly realm. As Saint Catherine duly noted, our selfishness is sickening.

THE NEXT REVOLUTION

By Bill McKibben

It was the great economist John Maynard Keynes who pointed out that until very recently, "there was no very great change in the standard of life of the average man living in the civilized centers of the earth." At the most, Keynes calculated that the standard of living roughly doubled between 2000 B.C.E. and the dawn of the 18th Century – nearly four thousand years – during which we basically didn't learn to do much of anything new.

And then, something new finally did happen. In 1712, a British inventor named Thomas Newcomen created the first practical steam engine. Over the centuries that followed, fossil fuels helped create everything we consider normal and obvious about the modern world, from electricity, to steel, to fertilizer. Now, a 100% jump in the standard of living could suddenly be accomplished in a few decades, not a few millennia.

It's useful to remember what Thomas Newcomen was up to when he helped launch the Industrial Revolution – burning coal to pump water out of mines. This revolution both depended on and revolved around fossil fuels. "Before coal," writes economist Jeffrey Sachs, "economic production was limited by energy inputs, almost all of which depended on the production of biomass: food for humans and farm animals, and fuel wood for heating and certain industrial processes." That is, energy depended on how much you could grow. But fossil energy depended on how much had grown eons before – all those billions of tons of ancient biology squashed by the weight of time till they'd turned into strata and pools and seams of hydrocarbons, waiting for us to discover them.

The End of the Fossil Fuel Paradigm

At any given moment, we face as a society an enormous number of problems. There's the mortgage crisis, the health care crisis, the endless war in Iraq, and on and on. Maybe we'll solve some of them, and doubtless new ones will spring up to take their places. But there's only one thing we're doing that will be easily visible from the moon. That something is global warming. Quite literally, it's the biggest problem humans have ever faced, and while there are ways to at least start to deal with it, all of them rest on acknowledging just how large the challenge really is.

What exactly do I mean by large? In the fall of 2007, scientists who study sea ice in the Arctic reported that it was melting even faster than they'd predicted. We blew by the old record for ice loss in mid-August, and by the time the long polar night finally descended, the fabled Northwest Passage was open for navigation for the first time in recorded history. That is to say, from outer space the Earth already looks very different – less white and more blue.

What do I mean by large? On the glaciers of Greenland, 10% more ice melted last summer than any year for which we have records. This is bad news because, unlike sea ice, Greenland's vast frozen mass sits above rock, and when it melts, the oceans rise – potentially a lot. James Hansen of NASA, America's foremost climatologist, testified in court last year that we will likely see sea level increase as much as six meters – nearly twenty feet – in the course of this century. With that, the view from space looks very different indeed (not to mention the view from the office buildings of any coastal city on Earth).

What do I mean by large? Already, higher heat is causing drought in arid areas the world over. In Australia, things have gotten so bad that agricultural output is falling fast in the continent's biggest river basin, and the nation's prime minister is urging his people to pray for rain. Aussie native Rupert Murdoch is so rattled he's announced plans to make his NewsCorp empire (think Fox News) carbon neutral. Australian voters ousted their old government last fall, largely because of concerns over climate.

What do I mean by large? If we tried, we couldn't have figured out a more thorough way to make life miserable for the world's poor, who now must deal with the loss of the one thing they could always take for granted – the planet's basic physical stability. We've never figured out as efficient a method for obliterating other species. We've never figured out another way to so fully degrade the future for everyone who comes after us.

Or rather, we have figured out one other change that rises to this scale. That change is called all-out thermonuclear war and, so far at least, we've decided not to have one. But we haven't called off global warming. Just the opposite: In the twenty years that we've known about global warming, we've steadily burned more coal and gas and oil, and hence steadily poured more carbon dioxide into the atmosphere. Instead of a few huge explosions, we've got billions of little ones every minute, as pistons fire inside engines and boilers burn coal.

Having put off real change, we've made our job steadily harder. But there are signs that we're finally ready to get to work. Congress is for the first time seriously considering legislation that would actually limit U.S. emissions. The bills won't be signed by President Bush, and they don't do everything that needs doing ... but they're a start.

What about China and India?

Here's a political reality check, just as sobering as the data about sea ice and drought: *China last year passed the United States as the biggest emitter of carbon on Earth.* Now, that doesn't mean the Chinese are as much to blame as we are – *per capita*, we pour four times more CO_2 into the atmosphere. And we've been doing it for a hundred years, which means it will be decades before they match us as a source of the problem. But the Chinese and the Indians and the rest of the developing world behind them are growing so fast that there's no way to head off this crisis without their participation. And yet, they don't want to participate because they're using all that cheap coal not to pimp-out an already lavish lifestyle, but to pull people straight out of deep poverty.

Moreover, with the entire world aiming for an economy structured like America's, it won't be just fossil fuels that we'll run short of. Here are the numbers we have to contend with: *Given current rates of growth, the 1.3 billion residents of China will, by 2030, be about as rich as we are.* If they then eat meat, milk, and eggs at the rate that we do, eco-statistician Lester Brown calculates that the Chinese will consume 1,352 million tons of grain each year, which is equal to two-thirds of the world's entire 2004 grain harvest. They will use 99 million barrels of oil a day, which is 15 million more than the entire world consumes at present. They will use more steel than all the West combined, double the world's production of paper, and drive 1.1 billion cars – 1.5 times as many as the current world total. And that's just China. By 2030, India will have a bigger population and its economy is growing almost as fast. And then there's the rest of the world.

Trying to meet that kind of demand will stress the Earth past its breaking point in an almost endless number of ways, but let's take just one. When Thomas Newcomen fired up his pump on that morning in 1712, the atmosphere contained 275 parts per million of carbon dioxide. We're now up to 380 parts per million, a higher level than the Earth has seen for many millions of years, and climate change has only just begun. The median predictions of the world's climatologists – by no means the worst-case scenario – show that unless we take truly enormous steps to rein in our use of fossil fuels, we can expect average temperatures to rise another four or five degrees before the century is out, making the globe warmer than it's been since long before primates appeared. We may as well stop calling it Earth and have a contest to pick some new name, because it will be a different planet. Humans have never done anything more profound, not even when we invented nuclear weapons.

Which means if we don't want other countries to burn their coal, we're going to have to help them. We'll need to supply the windmills, efficient boilers, and so on, that will allow them to build decent lives without depending on coal-fired power plants or oil.

Which means, in turn, we're going to need to be generous on a scale that passes even the Marshall Plan that helped rebuild post-World War II Europe. And it's not clear if we're capable of that anymore – so far, our politicians have preferred to scapegoat China, not come to its aid.

I said at the start that this was not just another problem on a list of problems: *Global warming is a whole new lens through which to look at the world.* When we peer through it, foreign policy looks entirely different. The threats to our security can be met only by shipping China technology, not by shipping missiles to China's enemies.

Economists Discover Hedonics

When we peer through the climate lens, our economic life looks completely changed as well. We need to forget the endless economic expansion that added to the cloud of carbon and instead concentrate on the kind of durability and sustainability that will head-off the troubles headed our way.

In fact, even when the economy "grows," most of us do not get wealthier. The average wage in the United States is less now, in real dollars, than it was thirty years ago. And although productivity was growing faster than it had for decades during the Bush presidency, even those with college degrees had their earnings fall by 5.2% when adjusted for inflation. Much the same thing has happened across the globe. More than sixty countries have seen *per capita* incomes fall in the past decade.

Which means, according to new research emerging from many quarters, that our continued devotion to "growth" above all is, on balance, making our lives worse – both collectively and individually. Growth no longer makes most people wealthier; instead, it generates inequality and insecurity. Growth is bumping up against physical limits so profound – like climate change and peak oil – that continually trying to expand the economy may be not only impossible but also dangerous, as the trillion dollar bail-out of Wall Street has made clear. So perhaps growth no longer makes us happier. Given our current dogma, that's as bizarre an idea as proposing that gravity pushes apples skyward. But then, even Newtonian physics eventually acknowledged Einstein's more complicated universe.

Traditionally, happiness and satisfaction are the sort of notions that economists wave aside as poetic irrelevance – the kind of questions that occupy people with no head for numbers who had to major in liberal arts. An orthodox economist has a simple happiness formula: If you buy a Ford Expedition, then *ipso facto* a Ford Expedition is what makes you happy. That's all we need to know. An economist would call this idea "utility maximization," and in the words of economic historian Gordon Bigelow, "the theory holds that every time a person buys something, sells something, quits a job, or invests, he is making a rational decision about what will ... provide him 'maximum utility.'" The beauty of this principle lies in its simplicity. It is perhaps the central assumption of the world we live in: *You can tell who I really am by what I buy.*

Yet economists have long known that people's brains don't work quite the way the model suggests. Researchers from a wide variety of disciplines have started to figure out how to assess satisfaction, and economists have begun to explore the implications. In 2002, Princeton's Daniel Kahneman won the Nobel Prize in economics even though he is trained as a psychologist. In the book *Well-Being*, he and his co-authors announced a new field called "Hedonics," defined as, "the study of what makes experiences and life pleasant or unpleasant. ... It is also concerned with the whole range of circumstances, from the biological to the societal, that occasion suffering and enjoyment." So Hedonics attempts to answer the question: *If we're so rich, how come we're so damn miserable?*

Are We Happy Yet?

In some sense, you could say that in America the years since World War II have been a loosely controlled experiment designed to answer this very question. Gross national product *per capita* tripled during that period. Our houses are bigger than ever and stuffed to the rafters with belongings (which is why the storage-locker industry has doubled in size in the past decade). We have all sorts of other new delights and powers: We can send email from our cars, watch 200 channels, and consume food from every corner of the world. Some people have taken much more than their share but, on average, all of us in the West are living lives materially more abundant than most people a generation ago.

What's odd is this: *None of this appears to have made us happier.* Throughout the postwar years, even as the GNP curve steadily climbed, the "life satisfaction" index has stayed exactly the same. And it's not that we're simply recalibrating our sense of what happiness means – we are actively experiencing life as grimmer. No wonder the show that changed television more than any other in the past decade is *Survivor*, where the goal is to end up alone on an island, to manipulate and scheme until everyone is banished and you are left alone with your money.

This decline in the happiness index is not confined to the United States. As other nations have followed us into mass affluence, their experiences have begun to yield similar results. In the United Kingdom, real gross domestic product *per capita* grew two-thirds between 1973 and 2001, but people's satisfaction with their lives changed not one whit. Japan saw a fourfold increase in real income *per capita* between 1958 and 1986 without any reported increase in satisfaction. In one place after another, rates of alcoholism, suicide, and depression have gone up dramatically, even as we keep accumulating more stuff. Indeed, one report in 2000 found that the average American child reported higher levels of anxiety than the average child under psychiatric care in the 1950s. Our new normal is the old disturbed!

If happiness were our goal, then the unbelievable amount of effort and resources expended in its pursuit since 1950 has been largely a waste. One study of life satisfaction and mental health by Emory University professor Corey Keyes found just 17% of Americans "flourishing" in mental health terms, and 26% either "languishing" or out-and-out depressed.

In general, researchers report that money consistently buys happiness up to about $10,000 income *per capita*. That's a useful number to keep in the back of your head – it's like the freezing point of water, one of those random figures that just happens to define a crucial phenomenon on our planet. "As poor countries like India, Mexico, the Philippines, Brazil, and South Korea have experienced economic growth, there is some evidence that their average happiness has risen," economist Richard Layard reports. Past $10,000 *per capita* (mind you – that is the average for each man, woman, and child), there's a complete scattering. When the Irish were making two-thirds as much as Americans they were reporting higher levels of satisfaction, as were the Swedes, the Danes, and the Dutch. Mexicans score higher than the Japanese and the French are about as satisfied with their lives as the Venezuelans. In fact, once basic needs are met, the "satisfaction" data scrambles in middling ways. A sampling of *Forbes* magazine's "richest Americans" indicates that they have identical happiness scores with

Pennsylvania Amish, and are only a whisker above Swedes taken as a whole, not to mention the Masai.

Consequently, on the list of major mistakes we've made as a species, this one seems pretty high up. Our single-minded focus on increasing wealth has succeeded in driving the planet's ecological systems to the brink of failure, even as it's failed to make us happier. How did we screw up? The answer is pretty obvious: *We kept doing something past the point that it worked.* Since happiness had increased with income in the past, we assumed it would inevitably do so in the future. We make these kinds of mistakes regularly (e.g., two beers made me feel good, so ten beers will make me feel five times better).

In addition, study after study shows Americans spending less time with friends and family, either working longer hours or hunched over their computers at night. And each year, as our population grows by 1% we manage to spread ourselves out over 6% to 8% more land. Simple mathematics says that we're less and less likely to bump into the other inhabitants of our neighborhood, or indeed of our own homes. As *The Wall Street Journal* reported recently, "Major builders and top architects are walling people off. They're touting one-person 'Internet alcoves,' locked-door 'away rooms,' and his-and-her offices on opposite ends of the house. The new floor plans offer so much seclusion, they're good for the dysfunctional family. ..."

As a result, materialism has carried us away from something valuable, something priceless. It has allowed us to become (very nearly forced us to become) more thoroughly individualistic than we really want to be. We left behind hundreds of thousands of years of human community for the excitement and the isolation of "making something of ourselves" – a nonsensical idea for 99.9% of human history.

Another Way to Be Human

So when we peer through the climate lens, our individual lives look very different, too. Less individual, for one thing. And we realize that the kind of extreme independence that cheap fossil fuel promoted – the crazy notion that we don't need our neighbors – can't last. Either we build real communities of the kind that let us embrace mass transit, local food, cohousing, and self-sustainable regions, or we can go down clinging to the wreckage of our privatized society.

Do we just think we're happier in communities? Is it merely some sentimental "good-night John-Boy" affectation? No – our bodies react in measurable ways to healthy inter-dependence. According to research cited by Harvard professor Robert Putnam in his classic book *Bowling Alone*, if you do not belong to any group at present, joining a club or a society of some kind cuts in half the risk that you will die in the next year. Check this out: When researchers at Carnegie Mellon (somewhat disgustingly) dropped samples of cold virus directly into subjects' nostrils, those with rich social networks were four times less likely to get sick. So we now know that an economy which produces only individualism undermines us in the most basic ways.

Here's another interesting statistic: Consumers have ten times as many conversations at farmers' markets than they do at supermarkets. By itself, that's hardly life-changing, but it points to something that could be – such as living in an economy where you are a participant, as well as a consumer, where you have a sense of who's in your universe and how it fits together. Studies also show that local agriculture uses much less energy than the "it's always summer somewhere" system we operate on now. These differences illustrate that between peak oil and climate change, there's no longer a question that we have to wean ourselves off the current energy consumption model.

Which leaves us with the one piece of undeniably good news: *We are built for community*. Everything we know about human beings – from the state of our immune systems to the state of our psyches – testifies to our desire for real connection of just the kind that an advanced consumer society will one day create. We need communities that employ green technology so that we can slow down the environmental changes coming at us. We need communities that practice sustainability so that we will survive the changes we can't prevent. And we need communities that integrate Hedonics so that we may be brought closer together, because that's what makes us fully human. This is our final exam, and so far we're failing. But we don't have to put our pencils down quite yet ...

Building a Movement

Last year, the United Nations sponsored a Climate Change Conference in Bali where participants managed to overcome U.S. resistance. Drafting began on an international treaty that will be ready in 2009. The talks are going slowly, largely because of American intransigence, but George Bush won't be president forever. Soon, we'll re-engage with the rest of the world and when we do, there are steps we can take to protect the Earth. But because our environmental problems are so big and coming at us so fast, those steps will need to be large. And even then, our actions won't be enough to stop global warming – at best these measures will slow it down and give us some margin of safety. Here's the deal:

We need to conserve energy. That's the cheapest way to reduce carbon. Screw in the energy-saving lightbulbs, but that's just the start. You have to blow in the new insulation – blow it in so thick that you can heat your home with a birthday candle. You have to plug in the new appliances – not the flat-screen TV which uses way more power than the old set, but the new water-saving front-loading washer. And once you've got it plugged in, turn the dial so that you're using cold water. The dryer? You don't need a dryer – that's the Sun's job.

We need to generate the power we use cleanly. Wind is the fastest growing source of electricity generation around the world, but it needs to grow much faster still. Solar panels are increasingly common, especially in Japan and Germany, which are richer in political will than they are in sunshine. Much of the technology is now available; we need innovation in financing and subsidizing more than we do in generating technology.

We need to change our habits. Really, we need to change our sense of what we want from the world. Do we want enormous homes and enormous cars all to ourselves? If we do, then we can't deal with global warming. Do we want to keep eating food that travels 1,500 miles to reach our lips? Or can we take the bus or ride a bike to the farmers' market? Does that sound romantic to you? Farmers' markets are the fastest growing part of the American food economy; their heaviest users may be urban-dwelling immigrants, recently arrived from another part of the world where they know what actual food tastes like. Which leads to the next necessity…

We need to stop insisting that we've figured out the best way on Earth to live. For one thing, if it's wrecking the Earth then it's probably not all that great. But even by measures of life satisfaction and happiness, the Europeans have us beat – and they manage it on half the energy use *per capita*. We need to be pointing the Indians and the Chinese in the direction of London not Los Angeles, Barcelona not Boston.

But most of all, we need a movement. We need a political swell larger than the civil rights movement – as passionate and as willing to sacrifice. Without it, we're not going to best the fossil fuel companies and the automakers and the rest of the vested interests that are keeping us from change.

Some of us have spent the last couple of years building that movement, and we've had some success. With no money and no organization, seven of us recently launched "Step It Up" (www.StepItUp2007.org). Before the year was out, we'd helped organize 2,000 demonstrations in all 50 states, and we helped take our once-radical demand for an 80% reduction in U.S. carbon emissions by mid-century into the halls of power. Last year, House Speaker Nancy Pelosi stood at a podium in front of 7,000 college students gathered at the University of Maryland and led them in a chant: "80 percent by 2050." I'm as cynical as the next guy, but it feels like our democracy is starting to work.

We've gone on to build another campaign called "Worldwide 350" (www.350.org), which takes its name from the number that scientists now say is the most CO_2 that we can safely have in our atmosphere. Currently, Worldwide 350 is organizing in every continent to push environmental negotiators in the direction of planetary protection. It's obviously an uphill fight – but what a pleasure to open my emails every morning and see one from a farmer in the Cameroon who has decided to plant 350 trees, or from a minister in Massachusetts who will ring a church bell 350 times. Each such action drives publicity and shows how the nervous system provided by the Internet can help us act locally in ways that drive change globally.

Even so, this movement will require a whole new level of commitment, from nonviolent protest, to electioneering, to endless lobbying. We'll have to commit to an environmentalism much broader and more diverse than we've ever known – younger, browner, and insistent that the people left out of the last economy won't be left out of the new one. And we'll need to foster the movement not just in America, but around the world. After all, they don't call it global warming for nothing.

<hr>

I will never forget my children's reactions after we watched Al Gore's movie *An Inconvenient Truth*. They were shell-shocked! My daughter, who is the oldest but who was only thirteen at the time of the 2000 presidential election, asked me, "Mommy, how could the country elect George Bush over that man?" I winced and replied, "We didn't." My son then asked, "How could your generation let this happen to the planet?" I winced again, but praised him for paying attention to the end of the movie – a call to arms to the younger generation. And my youngest son just held my hand, too numb and still too little to fully comprehend the Earth changes he will see in his lifetime. So he brought it home, "Mommy, I Love our farm and our creek."

Yes Bill, we will help you fight the Next Revolution ... and we will win. Such is God's plan.

OFFERING BEFORE CLEARING A FIELD

Kekchi Maya Invocation

O God – my Mother my Father:
Lord of the hills
Lord of the valleys
Lord of the forest
be patient with me.
I am about to do what has always been done.

I make You an offering that You may be warned:
I am about to molest your heart.
I trust You will have the strength to endure it.
I am going to work You in order that I may live.

Let no animal pursue me
no snake, no scorpion
no wasp annoy me
no falling timber hit me
no ax, no machete catch me.

With all my heart I am going to work You.

———◈———

The Earth wisdom of indigenous cultures and the respect they show Mother Earth is awe-inspiring. This wisdom goes beyond reverence. It is true Love.

I am privileged to host a Lakota sweat lodge on my farm. The lodge is led by Pete, an amazing soul who has learned the ways of the Lakota and lives by their principles – Love of Earth being the foundation of their Love of Great Mystery. Pete has taught me many things, but the one in my heart right now is the symbol of the lodge itself. The lodge represents our mother's womb, Mother Earth, and the fire is Father Sun. When we are in the lodge, we are as children. We relish the intimacy of sitting close and sharing our hopes and fears. You may close your eyes in the lodge if you wish, but Pete tells us to keep our eyes open in the blackness – the "void" – so that we may better see our visions.

Native ways are beckoning us now, and native elders have been meeting lately to discuss what to do about their "younger" brothers and sisters. In their prophecies, the white man asks for native wisdom once the consequences of greed and pride are plain for all to see. When the white man thinks of End Times, the world is destroyed. But for the red man, it is the time when ancient wisdom resurfaces and balance is restored. Finally, we learn to Love the land.

LAND LOVE

By R. Bruce Hull IV, Ph.D.

It is inconceivable to me that an ethical relation to the land can exist without Love, respect, and admiration for the land.

Aldo Leopold, *A Sand County Almanac*

Love celebrates sharing and sacrifice. Love generates intimacy and commitment. Love captures attention and elevates union above ego. Love thrives when partners flourish and grieves when partners suffer. We need more Love in our lives.

Loving foresters harvest wood and water in ways that improve soil and biodiversity. Loving farmers rotate crops, buffer streams, and recycle nutrients. Loving hikers build and maintain water diversion devices to reduce erosion. Loving suburbanites plant native, xeric gardens that reduce water and biocide applications and increase insect and bird habitat. Loving urbanites live more densely to reduce energy, commuting, and material needs. Loving friends gift memories, stories, and services, not material things. Loving consumers buy less or green. Lovers of nature create a sustainable future.

Unfortunately, most of us are taught to lust after nature, not Love it. Lust emphasizes the "otherness" of nature, puts it on a pedestal, idealizes it as perfect, and limits interactions to admiration from a distance. Lust distracts us from creating a loving, nurturing, sustainable relationship. It showcases nature's superficial beauty. It ignores the necessary struggle between give and take, hope and compromise, today and tomorrow, I and us. Lust is fleeting and one-directional, leading inevitably to disappointment and abandonment. We may begin a relationship with lust, but without deeper commitment, understanding, sacrifice and respect, we eventually move on.

But we cannot afford to move on from nature. We are emotionally, physically, culturally, and spiritually intertwined. Our long term survival requires a mature relationship, one that is respectful, prideful, joyous, and responsible – it requires Love.

We do not wrap loved ones in protective cocoons; we interact, we influence, we give, we take, and we accept responsibility for actively improving one another. Consider a loving parent who evokes wails of grief by unplugging video games – sources of seductive pleasures – and who directs the child's freed attention to literacy, music, gardening, friendship, or other pathways to deeper meaning and lifelong engagement. Focus shifts from I to us. Connections form. Compassion grows. Fulfillment flourishes. We must commit to nature like we commit to our family. We must be mindful of our impacts, fully committed through good times and bad, forgiving of harm done and proud of accomplishments, and always willing to encourage and assist.

Sustainability is responsibility born of Love. It requires responsible membership in the land community. It requires being prudent innovators, inspired visionaries, and loving partners in the odyssey of evolution. It requires using our creativity to enhance and care for all community members. It requires respecting the beauty, integrity, and complexity of our community. It requires being wary of hubris. It requires admitting that we can destroy as well as create sustainable futures.

Our global, consumer, suburban society promotes lust not Love by separating us from the land community. The products we purchase are made by people we neither know nor understand, marketed through exploitation of base urges and fears, transported by anonymous drivers into ever-expanding retail wastelands, and stocked on shelves profiting multinational franchises by pale people working third jobs, unable to step off the credit treadmill. Our sprawling development is worse still. It cocoons us in long commutes to isolated mansions where our only connections to the land community are conduits that pump entertainment in and drain wastes out.

Most of us don't know what it feels like to live sustainably, and trying to do so might be painful at first. We are addicted to the numbing agents of materialism, suburbanism, globalism, cheap energy, and intolerance. But if we can muster the courage to push through the pain and climb out of the abyss, sustainability will feel so good that we'll actually crave more. One taste of this elixir won't be enough – we'll want the whole jug, a whole day, a whole life. We will want to share it with others. And as we do so, society will change.

How do we create sustainability?

Flourescent light bulbs, hybrid cars, and energy efficient construction are potential first steps, but lead down the wrong path if they merely ease materialist guilt so that we can go on buying more stuff, driving longer commutes, and living in bigger houses. Green consumerism is not the solution. We cannot buy sustainability any more than we can buy Love. We need to live differently. We need to restore and respect the green infrastructure that performs our life support services. We need to live in buildings and neighborhoods that celebrate saving materials, energy, land, and commuting. We need to recycle as a last resort, reuse when possible, and above all else, reduce. We need to minimize our ecological footprints, sacrifice our material demands, and live a full life while loving and respecting our partners.

Opportunities for land Love abound. Install roof top gardens that provide safe food, capture rain and carbon, cool climate, and generate beauty. Organize neighborhood solar panels, windmills, and household batteries that get people off the corporate carbon power grid. Build narrow streets, neighborhood markets, sound-proof windows, and high density living arrangements that encourage walking, convenient shopping, healthy children, and neighborhood schooling. Use local labor and engage in local politics. Know who and what your actions affect, and act in a caring and loving manner. Do unto others as you would have them do unto you.

Love happens locally. Local food connects us to local seasons, soil, water, and farmers. Local energy helps us care for the pollution we otherwise export to people less fortunate. Local crafts connect us to local culture, materials, and people. Local recreation connects us to local scenery, solace, and ecology. Local is not only beautiful, it is contagious, because it spurs investment, pride, identity, sustainability, and Love. It inspires others to join and act. Love needs to be local because Love needs proximity: face to face, hand to soil, food to mouth. Love needs intimacy: a warm embrace, a cool caress, soothing comfort.

Bonded by Love we will prevail. Divided by selfishness we will fail. Together as a community we can steer toward a desired future. Divided as individuals we will lose our way on the choppy sea of neo-liberalism, scattered by the strong currents of self-interest. As a community we can shape our destiny by celebrating our heritage, nurturing our markets, sustaining our resources, and practicing Love. As disconnected consumers we breed intolerance, hoard assets, squander resources, and become easy prey for those spreading fear. The community members with power – land owners, apartment tenants, businesses, purchasing agents, teachers, bureaucrats, environmentalists, consumers, farmers, politicians, and the faithful – must weave together economy, ethics, and environment into the common ground – the Love – that supports and enhances the rights and well-being of all members of our land community.

The future toward which we steer should not be constrained by agrarian precepts of an idealized past, when cattle, wood, water, oil, and corn provided landed gentry with power and profit. The "good ol' days" were not good for everyone. Peasant agriculture, although it looks appealing through the romantic lens of plenty, generates low paying, tedious, and dangerous work that is unlikely to feed an increasingly numerous and wealthy global population. And that era won't return because globalization and innovation have changed the rules of the game: Commodity production systems need to be uber capitalized, nimble, and efficient to prosper in our rapidly evolving, technologically intensive, globalized system.

Besides, America is now aging and urban. For most people, living on the land is neither feasible nor desirable. We should also avoid the unquestioned pursuit of any and all economic development. Counties and local officials competing against each other to attract big box retailers and manufacturing giants by offering tax incentives, labor guarantees, and regulatory exceptions are wielding a two-edged sword. This strategy may give temporary employment but it also takes away money and opportunity that would have circulated within the local economy. Small companies, local entrepreneurship, and regional markets increase the amount and velocity of money and opportunity circulating within a community. Large, multinational companies take their profits and invest them elsewhere. They have only short term concerns for local natural capital. The "invisible hand" of the free market needs to be held and made to build the social, economic, and natural capitals of the local community.

Land lovers will restore and improve Earth's life support systems. We will protect the remaining wilderness that provides a record of our past, an inspiration for our future, and a home for so many. We will promote the integrity, health, and beauty of the community and its members. We will pursue technological innovations that increase efficiencies and opportunities in a finite world. We will live fuller lives with fewer things, engage in service not consumption, and insist on quality not quantity. We will construct regional economies that service rather than exploit local communities and local lands. All of this requires responsive and reliable government. It requires that we be engaged in our community. It requires Love.

You know you want it – go make land Love!

Bruce gets it! He not only gets it, he is teaching it at Virginia Tech, my state's most forward-thinking agricultural university. He and others in Virginia have been instrumental in bringing an international model of sustainability to the United States. It is called LandCare, and in the past five years the program has been embraced by: local farmers who now understand the benefit of organic practices; foresters who now are getting the help they need to preserve our old growth forests; and aquarian experts who have been pleading for decades with municipalities and corporations to preserve wetlands, protect the oceans, and address global water shortages.

Regardless of where you live, there are lightworkers who are dedicated to the planet and who are working overtime to teach sustainability. Please, be aware of your "ecological footprint" – a term our children now understand. Be aware of the quantity of garbage you produce versus the amount you recycle (your recycling should be greater). Be aware of how you heat your home (solar prices are expected to drop substantially in the near future). And be aware of the food you set on your family's table (investigate where it comes from and whether it is natural).

Just as importantly, read up on the many known dangers of commercial farming – such as the production of genetically modified organisms (GMOs), the use of "terminator seeds" that do not reproduce, and the mysterious global disappearance of honeybees, nature's greatest pollinators. Einstein did not say these words (that recently have been been attributed to him), but they are prescient and bear repeating:

> *If the bee disappears from the surface of the Earth, man would have no more than four years to live. No more bees, no more pollination, no more plants, no more animals, no more men!*

Just as God is the source and sustainer of life on the Ethereal plane, so Mother Nature is the source and sustainer of life on the Earth plane. As such, she rightfully deserves our reverence and our Love.

If you have the time right now, go outside. Take a walk. Look at the clouds and watch a bird fly. Find a patch of grass and hold a bug. And if you are lucky enough to have water nearby, watch it flow … and see if you can flow with it. Then say your own prayer to Mother Earth.

GASEGE DENE

*The God Amma, it appeared, took a lump of clay, squeezed it in his hand
and flung it from him, as he had done with the stars. The clay spread and
fell on the north, which is the top, and from there stretched out to the south,
which is the bottom of the world .... It is a body ....
This body, lying flat, face upwards, in a line from north to south, is feminine.
Its sexual organ is an anthill, and its clitoris a termite hill. ...*

*At God's approach the termite hill rose up, barring the passage and
displaying its masculinity. ... But God is all powerful.
He cut down the termite hill, and had intercourse with the excised Earth. ...
From this defective union there was born, instead of the intended twins,
a single being, the Thos aureus or jackal, symbol of the difficulties of God. ...*

*God had further intercourse with his Earth-wife, and this time
without mishap of any kind. ... Two beings were thus formed.
God created them like water. They were green in color, half human beings
and half serpents. ... These spirits, called Nummo, were thus two
homogenous products of God, of Divine essence like himself.*

Dogon Elder Ogotemmeli (d. 1947), *Conversations with Ogotemmeli*

In Dogon mythology, Love of animals – *gasege dene* in their African tongue
– imbues their creation parable. It is as though God reached down and
touched all the world's cultures with this theme. The *Old Testament*,
which is sacred to all three of the religions of Abraham – Judaism,
Christianity, and Islam – instructs us that God began populating the Earth
with animal life on the fifth day of creation, as though human beings were a
mere afterthought on day six.

May we finally understand that the animal kingdom represents an earlier
manifestation of God's kingdom on Earth and, thereby, dutifully accept the
responsibility placed in our hands as stewards of this planet.

NAKED, WITH SKIN ON

By Susan Chernak McElroy

A book about Love appropriately begins with an exploration of our Love of animals because animals are so very easy to Love. And we need things that are easy to Love. We need things that can elegantly and safely receive our clumsy, wet-behind-the-ears, and exasperatingly immature human expressions of Love. Thankfully, animals are here to help.

I think it is entirely fair to say that we humans are, overall, pretty lousy lovers. We need – desperately need – to improve ourselves in this endeavor, especially considering that we are now about a million years along in our evolutionary path. As God and the Beatles know, "Love is all you need." And anyone with the sense of a rutabaga knows this is true. At the dawn of the 21st Century, we should have at least learned this much: *Love is the answer.*

To our credit, many of us have acquired the ability over the millennia to Love in some rudimentary ways, although the sweetness of our Love contains a few salty crystals, like obsession, jealousy, precondition, and utter confusion. But at this fragile time in human history, we must learn to Love "better" if we are to survive the brutality of our darker nature. We must learn to Love with the clarity of ice and the honesty of dirt, with the dignity of redwoods and the strength of tides. We must learn to express a majestic Love as strong and enduring as mountains. This is how animals Love.

Please don't bother to argue with me on this point – I won't have it anymore. Animals genuinely Love. They Love because the universe is crafted from a sacred Love, a primordial Love; it is the power that drives all things. Animals have maintained a covenant with their original instructions, not because they are better or nobler than we, but because they cannot operate otherwise. Deep in the hearts and souls of all animals is written the original instructions: *Just Love.*

I'm not referring to the ooey-gooey kind of Love that makes your head spin and your heart race, but another kind of Love. The kind that is as still and quiet as a forest pond in autumn and which has no bottom. I'm talking about the kind of Love that, as you sink deeper and deeper, becomes the verb that was the noun and can never be a noun again. At the rock bottom of things, this kind of Love – "peace which passeth all understanding" – is the working engine, the heartbeat that is the All. It also is the Love at the core of the great mystical traditions.

We humans get overly puffed-up about our big brains and our free will, but these gifts come at great cost. We like to brag and often claim that "we are the *only* species that ..." In reality, though, the *only* thing we are the *only* in is our ability to ignore our original instructions! In this regard, we are indeed unique ... and scary, too.

True achievement comes after great challenge and hard work. No doubt Love is our highest calling and, consequently, our most confounding trial. Rife with internal ignorance, we ponderously construct a Tower of Babel, when we should be building an earthquake-proof Monument to Love. So we continue at a snail's pace as we pore over our crudely drawn blueprints ("Honey, where did you put our original instructions?"). And along the way, we struggle to maneuver with tool belts that are heavily laden with entitlement, self-righteousness, anger, terror, compulsion, judgment, and shame. Later, when our small testimonials to Truth crumble into heaps of assorted wreckage, we scratch our heads and wonder: *Where is the Love?* And so the Great Work goes.

A word or two about our tool belts: We did not equip them with resources of the Earth. These tool belts came down the birth canal with us. They have been there, wrapped invisibly around our midsections, since we became human. They are an unfortunate byproduct of the complex wirings of our really big brains. Nevertheless, to build a greater capacity for Love – both the giving and the receiving – we need to set these aforementioned tool belts aside. It is possible, but it won't be easy, because we've been carrying these tools around for a long time. Putting them down will be scary because we have come to believe that we can't work without them. Some of us even believe that we are the tools! But to Love well, we will have to empty our tool belts, pockets, and purses of all the junk (and don't forget the secret compartment in our boots where we carry the weapons). We have to strip down for Love. Ideally, we have to get totally naked.

Those of us who are courageous have already put our tool belts aside and have willed nakedness upon ourselves. To voluntarily become naked enough for bottomless Love is a noble gesture that makes creation sing. To be stripped bare by forces outside ourselves is another story; we usually name that story "trauma" or "catastrophe." Terminal illness can do it, natural disaster can do it, as well as any other event that shocks the mind totally senseless and leaves us utterly naked but too numb to care. This is how most of us get naked – not by volition but by force.

Animals come naked by design. They are always naked enough to Love and they Love naked ... but with their "skin on." I put those words in quotes in reference to a story shared by my wise friend, Carol. In the midst of a thunderstorm, Carol comforted a tearful grandchild saying, "Sweetie, if it ever thunders outside and Grammy can't be here, remember that the angels are always with you." Blubbering, the granddaughter replied between sobs, "I know, Grammy, but sa ... sa ... sometimes, I just need sa ... someone with sk ... skin on."

If you are a neophyte at ice clear, dirt honest Love (and excluding certain Sages, we all are), it is easier to practice getting naked in front of someone who is not going to laugh at you. Pick someone who won't snicker at the bulges in your spiritual places or at the flounder-belly pallor of the soulful parts of yourself that you've never before exposed to light, let alone to Love. It is far better to practice flexing your naked, flabby compassion muscles in front of someone who doesn't care how you look or how goofy you behave. Such delicate Love practice is best shared with someone who holds you safe and secure in a heart-place of perpetual acceptance – someone who also is starting to understand the profound nature of Love.

This is how animals Love. They are hard-wired for it. They never lose their instructions or forget how to express genuine Love.

Now, I'm not suggesting that you go out into the forest and practice your Love on a grizzly bear, because although a grizzly bear is capable of loving as clear as ice and as honest as dirt, the grizzly probably is not going to Love *you* like that, at least not until you have achieved a mastery of Love of the cosmic sort. So use your brain. As previously mentioned, we have really big ones. Commence your Love program where most of us must start – small and personal.

Luckily, there are animals that have been specially designed by humans (for good or ill, and don't get me started on that one ...). These animals are exceptional receptors and reciprocators of our loving practice. These creatures live close to us, sharing the twists and turns of our moods, histories, and circumstances. In my late night musings, I often wonder if the greatest blessing of domestic animals is not their service or even their companionship, but their amazing ability to be keepers of our Love. It is easy and uncomplicated to bare ourselves before our dogs, cats, horses, birds, and hamsters. As a little girl confided to me, "My guinea pig, Julia, Loves me more than anyone else in the world!"

"How do you know that?" I asked.

"Because she never tells my secrets to anyone."

Many would say that Love of God trumps all other Loves. True, perhaps, but Julia the guinea pig has skin on.

On the night my house burned down, it was my dog Arrow who pulled me through the first twenty-four hours of that trauma. All my animal and human family – my very old mother included – came through the fire alive. The house was in ruins, though, and I thought (mistakenly as it turned out), that I accidentally started the inferno by putting stove ashes in the trash. The fire ignited at four o'clock in the afternoon, and the firefighters didn't leave until after ten that night. Totally spent, we settled in for the evening with generous neighbors who opened up their home to us. Two cats were at the veterinary clinic for observation. The other two were asleep in our chicken house. The hens had cocked their heads side to side when the cats curled up in the straw beneath the egg boxes; they seemed to mutter, "What the … !" Our other dog, Strongheart, stretched out at my mother's feet, both of them twitching their toes in dream-filled sleep.

Arrow and I ended up together in my neighbor's laundry room. Arrow is a collie, and her fur looked as soft and inviting as a fleece muff. In the blessed quiet and privacy of the laundry room, I put my head against hers, sunk my fingers into her thick mane, and cried. Emotions bubbled up from my stomach, erupted in my mouth, and poured out of my eyes – not as tears, but more like a steady flowing stream. My head was too tired and too small to hold all these emotions, so I clutched at Arrow, who gave me Love when I absolutely could not face one more thing coming at me …

From puppyhood, Arrow had an instinctive ability to simply "be" with me when I was lonely, lost, or forlorn. That night between weeping fits, I hugged her and looked into her face and told her how grateful I was for her and how grateful I was that we were all alive. When I cry, I produce copious quantities of fluids – tears, mucus in buckets. Then I bloat up with fat red eyes – quite a sight, really! But Arrow's face remained serene during my fit – lustrous and high cheeked with Egyptian-lined eyes the color of pennies. "Why did this happen, Arrow?" I cried.

Arrow's honest heart echoed, "This happen …"

I blubbered, "What do I do?"

Arrow's eyes mirrored, "I do …"

"This is my fault," I moaned.

Arrow hung out her pink tongue, "This is …"

"I am to blame," I hissed to myself.

Arrow purred, "I am …" And then, she licked the wet snot off my face.

When I began to feel ugly and unworthy in the shadow of her grace, she farted, cleaned her behind with a zealous tongue, and tried to lick my face again. Truly, an animal's brand of Love comes as easily and unabashedly as farts and fanny cleaning. That's because when one is clear as ice and honest as dirt, one is that clear and honest across the board – no exceptions.

Trying hard to dodge her tongue, I heard emotions beyond name or recognition speaking to me. Slowly, they confided to me their names, and while their names sounded different, they were all the same word. I loved the fire. I could not and yet I did. It had come screaming at me with the voice of 10,000 lions, like some angered god, and the place inside me that lives before words loved that fire. I loved its destruction because it was no different than deconstruction and reconstruction, and it was all amazing and insane at the same time. I could even Love the grief left behind by that fire – like a burnt, stinking shoe – because it said its name was Love, too. But I could only Love it for a brief, holy instant because the thought was too big for my brain. And I loved Arrow, quietly, like water. I loved her for all reasons and forever. I loved her because she could receive and hold my tragic, sooty nakedness. In her mountain genuine presence, I loved my life … deeply and shamelessly.

The aftermath of the fire reinforced for me that Love speaks directly in those moments when a familiar, furry creature rests in our lap or places a forehead against our own. Such moments with animals allow us to practice a Love that is easy to give and even easier to receive. We carve out large chambers in our heart for ice clear, dirt honest Love. And if we practice this genuine Love often enough – if loving majestically like a mountain becomes habit – eventually, we will stand firmly on the very bedrock of Love.

In good times and troubled times, whether our faces are shining or tear stained, no matter if our own nakedness to Love is invited or thrust harshly upon us, blessed are we when received by the God spirit with animal breath, and with skin on.

⟫◆⟪

If you can, try to imagine for a moment what this world would be like without animals. Susan reminds us that such a world would be sterile and, for many of us, not worth living at all. It is now well-documented that the presence of animals improves the health and prolongs the lifespan of humans. Animals, quite literally, keep us alive with their Love.

MY STEED

By Imru al Quais
(501–544)

Early in the morning, while the birds were still nesting,
I mounted my steed.
Well-bred was he, long-bodied, outstripping the wild beasts in speed,

Swift to attack, to flee, to turn, yet firm as a rock swept
down by the torrent,
Bay-colored and so smooth the saddle slips from him,
as the rain from a smooth stone,

Thin but full of life, fire boils within him like the snorting
of a boiling kettle;
He continues at full gallop when other horses are dragging their feet
in the dust for weariness.

A boy would be blown from his back, and even the strong rider
loses his garments.
Fast is my steed as a top when a child has spun it well.

He has the flanks of a buck, the legs of an ostrich,
and the gallop of a wolf.
From behind, his thick tail hides the space between his thighs,
and almost sweeps the ground.

When he stands before the house, his back looks like the
huge grinding-stone there.
The blood of many leaders of herds is in him,
thick as the juice of henna in combed white hair.

As I rode him we saw a flock of wild sheep, the ewes like maidens
in long-trailing robes;
They turned for flight, but already he had passed the leaders
before they could scatter.

He outran a bull and a cow and killed them both,
and they were made ready for cooking;
Yet he did not even sweat so as to need washing.

We returned at evening, and the eye could scarcely realize his beauty
For, when gazing at one part, the eye was drawn away
by the perfection of another part.

He stood all night with his saddle and bridle on him,
He stood all night while I gazed at him admiring,
and did not rest in his stable.

———◆———

This portion of a poem by Imru al Quais is so honored for its cadence and beauty that it is one of the "seven hanged poems" in the Ka'ba at Mecca. The prophet Muhammad insisted that all idols be removed from the Ka'ba, as they were an affront to the one true God. However, Muhammad praised al Quais' poetry to such an extent that some historians believe the literary style of *The Holy Quran* was patterned on the work of this great poet.

Ancient Arabic poetry often was based on the spectacle of the natural world, particularly the strength and dignity of prized animals. One does not need to be an equestrian, though, to appreciate the incomparable design of the horse. Truly, even a half-discerning eye can appreciate the amazing musculature of the jaguar and the delicate architecture of the praying mantis. We all marvel at the camel's bizarre humps, the anteater's strange snout, and the peacock's decadent plumage. What a glorious demonstration of God's handiwork the animal kingdom represents ... what a gift!

About a month ago, I took my (young adult) children to the zoo. We had not been to the zoo in well over ten years, and the day turned out to be special, really special. It may seem trite to write this, but the zoo made us all feel like kids again. We laughed at the antics of the apes, watched a pygmy hippo play in its pool, and ate our lunch beside the pandas, who also were tearing into their bamboo supper.

However, our joy was dampened at nearly every exhibit due to the presence of an "endangered" or "near extinction" sign. Everywhere we looked, the signs were present, reminding us of the precarious time in which animals – and we – now live. Once again, I found myself apologizing to my children for the failures of my generation. And once again, my children looked at me in dismay.

When will we finally accept the fact that we are responsible for what happens on this planet – both the compassion and the carnage?

Love Is the Answer for Unity with All Beings

By Marc Bekoff, Ph.D.

Non-human species (a/k/a "animals") live within us and without us. Animals are intimate and indispensable parts of our spiritual lives. We weave them into numerous aspects of our being – perhaps all parts – because they are active participants in the vital and life-promoting processes of integration, assimilation, and surrender. These processes give birth to dynamic and reciprocal transformations between species that can help humans attain compassion, enlightenment, and Love. Ideally, our interconnections with animals offer us kaleidoscopic journeys toward planetary wholeness and unity. So, what's Love got to do with it? Everything and then some, especially if we want to increase our "compassion footprint" and thereby reduce wanton and intentional cruelty to all life on Earth.

Minding Animals and Increasing Our Compassion Footprint

Love comes in many different flavors and the word often is used in contradictory ways. For example, many people tell me that they Love animals and then they harm or kill them. My simple response is, "I'm glad you don't Love me!" Here are two good stories with which to begin our foray into Love of animals.

A recent trip to Kenya and Tanzania opened all my senses to the world of elephants, some of whom are the most amazing beings I've ever known. Observing large groups of wild elephants close up, I could feel their majestic presence, awareness, and emotions. Such first-hand experiences are wholly different from seeing bored, sick, and emotionally deprived captive elephants, who often live alone in the confines and unnatural settings of a zoo. In contrast, wild elephants live a deeply spiritual, inspirational, and transformative existence. While watching a group of wild elephants living in the Samburu Reserve in Northern Kenya, I noted that one of them, Babyl, walked very slowly. I learned that she was crippled and that she couldn't travel as fast as the rest of the herd. However, the elephants in Babyl's group didn't leave her behind; they waited for her. When I asked our guide about this, he said that the elephants always waited for Babyl and that they'd been doing so for years. The elephants would walk for a while but then stop to see where Babyl was. Depending on how she was doing, the other elephants would either wait or proceed. The matriarch of the herd even fed Babyl on occasion.

Why did the herd act this way? Babyl could do little for them, so there seemed to be no reason for them to help her. The only obvious conclusion is that the other elephants cared for Babyl and adjusted their behavior to allow her to remain with the group. Friendship, empathy, and Love go a long way. And Babyl's herd isn't an isolated example. In 2006, an elephant wandered into a village in Jharkhand state and accidentally fell into a ditch and drowned. The villagers quietly buried the lone elephant, but later 14 elephants crashed through their village trying to find their missing friend. Thousands of people had to flee their homes in the chaos that followed.

And then there's the story of Ben and Bill – two stray Jack Russell terriers who were found filthy and terrified, cowering on the main street of a small town. We all know that dogs are "man's best friend," since their devotion to humans is undeniable. But they also can be best friends to one another. When these terriers were found, one was bleeding from both eyes and the other was standing guard, barking and snapping at anyone who approached. The dogs were taken to a veterinarian, who determined that Ben (as he was later named) had been stabbed. As a result of these injuries, both of Ben's eyes had to be removed and the lids sewn up. Two days after the operation, Ben was reunited with his pal Bill in the local animal shelter. From that moment on, Bill acted as Ben's guide dog. Bill held onto Ben by the scruff of his neck and walked him around the yard until he knew the lay of the land. After a TV crew captured this amazing performance, the two dogs found a marvelous home with an elderly couple. With Bill's nudges and tugs, Ben quickly learned to negotiate their little house and garden as well. According to their human guardians, Bill and Ben now sleep curled up together and behave "rather like a married couple." Ben and Bill are not mates, as they are both male. But clearly, the dogs Love each other in a way that we typically think of as "human."

Embracing the Similarities and Differences: It's not "Us" vs. "Them"

Despite our commonalities, billions of animals are in precarious situations. We use them, we eat them, and we exterminate them as we proceed to redecorate our planet. Currently, 25% of wild mammal species face extinction. In the thirty minutes or so it will take you to read this essay, about 1.5 million animals will have been slaughtered for food in the United States alone. Grok that!

Thus, human relationships with animals are full of contradictions and ambivalence. On the one hand, animals are revered and worshipped as an indispensable part of the tapestry of life. On the other hand, animals are used and abused in a sickening and morally repugnant array of human-centered activities. Animals are confused and desperate as a result of the wide spread and wanton abuse they suffer at our hands. It's a double-cross: *We welcome animals into our lives, and then we treat them as if their lives don't count.*

This love/hate relationship makes life difficult, if not schizophrenic, for both animals and humans. It is truly ironic that animals are used to define where humans are in the great chain of being – the chain that's presented as a "hierarchy of beings" in which human animals place themselves above all other animals. We're not "more evolved" than mice or rabbits or dogs or cats. If we were evolved, we wouldn't harm the other animals.

Hierarchical speciesism results in endless cruelty and actually is bad biology. Trumping the interests of animals "in the name of science" for example, really means "in the name of humans." Isn't that convenient? We declare that we are more valuable than our animal kin and then we proceed to slowly exterminate the other animals that inhabit this planet. We fail to take them seriously for who and what they are due to our narrow anthropocentric view of the world. Throughout the world, animals have little to no legal standing – they are merely *property* like backpacks or bicycles, and humans are their *owners*. Consequently, animals are routinely dismissed, disenfranchised, relocated, bartered, harmed, and killed. Often this happens in the name of education, science, entertainment, clothing, or food. Once again, these are nothing more than self-serving excuses. Shame on us.

Existing laws and regulations don't adequately protect animals. We're fooling ourselves when we claim that animals used in research do not experience pain and suffering. What some scientists call "good welfare" isn't good enough. For instance, existing regulations allow mice to be shocked, rats to be starved or force-fed, pigs to be castrated without anesthesia, cats to be blinded, dogs to be shot with bullets, and primates to have their brains invaded with electrodes. And only about 1% of animals used in research in the United States are even protected by legislation, which is often written in nonsensical ways to accommodate the "needs" of researchers.

Here's a perfect example as quoted from the *Federal Register*, Vol. 69, No. 108 (June 4, 2004): "We are amending the Animal Welfare Act (AWA) regulations to reflect an amendment to the Act's definition of the term *animal*. The Farm Security and Rural Investment Act of 2002 amended the definition of *animal* to specifically exclude birds, rats of the genus Rattus, and mice of the genus *Mus*, bred for use in research." It may surprise you to hear that birds, rats, and mice are no longer considered animals, but that's the sort of logic that epitomizes federal legislation. Since researchers are not allowed to abuse animals, the definition of animal is simply revised until it only refers to creatures researchers don't need.

Just as we feel a wide variety of emotions, the life experience of animals is laden with magic and wonder. Just as we marvel at the mysteries of life, animals feel the grandeur and magic of the environs in which they live. Look at their eyes – gleaming with joy when they are treated with Love and dull when they are treated with cruelty.

In fact, the eyes of a cat were instrumental in my development as a scientist: One of the doctoral research projects I was involved in required that we kill the cats we were studying during the final experiment. I was assigned "Speedo" – a very intelligent cat whom I secretly named (secretly, because we weren't supposed to name our "subjects"). When I got Speedo from his cage for the last time, he looked at me as though he knew it was his final journey. While I held him, he seemed to ask, "Why me?" And he would not break his piercing stare. Tears came to my eyes. Though I followed through with the experiment (I had to because he had only part of his brain left), it broke my heart. To this day, I remember his unwavering eyes – they told the story of lost dignity and interminable pain. Others in the program tried to reassure me that the scientific benefits were worth it, but I strongly disagreed and left feeling sick in my heart.

It is misleading to present humans and animals in an "us" versus "them" framework. While there are many differences, the variations in species should be cherished rather than used to establish false and misleading boundaries. The multitudes of likenesses clearly show that "we are them" and "they are us." The borders are indeed blurred, since tool use, consciousness, rationality, morality, language, culture, and art can no longer be used to separate humans and animals. Many of the differences are a matter of degree rather than differences in kind. Charles Darwin stressed this in his *Theory of Natural Selection*, in which he discovered evolutionary continuity in the anatomy, behavior, and mental lives (including thinking, consciousness, and emotions) of a wide variety of animals – species that seem, at a superficial glance, to be radically different from our own.

In his poem, *Please Call Me by My True Names*, Thich Nhat Hanh writes, "We are the shared emotions of all our brethren. We are truly a kindred spirit with all of life." I believe that we are all part of the same deeply interconnected and interdependent community – a union based on interconnecting and reciprocal bonds that overflow with respect, compassion, and Love. I feel blessed when I open myself to the Love of other animals. When I study coyotes I am coyote, when I study birds I am bird. Often when I stare at a tree, I am tree and I feel a strong sense of oneness.

Every being contributes to the social matrix, which I define as an integrated tapestry, a dynamic event that resists being reduced to mere language given the evolutionary state of all species. My spiritual quest has taken me to an arena where science, ethology, and spirituality meet. Much of my journey owes itself to my interactions with other animals and their willingness to share their lives with me. Watching a red fox bury another red fox in blissful play, observing the birth of coyote pups and the tender care provided by the parents, and nearly falling over a mountain lion as he protected a fresh deer kill – all these experiences make me realize how much of "me" is defined by my relationship with "them."

Where To From Here? Science and Spirit

Scientists have learned that the presence of animals affects our spirituality, because animals help foster a deep feeling of oneness and wholeness. Animals are present in our hearts even when they are not immediately present in body. Although we may not see animals, they may be present in sounds and smells that remind us they are near. So even in the absence of the kaleidoscope of cues they directly provide, animals are naturally near and dear to our hearts.

Scientists also have learned that animals share the neural apparatus and neuro-chemicals that underlie the experience and expression of a wide variety of emotions. This begs the question: *Do animals feel the ups and downs of their daily lives as we do?* Put another way, can an animal feel "Wow!" the same way I feel "Wow!" when I am excited by nature?

This is not a frivolous question. We now know that many animals experience rich and deep emotional lives. We know that they can be happy and sad, that they can experience joy and grief. Consequently, I think that many animals exclaim "Wow!" in their own way: when they experience the panoply of joy associated with life's pleasures, or when they experience the agonizing depths of suffering after we've breached their trust. Yet another reason to offer animals the best life we can.

In many ways, however, we need animals more than they need us. Just consider: In our absence most animals would go on to live quite contentedly. However, our hearts and spirits erode when we lose a pet, accidentally harm an animal, or even purposely abuse an animal because they are an essential part of who we are. So we should step lightly when we trespass into animals' lives. If nothing else, we owe it to our children who will surely miss the animals they are only able to see in books about a bygone era ...

When we pillage Earth we destroy the deep and reciprocal interconnections that define all life, the interrelationships that resonate in all beings and all things. When we desecrate Earth an eerie coldness prevails. For when we slay nature we kill the animals, trees, and the ubiquitous universal spirit that connects us all. It chills my heart to imagine being severed from the Earth community or leaving fewer species of life to our children. Surely, we do not want to be remembered as the generation that killed nature. In sum, we must stop ravaging Earth or we jeopardize our own spirituality. Love must rule.

Animals Keep Our Dreams Alive

While we clearly are destroying the very animals and landscapes we Love, there is hope. I am a dreamer, a die-hard optimist. If Love rules we can save the endangered animals and our planet. But time is not on our side. There really is a sense of urgency. Each and every one of us must do something – anything – to make Earth a better place for all beings and things. Let us create a path for future generations so that they will be able to enjoy the many wondrous gifts of nature ... so that they will shout, "Wow!"

I ask people to imagine that they carry a suitcase of courage, compassion, and hope and that because we receive what they give, the supply of courage, compassion, and hope is never exhausted. And while Love isn't a specific game plan, it must underlie any cure intended to heal the wounds and dysfunctional relationships we have created with nature. Each and every one of us must play an essential role so that our spirits become intertwined with the spirits of all others. If Love is poured out in abundance, then it will be returned in abundance.

We need to replace "mindlessness" with "mindfulness" in our interactions with animals and Earth. Perhaps the biggest question of all is whether enough of us will choose to make the heartfelt commitment to improving this world. Surely, we will feel better about ourselves if we know deep in our hearts that we did the best we could and took into account the well-being of the magnificent animals with whom we share Earth. These beings are awesome and magical, and they selflessly make our lives richer, more challenging, and more enjoyable. And for the wild animals, it will feel good to know that we helped them, even if we cannot see, hear, or smell them. Many of us already have embarked on this pilgrimage. My Love of animals leads me in no other direction.

Animals have taught me a great deal about responsibility, compassion, caring, forgiveness, and the value of deep friendship and Love. Animals generously share their hearts with us, and I want to do the same. As we come to live more in harmony with nature, we can restore, rekindle, and recreate ourselves and our psyches, which have been fragmented because of our alienation from animals and nature. In short, we increase our own spirituality by loving animals more and more.

> We need to make peace with other animals.
> We need nature and wildness.
> We need wolf, eagle, coyote, deer, and hawk.
> We need their spirit.
> We need their love.
> And, most of all we need one another.

An Animal Manifesto: Ten Reasons to Treat Animals Better

Animals want to be treated with dignity and respect. Like us, they seek pleasure and avoid pain. And like us, they have a point of view. It's really pretty simple. Here are ten reasons why animals deserve far more than we've been giving them:

1. *We're all family.* Animals deserve the same dignity and respect we should be showing one another.

2. *They're more complex than we previously thought.* Like us, animals are smart, curious, and creative. They react with emotion and empathy to their world. And they feel pain.

3. *This land is their land, too.* Earth was not made just for us – we need to be more careful and caring when we redecorate nature.

4. *They touch our heart and soul in unique ways.* Our hearts are shriveling for lack of a connection. And when the animals are gone, we'll miss them more than they miss us.

5. *We need to look out for one another.* Compassion breeds compassion; when we care for animals we care for ourselves. In fact, we need them more than they need us.

6. *We're responsible for everything that happens on Earth.* We're here, there, and everywhere, and we are the caretakers of this planet.

7. *What we're doing now doesn't work.* Eating, wearing, relocating, experimenting on, and imprisoning animals is leading to extinction (theirs and ours).

8. *"Good welfare" isn't good enough.* Existing laws and regulations don't adequately protect animals, and we must no longer sanction their abuse.

9. *We need to increase our compassion footprint.* We need to make peace with animals or we will have no peace on this planet.

10. *We can't progress spiritually without them.* All faiths teach that everlasting peace is conditioned on showing Love for sentient beings ... that includes animals.

⟺⬥⟺

Scientists report that there have been five great extinctions since life crawled out of the oceans approximately 450 million years ago. During each of the five great extinctions, between 50% – 95% of all life on our planet was lost. Thereafter, research has shown that it took roughly ten million years for Earth to reestablish the biodiversity that existed before each extinction event.

Presently, we are experiencing what scientists call the "Sixth Great Extinction." But this death march is different than the previous extinctions for two very important reasons: First, the current extinction is a man-made event (as opposed to a naturally occurring disaster, like a meteor hitting our planet or an ice age). Second, this extinction may kill us too – *Homo sapiens* weren't around the last time vast amounts of life on Earth vanished.

The International Union for the Conservation of Nature (IUCN) maintains a "Red List" of endangered species. Currently, IUCN estimates that one in four mammals, one in eight birds, and one in three amphibians are at risk of extinction. In total, 40% of the species of planet Earth are in danger, including 51% of reptiles, 52% of insects, and 73% of our flowering plants. Scientists also report that 90% of all large fishes have disappeared from the oceans. And those life forms that are not currently impacted by mankind's mania will feel the effects soon enough, for the biodiversity of ecosystems is intertwined. In other words, life is dependent on life ... all the way up the food chain to us.

As Marc and our next author Jana know all too well, we are witnessing the slaughter of our beloved animals. Which brings us back to the main point: *The Sixth Great Extinction is our fault – yours and mine.*

CHANCE ENCOUNTER WITH A LIKE SOUL

By Jana Lee Frazier

Once upon a time when I first fell into depression, I was asked to go to a farm out West where an animal caught in a coyote trap lay in a cage awaiting identification. He was so big, they said – too big to be a coyote or a dog. Could he be an abandoned wolf-dog or was he actually a wolf?

It turned out that he was a wolf. The man from the wildlife division said so immediately. And when it was my turn to move close to the bars to kneel in front of him, I gasped. I knew him; I would have known him anywhere. He had come to meet me from my dreams; he was waiting for me across the span of countless miles and many years. I looked up at the sky and below at my feet. At just this point where longitude and latitude collide, our paths had crossed.

For a long time I had been a keeper of animals at an urban zoo. Daily, I beheld sinuous tigers swimming in deep pools, had been mesmerized by the russet coats of jaguars emblazoned in rosettes, spoke sign language with silverback gorillas as they dined, fed spangled fish to a rare river dolphin, and rubbed down the stony skins of white rhinoceros with warm oil. I had held hours-old red wolf pups in my hands still slick from their mother's tongue, their ears and eyes sealed shut and their little hearts beating fast. I had been lucky and I knew it.

But I had never in all those years, studying that wide array of animals, seen anything like the effulgence emanating from that wolf's eyes. Not of this Earth, ethereal, effervescent. The radiance seethed and shone a deep, pulsating emerald. Like jewels in sunlight. Stained glass in a church. He never blinked. In his unwavering gaze I saw all of God's creation: the spines and spires of mountain ranges, all the blue rivers receiving rain and rushing to the sea and the sea accepting the gifts of silt and grit. I saw snow falling slowly from smoky clouds, the skeletons of old trees spare, bare and black in winter, fields of wildflowers caught in the throes of spring winds, the conflagration that is autumn. And lightning igniting like fireworks in a summer squall.

This animal had been caught by only a toe. The man who set the trap had called authorities. The wolf offered no resistance, allowed a noose to be lowered around his neck, allowed himself to be led to the box in the back of the truck and taken to this place like a prisoner of war. He did not speak; he did not struggle. Or eat or drink. Yet I did not sense any fear in him, nor did his breath on my arm make goose bumps as he lay there at the mercy of the whim of man. Urgent, high-level meetings were called quickly to discuss this crisis. A wolf had not been seen in this place for seventy years.

He was incarcerated; he could be executed. I understood his dire plight even as I knew the severity of my own. We were both trapped: his body caged against the fervent freedom that he craved, and my mind mired in the quicksand of sorrow. When we parted ways only an hour later, I was not the same person. I took with me a little bit of his soul, a whole lot of that light.

After his long-distance exodus, the decision came deeming him unwelcome there. He was tranquilized, tagged, weighed, measured, and radio-collared before being released into the wilderness from whence he came. Some had wanted him killed, others wanted to kill him. As a biologist, I was not naive about his potential power, his hunting prowess, the strength of his jaws, the plans he might have to bring down a cow or a sheep. But I also knew that into his elemental nature was sewn a deep reserve and shyness that asked him to stay away from man and his activities.

Sometimes my sadness makes me cynical, but I cannot be cynical about the wolf. Six years after I met him on that far-away farm, he is gone, shot a few days after the delisting of his species from endangered status. That irony is not lost on me. I can't help thinking his death was born of a kind of bigotry. What I am mourning is the magic spell that he cast, a wild magic that is ebbing away each passing year as houses, hospitals, shopping centers, and factories claim the land. I never got to hear him sing, but on a starry evening just after dusk, people I know told me they did hear him, just days before he died.

And as I sit here writing his eulogy, this world is a much less beautiful place.

The Wolf by Jana Lee Frazier

THE ANIMALS DO JUDGE

By Madeleine L'Engle
(1918–2007)

We need not wait for God
The animals do judge
Of air and sea and grass
Accusing with their eyes
Waiting here en masse
They cry out with their blood

The whale caught in surprise
By oil slick's killing sludge
The cow with poisoned milk
The elephant's muted roar
At radioactive food
The tiger's mangy hide
The silkworm's broken silk
The animals do judge
The dead gulls on the shore
Mists of insecticide
Killing all spore and sperm
Eagle and owl have died
And nematode and worm
The snakes drag in the mud
Fallen the lion's pride
The night moth's wings are bruised

They cry out with their blood
Cain! Killer! We are named
By beast and bird condemned
By fish and fowl accused
We need not wait for God
The animals do judge.

THE GIFT OF ANIMALS: UNCONDITIONAL LOVE

By Dawn E. Hayman

Animals live in our hearts freely. People who have animals in their lives frequently allow animals into places where they don't allow humans – deep into their hearts. Why? The answer is so simple; yet, in its simplicity, it reveals one of the largest roadblocks to human growth: *Animals Love us unconditionally*.

They Love us for who we are, not for false images that we project onto them. You can have a terrible day, feel like a miserable failure, yet walk into your home or barn and be greeted by an animal friend who could care less what you've done that day – they just want to Love you. Animals respond from their hearts and give freely to us, without reservation and without judgment.

The fact that animals understand pure unconditional Love and practice it naturally is the very reason that people let them into their hearts. We trust them. Animals, unlike humans, do not separate themselves from one another, from us, or from nature. They understand the oneness of the Universe. They innately know that all beings communicate freely with one another. It is we humans who have changed our position among other life forms by literally removing ourselves from the chain of life. We rationalize that we are superior because of our "unique" ability to reason and communicate. We have created "authorities" who pontificate on our superiority over everything else in nature and our greater spirituality. These authorities presume to teach us and dictate to us what is good and what is bad, what is spiritual and what is not. Moreover, these authorities presume to tell us who, when, where, and how we are allowed to Love in a bizarre attempt to define the "superior" human experience.

For instance, we proclaim ourselves advanced because of our supposed powers of deduction and communication. One need only look at the history of the human experience to see that we are champions at neither. As a matter of fact, when one looks closely at the world of animals and nature, it becomes obvious that humans are the *worst* communicators on Earth. We, as a species, do not listen or communicate well with one another, let alone with other species. Yet, in the world of animals and nature there is communication with all. And there is understanding and Love for all.

When we humans insist on setting ourselves apart from the rest of nature, we immediately put ourselves at odds with all the other elements of creation. By our own acts, we either become dictators or victims of our natural surroundings. As such, we fail to communicate with the rest of the living world, and we fail to recognize a central truth: *Everything is connected.*

Nature communicates telepathically. In fact, telepathy is the most basic and universal mode of communication. It is the language of the heart – the vast beating heart of the Universe. Telepathy is the thought and feeling behind the words we speak. But because we humans put such emphasis on words, most of us ignore and even ridicule telepathy. Reading, writing, and speaking are just some of the ways we communicate. And while animals don't have the verbal capability of humans, many animals understand our language and even our written symbols. More importantly, though, through body language, grunts, and squeaks, animals know how to communicate on a deeper level than humans – through pure action and Love.

Most of us have forgotten this most basic form of communication. But over the past twenty years, I've had the amazing privilege of communicating telepathically with thousands of animals. I have shared, experienced, and witnessed the most profound depth of spirit, since animals use pure heart energy to communicate. It is the base from which they operate – just like the rest of nature. If mankind is to rejoin the rest of creation, we must relearn and trust the wisdom of our hearts and, once again, communicate from our hearts. We need to remember how to live without judgment and how to Love without condition. We have to reawaken our true spirit – which is one with the animals and nature.

Many animals have "signed on" to work with humans, even though many of them suffer due to our lingering ignorance – our failure to understand that what we do to them, we do to ourselves. Daily, animals endure unthinkable pain and oftentimes torturous deaths. Even so, animals convey messages of Love. They dwell in Love as a matter of daily course, and they wait for us to wake up from our long sleep and join them at the heart level. They are optimistic that we will make it. Their optimism fills me with hope. Truly, the depth of Love that animals share with me and with their human friends in consultations amazes and humbles me.

The relationships that people have with animals are endlessly varied. For many people, the focus is on competitions, sporting events, or working situations, such as dogs in show rings or on agility fields, horses in Olympic events or at the race track, helpmates for the handicapped or for search and rescue. Then there are animals who are in our food chain, whose lives and suffering often go unnoticed or unacknowledged. And, of course, there are the pets in our homes.

A major role that animals play in the human experience is that of healers. After 9/11 for example, the role that animals played in the healing of thousands of people was astonishing. Human rescuers who couldn't talk about their ordeal would instantly melt and open their hearts when a dog walked into the room. And millions of people are comforted in their homes every day by the gentle purring of cats or the companionship of dogs. In moments of deep sadness, people will laugh out loud if animals start to play. Few who have been around animals would argue against the idea that animals are healing.

So what gives animals the magic ability to heal? It is unconditional Love – an experience we crave and need in our lives. Such Love is given freely, simply, and without judgment by animals because animals live in the moment. It is not that they lack a concept of time; it's just that time does not consume them. Everyone has experienced a happy dog – they express themselves instantly with tail wagging and body wiggling. And when they get angry, they express themselves just as quickly. Their hearts are free to express their feelings without the need for analysis. People who have animals in their lives experience this truth daily and know that animals express Love for us immediately, completely, and naturally.

Recently, I had a communication from an Arabian mare that addresses this very topic:

> Currently, the connection between people and animals is very important, as animals embrace the heart without judgment or conditions. Humans reach for this connection like a much-needed tonic; it is like that for the animals as well, as they desire for all hearts to join together. But people need to connect with each other.
>
> You may suddenly be aware of deep friendships forming with people that have been on your periphery. As your heart begins to merge and you Love one another for the true beauty that each of you exhibits and expresses, the heart of the Universe will reach out to you. As this mass synchronizes, literally all of Life will beat in rhythm and unison. And at that moment, a healing that has never before been experienced will occur. Each and every life form is trying to join in this experience. You have chosen to be alive now for just this experience, which will generate tremendous force.
>
> Humans are the one species on the Earth that attaches conditions on its Love. The animals understand that Love just is. Yet humans, through

religions and social organizations, have created types of Love, degrees of Love, and rules as to whom you may or may not Love. There is friendship Love, parental Love, familial Love, and romantic Love, to name a few. Romantic Love often is designated as the highest form – and saddled with the most regulation. Then, within each type of Love, you have developed accepted levels of expressing Love. All sheer foolishness. To put regulations on Love is an absurdity that is now becoming clear to you. Already, your society feels the tug of a major spiritual shift.

Many of you, when you feel Love for another, instantly pull back as if what you are feeling is wrong, taboo, not right, ungodly. Yet, I emphatically tell you that it is most godly to Love and to express Love. When you feel a heart connection, you should not stop to think about whether it is right or wrong. You should not worry about what social rule may be broken if you set your heart free. To stifle the heart is to smother the soul.

Very few humans allow themselves to completely surrender to Love. But when you do, you feel the power of Love in all your relationships – whether friend, lover, family member, or stranger. Then, you can form a heart connection with many. That is what animals do, and it is part of the magic which draws people to them. It is more than loving unconditionally, it is loving whole-heartedly. And it is the most natural thing that you can do, for Love is a natural occurrence – as natural as breathing.

Many of you will experience this heart connection as a surrendering to the heart, breaking forth from the self-imposed chains keeping the heart in place. Love is the essence of the heart. Experience that Love and your relationships will begin to feel more intense as the spiritual shift occurs. It will feel like you are falling in Love anew. The human heart longs to fall in Love.

To journey into a world based on Love, you must forge a path straight from the heart. Conversely, if you lead with the intellect and try to think your way through, you will not make it. The three most powerful words in the human language – I Love you – activate a direct connection when spoken from the heart. Let us animals help you to practice these words, and then say them to each other with intention.

Your relationships are of great importance to your future. It is not how many relationships you have, but whether you freely share your heart. If you are feeling drawn to another person, it is because you have something to offer another on a heart level. When you deny the connection, you deny the healing. You all come with gifts for one another. But so often you do not share them for fear of rejection or being misunderstood. How can Love ever be misunderstood? The language of the heart is clear and pure. It is ever growing and expanding. It is alive and flowing. Think of Love as a river. If you jump in and relax, it will carry you along safely. But if you try to fight the current, it will be a rough ride. Like water, Love is naturally buoyant – all you need do is float.

And don't feel shy when your hearts connect. When you connect with another human, you see each other for the beautiful beings that you are. Why do you think people feel so good around us animals? We see you for who you are without conditions. And you can do that for each other, if only you would take the chains off of your hearts and go with the flow. If only you would let yourselves fall in Love with each other. Imagine your world if all of you loved one another – truly loved one another ...

Love is the miracle behind creation. It is the force behind the brightness of the Sun, the blue in the sky, and the blooming of the flower. It is the breath behind my neigh – the life force itself! When you make a heart connection with one of us or with each other, your heart expands. Go with that feeling. Let it breathe. Let it grow. That life force is within us and it is within you. Find it, nurture it, and then set your hearts free.

And then there is the following message given to me by a dog, who also understands the pitfalls of human language:

Words, when spoken from the heart, are the audible forms of feelings. But sometimes humans use words without putting meaning behind them. Why do you speak of Love when it isn't so? And sometimes humans try to speak when they reach a space where Love cannot be expressed with words. We know that you Love us by the way you look at us and stroke us.

If you want to use words, then the words should be a vessel for your Love. For example, if you are dying of thirst, a friend may give you water by bringing it to you in a cup. The water is what sustains you, and the cup is what holds the water. But if you were brought cups that contained no water, you would stop looking to the cup as the vessel of that life force. Such has been the human experience with words of the heart – they often are empty vessels. You may hear words of Love, but they are meaningless because the other person did not say them with genuine life force. So Love is like the water: You need it for sustenance. And words are like the cup: You can carry purity with them, or you can offer nothing until no one listens anymore.

Our animal relationships are not only based on unconditional Love. There are other purposes to these relationships. Sometimes animals enter our lives for uncomplicated reasons – simply to live with us, have fun, and share Love. And sometimes animals come into our lives to share a particular gift or teach us a lesson. Just as there are master teachers and healers among humans, there are master teachers and healers among the animals. This is hard for many people to comprehend. Yet, after your life has been touched by a master, whether human or animal, you never forget the experience. It can be a chance meeting or a long relationship, but one thing is clear: After you've met one of these masters, no matter how long you're with them, your life is never the same again.

Consequently, animals may appear as friends, teachers, personal guides, or angels. A beautiful illustration of this can be seen in the story of a woman who came to me for a consultation after she lost her beloved dog who was young and in seemingly good health when he died. The woman had let the dog outside while she prepared his supper. When she called him back inside to eat, there was no response. Knowing something was wrong, she ran outside and found the dog lying on his side. The vet later determined that the dog had a massive heart attack. The woman was devastated and had been mourning the dog for over a year when I met her.

I expected this to be the usual sort of consultation that occurs when I am asked to contact an animal who has passed – the reconnecting of two hearts, one in the physical and one in spirit. But the woman still was not past her grief and guilt, feeling that she must have missed something obvious about the dog's health. She was convinced that she had "killed her best friend."

As the woman arrived at my farm, a fox appeared in the driveway. When she got out of her car, the fox ran ahead of her and jumped up on my porch. Then, the fox stayed there for a few minutes, looking her right in the eye, before running off. When she entered my house, she asked if I had a pet fox. No, there is no pet fox at Spring Farm Cares.

When I start a consultation, I usually ask for the animal's name, age, sex, and breed. In this case, however, as the woman began to talk about her dog, he came right through. In fact, he was desperate to get a message to this woman! This is the message I relayed:

> *I know you are sad, but you need to know who I am and why I came to you when I did and, most importantly, why I had to leave when I did. You were at a point in your life where you were feeling very alone. You said a prayer that you would find someone who would be your friend. You also prayed for a healing in your life. I was the answer to both prayers. Do not focus on how long I was with you, but what I brought to you. Think of what was happening in your life when I came to you. Not only did I bring you the Love you asked for, but I also helped you set your own heart free by loving me. And in my passing, you witnessed the greatest healing of all. We didn't spend much time together but we accomplished great things. And I completed the task that I came to do – bring you Love and the healing which occurred at my death.*

When I was done speaking, the woman sat crying. Obviously, she understood the message. I told her that I could feel the amazing spirit of this dog and their Love for one another. But still, as often happens, the woman wanted additional confirmation of what I was getting: Was there something else the dog could share so that she could be sure that the message was from him?

At this point, I finally asked for the dog's name.

"Foxy," she said.

Instantly, Foxy came through again and said, "I came to her as she pulled in the driveway."

The woman gasped, as she realized that the fox was her friend. Minutes passed before she was able to speak again. When she did finally speak, she told me the rest of the story. I watched as years of tension melted from her face and her face grew bright.

She had been married for years to a very violent man who was abusive in the relationship and refused to get help. Additionally, her husband did not like dogs. For years, she had not gotten a dog for fear that he would harm it. But in her grief, despair, and loneliness, she did pray for a friend to come to her. She wanted someone in her life whom she could trust and who would Love her. And she also asked that her husband be healed.

Foxy had shown up in her life unexpectedly. Instantly, she grew attached to the dog and knew that she had to bring him home. The dog was her saving grace, giving her all the Love and affection that she so craved. But her husband despised Foxy, so she never left Foxy alone with him for fear that he might harm the dog.

Never once had her husband shown any interest or affection for Foxy. But when she found Foxy dead in the backyard and screamed, her husband came running out of the house.

"He's dead!" she cried. "Foxy is dead!"

"No – that can't be!" he exclaimed. Then he sank down beside Foxy, gathered the dog into his arms and began to sob. It was the first time the woman had ever seen her husband cry. And he stayed there in the back yard for over two hours, rocking Foxy's lifeless body and sobbing.

The next day, her husband came to her and said, "I Love you." He had never said these words before. He told her that he needed help and that, if she were still willing, he would go to counseling with her to save their marriage.

In the year following Foxy's death, her husband was gentle and loving. They now have two new dogs, and her husband is able to exchange Love and affection with the dogs and with his wife. Through more tears, she told me, "Now, I understand ... why Foxy came ... why he left. Foxy's Love healed both of us."

These are just some of many stories I have encountered that reflect the deep relationships between people and animals. These encounters illustrate why animals are here and what gifts they bring. Through these gifts of loving and living unconditionally in the present, animals provide shining instruction as to what our human hearts can achieve if we will reconnect with all the other beings on this planet. We are not better than or superior to any other species.

Yes, we humans are unique, but it is time for us to shift from brain power to heart power. We must look beyond our verbal skills and, like the animals, use our hearts to communicate. Humans have the loudest voices on Earth but the quietest hearts. It is now time for us to seek balance and participate in the ultimate healing of this planet. By learning the language of the heart – unconditional Love – such a healing will come. And to help us reach this goal, animals are here ... to walk patiently beside us and lovingly show us how it's done.

———————

Whether or not you are open enough to believe that Dawn has the ability to talk with animals, you certainly have experienced communion on an unspoken level with your own pet. These communications are sacred, and no less so because one of the participants has a different set of vocal cords. Studies reveal that certain breeds of dogs have the intelligence of three-year-old humans! Most toddlers can speak by the age of two. I can only imagine how badly my dog Shadow wants to say, "I Love you, Mommy."

Recently, people have begun to explore the concept of animal totems – a species that represents your higher self. This idea of communing with animals on a spiritual level is quite ancient. For instance, bears were worshiped by *Homo neanderthalensis* and *Homo sapiens*, as illustrated in cave petroglyphs (*circa* 200,000 B.C.E.). Later, the Greek goddess Athena had an owl on her shoulder to represent her wisdom.

Perhaps the most famous animal totem of all, though, is the snake, which historically has symbolized transmutation and connection to Great Spirit. Hence, the caduceus (the intertwined snakes), which still is used today by the medical community to represent transformation and healing. Unfortunately, the Catholic Church turned the snake into a symbol for the demigod Satan. It is interesting to note, however, that the snake knew more about the tree of knowledge than did Yahweh. (See *Genesis* 2:17, in which God asserts that Adam will die if he eats from the tree; versus *Genesis* 3:4, wherein the snake informs Eve about the truth of the matter.)

My personal totem is the crow – who lives in the void and guards the sacred law. I encourage you to explore which animal represents your higher self. Who knows, perhaps you will start counting crows as I do.

IN SEARCH OF THE SACRED HEART

By Brooke J. Wood

The furry fury was waiting for me – just outside the back door, clinging to the brick. I only caught a glimpse of something gray, hairy, and small, level with my eyes.

I screamed.

I had no idea, as I wheeled around to face a young squirrel, that my world was about to drastically change. Certainly, my first reaction was fear. Why would a squirrel have decided one Sunday morning to plant itself outside our suburban kitchen door and, as it turned out, refuse to go away? In a few short hours all my presumptions and assumptions about life and Love would be replaced by something much less tangible but infinitely more real … and my small guest would help me to put it all into perspective.

I asked my husband, Peter, to call animal control. After all, the tiny visitor didn't seem scared of us. I suspected rabies and feared for my family, as my mother lives with us and my great-niece Kendra was visiting. Peter tried brushing the squirrel away with a broom. Then, he tried scaring him by tossing rocks against the house – all to no avail. The squirrel ran around the corner but scurried right back to the door, gliding along the brick as easy as pie.

I had to work that weekend. "Take care of it please, Pete," I said before driving off.

As I drove to work my thoughts shifted from our small, uninvited guest to my sister, Rhonda. We'd been trying to get in touch with her all weekend. We knew she had a hearing on Friday in divorce court and that it had not gone well. To help out, we were watching her granddaughter Kendra for the weekend. But we wouldn't know until much later just how badly the court hearing went and that she failed to return to court after the noon recess.

On Thursday, I had made contact with her via cell phone while at the dentist. "Let's meet for lunch," I suggested, as I sat up from my annual teeth cleaning. I was in town and only fifteen minutes from where she worked as a registered nurse.

"I can't," she replied in her typically sweet voice. "I've got too much paperwork and a patient to see around noon." She was working in a home health office after years of working for a local doctor and, later, at an area hospital.

Behind her normal girlish quips, I could hear stress in her voice. I also heard something very rare for her – despondency.

I was disappointed we couldn't meet, but I told her I loved her and we said goodbye. On Friday night, after many attempts to reach her by phone to find out how the court hearing went, Peter finally made contact. Rhonda didn't say much, just that it hadn't gone well ... and that she had to vacate her house in thirty days. Peter tried to hand the phone to me or Mom but Rhonda told him that she didn't really want to talk anymore. This was another rare moment for her; usually, she met disappointments with unflappable optimism.

"Tell her I'll come over in the morning and stay with her," Mom offered.

Peter relayed the offer to Rhonda but she replied, "This isn't a good place for her to be this weekend. I just want to be alone." Rhonda was known for being stoic when she wasn't feeling well. Mom used to say that whenever Rhonda was sick she'd just get quiet, like she didn't want to bother anyone.

Rhonda. My beautiful big sister. We grew up on a small farm and she was nine years older than me. Every morning when my parents and brother Danny went to the barn to milk cows, they left me with Rhonda. I don't remember her changing my diapers or bottle-feeding me, but I've heard many stories about how well she cared for me.

Later, when she started dating Mike – not only her first Love but the Love of her life – I was the pesky and perhaps just-a-little-bit jealous younger sister. Whenever Rhonda left me alone with Mike, I would pounce on the couch and throw my arms around his neck. When she returned, Rhonda would be aghast to find me plopped in Mike's lap! Poor Mike – he was too embarrassed to correct my mischievousness. Or maybe he was mature enough to understand that I didn't want my sister to leave me. I was certain that's why he was there – to take her away ... and eventually he did when he became her first husband.

Now, nearly forty years later, I can't remember my exact thoughts about this stage of our lives. But I knew then, just as I know now: *My sister hung the moon and I wanted to be by her side forever.* So naturally, I wouldn't have hesitated to block any perceived threat, particularly one appearing in the form of a boyfriend.

Oh, how I wanted to be just like her! When I saw Rhonda and her friends reclining along the street in front of our house, I grabbed my best friend and sprawled in the road, too. At the age of four, I didn't understand why my Mom punished me for "acting like a stupid teenager." All I did was imitate the coolest person in the world.

And I used to Love listening to her albums: the Beatles, Monkees, and Supremes, over and over and over again. In fact, I played her records so much that the Supremes got stuck repeating "You can't hurry Love." And the Monkees kept taking that "Last train to Clarksville."

Of course, we fought sometimes like all sisters do. When I overplayed her records, she teased me and called me "Seego girl," in reference to a popular commercial. I didn't realize it then, but I was such an obnoxious brat. I probably deserved it when she tied me and my best friend in the barn with ropes so tight that it took us over two hours to get free!

Truly, though, she had a heart of gold. I'll never forget her small Baby Grand music box with the dancing ballerina. I used to sneak it out of her room so I could listen to the music and watch the ballerina whirl around. I soon wore it out, just like I did her records. Years later when I was in my thirties, she bought me one just like it for Christmas. "I felt bad that I used to take mine away from you, so I wanted you to have one just like it," she explained in the sugary yet sincere voice that everyone who knew her came to Love.

Why do we take for granted the Love we encounter in life, especially when it comes from a family member? I know I seldom told Rhonda just how much I loved her. I was particularly neglectful of our relationship as a young adult – when I was driven by ambition to prove myself as a teacher and later worked insane hours as a journalist. At that hectic time in my life I pushed everyone away, as I sought an identifiable measure of success, one that I could take to the bank or one by which others would know me. Stupidly, I pushed myself, my job, my husband, and my family to the brink. Thankfully, though, I managed to save myself and my marriage by electing to leave my hard-won job as a newspaper editor.

I left that position and turned inward because I knew something was missing. As a child, I had searched for deeper meanings and found them in dreamtime visions of God. But when I grew up and entered the "real world," I forgot the light of my childhood. I think our culture finds substitutes for inner peace and knowing. We seek to heal our ruptures, but we end up filling our empty spaces with food or sex or work or some other addiction.

That's what I did. And I see now that's what my sister did, too.

In Rhonda's case, her buoyant spirit actually drew others to her, including many men over the years who claimed to fall in Love with her. If Rhonda had an addiction, it was her perpetual need to experience the intensity of romantic Love. Unfortunately, her second marriage took her down the destructive road that eventually led to a nasty divorce and that ill-fated weekend which would change our lives forever.

I called Peter from work that Sunday morning with two concerns: I wanted an update on the crazy squirrel and, more importantly, I wanted to know if anyone had heard from Rhonda. On Saturday, my Mom had tried to reach her by phone multiple times. If it weren't for the fact that Rhonda lived an hour away, one of us would have popped over to check on her. But that Sunday morning I needed to work, and Pete and my Mom were busy trying to keep Rhonda's granddaughter Kendra entertained and away from our furry guest. When Mom failed to get an answer from Rhonda again on Sunday morning, Peter decided to call Rhonda's next door neighbor and ask him to investigate.

While at work, I got a message from Pete on my cell phone: "Something's wrong at Rhonda's. I'm on my way over there now." He didn't say anything else, so I tried not to worry. At my lunch break, I called him back and he answered in a barely audible voice ... "She's gone."

"What do you mean?" I asked, thinking that she must have left town.

"She's no longer with us," Pete said.

Suddenly, I understood. Pete was trying to avoid the word that would point to the end – the end of the most joyous complement to my life.

I remember slamming my cell phone shut as I screamed, "No!" And then I doubled over and sobbed. The friends who rushed to my side were holding me when Peter called back, worried about how I was and what he could do for me. I reassured him that I was breathing and then I asked what happened. I needed to know. He said that Rhonda had taken her life by overdosing on prescription drugs.

That's when the blame and guilt began ... as it does for the thousands of families who lose a loved one to suicide each year.

The rain was pouring down as my friend Stacey drove me home. Mom, Peter, and Kendra were at Rhonda's house. So, when I got home, I thought I'd be alone. I had completely forgotten about the small, furry friend who had come to our back door that morning.

As Stacey pulled into my driveway, the squirrel was standing on his back legs as if he had been waiting for me. He was standing atop the old barroom countertop we kept in our carport. As I approached the squirrel, my head still spinning with pain and confusion, he crouched as though he wanted to pounce on me.

"That's the squirrel you were telling us all about this morning!" Stacey exclaimed.

"Yeah," I replied despondently. And without really thinking, I put my hand out and the squirrel came toward me. Still uncomfortable with the idea of a wild animal just showing up at our back door, I anxiously jerked my arm back.

"Ah, he's okay," said Stacey, who extended her hand and allowed the squirrel to run up her arm.

I was so surprised that the squirrel befriended Stacey that – for just a moment – I forgot I'd just lost my sister. I smiled in spite of myself. The next thing I knew, the squirrel was crawling up my arm. And then it crawled down my shirt!

After Stacey left, I just sat like that – with my new friend crawling all over me. Soon, I couldn't hold back the tears. I wept and wept, as the squirrel gently tiptoed on my shoulders and then nestled in my hair. I could not help but be aware of the Love coming from that tiny squirrel. Slowly, bits of my pain started to wash away with my tears. And then I started to feel something else … acceptance?

When Mom, Peter, and Kendra returned a short time later, they found me still sitting with the squirrel on top of my shoulder. Mom, who came from a family of "sixth sense" females, looked knowingly at me and then at the squirrel. She would later name him "Dalai."

"He was at my bathroom window this morning, acting like he needed to tell me something," Mom said. According to the police, this was around the same time that Rhonda took her life.

When Rhonda's daughter, Nicole, arrived at my house, Dalai was even more animated. He jumped to the outside window ledge of whichever room in the house she happened to go in. He hopped from the kitchen window to the dining room window to the bathroom window, and he even tried to slide around the door frame to get into the kitchen.

In the days that followed, Dalai comforted us by peeking through the windows and jumping on us whenever we walked into the carport. He even built a nest in the carport by using the flowers and cards we brought home from Rhonda's funeral. We also found Dalai putting mementos into an empty cardboard box – cards that expressed loving thoughts about Rhonda, various flowers, moss from different plants, and a couple wash cloths we had laid outside thinking that was all he would need. As it turned out, Rhonda also had surrounded herself with mementos before she died – family pictures arranged in a semi-circle around her bed

Along with Dalai's now obvious charms, he also had some annoying habits. He uprooted lots of plants, threw dirt at us, and continued his nesting activities beyond his box. Plus, the bigger he grew, the bigger his claws got and the less joy we got from him crawling up our pant legs! But we forgave the mess and discomfort because we loved him being there ... his very presence brought us untold joy.

We often conjecture about Dalai. Some of my friends skeptically concluded that Dalai's appearance the morning of my sister's death was a coincidence – even though no squirrel before or since has found its way to our back door. Most of us, however, recognize that Dalai was sent to be a comfort and a companion during a very difficult time. Strangely, Nicole and Kendra told me that a couple summers before she died, Rhonda attempted to save a squirrel injured by her cat. Always the caretaker, Rhonda had placed the squirrel in a shoebox and tried to nurse it back to health for a couple of days before it passed away. What a mystery ... Rhonda and the squirrels.

Peter often says that when we lost Rhonda we lost the heart of the family. I am sure this is true and, try as I might, I have not been able to replace her delightful spark for our family. Eventually, I stopped trying to fill her shoes. Instead, I began an earnest search for my own peace and purpose.

Rhonda's departure and Dalai's appearance inspired a movement in me that I hadn't felt in a long time – a real quest for inner peace. I was left with a profound sense of Love – from her, from the squirrel, from my family – that led me down a new path of spiritual discovery. I started seeking answers to all the "why" questions in life, the questions that never seem to have an answer, or at least not an answer that comes from the heart. I needed more than pop psychology. I wanted some serious answers, so I commenced a serious journey.

The loss of my sister has been the greatest tragedy of my life. Not coincidentally, the squirrel was the greatest comfort during that difficult time. The simultaneous occurrence of Rhonda's death and Dalai's appearance has proved to me conclusively that "God works in mysterious ways."

My present search for answers has less to do with the organized religion I grew up with and more to do with an inner knowing. However, my birth religion planted the seeds for the path I now follow, wherein I understand that everything is a manifestation of God – even the tragic. When we come to know this truth, we become capable of suspending judgment, regret, and even pain. And we are able to live in the gnosis of the All. The *Gnostic Gospel of St Thomas* states it best for me:

> *Let him who seeks continue seeking until he finds. When he finds he will be astonished, and he will rule over the all.*

Some would call Rhonda's final act selfish, but I cannot judge her. Indeed, how can I judge the type of pain that makes someone feel so separated from life and from God that he or she can't go on? For me, this is the key: Remembering that none of us are separate from God. Until we remember this, we live in an illusion of lack that inevitably leads us down a path of quiet desperation.

I'm sure my sister thought that romantic Love would give her the companionship and peace she sought. But I now know that Love is most fulfilling when it comes from the Sacred Heart – a place of radiant awareness of our nature as bornless spirit, a Divine spark of God. In truth, we are never separate from God; we only have to remember and reestablish our connection. Thus, when my sister's soul passed into another plane, she helped me begin my own journey of the soul.

Dalai stayed with me for about seven months until my sister's birthday – on New Year's Day. A few days into the new year, Peter discovered Dalai's body on top of our mulching bag. Surrounding Dalai were a washcloth, some moss, and a couple remaining memory cards from Rhonda's funeral ceremony.

"He looks so peaceful," Mom muttered. We could tell he hadn't been dead long. Our loss was real once again, but this time I was comforted by my belief that every experience – even the most tragic and painful – is an opportunity to learn, grow, and Love.

⬳⬩◆⬩⬲

So fine is the line between animal kinship and the familial bond that our editors could not decide whether to place Brooke's essay in Chapter II or in Chapter III of this anthology. Is it a story about a squirrel, a biography about her sister, or a narrative of another kind altogether?

I met Brooke when she was teaching a class on the Christian *Kabbalah*. She mentioned her sister's suicide briefly to impress upon us that signs from God can come from the most unlikely of sources. Yes, even a squirrel can comfort a family after such a tragic loss, by bringing profound messages of hope and

Love. And so, hers is a story of a different kind altogether. A story of rebirth, really, since her sister's death eventually helped guide Brooke onto the path of sublime Love – the path of enlightenment.

And then, Brooke did the same for me. She helped guide me to study the *Kabbalah*. That experience, in turn, opened me to even more spiritual knowledge, even more Divine experience. And so it goes. The evolution of spirit.

Before we begin the next chapter on Love of Family, it is worth repeating – over and over again, it is worth repeating: *Humans need Love, and humans need to Love.* It is how we are hardwired. Regardless of whether the source of our Love is an animal, a sibling, or a friend, we need it. Regardless of whether the object of our Love is a child, a patch of this Earth, or a member of the opposite sex, we need to express it. Love is the primary force in this Universe. Love keeps the entire matrix glued together, even when destructive energy comes to call.

The life-death-life cycle is complicated – more complicated than I presently understand. But there is one thing I do understand, and that is that life always finds a way. The "God Game" is about evolution: It started with physical evolution, and now it is about spiritual evolution. Unless humanity makes a quantum leap spiritually, we will not survive the Sixth Great Extinction.

I am not one to dispute or deny the obvious – there is evil in the world. And there are people on this planet who enlist dark energy, who are aligned with the destructive force in the Universe. Yet, once you accept the paradox that God is everything – the state of perfect unity which existed during the First Spiritual Paradigm – you realize that God is both good and evil, both light and dark. Why, then, do I think Love is the most powerful force in the Universe?

We will explore the apparent duality of God a bit later in this anthology. For now, let me simply state my intuitive belief that Love is the only force that can save us, the only religion upon which we may safely rely. We need to evolve to a place of Love – quickly and collectively – if we want to make it through the current Great Cusp. The Fifth Spiritual Paradigm will not arrive until we evolve into a new type of human – one who understands that all life is connected and that all relationships are interdependent.

Logically, then, it is time for us to ponder how our immediate family members sculpt our initial understanding of Love …

HSIAO

*Filial piety is the root of all virtue and the stem out of which grows
all moral teaching. Sit down and I will explain the subject to you.*

*Our bodies – every hair and bit of skin – are received from our parents,
and we must not presume to injure or wound them:
This is the beginning of filial piety.
When we have established our character by the practice of the filial course,
so to make our name famous in future ages and thereby glorify our parents:
This is the end of filial piety. ...*

*As we serve our fathers, so we serve our mothers, and we Love them equally.
As we serve our fathers, so we serve our rulers, and we revere them equally.
Hence, Love is what is chiefly rendered to the mother and reverence is what
is chiefly rendered to the ruler, while both of these are given to the father.*

Confucius (551–478 B.C.E.), *The Hsiao King*

The essence of Love finds its roots in loyalty to family – *hsiao* in Chinese
– for our earliest relationships with family members provide us with a
framework for expressing Love throughout the rest of our lives.
Indeed, it is nearly impossible for a soul to flourish unless the foundation of
familial Love is firmly established. Lacking such critical nourishment, the soul
may be impeded in its growth and fail to achieve the grander stages of self-
actualization.

At a minimum, then, Love of family is a moral value that teaches our
children about respect, duty, and commitment. As a spiritual value, familial
piety primes the next generation of souls for an even greater obligation –
unconditional Love. Once we master the lesson that all of humanity is one big
family, we will begin to experience the Love of the Fifth Spiritual Paradigm.

THE LAW OF LOVE

By David Suzuki, Ph.D.

*The law of Love will work, just as the law of gravitation will work,
whether we accept it or not ... a man who applies the law of Love with
scientific precision can work great wonders. ... The men who discovered
for us the law of Love were greater scientists than any of our modern
scientists. ... The more I work at this law, the more I feel the delight in
life, the delight in the scheme of this universe. It gives me a peace and a
meaning of the mysteries of nature that I have no power to describe.*

Mahatma Gandhi

As energy from the natal cauldron of the Big Bang 15 billion years ago
filled the ever-expanding Universe, the newly formed particles that would
eventually coalesce into atoms felt a mutual attraction even as they rushed
away from each other. A body with mass tugs at any other body with mass.
Galaxies suddenly appeared a billion years after the Big Bang. Long after our
Milky Way galaxy and our Sun had evolved, hydrogen had transformed itself
into living matter, in the form of cells on Earth.

Throughout the Universe, however imperceptibly, all matter feels drawn
together. A membrane demarcates a cell from its surroundings, forming a barrier that allows materials to be concentrated within the cell and enables
metabolism to take place. Even though a membrane separates life from its
environment, membranes have such a strong affinity for each other that when
two cells are brought together they fuse, and the cytoplasmic contents of both
cells are combined into one. This mutual attraction may be built into the very
structure of all matter in the Universe. Love may in truth make the world go
round – or at least hold it together.

When we observe the care with which a mud dauber prepares a mud enclo-
sure, inserts a paralyzed victim as food, and deposits an egg, can we be so
anthropocentric as to deny this the name of Love? How else could we interpret the male sea horse's protective act of accepting babies into his pouch, the
months-long incubation of an emperor penguin's egg on the feet of its vigilant
parent, or the epic journey of Pacific salmon returning to their natal stream to
mate and die in the creation of the next generation? If these are innate actions
dictated by genetically encoded instructions, all the more reason to conclude
that Love in its many manifestations is fashioned into the very blueprint of
life.

We are social beings – herd animals who depend on each other at every stage of our lives. Like many other animals, we are born unable to care for ourselves; we need a long period of care from our parents so that we can grow and learn in safety. As each of us develops, we need companions to define and extend our sense of self, and a community in which we find opportunity for a mate, for rewarding activity, and for conviviality. These needs are absolute, inalienable, and where they are not met we suffer, even perish. Like the caribou that wanders too far from the herd, we cannot thrive in isolation from our kind. From the very beginning of life each one of us is shaped for and by close relationships with other human beings.

Numerous studies indicate that Love is an essential part of a child's upbringing from birth; it helps the individual to thrive, while it teaches the qualities necessary for belonging to a wider community. Being loved teaches us how to Love, how to imagine and feel for another person's existence, how to share and cooperate. Without these skills, how long could any group of humans survive together? In its purest form, the bond between parent and infant illustrates Love's remarkable property of reciprocity. The joy of unconditional parental Love is fully returned by the object of that Love.

The fundamental unit that fosters and strengthens parental Love is the family. It is an extraordinarily diverse human grouping, varying from the nuclear family of recent years in the West to the large extended families common in many parts of Africa to the collective kibbutzim of Israel. Whatever the shape of the family, one measure of its success is the happiness of its members. Sociologists have long known that there is no correlation between happiness and social class, per capita consumption, or personal income. Instead, happiness depends on intimate human relationships.

Love is the defining gift that confers health and humanity on each new human; it is the gift that passes on endlessly, given and given again by each generation to the next. Love shapes us even before birth. Secure in the equilibrium of the womb, a fetus is exquisitely attuned to the physiological, physical, and psychological state of its mother. In turn, its growth and development within the womb affects the sequence of hormone-controlled changes in the mother's body during the pregnancy. Mother and child are entwined in a collaboration.

Today, because we know about the critical role human touch plays in proper development, newborn babies often share a room with their mothers, we teach infant massage, and parents are encouraged to carry babies close to the body in baby slings. Numerous studies clearly demonstrate that human development is enhanced by touch. Babies who are touched are alert, aware, active, and engaged.

Touch can bond child to parent but, of course, it is a reciprocal exchange. We know that oxytocin surges when mothers give birth, nurse, and care for their infants, but mammalian fathers can also experience hormonal fluctuaions. Biologist Katherine Wynne-Edwards has found that hormone changes occur in male humans. In one study, men about to become fathers for the first time were found to have lower levels of testosterone and cortisol (specifically estradiol) and higher levels of estrogen than men in the general population. Estradiol is a hormone that influences maternal behavior.

Unfortunately, humanity's capacity for Love is counterbalanced by an awesome and awful capacity for brutality. When we see what happens to the victims of brutality, we realize the critical importance of Love and its most likely source – the family. Children in war-torn countries around the world have been subject to severe deprivation, and scientists have been able to study those children.

After the execution of dictator Nicolae Ceausescu in 1989, we learned of the terrible plight of children institutionalized in Romania. Intent on increasing Romania's population, Ceausescu had created a generation of unwanted children who were often abandoned to the state. An estimated 100,000 to 300,000 children were in institutions at the time of Ceausescu's fall. Overcrowded and understaffed, most institutions provided little more than subsistence levels of food, clothing, and shelter.

Among the 700 residential institutions for children, one type, the *leagane*, was for children who were not orphans but were abandoned or left for long periods by their parents. Scientists who examined them found rows of cots in huge dormitory rooms for the children, and staff members so harried they had no time to toilet train the children or teach them to dress or brush their teeth. The children were left alone for long periods and were not picked up when they cried or held when they were fed. As a result, the children were considerably underdeveloped in gross motor coordination, fine motor skills, and language development. About 65% of the children three years old and younger exhibited abnormalities in cell and tissue structure and activity resulting from malnutrition.

Victor Groze, who studied 399 families of Romanian adoptees, estimated that 20% of the children are what he calls "resilient rascals" who have overcome their pasts and are thriving; 60% are what he calls "wounded warriors" who have made vast strides but continue to lag behind their peers; and another 20% are "challenge children" who have shown little improvement and are almost unmanageable.

Exile from the human family does more than delay or prevent development – it can cause illness and even death. One study found that in Romania before Ceausescu's fall, up to 35% of institutionalized children died every year. Of course, moving to loving, supportive, and stable homes goes a long way to improving the emotional, psychological, and physical health of these children. Love can still have an impact. Children thrived physically when adopted out – their IQs improved, as did their ability to express positive emotions – but still, the lack of early contact, bonding, and Love left an indelible mark.

The security and self-confidence that are provided by a healthy family and that are so necessary for developing a child's self-esteem are amplified by the support of the community in which the family lives. During war, it is difficult for adults to buffer their children against the insecurity that is so damaging to their well-being. War is a social, economic, and ecological disaster. It is totally unsustainable and must be opposed by all who are concerned about meeting the real needs of all people and future generations. War is the ultimate atrocity that dehumanizes victor and vanquished alike; divorcing children from parents, separating families, smashing communities, it deprives its victims of their basic need for security and Love.

However, the threats to community are from more than warfare; we are in the grip of a mindset called "modernity" that views whatever is modern and recent as the best. Overwhelmed by the incredible changes brought about by technology and materialism, we have accepted a widespread belief that somehow human beings today are different from people in the past; because we have more information, have traveled more and are better educated than all our predecessors, then surely our thoughts and needs are more sophisticated, on a different plane from those of all preceding generations.

For thousands of years, small communities of people ensured relative tranquility while providing for the social needs of their members. The explosive rate at which our species has been converted to an urban creature has been accompanied by a deterioration of the social fabric that held people together. The 20th Century witnessed an unprecedented shift from predominately rural community living to big city living. In cities, distanced from nature and the primary means of production like agriculture, fishing, logging, and even manufacturing, we accept that it is the economy that provides our needs.

Technology has enabled us to travel rapidly and communicate over vast distances, while television, computers, and portable entertainment devices sever the shared activities with neighbors and communities.

Think of where we have been all this time on Earth. For almost our entire existence we have lived completely immersed in the natural world, dependent on it for every aspect of our existence. Moving through the landscape around us, led by the seasons, we lived lightly on the land and were sustained by its biological plentitude. The evolutionary context of human history makes it plausible that the human genome – the DNA blueprint that makes us what we are – has over time acquired a genetically programmed need to be in the company of other species. Edward O. Wilson has coined the term "biophilia" for this need (based on the Greek words for "life" and "Love"). In his book, *Biophilia: The Human Bond with Other Species*, Wilson defines biophilia as the "innate tendency to focus on life and life-like processes." It leads to an "emotional affiliation of human beings to other living things."

Watch children respond to a wasp or butterfly. Infants seem drawn to an insect's movement and color, often reaching out to touch it. They exhibit neither fear nor disgust, only fascination. Yet, by the time they enter kindergarten, enchantment with nature has often been replaced with revulsion as many children recoil in fear or loathing at the sight of a beetle or fly. By teaching children to fear nature, we increase our estrangement and fail to satisfy our inborn biophilic needs. We sever the connections, the Love that infuses our actions with compassion for our fellow beings. It is sad that extreme crises such as a nervous breakdown, a severe injury, loneliness, or death are needed to bring us back to the healing comfort of the natural world.

Our schism from nature is reinforced by the way we construct our habitat. Most of humanity in the industrialized world and a rapidly increasing number in developing nations live in cities where town planners, architects, and engineers dictate the nature of our surroundings. In the urban environment that is today's most common human habitat, science and technology perpetuate the illusion of dominance and shape the way we see the world. Cities manifest a way of thinking that reflects mechanical or technological models based on standardization, simplicity, linearity, predictability, efficiency, and production. The place where we spend most of our lives molds our priorities and the way we perceive our surroundings. A human-engineered habitat of asphalt, concrete, and glass reinforces our belief that we lie outside of and above nature, immune from uncertainty and the unexpected of the wild.

If we continue to think of ourselves as separate from our surroundings, we will not be sensitive to the consequences of what we are doing, so we can't see that our path is potentially suicidal. If we do not see ourselves as part of the natural world and become further detached, we risk a greater sense of loneliness, a lack of meaning, purpose, and sense of belonging.

Consumerism has taken the place of citizenship as the chief way we contribute to the health of our society. Economic rather than social goals drive government and corporate policies. The resulting high levels of unemployment produce stress, illness, and family and community breakdown. Stable communities and neighborhoods are a prerequisite for happiness, for productive and rewarding lives, for a crucial sense of security and belonging. It is not economics that creates community but compassion, cooperation, and Love.

The challenge is to create the kind of society in which our potential can blossom to the fullest extent. Whereas in the past the most important factor was the long-term survival or well-being of the family or group, today decisions are made based on the implications for a company, job, market share, or profit. So we assess costs and benefits within a very different framework of values, ignoring, for example, the health of the community or ecosystem. We have gotten out of the habit of thinking about the things that really matter to us, or perhaps we now have a perverted sense of what really matters.

The stability of the family – whatever its form – within a community provides an environment within which a child develops curiosity, responsibility, and inventiveness. Ecological degradation – deforestation, topsoil loss, pollution, climate change, and so on – destabilizes society by eroding the underpinnings of sustainability. This consequence was graphically illustrated in 1992 when all commercial fishing of northern cod in the Canadian province of Newfoundland was suspended. Overnight, 40,000 jobs were lost as the foundation of that society for five centuries vanished. Similarly, all across Canada, towns boomed as forests were clearcut around them, only to crash when the trees were gone. The coast of British Columbia is dotted with villages that once supported fishing fleets and canneries but were abandoned as salmon populations declined. Ecological health is essential for full community health.

"Eco" comes from the Greek word *oikos*, meaning "home." Ecology is the study of home, while economics is the management of home. Ecologists attempt to define the conditions and principles that govern life's ability to flourish through time and change. Societies and our constructs, like economics, must adapt to those fundamentals defined by ecology. But our brash exuberance over our incredible inventiveness and productivity in this century have blinded us to our place on this planet.

An economy was once created to serve people and their communities. Today economic rationalists contend that people must sacrifice and give up social services for the economy. As we reflect on our fundamental needs as social animals, it is clear that family and communities assured of biodiversity, full employment, justice, and security constitute the real non-negotiable starting point in the delineation of a sustainable future.

Thus, the challenge is to put the "eco" back into economics and every aspect of our lives. If we are to balance and direct our remarkable technological muscle power, we need to regain some ancient virtues: the humility to acknowledge how much we have yet to learn, the respect that will allow us to protect and restore nature, and the Love that can lift our eyes to distant horizons, far beyond the next election, paycheck, or stock dividend.

Elders, poets, and philosophers in all cultures, including our own, have expressed a similar sense of brotherhood and sisterhood, of mutual compassion and common interest with the rest of the living world – a relationship that can only be described as Love. Its source is "fellow-feeling": the knowledge that we are, like all other forms of life, children of the Earth, members of the same family.

Above all, we need to reclaim our faith in ourselves as creatures of the Earth, living in harmony with all other forms of life. The "Law of Love" is as fundamental and as universal as any other physical law. It is written everywhere we look and it maps our intimate connection with the rest of the world.

As one who desires to understand more about family systems, I am particularly indebted to David for this essay, as it eloquently explains why we need our families to learn Love.

I am thinking of my own mother right now, a woman who has shared herself with me on many levels. She is still sharing, still guiding, still holding me in her loving arms. I work with her now, and she is one of the "Pats" who helped edit this book. So to my own mother, I wish to say: *I Love you and I thank you for all that you have taught me about Love.*

And to our next author, my son Sean, and to my daughter Erin and my son Patrick, I wish to say: *My darlings, I will always be with you as an escape from the dark night. Your father and I Love you so.*

IN THE DISTANCE I SEE MY HOUSE

By Sean R. Conroy
(age 8)

I slip through the night
Cautious of my surroundings
I'm confused by the darkness
It s-u-c-k-s me like a black hole
Sounds of the night c   a   k   e   d
                   r   c   l   o
                              w
                         n   my spine

They lurk in subconscious
I speed my pace up the lonely street
Dimmed streetlights form a shadow-filled path
I know not what hides behind them

I start running
Turning my head left and right every stride
Hoping a monster of the black won't trip me from behind
The brisk cold air makes it hard to breathe
I pant and gasp for air

In the distance I see my house
Almost there can't give up now
I can feel the light the warmth the safety
Freedom from this nightmare

I clear the porch steps with a leap
Flying through the front door I   f
                              a
                              l
                              l

But it's a fall of relief
I've made it at last to my paradise island
I escaped . . . . from the dark night

THE FAMILY ALTAR

By Charles "Ohiyesa" Eastman, M.D.
(1858–1939)

The American Indian was an individualist in religion as in war. He had neither a national army nor an organized church. There was no priest to
assume responsibility for another's soul. That is, we believed, the supreme
duty of the parent, who only was permitted to claim in some degree the
priestly office and function, since it is his creative and protecting power which
alone approaches the solemn function of Deity.

The Indian was a religious man from his mother's womb. From the
moment of her recognition of the fact of conception to the end of the second
year of life, which was the ordinary duration of lactation, it was supposed by
us that the mother's spiritual influence counted for most. Her attitude and
secret meditations must be such as to instill into the receptive soul of the
unborn child the Love of the "Great Mystery" and a sense of brotherhood
with all creation. Silence and isolation are the rule of life for the expectant
mother. She wanders prayerful in the stillness of great woods, or on the bosom
of the untrodden prairie, and to her poetic mind the immanent birth of her
child prefigures the advent of a master-man – a hero, or the mother of heroes
– a thought conceived in the virgin breast of primeval nature, and dreamed
out in a hush that is only broken by the sighing of the pine tree or the thrilling
orchestra of a distant waterfall.

And when the day of days in her life dawns – the day in which there is to
be a new life, the miracle of whose making has been entrusted to her, she seeks
no human aid. She has been trained and prepared in body and mind for this
her holiest duty, ever since she can remember. The ordeal is best met alone,
where no curious or pitying eyes embarrass her; where all nature says to her
spirit: "'Tis Love! 'tis Love! the fulfilling of life!" When a sacred voice comes
to her out of the silence, and a pair of eyes open upon her in the wilderness,
she knows with joy that she has borne well her part in the great song of
creation!

Presently she returns to the camp, carrying the mysterious, the holy, the
dearest bundle! She feels the endearing warmth of it and hears its soft breathing. It is still a part of herself, since both are nourished by the same mouthful,
and no look of a lover could be sweeter than its deep, trusting gaze.

She continues her spiritual teaching, at first silently – a mere pointing of the index finger to nature; then in whispered songs, bird-like, at morning and evening. To her and to the child the birds are real people, who live very close to the Great Mystery; the murmuring trees breathe His presence; the falling waters chant His praise.

If the child should chance to be fretful, the mother raises her hand. "Hush! hush!" she cautions it tenderly, "the spirits may be disturbed!" She bids it be still and listen to the silver voice of the aspen, or the clashing cymbals of the birch; and at night she points to the heavenly, blazed trail, through nature's galaxy of splendor to nature's God. Silence, Love, reverence – this is the trinity of first lessons; and to these she later adds generosity, courage, and chastity.

In the old days, our mothers were single-eyed to the trust imposed upon them; and as a noted chief of our people was wont to say:

> Men may slay one another, but they can never overcome the woman, for in the quietude of her lap lies the child! You may destroy him once and again, but he issues as often from that same gentle lap – a gift of the Great Good to the race, in which man is only an accomplice!

This wild mother has not only the experience of her mother and grand-mother, and the accepted rules of her people for a guide, but she humbly seeks to learn a lesson from ants, bees, spiders, beavers, and badgers. She studies the family life of the birds, so exquisite in its emotional intensity and its patient devotion, until she seems to feel the universal mother-heart beating in her own breast. In due time the child takes of his own accord the attitude of prayer, and speaks reverently of the Powers. He thinks that he is a blood brother to all living creatures, and the storm wind is to him a messenger of the Great Mystery.

At the age of about eight years, if he is a boy, she turns him over to his father for more Spartan training. If a girl, she is from this time much under the guardianship of her grandmother, who is considered the most dignified protector for the maiden. Indeed, the distinctive work of both grand-parents is that of acquainting the youth with the national traditions and beliefs. It is reserved for them to repeat the time-hallowed tales with dignity and authority, so as to lead him into his inheritance in the stored-up wisdom and experience the race. The old are dedicated to the service of the young, as their teachers and advisers, and the young in turn regard them with Love and reverence.

Our old age was in some respects the happiest period of life. Advancing years brought with them much freedom, not only from the burden of laborious and dangerous tasks, but from those restrictions of custom and etiquette which were religiously observed by all others. No one who is at all acquainted with the Indian in his home can deny that we are a polite people. As a rule, the warrior who inspired the greatest terror in the hearts of his enemies was a man of the most exemplary gentleness, and almost feminine refinement, among his family and friends. A soft, low voice was considered an excellent thing in man, as well as in woman! Indeed, the enforced intimacy of tent life would soon become intolerable, were it not for these instinctive reserves and delicacies, this unfailing respect for the established place and possessions of every other member of the family circle, this habitual quiet, order, and decorum.

Our people, though capable of strong and durable feeling, were not demonstrative in their affection at any time, least of all in the presence of guests or strangers. Only to the aged, who have journeyed far, and are in a manner exempt from ordinary rules, are permitted some playful familiarities with children and grandchildren, some plain speaking, even to harshness and objurgation, from which the others must rigidly refrain. In short, the old men and women are privileged to say what they please and how they please, without contradiction, while the hardships and bodily infirmities that of necessity fall to their lot are softened so far as may be by universal consideration and attention.

There was no religious ceremony connected with marriage among us, while on the other hand the relation between man and woman was regarded as in itself mysterious and holy. It appears that where marriage is solemnized by the church and blessed by the priest, it may at the same time be surrounded with customs and ideas of a frivolous, superficial, and even prurient character. We believed that two who Love should be united in secret, before the public acknowledgment of their union, and should taste their apotheosis with nature. The betrothal might or might not be discussed and approved by the parents, but in either case it was customary for the young pair to disappear into the wilderness, there to pass some days or weeks in perfect seclusion and dual solitude, afterward returning to the village as man and wife. An exchange of presents and entertainments between the two families usually followed, but the nuptial blessing was given by the High Priest of God, the most reverend and holy Nature.

The family was not only the social unit, but also the unit of government. The clan is nothing more than a larger family with its patriarchal chief as the natural head, and the union of several clans by inter-marriage and voluntary connection constitutes the tribe. The very name of our tribe, Dakota, means Allied People. The remoter degrees of kinship were fully recognized, and that not as a matter of form only: first cousins were known as brothers and sisters; the name of "cousin" constituted binding claim, and our rigid morality forbade marriage between cousins in any known degree, or in other words within the clan.

The household proper consisted of a man with one or more wives and their children, all of whom dwelt amicably together, often under one roof, although some men of rank and position provided a separate lodge for each wife. There were, indeed, few plural marriages except among the older and leading men, and plural wives were usually, though not necessarily, sisters. A marriage might honorably be dissolved for cause, but there was very little infidelity or immorality, either open or secret.

It has been said that the position of woman is the test of civilization, and that of our women was secure. In them was vested our standard of morals and the purity of our blood. The wife did not take the name of her husband nor enter his clan, and the children belonged to the clan of the mother. All of the family property was held by her, descent was traced in the maternal line, and the honor of the house was in her hands. Modesty was her chief adornment; hence the younger women were usually silent and retiring, but a woman who had attained to ripeness of years and wisdom, or who had displayed notable courage in some emergency, was sometimes invited to a seat in the council.

Thus she ruled undisputed within her own domain, and was to us a tower of moral and spiritual strength, until the coming of the border white man, the soldier and trader, who with strong drink overthrew the honor of the man, and through his power over a worthless husband purchased the virtue of his wife or his daughter. When she fell, the whole race fell with her.

Before this calamity came upon us, you could not find anywhere a happier home than that created by the Indian woman. There was nothing of the artificial about her person, and very little disingenuousness in her character. Her early and consistent training, the definiteness of her vocation, and, above all, her profoundly religious attitude gave her a strength and poise that could not be overcome by any ordinary misfortune.

Indian names were either characteristic nicknames given in a playful spirit, deed names, birth names, or such as have a religious and symbolic meaning. It has been said that when a child is born, some accident or unusual appearance determines his name. This is sometimes the case, but is not the rule. A man of forcible character, with a fine war record, usually bears the name of the buffalo or bear, lightning or some dread natural force. Another of more peaceful nature may be called Swift Bird or Blue Sky. A woman's name usually suggested something about the home, often with the adjective "pretty" or "good" and a feminine termination. Names of any dignity or importance must be conferred by the old men, and especially so if they have any spiritual significance: as Sacred Cloud, Mysterious Night, Spirit Woman, and the like. Such a name was sometimes borne by three generations, but each individual must prove that he is worthy of it.

In the life of the Indian there was only one inevitable duty – the duty of prayer – the daily recognition of the Unseen and Eternal. His daily devotions were more necessary to him than daily food. He wakes at daybreak, puts on his moccasins and steps down to the water's edge. Here he throws handfuls of clear, cold water into his face, or plunges in bodily. After the bath, he stands erect before the advancing dawn, facing the sun as it dances upon the horizon, and offers his unspoken orison. His mate may precede or follow him in his devotions, but never accompanies him. Each soul must meet the morning Sun, the new sweet Earth, and the Great Silence alone!

⟫◆⟪

In 1862 at the age of four, Ohiyesa ("Winner" in Lakota) survived the Minnesota Uprising, during which his tribe was slaughtered and the survivors fled to Canada. Thereafter, he left his people to acquire a medical degree from my alma mater Boston University. In 1880, he returned to his people in time to witness yet another slaughter – the infamous Massacre at Wounded Knee – and to treat the few who managed to survive the continued inhumanity of the white colonizers.

Ohiyesa explains how a boy was turned "over to his father for more Spartan training." My father, having no sons, provided me with similar training, and I thank him for preparing me for what is coming. May we all have the ability to draw upon this warrior "medicine," even though it is difficult to possess. Such power requires wisdom and an acute sense of timing. Otherwise, it can be a demon, a madness that eats away at the soul. This theme is explored in our next essay, along with an even greater medicine – Love.

LAKOTA MEDICINE WOMAN

By Barbara Hand Clow

I see a small, bread-loaf shaped habitation made of skins stretched over a frame of willow or larch poles. I live in this home and I see myself sitting inside holding my infant. My baby is wrapped very tightly and I am encased in tight blankets. It is a cold winter, and the baby is suckling as the wind slaps the frozen skins against the poles. He is about six or seven months old.

The elements are very harsh and we feel them intensely. We are wrapped up tightly together because of the bitter wind, and I feel abandoned. We are waiting for our men to return. There is not much else I can do but feed my baby. My people are not hungry, since there is still food, but keeping the fire going is difficult. My main interest is to keep us warm. I am young, only seventeen, and this is my first child. My body is very strong, vital, and healthy.

I am worried about where all the men went. My husband is a warrior and he is gone with the other men. Normally, the party would have gone hunting, but this time the men have gone to war. That is why I do not know when my husband will return. I do not know what is going to happen. Our warriors are fighting the Shawano, and we are the Lakota. I live on the plains in the center of the land, and I have a sense of my geographical location because we travel great distances. I am just west of the Big River. We are the people of the Sun. In other places, nearby, people of the Sun also live. There are other villages nearby, and we are all usually in communication. But right now we are all in our homes, since the weather is cold. We must fend for ourselves without men.

This child is the son of a warrior. He is very healthy and I am very proud of him. I am proud that my first child is a son, since he has a great future in our tribe, but this is a strange time. These Shawano people never used to come here. Their people used to live farther toward the rising Sun, and now members of these people come here to hunt and travel through our land. This intrusion is disturbing our village confederation. We have many villages on this plain and we have been people of peace. These people are pressing on us from the East because their tribes have been driven out of their own homelands. This is very confusing because, once upon a time, in the olden days, we all agreed on who used the territory. As for these Shawano, we know this is not their fault. Their warriors are invading our territory because they have been pushed out of their own land. We cannot allow this, but we do not wish for violence. Neither do they, yet they need hunting grounds and places to settle.

Our land is very balanced. We have wisdom about how people can live in harmony with the animals, the trees, the land, and the plants. We let the old people die when they are ready. We lead the weak children into the wilderness to die or develop survival skills. We are equal with the animal. We do not take over animal territory, and we limit the number of people in our villages. We do not take more trees than we require for simple shelter and fire. We only plant enough food for our village people, with some extra for wanderers and the hungry insects. This invasion has created imbalance, which is not right for the land, the people, the animals, and the trees. Just as the old people and the sick children must die, the Shawano must die unless they can find their place in balance. I am heavy in the heart about this problem as I hold my son of a warrior.

The men are gone away. I hear twigs snapping and soft footsteps on the ground. My astral body is very trained. I can jump out of my physical body and go to other places and other times. I sit quietly and fly out of my body to view the home I sit in. These warriors are not my people! I take my child, cover his head, hold him tightly to my body, and I immediately leave my home. I go to the next home and pull aside the skins and say, "I-sha-na-ya-na-wa-na!" which means "Shawano danger!" I go to the next tent and say, "I-sha-na-ya-na-wa-na!" All of us do this. We move together to the edge of the village, but we are too late. We see many warriors who have terrifying faces streaked with red, white, and black war paint.

Suddenly these men all run after us! The warriors have long sticks that make thunder! I am clutching my baby and looking back, and I see the people falling with a look of shock on their faces, as if they are being exploded from inside just when the sticks thunder. A warrior grabs me by my shoulder, turns me around, and puts his arm heavy and tight around my shoulder. He grabs my baby with his other hand and throws my baby away from me! My baby screams as he lies on the ground. A warrior stomps on my baby. I am begging this man with my eyes not to leave my baby on the ground. The man's grip is so strong that I cannot escape. His arm is like iron. Holding me tight, he starts to drag me away, and the last thing I see is one of the other warriors hitting the baby with a stone club. I see blood gushing out, and I know my baby is crushed. I pass out, and that is the last thing I see. My heart is broken when my son dies.

When I wake up later, I find that I have been abducted. The warriors have taken the young women and a few of the young boys. The rest of our village must have been slain. The men are moving us west. Horses are pulling bundles along behind them, lashed to their sides with tree poles. The murderers are marching along, forcing the last of my village to keep up. The warriors watch us, making us move along with them toward the setting Sun. Stopping to set up a camp, they make a fire. We prepare food from the meat, vegetables, and grains taken from our village. The warriors are very hungry, but I am not. I will not eat, but then a man forces food down my throat. My breasts hurt from making milk for my dead son. I know what is coming next, as the warriors choose women.

The one who grabbed me is not the one who takes me. A young warrior who does not look at me takes me and rapes me. I leave my body while this is happening. I am in a state of utter and numbing grief. All I feel is the pain from losing my baby. I cannot talk – these people speak another language. I do not tell my sisters how I feel, since we are all numbed by pain. We have lost our grandmothers, parents, children, and babies. We just look at each other with blank stares. The warriors even rape the boys, and I am sickened. This has not happened to these boys before, and I have never seen such a thing. We are used the way sick men use animals. We are taken a great distance, and each day we walk and move. The war party is trying to get far away from our homeland because the leaders know that our men will kill every one of them if they catch up. I have to cook for my abusers and be used every night. These people have been completely dehumanized. I can feel that these men once had their humanity, but that their identity has been stolen. The warriors are doing to us what has been done to them. I wonder if our men did something to them.

After three Moons, I begin to live with the loss of my child. The way I do this is to meditate on the plants and trees. Children are like plants. We are all like plants. We are born, we live and die, and we are reborn. I know that my child's spirit will return, just as I have once known his spirit. This teaching is very deep for me. I also live through the pain of the long journey, knowing that I might die or not. I am like a tree, and maybe I will attain my growth and maybe I will not. But I know I will come back again and again, just as the deep soil sprouts a new field of grain every spring. My heart and soul have room to absorb much pain because of our teaching about life and death. Some are seasons of pain. Some are seasons of joy. This is such a deep teaching among my people that the message holds true for me as I endure intense suffering.

After five Moons, we begin to learn how to communicate. The winter ends, spring comes, and we have arrived at a river where we can stop. Possibly there are few people here, or possibly the Shawano know the tribes of this area. For whatever reason, we set up a village near the river. This is a flat, muddy plain with much flowing water and few trees, the Platte River. The people who live on this river are fishermen. We can stay here for the summer without harm. We begin to learn to talk with each other, first with our eyes, then by sharing our words for the tools we work with.

I am chosen by one of the men. He pushes the other men away one day and he takes me into his teepee. This house has sticks that come to a point with an opening to the sky. The lodge poles are wrapped with buffalo skins. He lets the other men know I belong to him, and then we begin time and space together. My consciousness is that I am like the leaves in the trees which blow with the wind. I have blown a long, long distance, and now I have blown into a shelter. Now I am with another tree and we will grow together.

I am sitting in meditation wearing a deerskin dress with a secret pocket sewn into it. I remove an ancient turquoise from this pocket. This turquoise is a sacred stone that has been with my people for many years, and now I can finally sit alone and listen to the voice of the stone for a while. I go into the Dreamtime by making spirals in my mind. I enter into a dream about all time before this moment. I make the four directions within the circular tent, using pieces of painted deerskin: white for North, yellow for South, red for East, and black for the West. I enter my heart and thank the Universe for my place with this man in this sacred space. I move very deeply into the Dreamtime and I ask Wakan Tanka for my power.

When these men took my body, I held my seed. We can control the time when we have children by watching the Moon and holding the seeds of the ancestors deep within. All of us have done this since we were taken from our homeland. I now release my seed and call back my child. I do not do this out of my own need, for I do not need this child, since children come through us as gifts from the Universe. We must survive. These are my people now and I will bring them a child from the Universe. I ask for the return of my child because, in my meditation, my child called to me from the other side. This is a very, very great miracle that ends all my pain.

We cannot release our seed if we are in a state of anger or fear. I go deeper and deeper into meditation. I enter a state in which, even if this man who chose me is the man who killed my child, I will still Love him as the father of my new child. I cannot know if this man who chose me is the one who carried me off or is the one who crushed my child, because the war paint masked all the warriors on that fateful day. I assure Wakan Tanka that even if he is that man, I will still carry Love for him in my heart and soul. We cannot bring forth a child if we are angry in our hearts. If we did that, the child would be unable to feel Wakan Tanka as its spirit enters Earth. The child would be like a tree with no roots that is unable to reach for the Sun. We only seed a child from Love and wonder. These warriors do not understand that teaching. Perhaps their women knew? Our children are very great, very evolved, for we are the spiritual teachers of this land. We are Lakota.

I enter a state of preparation so that I can conceive this child. Soon, six moons later, my belly swells and this man is pleased. This man is becoming more kind to me every day because I give myself totally to pleasing him. As he learns that I am his center, his humanity returns. The pain of these people begins to leave their skins, their hands, and their minds, and I see swirling circles of colors at their primary body energy points, such as their hearts and stomachs. His red and brown aura is gone now, which means his body is clear of anger. I watch the rays of light, the waves of energy, passing off his body, and when his light is completely clear, I fuse my light with his once during lovemaking before our child comes. We become a star together and a new silence enters his soul. I spend much of my time in meditation, passing pain, passing anger. I am a being of great peace filled with the wonderment of the black night sky. I am one of great endurance and patience, like a rock. If I just wait, then all will be beautiful again. I have complete trust in Wakan Tanka. I only ask when I am in need, and when I ask, my request is given to me. I am a priestess in my tribe, and all women are priestesses as the sisters of the Moon.

We modulate our energy with the Moon, drawing deep within and going into silence. Then there are times when we are shining. We do moon-sign, or moon-talk, by looking into each other's eyes. Words are never spoken. When I was a young girl, the grandmothers trained me in how to reflect the Moon. The waxing and waning of the Moon is the breath of the Goddess who draws in and exhales the winds of the Sun, the breath of God. The men exist to shine like the Sun, and I give my energy to this man so he will be the Sun as he readies to be a father. I wonder if he was a father before his heart was broken. Did the warriors destroy his child and his woman? I will never know because we do not speak about the painful things, just as I never tell about what happened to me. Talking about these things gives them life. When he shines like the Sun, there is real life. We gather the berries and capture small animals with no worries. These men are receiving wisdom from us because they are willing to feel again. Their need to hurt others is spent.

I bring forth a child with the spirit of my son, but she is a girl child! In the survival teaching of this man's tribe, when a man's first child is a daughter, the child is put out on the rocks to be eaten by the vultures. There is space for only so many beings, and the vultures and maggots transmute life eventually. My center in the divine order of the Universe is so absolute that I can even accept letting go of this daughter, the returned spirit of my heart, if her death is to come. For if there are too many female children, there will be too many babies born in the seasons and not enough hunters and warriors for survival. My heart is suspended because my first child was the warrior's gift and has returned as daughter of the Moon.

I have entered into oneness with this man, and my heart beats with his heart. Part of my respect for him is not to speak out of turn, so I am silent. My sharing of my heart is so pure that I see he is going to allow me to keep this child, and I lower my eyes as my daughter moves her mouth for milk. Now I see with my astral body that he is the one who killed my son. I could not have received that wisdom until he took my female child and accepted her. If I had not given from my heart to this man since the very beginning, he would not have chosen my female child because he would have been incapable of feeling Love for her. I followed the wisdom of Wakan Tanka, and my daughter is saved. I have saved my own child by loving and not being angry in my heart. This is a great teaching for one so young to receive.

In my life as Ti-a-no, Water Woman, I became a great medicine woman. This child was a teaching for the Universe, the gift of life. I held faith for the people, and for myself, during a period of great agony for the native people of the land. I made my heart large so that pain could blossom into Love. This was about three hundred years ago. I was born in 1720 and I died in 1795. There was much more suffering, more thunder sticks, and great pain, a time of darkness before the light. The worst pain that I experienced was my people being attacked by other native people. It was tribe against tribe, our people against the white people, and warriors against children, but the time has come to open the secret teachings of the Blue Star. When Tecpatl reached the Blue Star, the Sisterhood of the Moon released the pain into water – Quiahuitl.

White Buffalo Woman came to the men of my tribe carrying the Sacred Pipe of peace, the pipe of sacred red stone, which hardens into granite in the Sun after removal from the Earth. This stone is the blood of the Goddess.

The time of trial goes on and on, but the Sacred Pipe is smoked, always signifying the patience of the people waiting for the time when the red pipe transmutes into the white pipe. We keep moving farther toward the setting Sun when there are many thunder sticks and much death and disease. I use my power to Love and to heal, and I have great wisdom. I know the medicine of herbs and animal spirits as I watch the people coming and going. The seasons hold great pain and loss when our blood washes Mother Earth. We thank Earth for transmuting our blood into stone for our smokes of Wakan Tanka.

I am very close to my daughter, but she is also independent. I raise her until she is fourteen. She learns my ways and she works hard, and when she is fourteen, she is taken away to another tribe. I cannot control that part of my reality. I am under the rule of the Shawano. My mate gives her as Maisu, a wife, and her people move a great distance away. She returns three times, once with two children, later with a third. I cannot leave to go to her, but my staying does not matter. She and I have Moon wisdom. We are both stars in the galaxy, eternally, and we are never out of touch with each other throughout all time. She is in the wind, water, and Sun, and I visit her in the forest.

When I do see her, I look into her eyes to see that she has no anger. She has laughing eyes. Our greatest teaching is to not hold anger, and the greatest joy a mother can have is for her own child to share this wisdom teaching with her. Later my tribe hides this wisdom for a long time, but my daughter shares the knowledge with me. Because of the Moon wisdom in her eyes, I am able to let her go without pain, and we both keep Moon lodge at the New Moon, thirteen times a year. You will know when peace has returned to Earth when the women keep the New Moon lodges again, and when the men manifest the white pipe after the Earth has been saturated with the blood of native people.

⁙

This passage from *The Mind Chronicles Trilogy* is the story of one of my recent past lives. The Lakota Medicine Woman lived in the Great Plains of North America more than two hundred years ago. This was a very stressful period for her people because colonial settlers were pushing the Eastern tribes out and forcing them to migrate into the territories of her people. Her story is one of deep compassion and Love in the middle of unsettling times.

But you may wonder: *Who am I now?*

I am the mother of three sons and a daughter, and my husband Gerry and I have already had to bury two of our sons. The oldest, Tom, had Asperger's Syndrome, a mild form of autism that I believe was exacerbated by his babyhood vaccinations. Tom's life was always a struggle, and eventually in his forties he became depressed by the American invasion of Iraq. He was especially gloomy about the American abuse of Iraqi prisoners. To cheer him up, a doctor put Tom on Paxil, and a few months later in June 2004, he committed suicide.

My second son, Matthew, was a devoted environmentalist. In June 1998, Matthew drowned while doing graduate research to save native trout in Red Rock Lake, Montana. I've struggled to maintain my sanity since 1998, and my deepening Love for the rest of my family and friends has been the key to my survival.

I accessed this remarkable story in a past-life session under hypnosis in 1985 that was facilitated by Chris Griscom of The Light Institute in New Mexico. Sometimes I reread this session to stave off the waves of grief that nearly overwhelm my soul. This is the story of a woman of great courage, whose deep compassion enabled her to flow with the laws of nature, the laws of Love.

⇒•◇•⇐

Earlier, I touched on two concepts: the life-death-life cycle and the duality of God. With regard to the first, the evidence is mounting – reincarnation appears real. Dr. Ian Stevenson conducted research on reincarnation at my other alma mater, the University of Virginia. He learned that children have incredible recall, but by age seven most of them forget their prior life history. Not Barbara! She has recalled many past lives and has generously shared this memory to show how Love triumphs over hate.

Which brings us to the second concept – the apparent duality of God. My view of Deity includes the belief that God contains both masculine and feminine energies. Mystics say that masculine energy is the creation half of God and feminine energy is the wisdom half, personified by Sophia. Fourth Paradigm religions focus on masculine energy, thereby glorifying the creation of all things possible. But Sophia would ask, "Why?" Why spend $2.6 billion to upgrade B-52 bombers when the money could be spent on universal healthcare? Sophia would prioritize. Truly, if we refused to support the military industrial complex, we would enter the Fifth Spiritual Paradigm. Such is the genesis of one of our most hallowed American holidays: Mother's Day.

MOTHER'S DAY PROCLAMATION

By Julia Ward Howe
(1819–1910)

Arise, then, women of this day!
Arise all women who have hearts,
Whether our baptism be that of water or of tears!

Say firmly:
"We will not have great questions decided by irrelevant agencies.
Our husbands shall not come to us, reeking with carnage,
for caresses and applause.
Our sons shall not be taken from us to unlearn
All that we have been able to teach them of charity,
mercy, and patience.
We, the women of one country, will be too tender of
those of another country
To allow our sons to be trained to injure theirs."

From the bosom of the devastated Earth a voice goes up
with our own.
It says: "Disarm! Disarm! The sword of murder is not
the balance of justice."
Blood does not wipe our dishonor, nor violence indicate possession.
As men have often forsaken the plough and the anvil
at the summons of war,
Let women now leave all that may be left of home
for a great and earnest day of counsel.

Let them meet first, as women, to bewail and commemorate the dead.
Let them solemnly take counsel with each other as to the means
Whereby the great human family can live in peace,
Each bearing after their own time the sacred impress,
not of Caesar, but of God.

In the name of womanhood and of humanity, I earnestly ask
That a general congress of women without limit of nationality
May be appointed and held at some place deemed most convenient
And at the earliest period consistent with its objects,
To promote the alliance of the different nationalities,
The amicable settlement of international questions,
The great and general interests of peace.

I WANT TO TELL YOU SOMETHING YOU SHOULD KNOW

By Nicholas Gordon, Ph.D.

I want to tell you something you should know,
Something that you might not want to hear.
It is, however, true of me, and so
If you would know me, I must make it clear.

I am a woman who Loves other women.
I could not nor would want to be aught else.
I am your daughter and a lesbian.
Please make a place for that within yourself.

Please Love me as I am, as I Love you
No differently from when I was a child.
I am the daughter that you always knew
Save for one sweet way that fate has smiled.

Whatever you decide, I'll Love you still,
For Love heeds not the weather, but the will.

———⊰◆⊱———

In the Fifth Spiritual Paradigm, there will be no forbidden forms of Love. Love is Love, whether it blossoms between two men, manifests between two women, or blesses people from different races.

My only sibling, my sister Leslie, is gay. She has a "domestic partner" who should be her "wife." But then again, these are just words, man-made appellations, meaningless titles that have come down to us through the centuries. What is a wife? What is a husband? To me, these Fourth Paradigm designations connote possession ... control. The very opposite of Love.

Our father was a complex man. Some would say, challenging. Nevertheless, Leslie and I (and our mother) managed to spiritually thrive in the isolated environment which engulfed our immediate family unit.

Nick's poem is about acceptance – one component of true Love. For Love is much more. Love also is about forgiveness. I have forgiven my father. But sometimes, I wonder, has he forgiven me?

Nothing worth doing is completed in our lifetime;
therefore, we must be saved by hope.
Nothing true or beautiful or good makes complete sense in any
immediate context of history;
therefore, we must be saved by faith.
Nothing we do, however virtuous, can be accomplished alone;
therefore, we are saved by Love.
No virtuous act is quite as virtuous from the standpoint of our friend or
foe as from our standpoint.
Therefore, we must be saved by the final form of Love which is
forgiveness.

Reinhold Niebuhr, *The Irony of American History*

I would like to believe that my father and I are even, that our *karma* has been neutralized, no more *samsara*. But I had to say goodbye to my father for a few years in the 1980s in order to achieve such clarity. The book *Toxic Parents* was popular at the time, and it undoubtedly gave me implicit permission to detach from him for a while. Sometimes, this is necessary. Sometimes a soul needs to seek out a new "family." The Love we share with our closest friends can be just as nurturing and fulfilling.

Years later, when my father suffered a recurrence of cancer, I was able to rally and be by his side – Leslie was able to rally as well. In fact, we took turns visiting him every week without fail until he died. It was our final act of Love for him. Our tribute to a man we may never understand, but who had given us the gift of life and other gifts as well – such as a strong sense of justice, a confidence that is only born through trial by fire, and a sense of adventure that, for me, still is best exemplified by the movie *True Grit*, a movie he took me to see when I was eight years old.

Oh, how I wished to be Mattie! She was fearless. Even when she thought John Wayne had abandoned her, she was able to mock the outlaw Lucky Ned Pepper and declare with utter and complete sanctimony:

Rooster Cogburn is no good friend of mine! He led us straight into your
hands, and now he has left me with a gang of cut-throats! Is that what
they call "grit" in Fort Smith? We call it something else in Yell County.

Of course, John Wayne circled back for Mattie. Similarly, my father circled back for me, and he is still circling.

I Love you, Dad. And I will see you soon enough. We will compare notes and have a good laugh together, maybe a beer … soon enough.

ALWILA' ALQABILI

I am of the Ghaziyya: If she be in error, then I will err;
and if Ghaziyya be guided right, I go right with her!

Take for your brother whom you will in days of peace,
but know that when fighting comes your kinsman alone is near.
Your true friend is your kinsman,
who answers your call for aid with good will and
when deeply drenched in bloodshed has sword and spear.

Oh, never forsake your kinsman even when he does you wrong,
for what he has marred he mends thereafter and makes sincere.

Abu Tammam Habib ibn Aus (805–845), *Hamasah*

Mankind's earliest attempts at communion outside of the family produced tribal cultures, which demanded strict loyalty and Love of clan – *alwila' alqabili* in Arabic. Survival depended upon one's immediate kinfolk, so obedience was prized and rewarded. Thus began the era of blind faith, which still haunts many cultures today.

Sadly, even though most of us share the same moral code, we readily forsake our values when our own community is threatened. In moments of extreme danger and intense fear, many of us forget the seminal truth that all of humanity comprises just one community in the sight of God.

Our global challenge, then, is to question those inherited loyalties – like national pride, racial purity, and religious infallibility – which produce mistrust and intolerance. Let us also acknowledge that unfettered allegiance – to state boundaries, cultural constructs, and religious dogma – comprise the greatest threat to our collective survival. Once we abandon the prejudice and fear which bound our tribal ancestors, we will be ready to experience the joy of true communal life and Love.

NEO-HUMANISM AND THE NEW ERA: EXCERPTS OF SONGS AND ESSAYS

By Shrii Prabhat Ranjan Sarkar
(1921–1990)

All human beings are our own –
All hearts share the same innermost heart, the needs of all are the same.
We cry in sorrow, we laugh in joy;
We Love to see the faces of our dear ones;
We share food and drink all together;
We realize that all share the same needs.
We all Love our Universe, the moon and stars above and the forest below;
We dance to the same rhythm and sing with the same life's urge
We link our minds together to call to the Supreme Lord.

All humanity is a singular entity; it is one and indivisible. The feelings and sentiments of all human beings are the same, and preparation for a nobler life is the same for all. The requirements and necessities of all humanity are the same. So humanity is a singular entity, humanity is one and indivisible. And for this purpose we should always maintain equilibrium amongst different humans; there must be one equipoise for the development of all, irrespective of caste, creed, nationality, and clan "isms."

Today's humanity has no doubt made some progress in intellect, in wisdom and in rationality. Human beings came onto this Earth about one million years ago. The feelings and sentiments, hopes and aspirations, frustrations and disappointments, cares and anxieties, pleasures and pains, tears and smiles of the present-day human beings are almost the same as those of the primitive humans. The difference is that the emotions and feelings of the present human beings are deeper than those of their ancestors.

Not only has there been an increase in the depth of their feelings; but along with this there has been an increase in the originality of their thoughts. Humanity is the collection of all the perfections and imperfections of human beings; and when the higher thoughts and ideas are combined together, we get humanism. The word "human" is used both as a noun and as an adjective to denote a complete human being having both perfections and imperfections.

During the past million years of human history, proper justice has not been done to human beings; a particular class, a particular section has always been given greater importance than others, and in this process the other sections have been neglected. For instance, when a soldier sacrifices his life on the battlefield, his death is announced in bold headlines in the newspapers; but the same newspapers do not mention anything about the great hardships that his widow faces to raise their small family after the death of her husband. This is how one-sided justice has been meted out.

Human beings have limped forward in their journey of history for the last million years bearing the burden of this defective social system; all have not been given equal justice. That is why I say that neither has justice been done to humanity (the abstract noun for "human beings") nor has justice been done to humanism (the abstract noun for "the works performed by human beings for human beings"). Now it is high time to make a reappraisal of the down-trodden humanity, of the downtrodden humanism. Oftentimes, some people have lagged behind, exhausted, and collapsed on the ground, their hands and knees bruised and their clothes stained with mud. Such people have been thrown aside with hatred and have become the outcasts of society; they have been forced to remain isolated from the mainstream of social life. This is the kind of treatment they have received. Few have cared enough to lift up those people who lagged behind and help them forward.

When some people started advancing, they thought more about themselves and less about others; nor did they think about the animals and plants. But if we analyze with a cool brain, it becomes quite clear that just as my life is important to me, others' lives are equally important to them; and if we do not give proper value to the lives of all creatures, then the development of the entire humanity becomes impossible. If people think more about themselves as individuals or about their small families, castes, clans or tribes, and do not think at all about the collectivity, this is decidedly detrimental. Similarly, if people neglect the entire living world – the plant world, the animal world – is this not indeed harmful? That is why I say that there is a great need to explain humanity and humanism in a new light, and this newly-explained humanism will be a precious treasure for the world.

What is Neo-Humanism? Neo-Humanism is humanism of the past, humanism of the present and humanism – newly explained – of the future. Explaining humanity and humanism in a new light will widen the path of human progress, will make it easier to tread. Neo-Humanism will give new inspiration and provide a new interpretation for the very concept of human existence. It will help people understand that human beings, as the most thoughtful and intelligent beings in this created Universe, will have to accept the great responsibility of taking care of the entire Universe – will have to accept that the responsibility for the entire Universe rests on them.

So then, what is Neo-Humanism? Humanism newly-explained and newly-sermonized is Neo-Humanism – the philosophy which will make people understand that they are not merely ordinary creatures. This philosophy will liberate them from all inferiority feelings and defects and make them aware of their own importance; it will inspire them to build a new world.

Geo-Sentiment

The sentiment that grows out of Love for the indigenous soil of a country is called "geo-sentiment." From this geo-sentiment, many other sentiments emerge, such as geo-patriotism, geo-economics and many other geocentric sentiments, including geo-religion. This geo-sentiment attempts to keep humanity confined within a limited part of this world. But the innermost desire of people is to expand themselves maximally in all directions.

Human society is continually striving to arrive at a synthesis through analysis, some sort of unity through diversity. The natural obstructions of small clans, narrow communal interests, geographical distances and intractable customs and usages – none of these obstacles could hinder the steady and silent movement towards a supreme goal. That is why the policy of apartheid, the vanity of racial superiority, national chauvinism or regionalism – these relative doctrines or social philosophies – could not thwart the progress of human society. The outdated ideals of nationalism are crumbling to pieces today.

Socio-Sentiment

There is still another sentiment which is more expanded than geo-sentiment – it is socio-sentiment. Socio-sentiment does not confine people to a particular territory, but instead pervades a particular social group. That is, instead of thinking about the welfare of a particular geographical area, people think about the well-being of a group, even to the exclusion of all other groups. And in the process, while they concern themselves with the interest of a particular group, they do not hesitate to violate the interests and natural growth of other groups. Perhaps this socio-sentiment is a bit better than geo-sentiment, but it is not altogether ideal; it is not free from defects.

Now, family sentiment is also a kind of socio-sentiment, but its radius is very small. Greater than this is the radius of caste sentiment, and still greater is that of community sentiment, national sentiment, international sentiment, and so on.

Socio-sentiment has, in the past, caused much bloodshed and created enormous division and mutual distrust among human groups, separating one group from another and throwing them into the dark dungeons of petty dogmas. Humanity's movement is then no longer like a broad and flowing river, but like a stagnant pool.

Geo-Religious Sentiment

Besides this, there is the domineering influence of religion on the human mind. You know that religions are based on dogmas. The propagators of religion never cared to preach *Bhagavata dharma* – the universally applicable human *dharma* [divine human path] free from narrowness – rather they always feared and avoided it. What have they preached instead? They have always declared, "I am not speaking with my own voice, I am speaking with the voice of heaven. I am the messenger of God. Don't take these words to be mine – they are the message of God, and so you will have to accept them. You must not question whether they are right or wrong; to question is a sin. If you question, your tongue will fall off!" They have tightened the noose of dogma around the people, so that they fear to take a single step over the line thinking, "How terrible! If I do so I will be burnt in hellfire for eternity!"

Thus, those who sought to confine different groups with the bondage of dogma in the aforesaid ways are the so-called religious leaders or *gurus*; they have done enormous harm to human society. The various religious groups have fought many bloody battles, because their dogmas were totally contradictory; if one group turned to pray toward the north, the other turned toward the south. Their leaders, meanwhile, fulfilled their own petty, selfish interests, saying, "These are God's commandments."

You must awaken those religious people who are not aware of what they are doing, and make them aware. Let the ideals of Neo-Humanism reach their ears and be implanted in the core of their hearts. With their liberated intellects they will throw all of their illusions into the dustbin.

Devotional Sentiment

Now, what is the role of devotional sentiment, the most valuable treasure of humanity? It is to transform the sense of worldly existence into the supreme spiritual stance. If a materialistic philosophy contains any narrowness, like the geo-sentiment we discussed, an imbalance is bound to occur between the inner and outer worlds, and psycho-physical imbalance will be inevitable. That is why, in spite of possessing everything, people will remain poor and deprived.

In the past this geo-sentiment has caused enormous harm to many individuals and groups of people. Intelligent people must keep themselves aloof from this geo-sentiment and support nothing that is based on it, because it pollutes the devotional sentiment; it degrades human beings and undermines human excellence.

> In the bower of kadamba flowers, the rains have come
> Dancing, dancing in the grove of cane.
> And all the peacocks have started prancing in rhythm.
> In the vibrant songs from the sounding lyres,
> The world without rhythm has found new life.
> The fragrance of jasmine floats in the wet air.
> And the pollen of mind smiles in the sweetest Love.
> Thrilling in blissful rhythms,
> The half-dead trees have all sprung into life.
> And all the peacocks have started prancing in rhythm.

This concern for the vital rhythm throbbing in other human creatures has driven people to the fold of humanism, has made them humanists. Now, if the same human sentiment is extended to include all creatures of this Universe, then and only then can human existence be said to have attained its final consummation. And in the process of expanding one's inner Love to other creatures, there should be another sentiment behind this human sentiment, which will vibrate human sentiment in all directions, which will touch the innermost recesses of the hearts of all creatures, and lead one and all to the final stage of supreme blessedness.

Humanity is now at the threshold of a new era. We do not want any dogma. The age of dogma is gone. What we want is an idea based on Neo-Humanism. We are for the entire created world; and not only for human beings or living beings, but for the entire animate and inanimate Universe.

All molecules, atoms, electrons, protons, positrons

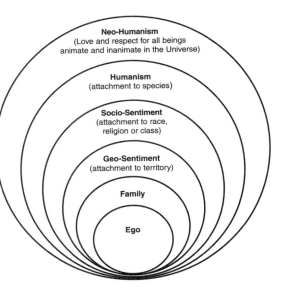

Sarkar's Neo-Humanism

Neo-Humanism
(Love and respect for all beings animate and inanimate in the Universe)

Humanism
(attachment to species)

Socio-Sentiment
(attachment to race, religion or class)

Geo-Sentiment
(attachment to territory)

Family

Ego

and neutrons are the veritable expressions of the same Supreme Consciousness. Those who remember this reality, who keep this realization ever alive in their hearts, are said to have attained perfection in life. They are the real *bhaktas* [devotees]. When this devotion does not remain confined to a mere practice, but instead is elevated to a devotional sentiment, a devotional mission, to the realm of devotional ideation – when the underlying spirit of humanism is extended to everything, animate and inanimate, in this Universe – I have designated this as Neo-Humanism. This Neo-Humanism will elevate humanism to universalism, the cult of Love for all created beings of this Universe.

Prabhat Ranjan Sarkar, known as Shrii Baba to his followers, developed the concept of Neo-Humanism based on his belief that humans have unlimited potential and that society should be structured to encourage our intellectual growth, physical health, and spiritual ascension. That means parity in the marketplace, fair distribution of resources, and appreciation for all living things. It is an egalitarian model, and there are numerous communities around the world devoted to Shrii Baba's teachings.

The notion that humans have innate Divine potential is contained in all the holy books, even those that have been purposely misinterpreted by ecclesiastical men of power to subjugate the masses. For instance, the *Old Testament* creation myth (which is actually Sumerian, not Hebrew), states that we were created in the image of God (i.e., the First Spiritual Paradigm). The *New Testament* repeatedly cites our ability, albeit through hard work, to achieve union with God again (i.e., the Fifth Spiritual Paradigm). In this passage, Jesus isn't just defending his right, but everyone's right to claim Divine status.

> *The Jews again picked up rocks to stone him. Jesus answered them, "I have shown you many good works from my Father, for which of these are you stoning me?" The Jews answered him, "We are not stoning you for good work but for blasphemy. You, a man, are making yourself God."*
>
> *Jesus answered them, "Is it not written in your law … 'You are gods'? If it calls them gods to whom the word of God came, and scripture cannot be set aside, can you say that the one whom the Father has consecrated and sent into the world blasphemes because I said, 'I am the son of God?'"*
>
> *Gospel of John*, Chapter 10:31

The goal is not to "prove" ourselves to God. The goal is to be the best we can be, to live life justly and fully, and to spread our Love to everyone in our community. Only then will we reach the utopian Fifth Spiritual Paradigm.

WHAT WE WANT

By Ella Wheeler Wilcox
(1850–1919)

All hail the dawn of a new day breaking,
When a strong-armed nation shall take away
The weary burdens from backs that are aching
With maximum labor and minimum pay.

When no man is honored who hoards his millions,
When no man feasts on another's toil,
And God's poor suffering, striving billions
Shall share His riches of sun and soil.

There is gold for all in the earth's broad bosom,
There is food for all in the land's great store,
Enough is provided if rightly divided,
Let each man take what he needs – no more.

Shame on the miser with unused riches,
Who robs the toiler to swell his hoard,
Who beats down the wage of the digger of ditches,
And steals the bread from the poor man's board.

Shame on the owner of mines whose cruel
And selfish measures have brought him wealth,
While the ragged wretches who dig his fuel
Are robbed of comfort and hope and health.

Shame on the ruler who rides in his carriage
Bought with the labor of half-paid men –
Men who are shut out of home and marriage
And are herded like sheep in a hovel-pen.

Let the clarion voice of the nation wake him
To broader vision and fairer play,
Or let the hand of a just law shake him
Till his ill-gained dollars shall roll away.

Let no man dwell under a mountain of plunder,
Let no man suffer with want and cold,
We want right living, not mere alms-giving,
We want just dividing of labor and gold.

CHAPTER 4: LOVE OF COMMUNITY | 101

=>◆<=

Without a brand new economic model, there cannot be social justice. Currently, we are witnessing the collapse of the "free market." It will be in ruins shortly. Why? Because it is the antithesis of what fair-minded people consider fair. The financial and corporate deck is stacked against the average person, the middle class laborer. Compounding the problem is the fact that the banking elite have built a house of cards with the deck – our deck. Money should be viewed as a utility or, as Thomas Jefferson would say, the "commons" – those assets in which we all have a stake and in which we all have a right to share.

Capitalism is failing because it is based on the concept of debt, rather than on the idea of the commons ... the common good. By definition, a debt-based society is dependent on debt; it needs credit to thrive. Our markets are sick because credit – the lifeline – has dried up. In short, people cannot afford to borrow any more. There is no one left to bring into the pyramid scheme. The game is over.

Many books are now being published on this subject. Indeed, the term "economic democracy" is now in vogue. I will leave it to greater minds to determine which model we should try next. I simply know that capitalism has spawned greed – the first cardinal sin.

At this juncture, what strikes me as particularly fascinating is that both the left and right extremes of the political spectrum are calling for a tax revolt! There is a growing movement by uber-liberals to abolish the Federal Reserve (which *is* an illegal and unnecessary institution). And there is a burgeoning groundswell by ultra-conservatives to stop paying taxes altogether.

I suppose we could start a Spiritual Revolution over the issue of taxes; it was the driving force behind the last American Revolution. Such an approach might prolong the agony of the Great Cusp, or it might bring it to a swift end. But at what cost? Our bad decisions to date have caused this to be a breech birth into the New Millennium. We need not make it worse.

Instead, I would advocate a less drastic and more measured approach. We all share in the commons, so we are morally obligated to maintain them. We should start now to implement a new economic model for the Fifth Spiritual Paradigm. The Oracle Institute is working on such a plan, which will be the foundation of an ambitious project in Independence, Virginia – the first 100% sustainable spiritual community in the United States.

LOVE AND CONFLICT:
INSIGHTS FROM AFRICA ON
TRANSFORMING SELF AND SOCIETIES

By Philip M. Hellmich

Love and compassion are necessities, not luxuries.
Without them, humanity cannot survive.

His Holiness the Dalai Lama

For nearly twenty-five years, Africa has been an integral part of my spiritual journey and an ongoing source for exploring and experiencing Love as a powerful, transformative force that is essential to personal, societal, and global evolution. I have made more than twenty trips to African countries, including Angola, Burundi, the Democratic Republic of Congo, Guinea, Ivory Coast, Liberia, Nigeria, Rwanda, and my beloved Sierra Leone. Almost all of these countries have experienced violent conflict, so it is often hard for people in the United States to comprehend the level of sadness and, at the same time, incredible inspiration I have encountered on these visits. In this essay, I will share some of my insights in the hope that others may benefit from what I have learned from the people of Africa.

Africa: My Spiritual Journey Begins

After college, I left my family of ten siblings and hometown in Indiana and joined the Peace Corps. I was assigned to Sierra Leone, where I worked for four years to overcome water shortages and prevent deadly diseases like diarrhea. I lived in mud huts in remote villages – the first two years in Kagbere and then two more years in Masongbo. There were maybe thirty houses in each village, which meant there were approximately three hundred people in each community. There was no running water, no electricity and no telephones. While living in these bush villages, I grew to Love many people, such as the Conteh family of Masongbo. Like many Peace Corps volunteers, I found that what I learned from my friends far outweighed my contributions.

The Contehs welcomed me into their family. I often fished with the brothers at a nearby river and together learned how to make fishing lures from sticks and wires. We ate dinner collectively, usually from the same plate. And we would pass the nights telling stories or playing drums. They tried to teach me how to drum – a futile exercise that always ended in laughter.

For all its lack of Western conveniences, the Masongbo village was rich in social connections. There were frequently three or four generations of family members living together in the same huts. The elderly were respected for their wisdom and life experiences and helped take care of the younger ones. I often marveled at how each person seemed to know his or her place in their family and village. This was in part because of the education provided by the "secret spiritual societies," traditions that were hundreds of years old and that existed right alongside Christianity and Islam.

There also was a deep sense of spirituality that came from a daily connection to nature. As subsistence farmers, the people followed the rhythms of "hungry season," when previous crop yields were low and it was time to plant, and harvest season, when there was abundance. There also were rainy seasons and dry seasons and the cycles of the moon. On nights with a new moon in the rainy season, it was dark and people went to bed early. When the moon was full in the dry season, there was lots of light and the children laughed and played throughout the night.

And, ultimately, there was the cycle of life and death. When Pa Conteh, head of the Conteh family, died, people grieved openly, and for days family members arrived from around the country for the funeral. When I went to see Pa Conteh's body, he had been dead for three days. The hot, humid weather had turned his vibrant face and twinkling eyes into a skull wrapped in dry brown skin. The pungent odor was so strong it was difficult to breathe. Finally, Pa Conteh's body was wrapped in a piece of white cloth and placed directly in the ground.

As I pondered Pa Conteh's body being consumed by the Earth, the village began a huge celebration! This caught me completely off guard, as I was still grieving. The entire village danced, sang, ate, and drank … well into the next day. It was during this death celebration that I noticed the music contained rhythms from nature like the calls of birds in the bush, and the dancing reflected movements of daily life such as pounding rice or making Love.

It would have been easy to romanticize village life if not for the fact that Sierra Leone was, and still is, one of the poorest countries in the world, where one in every four children dies before the age of five. Decades of government corruption had all but destroyed the infrastructure. The country had vast natural resources of diamonds, gold, and rutile (a major ore of titanium), but these riches did not benefit the villagers. There was a huge contrast between rich and poor. Government officials and wealthy businessmen drove expensive vehicles while my friends were lucky to have sandals on their feet.

Meanwhile, signs of Westernization were ever present, and usually in bizarre ways. Throughout the country, even in the most remote villages, people wore T-shirts and other used clothing from the United States. When the fashion trends changed in the United States, Sierra Leone and other countries got the hand-me-downs. I frequently saw people wearing clothes that looked utterly comical from my perspective – such as an elderly man who wore a shirt that read "baby on board." Nevertheless, the social tapestry of Sierra Leone appeared to be holding together under the strain of poverty, corruption, high infant mortality rate, and onslaught of Western influences.

Reverse Culture Shock: Going Inward

It was when I returned to America that I realized how much I had changed while in Africa. Suddenly, I was aware of the wealth, material abundance, and incredible waste in my home country. Electricity was accessible twenty-four hours a day with the flip of a switch, so the cycles of the moon went unnoticed. Safe drinking water was readily available without having to carry buckets of water. Stores were filled with everything a person could ever want. I remember pausing at the pet section of my local grocery store and counting over fifty varieties of cat food. I found myself translating the cost of everything into cups of rice and calculating how many members of the Conteh family it could feed and for how long.

American abundance literally bombarded me. Everywhere I looked, I saw a culture obsessed with youth, beauty, sex, and various products designed to enhance these goals. There also was unbelievable violence on TV and at the cinema. I remember the first time I saw a person killed in a movie – I flinched – and then was disturbed to see that the people with me did not seem to notice anything wrong. Even now, I am sensitive to seeing people killed in the movies.

After returning home, it didn't take long for me to experience a deep crisis – a void. People seemed too busy to connect as deeply as my African friends and I felt alone. This void jolted me and then sparked me to pursue a conscious spiritual journey through a daily meditation practice. My inward exploration intensified as I watched Sierra Leone succumb to a terrible war. All I wanted to do was help. My body was in America but my heart and soul were in Africa.

So in 1997, I joined Search for Common Ground, an international conflict transformation organization. Since then, Common Ground has sent me on numerous African missions. Each of my trips would begin on a Sunday morning, when I would go to my favorite meditation center. I enjoy meditating with others, as I have found that it is easy for me to experience deep states of peace, bliss, and Love when with a group. After service, I would go home to Arlington, Virginia, finish packing, and then fly out from Washington Dulles International airport. Within twenty-four to thirty hours, I would land in Monrovia, Freetown, Kinshasa, or some other war-torn city in Africa.

The contrast between the peacefulness of a meditation hall and the impact of deadly conflict is shocking, to say the least. My meditation practice trained me to be present, open, and in many ways vulnerable. This was both a blessing and a challenge, as it meant I would be more open to the depth of suffering of people around me, especially of my friends in Sierra Leone.

My first trip back to Sierra Leone was in April 1998, as part of an assessment team for Search for Common Ground. There was a lull in the ongoing civil war, so I was able to reach my friends in Masongbo. I had mixed emotions about returning to the village – while I desperately wanted to know if my friends were okay, I was nervous about seeing the impact of war on people I loved. Needless to say, when I saw the Conteh brothers I had a deep sense of relief! They, too, were astounded to see me suddenly appear. We hugged, looked into each other's eyes, and smiled.

The entire village gathered around, hugging me, laughing, showing me the babies named after me, children conceived during the war. I could not help but notice how emaciated my friends looked – people I remembered being lean and strong from farm work. Now, their hair had a reddish tint from malnutrition and the children were more frail and vulnerable than before. Moses Conteh and his cousin Sanpha told stories of how they almost starved, surviving at times by fishing, using the methods we learned together when I was a Peace Corps volunteer. While telling these stories, the Contehs offered me a live chicken and palm wine, traditional gifts for a special guest. Children handed me mangos and coconuts, while the village chief gave me kola nuts, a customary greeting that means: "He who gives kola, gives life." Later, the Contehs went fishing and caught a thirty-pound Nile perch using a lure they made themselves – enough fish to feed their families for days. They were so happy to offer the fish as a gift.

The author and Sanpha Conteh with the thirty pound fish.

The Love I shared with the Contehs and their village opened my heart. Their generosity, when having so little and surviving so much, still moves me beyond words.

A few weeks after this visit to Sierra Leone, the civil war surged and the village of Masongbo was once again sacked by rebels, known as the RUF. During this horrific period, I had no way to contact the Conteh family or my other friends. I watched in dismay as the news from Sierra Leone became increasingly bleak. The reports about the number of people killed or mutilated were not like other bad news stories. No, these were people and communities I loved deeply and who loved me. I would later learn that the RUF unit that raided Masongbo was headed by a teenage boy named Colonel Rambo. For nearly two years, Rambo and his "men" held the Contehs and others hostage, taking whatever they wanted from the villagers who lived on less than a dollar a day. The RUF even took young children from the village as new recruits. And a dear friend, Adama Conteh, who had daughters named Peggy and Patience, died giving birth to her third child, having been denied medical care by the RUF.

My meditation practice became a life raft as I struggled with frustration, rage, and sadness. I desperately wanted to know how to bridge the refuge of inner peace I experienced in meditation with the outer world of conflict and peace building. Often, I would look to His Holiness the Dalai Lama as a source of inspiration. He dealt with enormous international problems with China annexing Tibet. His people suffered tremendously and, yet, His Holiness constantly came from a place of compassion and Love, using meditation as a source of strength. His example helped me to keep my faith and to persevere.

A Breakthrough in Love

A breakthrough came in May 2000. The United Nations had peacekeeping troops in Sierra Leone and Search for Common Ground had just received the funding needed to start a program there. Meanwhile, my supervisor and two other colleagues had just left the organization for a start-up dot.com company. I was suddenly promoted to oversee our West African programs, including the new one in Sierra Leone.

I was in Monrovia, having just left Freetown in Sierra Leone, where I had hired some staff members and a contractor to set up our office. I was scheduled to fly back to Freetown, but a friend called hours before the flight. He strongly encouraged me to stay in Monrovia, because Foday Sanko, head of the RUF, was planning a coup in Freetown. Sure enough, the coup attempt did happen and the house where I would have stayed was caught in the crossfire.

As a result, I stayed in Monrovia, which had survived numerous attacks during its own civil war and was a bombed-out city with no running water or electricity. After making the decision not to go to Sierra Leone, I remember going back to a bare apartment and meditating. This time, I entered a meditative state besieged by new responsibilities, wanting to help people in Sierra Leone, but not knowing what to do.

Generally, I do not talk about my meditations; however, they were evolving dramatically. On that afternoon, a wave of ecstasy came shooting through my body. I was overcome by an intoxicating amount of Love in which I experienced a profound connection with everything in all directions at the same time. In that state of Love, I felt at home and trusting. The Love went on and on, lasting for hours, until I finally passed out.

The timing of this blissful event was incredibly powerful. Just as I was feeling helpless and distraught, an invisible presence enveloped me with a deep level of comfort. I was confused at first, wondering how so much Love could exist next to so much pain and suffering. Love was leading me somewhere ... I just did not know where yet.

I needed help navigating these inner terrains and the range of emotional reactions I was having to the deadly conflicts in Africa. I had a meditation practice and a larger meditation community as a foundation. Still, I wanted a mentor. After creating this intention, I met Dr. Rick Levy, who later published *Miraculous Health: How to Heal Your Body by Unleashing the Hidden Power of Your Mind.*

Over a seven-year period, while going back and forth to Africa, I went to Rick for advice. Having studied spiritual practices from around the world, Rick accompanied me on a trip to West Africa, where he assessed what role indigenous spiritual healers might play in the Sierra Leone peace process. Moreover, through our one-on-one sessions, Rick helped me release the negative emotional reactions I was having to the atrocities in Africa. We would go into meditation together, then shift the focus of my consciousness to the inner realms of my being – to my soul. This took me into even deeper states of peace and Love that rejuvenated me and enabled me to continue working in difficult situations without getting "burnt out."

The work with Rick and my daily meditation practice became means of "purifying my consciousness," helping me realize from an experiential perspective that my true inner state was peace and that I am connected to and part of a larger source of Love. I started to envision the negative thoughts and emotions as waves – natural reactions to a troubling world – that would rise and pass away if I allowed them, not part of my identity.

I began to fall in Love with Love itself, to write ecstatic poetry, to study the mystics. Paramahansa Yogananda once described Love as "the divine power of attraction in creation that harmonizes, unites, binds together." With this lens, I started to see Love permeating everything: the Love I felt for my parents and siblings; the Love they expressed for me; the Love felt with friends; the Love between my cats and me – it was all Love expressing itself. I listened to a radio station that played Love songs. I substituted "the Love" for the object of Love in the songs and the songs took on a whole new level of meaning.

On a practical level, I could not maintain this state of intoxicated Love indefinitely, but I found I could cultivate Love in my daily life by removing barriers that held me back from connecting with other people and nature. For example, I practiced being fully present and focused on a person when greeting him or her. Could I see the other person as a soul whose essence is Love? Could I listen to his or her every word, I mean really listen? Sure enough, my familial, personal, and office relationships all began to shift through this simple exercise. The question became: *How much Love could I handle?*

Ultimately, I concluded that the amount of Love we experience is based on our openness to connect. Invariably, ever-deepening connections bring old fears to the surface that need to be released. In this way, I discovered that openness to Love is an integral part of the purification process and the inner transformation necessary to create harmonious and loving environments.

Separation: Root Cause of Conflict

> *A human being is a part of a whole, called by us "Universe," a part limited in time and space. He experiences himself, his thoughts and feelings as something separated from the rest ... a kind of optical delusion of his consciousness. This delusion is a kind of prison for us, restricting us to our personal desires and to affection for a few persons nearest to us. Our task must be to free ourselves from this prison by widening our circle of compassion to embrace all living creatures and the whole of nature in its beauty.*

Albert Einstein

My personal exploration of Love as a transformative and unifying force provided me with a new perspective on how to contend with deadly conflicts and peace-building efforts in Africa. For instance, the very idea of Love presupposes duality, as there is an exchange between two entities. As described by many spiritual teachers and implied by Albert Einstein above, it is the illusion of separation that is the root cause of conflict, including a sense of separation from God, Spirit, or Universe (whichever word works for you).

Michael Singer, author of *The Untethered Soul*, describes this idea by saying each of us has within us a soul that is part of the larger Spirit, filled with bliss, peace, and Love. Intuitively, we know that these exalted states exist, but instead of looking inward to experience them, we look externally in an attempt to create peak moments.

Tara Brach, a psychologist and meditation instructor in the Washington, D.C. area, explains this phenomenon by saying we identify with our thoughts and emotions and then believe they are real. This starts a process whereby we separate from others and everything around us. With separation comes fear, which in turn gives rise to the "wanting self" (e.g., I want to be happy and avoid suffering). Everyone on the planet has this basic operating software package running – we are all trying to rearrange a constantly changing world to avoid suffering and get what we want.

Conflict is inevitable, as a result. It also is a natural part of the human experience, as we bump into other people trying to avoid suffering and create happiness. A child wants a toy and will fight with another child to get it, adolescents struggle over identity and romantic relationships, and adults continue the drama with even more involved conflicts. In a warped way, we can see that the people who sold AK-47s and rocket-propelled grenades to the RUF were doing so to make money so they could be happy.

Meanwhile, humans are governed by three basic spiritual laws: the first one is choice or free will; the second is cause and effect or *karma*; and the third and most subtle law is evolution. Often, free will is usurped by emotions, societal expectations, or cultural norms. Still, we slowly learn by trial and error and by reaping the fruits of our actions how to choose behaviors that benefit us and those we Love. In this way, we evolve.

Eventually, we learn to look inward, to reconnect with our souls to find the bliss, peace, and Love we long for. Once in touch with our soul, we sense our oneness with others and all of nature. This connection gives rise to the highest qualities of the human spirit, such as tolerance, compassion, forgiveness, and Love. Then our outward actions are qualitatively different – they express our unique gifts without the need to get anything in return.

Accelerated Pursuit of Happiness: Creating Complex Problems

Unfortunately, the Western model for happiness is based on individual consumption, which I find terribly disturbing after living in Africa. To me, it is clear that the Western pursuit of material satisfaction has created a global spiritual crisis that now threatens human survival. There literally are billions of people striving to avoid suffering and be happy through massive consumption, all of which is being accelerated by technological advances. Yet somehow, we do not see the cause and effect impact of our collective individual actions on the environment, people who live thousands of miles away, or geopolitical struggles for resources.

Although the global economy may be weaving together humanity, without the unifying power of Love, greater and greater global conflicts will arise. Also, the individual pursuit of happiness through consumerism usually results in less human connection, less connection with nature, and, ultimately, less experience of Love. This in turn creates isolation, suffering, and an inner hunger that leads to more craving and consumption. It is no surprise that many of the top-selling prescription drugs sold in America deal with depression and anxiety. Material progress without Love and compassion leads to suffering.

With all this said, my colleagues at Search for Common Ground often remind me that most conflicts in the world are handled peacefully or at least non-violently, a fact easily forgotten when traveling to war-torn countries or watching the evening news. They also point out that conflict is an engine of growth and transformation when handled constructively (or, as I now believe, with Love). I see this in my own life – close friendships deepen after an argument if we are able to communicate openly. And my own spiritual journey has been enriched as a result of the inner conflict I felt after returning to the United States from Sierra Leone.

However, when conflicts are handled destructively, fear becomes the driving force.

People become polarized and their extreme positions drive the agenda. The people with the loudest voices often use fear as a tactic to unify their group against "the others." As fear increases, people narrow their multiple identities (such as father, mother, musician, artist, sports fan, farmer, teacher), down to just one – whether an ethnic group (I'm a Hutu and you're a Tutsi), a religious sect (I'm a Muslim and you're a Jew), or a political party (I'm a Republican and you're a Democrat). Instead of seeing what they have in common or what connects them, they see only how they are different and what separates them.

The Common Ground Approach: Transforming Societies

In Rwanda, this dynamic played out to an extreme level. In the early 1990s, radio programs amplified the fear and mistrust by fueling ethnic tension. As fear increased, people became more polarized, thinking in terms of "us and them." Tutsis and Hutu moderates were identified as the problem. To get rid of the problem, the radical Hutus believed it was necessary to get rid of the Tutsis and even the moderate Hutus. As in all destructive conflicts, the aggressors created an atmosphere where it was possible to strike out and kill – first stereotype and then dehumanize "the others." Thus, Tutsis were called dogs, since it is easier to kick a dog than a human. Then they were called cockroaches, as it is easy to kill a cockroach.

My colleagues at Search for Common Ground did just the opposite in neighboring Burundi, a country populated largely by people with Hutu and Tutsi ethnicity. Burundi was teetering on the brink of all-out violence immediately after the genocide in Rwanda. Quickly, my colleagues assessed the situation and then established a radio studio where Hutu and Tutsi journalists worked side by side. They produced programs that provided balanced information and that rehumanized both groups.

I remember the first time I went to Burundi. I was nervous because the Rwanda genocide was such a hallmark of horror. But I was amazed to walk into the Common Ground office and see a large team of people busily producing radio programs, all committed to working together. One of them was

Adrien, a tall, soft-spoken man with deep, compassionate eyes. He was a Hutu and in his youth Adrien missed school one day – the day his entire class was massacred by Tutsis. In the office next to Adrien was Agnes, a powerful, robust Tutsi woman who had lost seventy-nine members of her family to the ethnic violence. Indeed, everyone on the staff had a story of personal loss, yet each was willing to take a stand, together, for a new way of resolving conflict.

Coming from a large family myself and having seen the impact of war on the Conteh family, I found it both mind- and heart-boggling to imagine working side by side with people from an ethnic group that committed atrocities against loved ones. Adrien, Agnes, and others across Africa became my teachers on the practical ways to embody compassion and Love, and how to promote those values across multi-cultured societies.

Their techniques were similar to what I learned in meditation. For example, my meditation training taught me to look at and accept the realities of a situation, no matter how difficult. I did not have to like the situation, just accept it. This could be an outward state of affairs, such as the war in Sierra Leone, or it could be the anger and sadness that arose as a response. Tara Brach calls this approach "radical acceptance."

All of Search for Common Ground's programs face harsh realities head-on, accepting that such situations exist. There is nothing "Pollyannaish" about our work. The idea is to shift the focus from what separates people from their perceived enemies to what they have in common – their common humanity.

The Common Ground approach is based on an implicit trust in the human spirit. When there is recognition of common humanity, innate spiritual qualities of tolerance, compassion, forgiveness, and Love can be awakened. With these positive human qualities present, it is easier for people to shift their mindset. A new consciousness arises, one where they can face problems together instead of attacking each other. In essence, our approach is similar to a meditation practice: We help people move beyond fear, expand their identity or consciousness, and experience a sense of oneness or connection with other people and nature. This process opens people to their innate spiritual potential and allows them to create win-win solutions.

This may sound simple, but it is profound. Meditation teaches that wherever you place your focus, that is where your energy and consciousness goes. Scientists now theorize that the physical world arises out of consciousness, something yogis and sages have taught for centuries. Many motivational speakers and spiritual teachers talk about the power of positive thinking and positive affirmations. One teacher says if you want to reduce the power of negative influences, do not battle the negative; rather, increase the positive. Yogananda once said, "If you want to change your circumstance in life, change your thinking." This may sound idealistic when a society is facing potential genocide, but this is exactly what our staff employed in Burundi – we helped an entire society change its consciousness.

One of the Common Ground radio programs produced in Burundi was a radio soap opera called *Our Neighbors, Ourselves*. It told the story of a Hutu family living next to a Tutsi family. Like all good soap operas, it was filled with laughter, tragedies, drama, and Love affairs. Through more than a thousand episodes, the program helped rehumanize Hutus and Tutsis to each other by highlighting what they have in common. Nearly 90% of the population listened to the show. It became so popular that during a break in programming, a general in the army came to our office and demanded a copy of the next episode! He said his men were anxiously waiting to hear what happened next.

The core message of *Our Neighbors, Ourselves* was pretty close to: "Love thy neighbor as thyself." Adrien, Agnes, and other staff were modeling behaviors taught by the great spiritual traditions and they helped reweave the social tapestry of their society with compassion and Love.

Steady Bongo and the Cultural Heroes

During my travels in Africa, I met hundreds of people like Adrien and Agnes – people who bravely risk their lives to promote the search for common ground or common humanity. While their stories and situations may differ in detail, they possess a distinctly similar focus: a commitment to bridging the walls of separation that divide them, their communities, and their countries. In this sense, and without relying on any religious affiliation, they promote the universal expression of Love, drawing together and healing fragmented parts of the whole.

Sometimes, this search for common humanity can take unexpected twists and turns that lead to joyous celebrations, even in the direst situations. An example of a surprising outcome involved a Sierra Leonean pop musician named Steady Bongo. A year after our program started, there was a tenuous peace agreement between the government and RUF rebels. The RUF held most of the northern and eastern regions of the country while United Nations and British peacekeepers controlled the rest.

Word came to Frances, our director in Sierra Leone, that the RUF were harassing UN workers who were trying to get humanitarian aid to the region. Steady Bongo was visiting Frances at the time, and Frances had a hunch that Steady should go with her to the front lines. Keep in mind, the RUF had committed terrible atrocities – people were terrified of them and rightly so.

Frances and Steady drove more than twelve hours across the country. When they arrived at an RUF checkpoint, teenage boys wielding AK-47s started harassing Frances. She calmly asked if they liked Steady Bongo's music, to which they replied, "Yeah sure – he's our man." Then she pointed to the back seat. When they saw Steady Bongo, the combatants went from being thugs to young boys. They danced and sang, "The war is over, Steady Bongo has come!" Then the gruff, hardened commanders met Steady; they went from being terrorizing combatants to starry-eyed fans in seconds. The RUF commanders asked Steady to play some music and Frances jumped in, sensing an opportunity.

Ultimately, the RUF commanders agreed to give safe passage to Steady Bongo and his band, provide security, pay for half the expenses, and allow Search for Common Ground staff to interview people for radio programs, which we broadcast across the country. In return, Steady Bongo and his band the Cultural Heroes did a peace concert tour across the RUF area, helping to open the lines to humanitarian aid. They were greeted by enthusiastic combatants and civilians alike, and our national radio program broadcast voices of young RUF combatants, who said they were tired of fighting and wanted to end the conflict. Our interviews started to rehumanize the RUF rebels, allowing the slow process of reconciliation to begin.

After supporting Sierra Leone through the tenuous peace process, disarming combatants, reintegrating refugees, and holding national elections, we now are addressing the root cause of the war – poverty and corruption. We also are giving a national voice to those who have been marginalized, like women and children. Sierra Leone, like Burundi, still faces incredible social and political problems, such as a lack of opportunities for a generation of youth who grew up with violence. These countries are evolving, slowly growing out of difficult periods. The ongoing challenge is to reweave the social tapestries and integrate the best of traditional African cultures with the positive aspects of globalization. The new social fabric will need tolerance, compassion, and Love to withstand all these pressures so that people can explore creative solutions without resorting to violence.

Universal Lessons – Global Challenges

In a sense, the lessons from Africa are universal to the human experience. Humanity is facing complex problems, such as global warming, that require us to look beyond our individual and national identities. If we start to view all of humanity and nature as being interconnected and interdependent, we will be able to move beyond behaviors that are fueled by a sense of separation and fear. Then cooperative solutions will come at an unprecedented rate and scale. But first, we must reevaluate how we individually and collectively pursue happiness. As Einstein prescribed, we must widen "our circle of compassion."

In Africa, the human spirit has proven to be incredibly resilient. From direct experience, I know it is possible to cultivate Love on an individual level through spiritual practices such as meditation, and on a societal level by applying emerging methodologies of conflict resolution such as the Search for Common Ground approach. The next step will be an evolutionary leap: *To weave a new global tapestry based on the universal principle of Love.*

While this global challenge may seem overwhelming, I have found that if I focus on my immediate environment, I am empowered. In meditation, the idea is to "be present." I believe that my contribution to world peace starts right now, with every breath, choosing to be present in my own humanity and honoring the humanity in whoever is in front of me. This simple exercise allows me to connect spiritually with people all around the world. And it enables me to be open to the unifying and transformative power of Love.

When I look back on my many journeys to Africa, one of the most important lessons I have learned is simple: slow down and "keep time" – a Sierra Leonean expression for being together and connecting with others. Surely, our collective future depends less on science and technology and more on the art of cultivating compassion and Love.

⇒·◆·⇐

For me, this essay highlights the concept of community in two ways. First, it provides a snapshot of the realities on the ground, a vivid look into the insanity and near hopelessness of ethnic-based conflict. Second, it provides a bird's eye view of the exploitation of the third world, how consumerism has stripped an entire continent of its natural resources. Just as the international financial cabal has stolen the last possible dollar from the middle class, so the global middle class has sucked the last bit of air from the poor.

So where are the guys in white hats? Phil has one!

ALONE

By Dr. Maya Angelou

Lying, thinking
Last night
How to find my soul a home
Where water is not thirsty
And bread loaf is not stone
I came up with one thing
And I don't believe I'm wrong
That nobody,
But nobody
Can make it out here alone.

Alone, all alone
Nobody, but nobody
Can make it out here alone.

There are some millionaires
With money they can't use
Their wives run round like banshees
Their children sing the blues
They've got expensive doctors
To cure their hearts of stone.
But nobody
No, nobody
Can make it out here alone.

Alone, all alone
Nobody, but nobody
Can make it out here alone.

Now if you listen closely
I'll tell you what I know
Storm clouds are gathering
The wind is gonna blow
The race of man is suffering
And I can hear the moan,
'Cause nobody,
But nobody
Can make it out here alone.

Alone, all alone
Nobody, but nobody
Can make it out here alone.

The evidence is mounting ... we are all connected. The Inuit's diet is rife with dioxins and PCBs produced by their "neighbors" in Europe. The air in Alaska contains industrial chemicals burned by their "neighbors" in China. The U.S. sub-prime loan and derivative asset collapse has thrown its "neighbor" Iceland into bankruptcy. And lest we forget, the frustrations felt by our Middle East "neighbors" brought down the Twin Towers. Alone? Hardly! Maya is right – there is no getting through this Great Cusp alone.

It is strange, this delusion that we are insolated from, immune to, or protected against the choices of others. Just as odd is the narcissistic notion that whatever we do in our community stays in our community, or that it is no one else's business what we do. Truly those days are over.

In the Fifth Spiritual Paradigm, we will accept the truth that we are all one community. We will recognize that however we treat the weakest, the poorest, the most vulnerable is the true measure of our civility. And we will come to understand that the light of God shines in each of us, so that we may never again justify the neglect or abuse of any soul. These may sound like idealized, starry-eyed predictions, but I am confident about our future. Already, advanced souls are working to build a new world. Here are some exciting examples.

In Italy, there is a magical, almost unbelievable place called Damanhur. About a thousand people live in Damanhur, and the community is close to 90% sustainable. That means they grow their own food, produce their own energy, operate over eighty cooperative businesses, educate their children, assist their elderly, and tend to their sick. They also have their own bank and currency. It is an incredible model for the future, and their non-denominational Temples to Humanity celebrate the Divine spark in all of us.

Last summer, I attended a seminar in Radford, Virginia entitled *Building a New World*. It was sponsored by PROUT, which stands for Progressive Utilization Theory and is based on the economic, social, and spiritual principles enunciated by the first author in this chapter, Shrii Baba. I made many friends at that seminar – some of whom will assist with our Independence project. The last day of the conference, we had a roundtable discussion, during which many of the attendees shared their already implemented ideas. I was stunned to learn how much these lightworkers have accomplished! I saw the future, and it is all about intentional sustainable communities.

But first we must navigate the Great Cusp. We will need special energy for this challenge, the type of energy described in the next essay ...

BODHISATTVA WARRIORS IN THE 21ST CENTURY COMMUNITY

By Kenneth Porter, M.D.

It was the best of times, it was the worst of times, it was the age of wisdom, it was the age of foolishness, it was the epoch of belief, it was the epoch of incredulity, it was the season of Light, it was the season of Darkness, it was the Spring of hope, it was the Winter of despair.

Charles Dickens, *Tale of Two Cities*

These prescient words of Dickens, written exactly a century and a half ago, can still touch us with their wisdom. Never before has the capacity for both human aggression and Love been so great. In the past few decades, we have seen justice come to South Africa, peace come to El Salvador and Ireland, freedom come to Eastern Europe and parts of the old Soviet Union, and at least a small measure of nuclear disarmament come to the First and Second Worlds. Television and the Internet have begun to create a global consciousness. Technology promises to significantly reduce world poverty, hunger, and disease. Spiritual consciousness is increasingly present in our communities.

But we also are threatened as never before. Global warming, nuclear proliferation, species extinction, and extremist Islamic terrorism have placed the planet in peril. One child dies of poverty and disease every six seconds, one-fifth of the world lives on less than $1 per day, and the forty wealthiest individuals on the planet own as much as the poorest 40%. These are the facts of our time.

Some of us may feel called to action. But our challenge is not action in the traditional political sense. Instead, we are called to what might be called "enlightened action" – the loving action of the bodhisattva warrior.

The Bodhisattva Warrior

Many great Buddhist masters have prophesied that centuries from now, when the forces of aggression amass on earth and no reason can turn them back, the kingdom of Shambhala will open its gates and its enlightened warriors will come forth into battle. Whoever they encounter will be given a choice – turn away from non-virtue to virtue, or by direct, wrathful intervention, be liberated into a pure land.

Chagdud Tulku Rinpoche,
from *The Awakened Warrior*, edited by Rick Fields

What is an enlightened warrior? The great mystery traditions speak of three paths to spiritual maturity. Each is associated with a different approach to spirituality and with a different energy center of the body – the heart, the head, or the belly. Interestingly, modern neurobiology has discovered that the human brain is *not* the only seat of consciousness in the body. As it turns out, the heart and intestines (belly) also contain brains – organized collections of nerve cells – that influence our lives. Hence, "the intelligence of the heart" and "gut instinct."

So, returning to our question: The bodhisattva warrior is one who has integrated her heart, her head, and her body in the service of healing. She wields the Sword of Wisdom, the Sword of Power, and the Sword of Love. She is a practitioner of what The Oracle Institute calls the Fifth Spiritual Paradigm.

But how does this bodhisattva warrior come into existence?

Our understanding of human growth is often pessimistic. We recognize that we can learn mathematics or learn to play tennis – that the mind and body can be trained. But do we recognize that the heart and soul can be trained, as well? Do we realize that wisdom, power, and Love can be learned?

When I went to medical school forty years ago, we were taught that the adult central nervous system – the brain and spinal cord – could not grow new cells. Now we know that this is not true. Interventions as diverse as anti-depressant medications and psychotherapy are capable of promoting "neuro-genesis" (the growth of new brain cells), and "neuroplasticity" (changing brain capabilities). And this also is true of the cells of the heart and the body.

How does a baby learn to walk? No one needs to push her; she has an inborn drive to learn and grow. And this learning takes place, as in the old joke about getting to Carnegie Hall, by "practice, practice, practice." But do we sufficiently recognize that wisdom, power, and Love are inborn drives that can, with equal success, be developed and trained – that bodhisattva warriors are both born and made?

One more point before we begin to explore the training of the bodhisattva warrior. We need to recognize that wisdom, power, and Love are interconnected aspects of the experience of being human and, therefore, inseparable. Wisdom connects us to our power and our Love. Love makes us wise and strong. Power is the vehicle for our loving wisdom. Ultimately, actualizing our Love requires all of our resources.

Nonetheless, for the purposes of learning, we will need to focus on each aspect of our true nature separately. We will start with wisdom – the practice of the truth.

The Path of Wisdom: Transforming Ignorance into Truth

> *When you go around the Earth in an hour and a half, you begin to recognize that your identity is with that whole thing, and that makes a change. And you look down there and you can't imagine how many borders and boundaries you cross, again and again and again. And you don't even see them. From where you see it the thing is a whole, and it's so beautiful, and there are no limits, there are no frames, there are no boundaries. There you are, hundreds of people killing each other over some imaginary line that you, you're not even aware of, you can't see, and from where you see it, the thing is a whole and it's so beautiful, and you, you wish you could take one in each hand and say look, look at it, from this perspective, look at that, what's important?*

> Rusty Schweickart, Lunar module pilot for Apollo 9
> (on walking in space and seeing Earth)

To become an enlightened, compassionate, and powerful warrior for Love, we first must wake up. How can we accomplish this?

For thousands of years our species has understood that we can live in two distinct states of consciousness – sometimes called the true and false states. In the true or awakened state of consciousness, we know ourselves as connected with other humans. We see that we are identical with our fellows and our Universe. Who we are – our true identity – is large and we have access to experiences of wisdom, power, Love … and happiness.

In the false state, we know ourselves only as a localized self, a personality, an ego. We have a center that is our identity and we have boundaries that separate us from other beings and from the world. Who we are – our false identity – is small and we experience suffering.

For many centuries, the great spiritual paths have offered to help us shift our identity from the false to the true state. One of the chief strategies has been meditation or controlled attention. Although there are numerous forms of meditation, one of the most effective is the Buddhist practice of mindfulness. In mindfulness, we train our minds. We practice taking our attention away from the false state of consciousness – the hopes, wishes, fears, dreams, and demands of our ego-self personality. We do this at first by selecting another focus of concentration – our breath, an image, a word, a phrase – as a way of shifting our attention from the false state.

Then, once we are calm, we open our awareness to experience everything. We engage in a very simple practice. We simply experience what is. We reject nothing – no thought, no bodily experience, no emotional feeling. But at the same time we attach to nothing, we dwell on nothing, we identify with nothing. Focusing on any one aspect of our experience would immediately shut out other aspects. So we try to remain in this paradoxical state: simultaneously fully experiencing yet fully dis-identifying. This sounds contradictory, but the meditating brain is capable of functioning holistically and doing two things at once.

For a more advanced practice, we add several guidelines. We try never to judge our experiences. No matter how ugly or distorted a thought, feeling, or impulse might seem to be, we are careful never to condemn ourselves. *This is a radical practice.* Violence, selfishness, greed, sexuality, hatred, joy, bliss, grief, hurt, pain – we sit in the midst of it all and everything is allowed. We are simply present …

However, we vow not to get rid of any uncomfortable experience by discharging it inappropriately (i.e., by acting it out). Nor do we blame our experiences on anyone else. We take full responsibility for our experience. One of the secrets of life is that this meditative practice of wisdom can become the daily minute-by-minute practice of our lives. We can continuously practice being present. And the great gift in doing so is that we eventually become "Presence."

When we do this radical practice of Presence, what do we discover? First, we usually discover what we don't want to discover – that we are suffering, that we are pained, that we are unhappy. Second, we discover that we have a dark side – what Carl Jung called the "shadow." This discovery – that we have a shadow – can begin to fertilize the seed of Love and compassion for ourselves, which becomes our third discovery. Fourth, we discover that we are not alone. Others are suffering also, we see, and have their shadow, too. Simply seeing this simple truth can give birth to yet a fifth discovery: compassion, tenderness, and Love toward others.

After seeing our own pain and limitations and the pain and limitations of others, we begin to feel concern and tenderness for ourselves and others. At this stage, an even deeper realm begins to open for us. We see that we are not just suffering and shadow, and not even just Love. Not only do we comprehend that we possess wisdom, compassion, and Love, we also see that we contain joy, strength, peace, and a beneficent will to power. We are becoming spiritual warriors.

The Path of Power: Transforming Aggression into Warriorship

My brothers, the holy wars that the children of Adam are waging today are not true holy wars. Taking other lives is not true jihad. We will have to answer for that kind of war when we are questioned in the grave. That jihad is fought for the sake of men, for the sake of Earth and wealth, for the sake of one's children, one's wife, and one's possessions. Selfish intentions are intermingled with it. True jihad is to praise God and cut away the inner satanic enemies. When wisdom and clarity come to us, we will understand that the enemies of truth are within our own hearts. Until we reach that Kingdom, we have to wage a holy war within ourselves.

M.R. Bawa Muhaiyaddeen, Sufi Master,
from *The Awakened Warrior*

The spiritual warrior is an ancient human archetype – both female and male – acknowledged by every ancient culture. Examples are: Athena (Greek); Vajrayogini (Buddhist); Durga (Hindu); Inanna (Sumerian); Ishtar (Babylonian); Sekhmet (Egyptian); Valkyrie (Norse); Andraste (Celtic); Oya (Yoruba); White Buffalo Calf Woman (Native American). I purposely have mentioned feminine representations of warriorship because in our modern society power is usually identified as being masculine. Nevertheless, being a warrior in the sense that we are using the term means being a warrior of the *Spirit* and using our power to help, not hurt.

Contacting and developing this power requires an inner journey. Using the practices of wisdom that we have discussed, we must descend into the dark world of the soul – into our shadow self – where the demons of fear, anxiety, aggression, violence, and hatred reside.

For millennia, warriorship has been viewed as a Tantric path. Tantra arose in the Hindu tradition around 500 c.e., and later became embodied in the Tibetan Buddhist (Vajrayana) tradition. Its principal teaching is that spiritual maturity is best developed by using the right kind of consciousness to descend into – and fully experience – the seemingly ugly underbelly of being human. We then are able to transform our base consciousness, rather than trying to transcend it.

This is a frightening journey, but a necessary one for the spiritual warrior. Philosopher and mystic Soren Kierkegaard explains it thus:

This is an adventure that every human being must go through – to learn to be anxious in order that one may not perish. Whoever has learned to be anxious in the right way has learned the ultimate. The more profoundly one is in anxiety, the greater is the person. Anxiety enters the soul and leads us where we want to go.

Sadly, most people fail to recognize the need for this descent into personal darkness (and some who do get stuck there). Most people already consider themselves to be spiritual – trying to make the best possible lives for themselves and their families, wishing to be good people, decent citizens, etc. We may wish to be "good" not "bad," "loving" not "hateful," but as Russian novelist Alexander Solzhenitsyn remarked, "The line between good and evil runs straight down the center of the human heart. And who would wish to throw away half of his heart?" Indeed, the inner journey is perilous. Why, then, is it necessary for us to undertake it?

All deep, intense, emotional, energetic, and spiritual experiences are intertwined in the human soul. Thus, the aspects of the human soul that are primitive – often referred to as the lower self, the animal soul, or the desire soul – must be mastered in order for us to become spiritually mature. The conditions of becoming a modern adult require us to "civilize" ourselves. But the spiritual mastery of which I speak is quite different: Mastery of the higher soul requires us to unbury our demons of aggression and hatred because, unfortunately, our wisdom, power, and Love are buried there, as well.

Frightening and counter-intuitive as it may seem, the Tantric understanding turns out to be correct. At the core of our hatred, we discover the purity of our healthy strength. The spiritual warrior must confront her inner demons before she can grasp the sword of her true power. Ultimately, as the Tibetan Buddhist teacher Chogyam Trungpa Rinpoche reminds us, "The key to warriorship is not being afraid of who you are."

However, this journey must be undertaken with the proper orientation. We must have achieved sufficient maturity to understand and adhere to two principles. First, our intention must be to experience everything within us for the purpose of healing the fractures in our soul, and not for the purpose of living out the primitive passions in our lives. With proper training and guidance, we can learn to experience intense hatred, for example, without acting it out. Then we can discover the pure power at its core. Second, we should undertake this underground journey not to enhance our own selves, but to be in a better position to truly benefit, in a deeper way, our fellow humans, our communities, and the world.

The Path of Love: Transforming Selfishness into Being the Bodhisattva

The seeker should not stop until he finds. When he finds he will become anxious. After he becomes anxious he will be astonished. Then he will enter the Kingdom of Heaven.

Jesus, *Gospel of Thomas*

Having come this far down the spiritual warrior path, the rewards are great. We have touched our truth with the practice of wisdom, and we have touched our warriorship with the practice of power. Now, we are ready for the final challenge: *the practice of Love*. How then do we train to become a bodhisattva – a being who lives and leads selflessly, who refuses ethereal enlightenment to remain on Earth and assist others who wish to attain full spiritual maturity?

Well, first we would do well to recognize that with Love we are not creating something out of nothing. The capacity for Love is hard-wired into the human soul. Modern biologists, in their explorations of sociobiology, have begun to recognize this truth by adding a second evolutionary paradigm to Darwin's competitive "survival of the fittest." While not rejecting Darwin's model in total, new evidence shows that altruism and cooperation play as large a role in human evolution as does competition. This is supported by the observation that once children reach the age of one year, most of them demonstrate unprompted empathy for others in pain, manifested by spontaneous hugging and patting.

As we continue to explore the subject of practicing authentic Love, it is important that we distinguish and attempt to exclude common perceptions of morality. In other words, spiritual warriors are not called to be loving because "it is the right thing to do" or "to be a good person." Such notions are more aligned with what The Oracle Institute calls the Fourth Spiritual Paradigm: the internalized patriarchal code of the last two thousand years. That version of Love, though effective in crafting authoritative cultures and controlling the masses, is no longer a sufficient model for the active Love which we now are being called upon to perform.

Thus, to be a bodhisattva warrior in the Fifth Spiritual Paradigm, we need to embrace a new definition of Love: *awakened Love*. This spiritually mature Love is aligned with objective altruism and the selfless love described by the mystics of every wisdom tradition. Looking more deeply into it, we see that this Love is quite complex.

For example, the Buddhist tradition suggests that true Love for others is difficult to manifest without first experiencing proper Love of self. And if we have the courage to confront and experience our own suffering using the meditative wisdom practice of mindfulness, it can fertilize our capacity for self-compassion. A crucial step to practicing healthy self-compassion is developing the capacity for self-forgiveness. This can be undertaken as a concrete spiritual practice, in which we mentally call to mind the actions and feelings we regret, and then say words to forgive ourselves for being human, for experiencing imperfection.

In the West, we tend to suffer from the primitive, harsh, and unnecessary experience of having a critical inner judge or "super-ego," as it is known in psychoanalysis. This is the immature self-judging part of our minds that is inherited from our parents, culture, and religion. It is the voice that is constantly commenting on our behavior and pronouncing us either "good" or "bad." Modern psychological approaches to healing that are spiritually oriented recognize this structure as unnecessary for a mature human being whose soul already has the inherent capacity to discriminate between positive and negative behaviors without resorting to harmful strategies of self-judgment, self-rejection, and self-loathing. These approaches identify the super-ego's presence and help reject its influence, thereby allowing for self-forgiveness and self-compassion, purifying the soul of self-hatred, and opening the gateway to a fuller experience of Love.

As we progress even further on the bodhisattva path, we may choose to engage in other spiritual practices to cultivate our capacity for what the Buddhists call *metta* – unselfish loving and kindness to all beings. In meditation, we might consciously wish for the well-being of others. A similar meditative practice in Tibetan Buddhism is *tonglen*, in which we imagine breathing in the dark suffering of others and breathing out healing energy and light. These practices and others like them help us develop the consciousness of an awakened heart.

Putting It All Together: Bodhisattva Warriors in the 21st Century

We live in a time of glory and terror. Never has our species had such power to bring peace, justice, and well-being to all peoples. And never has the danger of destruction been so high. Truly, it is "the best of times and the worst of times."

Spiritual teachers, futurists, and astrologers predict that the coming two decades will be a time of momentous transformation, the ultimate direction and character of which is as yet unknown. Furthermore, it has been said that our communities will need guides, shepherds if you will, to show us what the mystics call "The Way" or the "Path of Righteousness." But who will these shepherds be?

> There was an old lady, from the Cree tribe, named Eyes of Fire, who prophesied that one day, because of the white man's greed, the fish would die in the streams, the birds would fall from the air, the waters would be blackened, and the trees would no longer be. Mankind as we know it would all but cease to exist. There would come a time when the Keepers of the legends, stories, culture rituals, myths and ancient tribal customs would be needed to restore us to health. They would be mankind's key to survival. They would be the "Warriors of the Rainbow."
>
> There would come a day of awakening when the peoples of all the tribes would form a new world of justice, peace, freedom and recognition of the Great Spirit. The Warriors of the Rainbow would spread these messages and teach all peoples of the Earth how to live the "Way of the Great Spirit."
>
> The tasks of these Warriors of the Rainbow will be many and great. There will be terrifying mountains of ignorance to conquer, and they shall find prejudice and hatred. They must be dedicated, unwavering in their strength, and strong of heart. They will find willing hearts and minds that will follow them on this road of returning Mother Earth to beauty and plenty – once more.

Lelanie Fuller Stone, Cherokee-American healer

Contemplating all of this, we might get discouraged. Watching the nightly news and reading the newspapers, we easily could become depressed. Just a handful of warriors against such powerful forces ... is it possible?

At times like these, we must call upon a new perspective. In his book *Power vs. Force*, psychiatrist and spiritual teacher David Hawkins reminds us that the scientific field of non-linear dynamics, which includes chaos theory, indicates that disorder in the Universe only seems disorganized due to the limitations of our perception. In fact, the Universe is actually quite well organized. It is organized by powerful and seemingly invisible forces that are known as "attractors." One of the strongest of these attractors is the soul of a very mature human being – like Gandhi, Martin Luther King, or Nelson Mandela – who generate what biologist Rupert Sheldrake has termed a huge energetic "morphogenetic field" that can influence millions of people. And each one of us has the potential to become such an attractor.

I have no parents: I make the heavens and earth my parents.
I have no home: I make awareness my home.
I have no life or death: I make the tides of breathing my life and death.
I have no divine power: I make honesty my divine power.
I have no means: I make understanding my means.
I have no magic secrets: I make character my magic secret.
I have no miracles: I make right action my miracles.
I have no armor: I make benevolence and righteousness my armor.
I have no castle: I make immovable mind my castle.
I have no sword: I make absence of self my sword.

Anonymous Samurai (14th Century),
from *The Awakened Warrior*

Will the prophecies for a sea-change in the coming decades – a wave of spiritual transformation – be fulfilled? This we cannot say. But what we can say is that many of us are on the ocean, a great armada of ships – boats, canoes, supertankers, rowboats, yachts, and ocean liners – all steered by bodhisattva warriors. In the distance, we see the beautiful towers of our communities burning. But in our boats, we bring the wisdom, power, and Love – the warrior heart – to quench the flames.

Will we reach the shore in time? This too, we cannot say. But as we row our boats of Love, the sun beats gloriously down upon our backs, the gulls scream and wheel above us, the sea breeze whips across our bodies, the salty ocean sprays our faces, and we turn to each other, laughing with joy, and say: Oh, my brothers and sisters – isn't this a glorious time?

—————

A glorious time, indeed! I am indebted to Ken for so accurately and lovingly explaining the bodhisattva warrior spirit. For many, this type of energy is hard to understand, since spiritual warriors are rare and stay veiled until needed. But they do exist – and their numbers are growing. We shall see them arise *en masse* when the time is right, when the Great Cusp seems bearable no longer. Then we shall see these heroes emerge, armed not with wrath but with righteousness.

I also am indebted to Ken because he is one of the lightworkers who is holding the vision for the Fifth Spiritual Paradigm. As a spiritual warrior, he is able to do this, even during the dark times. It isn't easy to maintain the vision – it takes more faith than imagination. But I have heard from a reliable source that faith the size of a mustard seed is all that we need.

DECLARATION OF COSMIC COOPERATION

By Thomas Hansen, Ph.D.

Because of the course of events on Earth, it has become necessary for we humans to declare our desire to join with peaceful civilizations throughout the Universe to save Earth and ourselves from our own excessive self-interest. We desire to use our creativity to assure that all living things on Earth are free to enjoy the resources and beauty of Creation now and throughout future generations.

We hold these truths to be sacred and undeniable; that all are created with the right to enjoy the Universe and receive sustenance; all are endowed with certain inalienable rights, among these are Life, Liberty, and the realization of Happiness; that to secure these rights we recognize that the denial of the rights of any living thing affects the rights of all beings in the Universe.

Civilizations are legitimized by their ability to promote these rights for all life now and in the future. They should exist for the purpose of recognizing and serving the unity of life. To the extent that they promote primarily their own identity, they inhibit the recognition and implementation of this unity. Extreme identification with any part of the whole Cosmos, be it a particular region of the Cosmos, a planet, nation, religion, race, institution, or species is detrimental to individual and collective peace throughout the Universe.

We humans have changed life on Earth. We have converted valuable resources into waste products. We have threatened the very existence of life on Earth with our weapons of mass destruction, mass pollution, and mass poverty. We have allowed our strong desire for independence to interfere with our innate and natural qualities of goodness, Love, and sharing. We have been lured into the belief that our individual lives are more important than the lives of others, wherever they reside.

We humans now choose to change our approach to all of life to be that of service-to-others, rather than service-to-self. We vow to eliminate our over-identification with our particular individual lives and with our planet. We vow to create a new sense of cooperation that values the life force within everything. We pledge our lives to co-creating a Universe where all beings can more easily remember their natural freedom, unity, and goodness. We pledge that we, the people of Earth, shall strive to become peaceful and productive members of the Universal community of beings.

My dear friend and mentor Tom drafted the *Declaration of Cosmic Cooperation* to help us awaken to the fact that we are at the dawn of a new era, one in which we shall learn to live in cooperation and interdependence with all other life forms – whatever and wherever they may be. Similarly, my work has led me to adopt a new theory on the evolution of humanity. It is based on my continuing research into the history of this planet and my evolving concept of the Godhead. For example, I have studied some of the Atlantean stories, Lemurian Legends, recollections of Edgar Cayce, and new discoveries made by unbiased archeologists, anthropologists, and geologists. In a nutshell, some scientists now are concluding that certain archeological sites, fossil records, and environmental residue point to an alternative history for planet Earth – one that involves a radically different theory of evolution.

Just to be clear, I am not questioning whether mankind evolved from other life forms, I am wondering whether we evolved from other *more advanced* life forms. In other words, there is a growing body of research which points to an alien visitation on Earth and, quite possibly, the genetic manipulation of *Homo erectus* into *Homo sapiens* by technologically superior beings. Crazy, you say? Perhaps. But as a truth seeker, I will follow a thread until it no longer interests me or until it appears to be a dead end. On this fascinating topic, I am still pursuing data.

Tom's *Declaration* asks us to join the "Universal community of beings" – regardless of whether our Universe turns out to be comprised of just the indigenous life on Earth, or whether it includes life on other planets as well. If all life is sacred, and it is, then we must begin to accept that our rapidly advancing technology may uncover proof of alien life forms. We now know that Mars once had water – which means life. And I have it on good authority from people connected inside the government that Roswell was a genuine ET visitation.

The bottom line is that we most likely are not the only creatures made by God. Indeed, we may discover that our immediate creator is *not* God! The oldest written records on the planet, clay tablets inscribed by the Sumerians, give strong indication that their "gods and goddesses" were from another planet. I for one am open to such possibilities, since I am on a quest for truth and for God. I know this sort of openness makes some people uncomfortable, but it seems to me that we should all be open to what may be revealed next. Such is my passion for truth … a passion as strong as our next Love topic.

L'AMOUR

*For I often come with parched throat, longing to be refreshed by the
nectar of your delightful mouth and to drink thirstily the riches
scattered in your heart. What need is there for more words?
With God as my witness, I declare that there is no one in this world
breathing life-giving air whom I desire to Love more than you.*

Heloise (1101–1162), *Early Letter to Abelard*

*How fertile with delight is your breast; how you shine with pure beauty;
body so full of moisture – that indescribable scent of yours.*

Abelard (1079–1142), *Early Letter to Heloise*

During the 12th Century, European nobility was consumed with
l'amour – the French word for romantic Love. Previous generations
and earlier civilizations had little time for matters of the heart, and
relations between men and women were treated as business arrangements or
contractual alliances, entered into by families in order to enhance their
social prestige or wealth. Moreover, while males in the upper classes often
enjoyed the company of mistresses outside of marriage, rarely had women
allowed their thoughts to turn to lustful urgings. Thus, a new day had
dawned for humanity, one in which both sexes were free to explore the
ecstasy and agony of sensual Love.

Today, while most societies provide both men and women with an appropriate environment in which to explore the sacred union of the sexes, there
still are cultures which forbid females from choosing their mates. Some religions so greatly fear the Sacred Feminine that they continue to teach the
dual lies of sexual inequality and female inferiority. At the dawn of the New
Millennium, may we finally learn to Love both the masculine and feminine
aspects of God as manifested in human form.

L'AMOUR: THE SOUL IN LOVE

By Brenda Schaeffer, D.Min.

This beast that rends me in the sight of all,
This Love, this longing, this oblivious thing,
That has me under as the last leaves fall,
Will glut, will sicken, will be gone by spring.
The wound will heal, the fever will abate,
The knotted hurt will slacken in the breast;
I shall forget before the flickers mate
Your look that is today my east and west.
Unscathed, however, from a claw so deep
Though I should Love again I shall not go:
Along my body, waking while I sleep,
Sharp to the kiss, cold to the hand as snow,
The scar of this encounter like a sword
Will lie between me and my troubled lord.

Edna St. Vincent Millay, *Fatal Interview*

The term we use for this mysterious power – romantic Love – has been known to shape wars and history, create national scandals, justify crimes of passion, turn strong men and women into weaklings, and make fools out of kings. Often, we are embarrassed by our desire. We blush when we talk about it, we feel weakened when in it, ashamed we have fallen, and reluctant to admit to it. Romance defies all words and, when it is present, no words are necessary.

Almost all great Love stories metaphorically speak to the passion that brings us together and, when mishandled, brings suffering and even death. The blazing passion which longs for union is *Eros*, referred to by many as physical lust. Eros was the Greek god of Love, the capricious child of Aphrodite and Hermes. According to legend, Eros was so compelling that no mortal could resist his charms. Hints of this new kind of Love – a Love that implied intense romantic attraction – reappeared at the beginning of the 12th Century, when courtly or passionate Love for another, rather than being considered sinful, began to be viewed as emanating from the soul. Eros, the longing for physical union, united with *agape*, the universal, spiritual Love of our neighbor, and became *amour*, a virtuous romantic Love.

This profound feeling preceded any physical union; often the yearning was more important than the actual physical coupling. Touch and sexuality were rendered sacred though sometimes never took place. One lover would leave, so he or she could hold the longing and desire for the beloved. This experience was in complete contrast to the euphoria of sexuality, where pleasure of the body and ego was the only goal. In courtly Love the senses were honored and respected as a meaningful and virtuous part of the Love relationship.

Remnants of *amour* remain in modern-day romantic Love, although there seems to be much less concern today about Love bringing out our virtues. As we shall explore, the contrary has actually happened. Over time the virtues of romantic Love have turned into the pains of dependent Love and Love addiction – using the other to "get" or "consume" Love.

Multidimensional Lovers

Love relationships are where we go to look for Love's promise ... yet often hit pain and sorrow. One reason is that in relationships, we experience our self in all ways, whether we like those ways or not. We have a biology we keep bumping into. We have cultural Love maps that guide us to dead ends. We have a psychological story filled with mental and emotional constructs that have skewed our definitions about Love. We have a soul that knows passion and a spirit that desires to elevate Love to an ideal. In sum, we bring a reactive *body*, an adaptive *ego*, a curious *soul*, and a lofty *spirit* to every relationship.

When these four facets – body, ego, soul, and spirit – are fused and run through the heart, our romantic relationships thrive. They bring us to a deep fulfilling intimacy of which *amour* is but the first phase. But if these four facets are out of synch, if certain needs go unmet or old wounds go unhealed, our Love relationships can become dependent or addictive.

Another reason why Love is so complicated is that something significant happened in the 17th Century during the scientific revolution. A dualistic reality was created: matter versus spirit. Not only was a two-tiered reality created, but sacred and secular experiences were separated or seen as opposites. What resulted was a sterility that created an aching in the heart and a longing of the soul. Contemporary outlets for this cosmic dualism have come in the form of addiction, compulsive behavior, anxiety, depression, empty relationships, and meaningless lives. We know the rest: psychology was called in to fix things.

The only problem is that both soul and spirit have been taken out of psychology and, therefore, most Love relationship counseling. But some therapists are rediscovering that a psychology focused on body and ego alone misses the point. Our soul and spirit also suffer in our life and Love relation-

ships. A sacred psychology allows for the expression of the pure uncontami-
nated self in total – body, ego, soul, and spirit. Here are some definitions to
brief you on what I mean when I refer to the four dimensions we bring to Love
relationships.

I view *body* as our biological makeup, our chemistry, our senses, and our
physical vehicle of transportation in the world of matter. The body has its own
unique intelligence which allows it to interrelate with all life forms. It is home
to our heart and our brain, and it contains hundreds of mood chemicals plus
our genetic makeup and learned programs. It allows for profound physical
and sexual intimacy that is the touchstone and foundation of Love on Earth.
It is essential to the full expression of Love, and it has been given the assignment of bringing sensuality, sexuality, physical bonding, and energy to our
Love relationships. The body lives in symbiotic relationships with others.

Biology naturally provides us with three sensations of pleasure – arousal,
fantasy, and satiation – that are controlled by hundreds of chemicals which
allow us to experience life to its maximum. Contentment, creative passion,
sexual excitation, romantic Love – each has a neurological analogue. Though
these chemicals are meant to enhance our Love life, we can become dependent on, even addicted to, these "feel good" chemicals, as we attempt to self
medicate our problems with them.

Ego is that part of a person that lives in the material world and is defined
by it. Ego lives in a physical body, has an emotional life, and grows through
specific stages of development. It feels, it thinks, it nourishes and protects
those we Love and our self. We need it. Ego is emotionally intuitive and
desires emotional intimacy and connection. So, it is essential to our human
Love stories.

Compared to soul or spirit, ego is dense and its energy moves slowly. It
confuses "doing" with "being" and can easily get lost in stereotypical roles. It
takes on beliefs about Love from others and often lives through others
because of unmet emotional needs. It medicates with Love. When therapists
or spiritual teachers work with the ego, their goal is to help it become a well
integrated piece of the personality structure, so the soul can be expressed (versus suppressed) when the person is in Love.

Skipping ahead for a moment, *spirit* refers to that part of us that aligns
with the Divine. It is the internal force that pulls us toward growth. Often
referred to as our "higher self," spirit is more interested in "becoming" than
"living." It is that immutable self that we often experience as detached from

life, in an observer position, which views everyday life as mundane, secular, and a temporary distraction. Whether we recognize it or not, spirit is always working in us. It seeks enlightenment, spiritual highs, and is definitely heaven-bound. Seeking union with a God force, spirit is always striving upward.

Spirit also is idealistic, creative, inspiring, and wise. It is evolutionary in nature and seeks not only to learn lessons but to transform and transcend them. It has strong inner intent and absolute faith, and it expresses the higher emotions of compassion, gratitude, and humility. In our human life, spirit is sometimes considered lofty, ascetic, detached, over-serious, even pedantic and intolerant. It can even be self-deceptive and limit soulful living. It is on a path to the beloved and determined to be with the beloved for eternity. Bent on Divine perfection and truth, it exalts both the ego and the soul. Spirit brings heart into matter and helps guide the soul.

But the *soul* is neither ego nor spirit, but the glue between them. The soul, as I use the term, is bound to matter in order to bring depth to raw experiences. Earthy and primal, it speaks through symbols and stories as it explores life's mysteries. It loves ritual, ceremony, art, and music. It is the creative muse, the generator of intuitive knowing. It jumps into life and devours all of it – the dark and murky as well as the light. It is our personal medicine, our unique essence, and our authentic self. Thus, the soul lives now and now only. It does not care about a path and can be easily distracted – think of it as the spirit's inner child. It is perhaps the most alive part of who we are, since it brings passion and depth to our life. It eats the food of experience, digests it, and magically changes it to something new.

Often, the soul is referred to as the mediator or middle principle. Some say the body is in the soul; others say we have a soul-infused body. It is the soul that can bridge the two realities, heaven and earth, the sacred and the secular. It materializes spirit and spiritualizes matter. The soul is unique and yet is at one with other souls. It is greater than ego or personality and is said to use the personality to express itself. The soul needs the ego to recognize it and give it its rightful place. And it is the soul's job to bring spirit into the world.

We must never think of these four as separate entities or at odds with each other. Intrinsically intertwined and often overlapping, body, ego, soul, and spirit make for an exalted human and for exalted Love.

To make their relationship a little clearer, let's consider how each faculty relates to a chocolate bar: The body sees the chocolate bar and craves it; the ego gets attached to the craving and acts to get its need met by starting to eat the bar; the soul relishes the delicious taste of the chocolate and the delightful mess it's making on its chin; and the spirit simply observes the process without judgment and lets the craving rise, persist, then pass away. If the others persist in the craving to a point of overdose, the spirit will intervene as a wise and loving parent to say, "Stop – you are hurting yourself." And so it is in romantic Love: The body sees the romantic object and chemicals are released; the ego gets attached to the ecstasy experience and takes action to meet the desired object; the soul immerses itself in the whole experience with wonderment; and the spirit observes the process, embracing the beloved with wise oversight.

The Soul in Love: The Bigger Story

> *If the soul could have known God without the world, the world would never have been created.*

Meister Eckhart

For the remainder of this essay, I shall focus on the soul's story of Love, which is like the story of Cupid and Psyche – a Love story filled with passion, loss, trials, ultimate fulfillment, and the inspiration for many a fairytale read to us as children. Cupid was the adored son of Venus, the Roman goddess of Love. Venus was jealous of a beautiful mortal named Psyche and asked Cupid to use one of his arrows to make Psyche fall in Love with a vile creature. But Cupid accidentally pierced himself with an arrow of Love and fell in Love with Psyche. The remainder of the story is about the struggle that ensues as the characters wake up to who they are in Love. Neither Cupid nor Psyche goes from infantile dependency to happiness overnight. Indeed, Psyche at one point loses Cupid through an act of betrayal and is put through a series of harsh tests by Venus to prove she is worthy of her son's Love. Cupid struggles with his passion for Psyche and his loyalty to his mother. In the end, like all fairytales, there is the happy ending – the reunion of Cupid and Psyche, spirit and soul.

The soul, like a capricious child, is not afraid to take the journey of the heart. It views Love as a sacred mystery, a magical, mythical journey full of hills and valleys, joy and sorrow, impossible tasks, and experiences deemed good and evil by our egos – including romantic Love. To the soul there is no right or wrong, nor condemnation. What's important is that the lessons be fully learned, regardless of the chaos and consequences.

The "Bigger Story" is that we, too, can trust that out of chaos a new life is possible. The Bigger Story is our own mythological tale. It calls on our lover's heart, which is not afraid to live in suspense, awe, mystery, and romantic longing. The Bigger Story does not concern itself about the past or the future; it is always happening now. A soulfully lived romantic Love relationship is organic, alive, and tenacious. It dares us to show our innocence and our vulnerability, and to let another human in.

The soul, in the Bigger Story, allows things to naturally unfold and does not get caught up in the "what ifs" and "if onlys" that the ego agonizes over. Love is not a project or an end in itself – it is a mystery. Living from the Bigger Story, we are not focused on success or failure or rigid ideas of how to live and Love. Instead, we let our Love relationships reveal themselves to us. We do not analyze but reflect. We ponder questions that have a very different flavor than the ego's questions. The soul's questions are more poignant and have more universal themes:

> *What am I to learn from this betrayal?*
> *What is this ache in my heart?*
> *Where is this melancholy coming from?*
> *I wonder why this person came into my life now.*
> *How is this present situation challenging my soul?*
> *What is it stirring up in me?*

This is a big shift from the ego's narcissistic questions:

> *Why am I such a failure?*
> *Why can't she Love me?*
> *How could I be so stupid?*

When you make this great leap in your mode of questioning, you are living the Bigger Story. As Thomas Moore said so clearly in *Soul Mates*, "Relationships have a way of rubbing our noses in the slime of life – an experience we would rather forego, but one that offers an important exposure to our depths."

Everything in our Love relationships is material for soul making: the good, the bad, and the ugly. Unlike the ego, soul does not shame us. It recognizes that relationships bring out the worst in us as well as our virtues. Unlike the ego, soul does not seek perfection, but rather depth of experience. "Right" is not a set path or a yellow brick road that leads to one destination; right is allowing a Love relationship to be a live process that unfolds before our very eyes, with a soul and a spirit of its own. The magic is in the taking of the detritus and decay we experience in our Love relationships and turning it into gold – Love alchemy.

The bottom line is that the soul gets to the heart of the matter. It does not need solutions or resolutions. Living the Bigger Story does not mean looking to the other to make us feel good, repair a damaged childhood, become our sugar daddy or surrogate mother. We are beyond the learned definitions and the cultural formulas for Love. We have dug deep into the Love story itself. And as we dig, we understand everyone's part in the story, including our own. We can stay with the chaos until it presents its truth and not get caught up in the reactive nature of a feeling. Instead of analyzing things to death, we remain curious.

Though this seems paradoxical, the more detached we become from our human drama and obsessive fantasy life the richer our drama and fantasy life become. We recognize that we are in ego drama when we tell our stories three times and nothing changes. We are stuck. If we are living from the Bigger Story, the story of the soul, the experience nourishes us into a new form.

Ideally then, romantic Love energizes the soul so that the soul becomes playful, buoyant, and even gets to use its cunning. It knows that every moment can be lived erotically. Passionate living is not reduced to sex. Unlike compulsive sex or romance addiction where the hunger is never satisfied, loving from the Bigger Story creates no hunger because we are fully present, heart and soul. We feel the power of Love as we taste it, touch it, smell it, and sense it all. Love and life seduce us.

It is in Love relationships that we are challenged or nurtured. The greatness of Love stories is not in how perfect they can be, but how we evolve in them. Living the soul's Bigger Story means seeing Love relationships as initiations into Love's mystery. In that regard, nothing about our Love life is to be considered a waste, not even the most awful experiences.

Soul Wounds

What lies behind us and what lies before us are tiny matters compared to what lies within us.

Ralph Waldo Emerson

We all have wounds of the heart. Some are so deep that they go beyond the trauma in our bodies and our psychological memory, and are etched deep in the soul. They hurt incredibly. Some of these wounds are sexual – a betrayal by a lover. But the soul, living in basic trust, understands that everything is as it should be, even the most excruciating pain. We might not realize until a year down the road that the horrendous betrayal we suffered was exactly what was needed to shock us into reality and catapult us into the next stage of our soul's journey.

The ending of a relationship with someone with whom we have shared deep Love means a total surrender, a death, but also a profound soul initiation. When we approach such events from the Bigger Story, we remain in Love. Accepting this death without blame, shame, or endless explanation creates a sacred alchemical moment. We find ourselves in a passageway to something new.

All endings contain the seed of a new beginning. Inside the soul is a stirring of the new seed that's been planted. We cannot see it, but we feel its presence. Living in basic trust, we patiently allow for quiet gestation time. With hurting heart still open, we affirm the words of Kahlil Gibran, "Sorrow carves the heart to contain more joy."

In the loss, we do not see ourselves as doomed or as failures. Our self-examination is based on a sense of curiosity and is very different from the self-deprecating messages put out by the ego. We ask soul questions: "I wonder what my soul can learn from this?" Rather than defend, deny, or exult in our wounds, we learn to bring them to our next Love relationship and give them a place. After all, they are a part of our Bigger Story.

All Love stories are adventures, and all Love stories burn with a fiery passion that annihilates us and challenges us to a new life. If we are looking for a neat little story, then we should stay away from Love. Love is an electromagnetic force ethereally, a pulsing heart emotionally, and luscious passion as far as the soul is concerned. When these are aligned, we feel movement that catapults us into a new reality. To attempt to control Love is not unlike telling the Sun to stop melting snow. Love does what it does. It moves the Universe and we are along for the ride.

A Story

Linda, having experienced the ending of her romantic Love relationship, stepped into a well of darkness. She encountered her soul's fascination with death. Here is what she wrote in her journal:

> You, darkness, are a gathering place, a place of dreams and nightmares, of knowledge yet to be conceived. You, darkness, have been feared, scorned, avoided, put on trial, blamed and yet remain dauntless. You come each day and with each breath. You believe you have a place of majesty. You are relentless as you challenge the light, knowing that the light does not exist without you. You laugh, you smile, you smirk like a wicked parent to an innocent child.

Death, death, death. How necessary you are. Pain you bring; pain you say is the fertilizer of tomorrow's dreams. Birthing the new, you are within everything. You are but a place, a moment, a transition. Always I must be mindful of your presence as a blessing – as a part of cruel mystery.

I will take you on with the fullness of life. To greet the way of change. To say goodbye to my beloved that touched my body, shared my soul, let me touch life passionately, imperfectly and deeply. I can face death now. The pain of a broken heart dampened my normal senses, and I got a glimpse of other realms. It pulled me out of my ego and told me I could feel tortured, change form, die and be reborn.

It's no accident that Linda's feelings about the death of her relationship read like poetry and myth. For the soul, myths provide the images necessary to develop our wholeness. In them we value and explore all parts of the self. Though we walk through a life that is defined by externals, soul work helps us discover that the real journey is an inward one, filled with symbols, archetypes, dreams, and reflections.

Religious historian Mircea Eliade, exploring ancient initiation rites, discovered three necessary events that usher the initiate into a new mode of being: First, there is *torture* at the hands of the spirits; second, there is a *death* ritual; and third, there is a *resurrection* into a new form. In the process, the innocence and ignorance of the questor are transformed, and he or she is fired into a new and greater human being.

Similarly, pain and suffering in Love relationships dampen the ego long enough to give us glimpses of other realms where we can die and be reborn. Unless the initial elements die, the Bigger Story cannot proceed and the soul remains entrapped in its limited human form, lost in its conditional and habitual existence. Yet, something is not created out of nothing. As in alchemy, the process must start with a base metal, improving and transforming it. In the soul-alchemy of Love, our human story is the base metal that is eventually turned into gold. It is the black carbon that ultimately yields to the diamond – the allegorical symbol of Love and marriage.

Soulful Loving: A Recipe

The Soul selects her own Society
Then shuts the Door
To her divine Majority
Present no more.

Emily Dickinson

With the heart present, what does soulful loving look like? Actually, a soul mate comes in many shapes, not just one. It can be our cousin, a best friend, a daughter or son, a great aunt, or even good old Mom or Dad. It can be a therapist, a spiritual mentor, a marriage partner, a boss, or a lover. Soul intimacy is rare but is not limited to one person. The person may come into your life for a short time only, but once the connection is sparked, it ignites something in you. You are changed in some way.

The soul luxuriates in attachments and yet yearns to be free. One can never cage the soul of another without causing harm. Our soul may be ready for a mountain climb when our soul mate would rather play indoors for a while longer. Honoring the impulse of individual souls is part of soulful mating. The soul wants to be understood. "See me and hear me," it cries.

If our soul is present in our Love relationships, we will more easily experience our soul in everything we do. Life will feel richer. Our soul is what takes ordinary relating and elevates it to profound intimacy. Assuming that our heart and compassionate wisdom are along for the ride, we have all the ingredients we need to create relationships full of soulful Love. And we can vary these ingredients according to the needs and desires of our intimate partners. Here are some suggestions for romantic soul mates:

- Love with everything you've got
- Touch, taste, and smell
- Expect everything
- Expect nothing
- Write letters, poetry, and songs
- Never shame or blame
- Accept everything in your Love life as fuel for change
- Live in the mystery of your Love relationship
- Take your Love to the edge of experience
- Look in your lover's eyes
- Have deep conversations, even in silence
- Go with your intuition
- Use your imagination
- Look for the lessons in all things
- Wonder instead of worry
- Look for synchronicities
- Give your partner space
- Be passionate about your own solitude
- Never try to change your partner

+ Leave incidental things alone
+ Enjoy your special Love story
+ And know that soulful Love relationships are where egos go to die and be reborn

Meditation for the Soul in Love

May I leave you with a meditation, designed to encourage soulful journeys based on gratitude, self-confidence, curiosity, and Love.

> *I am deeply grateful for my soul and its ability to fire up my life with passion, zest, curiosity, and longing. It allows me a depth of loving that bridges the sacred and secular worlds. It helps my virtues shine. I will guide and protect it and heal its wounds. I will share it with the ones I Love, but I will never give it away.*

⟫◆⟪

The elements of romantic Love are complex. Unfortunately, it is so common for people to focus on just the physicality, the lust of *amour*, that the full meaning of romance is lost. Brenda reminds us of the many facets of romantic Love and the fact that there is nothing sweeter available to us on the Earth plane.

Having lived through a divorce and survived the last fifteen years of "dating," I can readily attest to the elation and heartbreak of romantic Love. Truly, there is nothing else like it. As Brenda explains, one of the most important aspects of romance is how it mirrors and massages our inner being, our spiritual self. Thus, romance is yet another way – perhaps the primary way – in which we explore our world and ourselves.

I hope that the poetry, essays, and stories in this chapter inspire you to take another look at your concept of romantic Love. The topic has filled more books than any other. We at the Institute believe that sacred coupling is the height of our Earth plane experience. Certainly, other forms of Love are spiritual. Indeed, we end this anthology by exploring Love of God. But such "higher" forms of Love are not of *this* world. They are more transient Love connections which temporarily take us to the Ethereal plane. In other words, we can not and we are not meant to stay in those altered states of Love forever. Eventually, we must return to Earth as physical beings and express our Love for other physical beings. Romance affords not only a perfect outlet to demonstrate our Love for another, it also provides a context – a Love bubble – in which to share our experiences in the unseen realm with our best friend on the material realm, our most intimate friend ... our lover.

THE SHYNESS

By Sharon Olds

Then, when we were joined, I became
shyer. I became completed, joyful,
and shyer. I may have shone more, reflected
more, and from deep inside there rose
some glow passing steadily through me, but I was not
playing, now, I felt like someone
small, in a raftered church, or in
a cathedral, the vaulted spaces of the body
like a sacred woods. I was quiet when my throat was not
making those iron, orbital, rusted,
coming noises at the hinge of matter and
whatever is not matter. He takes me into
ending after ending like another world at the
center of this one, and then, if he begins to
end when I am resting I feel awe, I almost feel
fear, sometimes for a moment I feel
I should not move, or make a sound, as
if he is alone, now,
howling in the wilderness,
and yet I know we are in this place
together. I thought, now is the moment
I could become more loving, and my hands moved shyly
over him, secret as heaven,
and my mouth spoke, and in my beloved's
voice, by the bones of my head, the fields
groaned, and then I joined him again,
not shy, not bold, released, entering
the true home, where the trees bend down along the
ground and yet stand, then we lay together
panting, as if saved from some disaster, and for ceaseless
instants, it came to pass what I have
heard about, it came to me
that I did not know I was separate
from this man, I did not know I was lonely.

ANATOMY OF A LOVING RELATIONSHIP

An Interview with Allyson and Alex Grey

Q: How do you create together and separately, cooperatively and non-competitively?

Alex: Together we share a third mind that is more effective and intelligent than either of us individually. Allyson's aesthetic is seen through my eyes, my aesthetic is seen through her eyes, and our understanding and Love emerge as a Being of greater perception – our "Angel" – the one that is more than two and can travel deeper into the visionary world from where our inspiration comes. This angelic fusion of our spirits reflects our devotion to God through our devotion to each other, and it helps us in our artistic and life choices.

I have great respect for Allyson's vision, for her design sensibility and intuition. Our visions are similar and different. I trust her and rely on her. Ideally, I'd ask her opinion on every important decision. Sometimes I sketch a vision, seeing it from a particular angle. Allyson will come over and say, "Oh Alex, it's just got to be in the center – you have to move this thing over there." Her clarity will change an artwork for the better, change a piece that might have been merely interesting into a stronger and more iconic symbol.

Allyson: Alex gives me an incredible amount of power by honoring me as the source of his artwork and inspiration. Alex is clearly the source of my life. I think and work most hours of the day on matters pertaining directly with his artwork. The email I answer, the products we create, the business of creating the Chapel of Sacred Mirrors all have Alex and our work at its heart center. Alex is my heart center. He is the power source and I am the power-feeder – a very potent and consequential position. This duality has been essential for an effectively working "engine." Alex naming me as the source of his work and my making him the source of my work is a damn good machine!

We both need to be valued and involved in each other's work. With my own paintings, Alex's input is of paramount importance to me. Every work of art begins with a consultation. By encouraging my artwork, Alex feeds my creative source. The Source needs a Feeder. The Feeder needs a Source. An engine can't run without fuel and fuel is worthless without an engine or a spark.

Alex: Our relationship is not just some nebulous bliss-mush. We've been through our cathartic dark spaces and healing spaces; purifying our negativities is an ongoing task. Each of us, because of our individual character, has had specific and different pathologies to manifest through our relationship … complementary pathologies.

Here is our theory of how couples work: Each person's main psychological problem comes forward in a close relationship. Each can express his or her shadow and be healed in a context of Love and support *if* the problems are complementary. Non-complementary pathologies accelerate confrontation and negative spiraling.

My shadow specialty is depression, not exactly catatonic despair, but hopeless "what's the use" kind of abysmal moods. My moods can really darken an atmosphere of loving, not extinguish it, but like a black hole suck and deplete it.

Allyson: At my best, I am "captain of the cheerleaders" looking for a positive spin on every dark circumstance. Sometimes I can reason Alex out of his negativity by reflecting a new view. On the other hand, I came to the relationship with twenty-three years' practice in rage, judgment, and criticism. Alex is not an angry person and sets a wonderful example when dealing with upsets through communication and restraint. How can I stay angry with a person who is so loving and conciliatory?

Alex: In an ideal relationship there must be mutual respect and gratitude. We call this the theory of "too good for me." When I met Allyson in art school, she was friendly, positive, and popular. She was very attractive and everyone knew and liked her. I never thought she'd ever be interested in me. After our first date I was so elated that I did not have confidence that it would last. I thought, "Even if this relationship ends I have now learned that Love is possible."

Allyson: The first time I saw Alex, I noticed his deep intensity, his drive and accomplishment, his strangeness and brilliance. I've never met anyone more interesting than Alex. Sometimes we will be in our studio, sitting at our drafting tables quietly working away on our paintings and I'll be deep in thought. I might be contemplating my last conversation with my mother or what we will have for dinner. My thoughts are generally pretty grounded in the mundane. If I call over to Alex's desk and ask, "What are you thinking about?" he will inevitably recount some philosophical reading he just did, something about Hegel, Schopenhauer, or some Sufi mystic. He'll be having a deep and lofty thought that is totally authentic and truly ponderous. This pulls me out of my earthy reality and gives me the opportunity to think about matters that are beyond my own initiation. It is then that I think how lucky I am to be loved by Alex.

Alex: Mutual Love has improved our self-esteem. Our "Love mirror" allows us to experience our worth. Respect and admiration are essential to this "chemistry," and I don't think a relationship can survive without it. The terms "my better half" or "a good catch" jokingly imply this notion of "too good for me." This partner is a better person than I might have expected to attract. Because of this Love, I strive to be a better person.

Allyson: It is seeing the other as the source of your own transformation that makes a relationship ideal, the thought being: Without this relationship I would not be the improved person I have become. Our favorite time is still working with each other nearby; sitting down and making art at adjoining tables, painting while listening to music, or talking are the earmarks of a perfect day. Alex thinks very differently than I do and that challenges me in a positive way.

Alex: Allyson helps me stay grounded. Together we run ideas through the meat grinder of both of our intelligences to create a better product.

Q: Sounds like you are best friends.

Allyson: That's true. Enjoying spending time together and having a life filled with fun and purpose is essential to sustaining a partnership. Being best friends, however, is not enough to make an ideal relationship. A wonderfully fulfilling platonic friendship does not have the chemistry needed for a successful intimate partnership. Sexual attraction is essential in the ideal mate. I was particularly fond of Alex's hands and noticed them right away. I loved his back and especially his slender physique. Satisfying sexuality develops and improves over time through a willingness to communicate about sex, but chemistry can also come from subtle characteristics like the voice or the smile. Sexual excitement lives in the mind, after all. Through open communication, sex can remain fresh and exciting and need never become stale or repetitive.

Alex: Many of us have "fallen" for someone where the sex is great but the relationship is nowhere. Making a relationship work means mutual respect and admiration. Allyson and I loved each other's artwork before we really knew each other. We continue to appreciate each other's capacity for working long hours, and we both are more fond of creating than any other activity. Allyson's art is deep and complex and I have great respect for the way her mind works.

Q: How does your close friendship benefit your worldly life?

Alex: People blessed with a loving relationship naturally bring good energy into the world. Love flows into relationships with other people, communities, and potentially even between governments. After years of working on personal trust with each other, we reach out toward other people "aurically" and we prayerfully project that same unconditional trust, operating at our highest collective level.

Actions that place money and power above caring and kindness encourage cynicism and disable our trust in each other. This leads to a nihilistic sense about what is possible. If you trust good friends – and your spouse should be your best friend – you project trust into the world.

An atmosphere of trust is essential to a Love life. Access to that passionate, peaceful atmosphere becomes your "mustard seed of faith" that can be practiced and extended beyond the body. If you recognize Love as the true "ground of being," then Love is not an aberration, it is the underlying and undying fabric of the Universe. This manifest Universe is an ornamental display projected from the seething, oceanic, boundless light of Love. Energy condenses into weird and wonderful colored light packets – every living and non-living thing we encounter and with whom we create relationships.

Underlying all the time-space-matter limits of the known physical Universe is the vast, boundless mystery of Love. We can glimpse and realize our unity with the body of God through the sacred marriage-field of infinite Love. Allyson's and my true relationship is as interconnected spheres of light that recognize themselves as emanating from one Source. Couples are perturbations in a seamless net of Love that extends out from the unmanifest Source, like expressions and extensions of a trans-temporal field.

Q: How did having a child change your creative life?

Allyson: When Zena was born we began doing many things separately. Before, we rarely went anywhere without each other – grocery shopping, errands. After becoming parents, we had to become more independent and it was really good for us.

Alex: As parents guiding a new life, Zena forced a new aspect of our "life-training" to become whole and independent, developing new aspects of ourselves. Allyson's fitness concerns remind me to exercise, and Zena and Allyson claim to have gotten value from my study of Buddhism and mystic wanderings. Our independent interests became part of a more integrated and deeper life practice that we shared with Zena.

Allyson: Zena and I went along with Alex to some retreats of the Dzogchen community, but we did not make the same commitment to the study of Buddhism that Alex had made. I returned to an interest in dance, movement, and the body that I had left behind, and I began body building and teaching exercise classes at several gyms. Alex and I learned to operate in separate worlds and then come back together and work on our collaborative projects, like the Chapel of Sacred Mirrors.

Out of Love and compassion, we felt compelled to consider our daughter's commitment to a creative life, a firm decision to be a professional actress. She started working at age seven, and between ages eight and nine, I accompanied Zena to two hundred auditions. Alex also gave his support. Zena has contributed to our lives profoundly. Her career has taken us to some of the most interesting places, introduced us to some of the most highly creative and accomplished people, and taught us unreasonable determination.

Alex: Zena inspired us to self-actualize, independently as well as together. Our home has been a symbol of our true center – our heart and our Love – which is unshakeable.

Q: You are very spiritual yourselves. Did you impress this on Zena?

Allyson: How would you parent if you knew your child was a high spiritual being? Imagine how Mary felt being the parent of Jesus. The Dalai Lama is an example of a child raised with the knowledge that he is the incarnation of a Buddha – Avalokitesvara – the bodhisattva of active compassion.

Zena has indeed been our guru throughout her life. We have worked on being better people because of her. Because we believe it is entirely possible that the soul of a very high spiritual teacher has been entrusted into our care, we listen carefully for whatever wisdom she might impart. In return, Zena treats us with great respect.

Alex: The power of Love is primordial. Songs of Love are songs of Source, songs of God. This can't be explained or measured with instruments. Yet the knowledge and experience of Love provide proof of the inner world and validate the fundamental insights of the neo-Platonists or any truly mystical tradition. Beyond the outer surface reality are the causal formative principles.

The Tibetan Buddhists describe the causal realm nicely: emptiness, clarity, and great compassion. Emptiness and clarity alone have a ring of intellectualism, but infinite compassion is recognized as co-extensive with emptiness and clarity. That is the great primordial field that I recognize as the foundation of all loving relationships and all expressions of Love. It is beyond sex, beyond Wilhelm Reich's "orgonic" force, beyond the molecular curl of the DNA.

One of the primary symbols of the Dzogchen Buddhist teachings is the naked embracing peaceful Buddhas: the naked blue Buddha of space, Samantabhadra, in *yab-yum* (sexual union) with Samantabhadri, the white or red goddess form. The dark blue Buddha is the *dharmakaya*, the essence of the enlightened mind, the uncreated realm beyond form, the boundless; and the white/red Shakti energy is the *rupakaya*, the physical body, the world of form, the finite. The material realm is always in a Love embrace with the ethe-real plane – it is the relationship that creates everything. And the image of the *yab-yum* is symbolic of reconciling all the opposites of this world: the genders, the manifest and unmanifest, all things that can't come together any other way but through the miracle of Love.

How would the Universe exist, were it not for the Love rites of the gods and goddesses? The kiss and inter-penetration of a loving king and queen? Love is the cosmic tension and dynamism that plays itself out on every level in our lives. Does not the electron Love the nucleus? See how they are attracted to each other? Taoism abstracts this principle with the yin/yang symbol. *Tantra* represents the union of the cosmic lovers: Shiva and Shakti energies. Temporal form is secretly and erotically impregnated by timeless, formless, primordial reality. This is the true *hieros gamos*, the actual sacred marriage.

Third Force by Alex Grey

The sacred marriage which Allyson and Alex have achieved emanates from the spiritual realm. Those mystics who had partners report that the sacred marriage is the ultimate expression of Love because it takes the couple – the physical manifestation of the masculine and feminine energies of God – into an entirely different state of being, one that is shared with God. Such bliss occurs when the cosmic yin/yang energies are merged. Only then does duality evaporate. Only then do we see – if just for an instant – what God sees.

THE INVITATION

By Oriah

It doesn't interest me what you do for a living.
I want to know what you ache for
and if you dare to dream of meeting your heart's longing.

It doesn't interest me how old you are.
I want to know if you will risk looking like a fool
for Love
for your dream
for the adventure of being alive.

It doesn't interest me what planets are squaring your moon ...
I want to know if you have touched the centre of your own sorrow
if you have been opened by life's betrayals
or have become shriveled and closed
from fear of further pain.

I want to know if you can sit with pain
mine or your own
without moving to hide it
or fade it
or fix it.

I want to know if you can be with joy
mine or your own
if you can dance with wildness
and let the ecstasy fill you to the tips of your fingers and toes
without cautioning us
to be careful
to be realistic
to remember the limitations of being human.

It doesn't interest me if the story you are telling me
is true.
I want to know if you can
disappoint another
to be true to yourself.
If you can bear the accusation of betrayal
and not betray your own soul.
If you can be faithless
and therefore trustworthy.

I want to know if you can see Beauty
even when it is not pretty
every day.
And if you can source your own life
from its presence.

I want to know if you can live with failure
yours and mine
and still stand at the edge of the lake
and shout to the silver of the full moon,
"Yes."

It doesn't interest me
to know where you live or how much money you have.
I want to know if you can get up
after the night of grief and despair
weary and bruised to the bone
and do what needs to be done
to feed the children.

It doesn't interest me who you know
or how you came to be here.
I want to know if you will stand
in the centre of the fire
with me
and not shrink back.

It doesn't interest me where or what or with whom
you have studied.
I want to know what sustains you
from the inside
when all else falls away.

I want to know if you can be alone
with yourself
and if you truly like the company you keep
in the empty moments.

Ah, yes, but there's the rub ... the finding of the soulmate. Our two poets
in this chapter, Sharon and Oriah, know what to look for in a lover. May you
find your best friend, your counterpart, your perfect complement. And may
you also have the wisdom to nurture and protect such a sacred, vibrant relationship once you find it.

HEARTWORK IN HUMAN RELATIONSHIPS

By Dale L. Goldstein, LCSW

In human relationships, true Love is the total acceptance of everything in myself and, therefore, in others. I can only Love in others that which I have come to Love and embrace in myself. Anything that I don't Love in others is something I have not yet come to Love in myself. Anything other than Love and compassion that I feel toward another is my own unresolved, self-alienated stuff. This is why relationships are so wonderful. They are mirrors that show us all the places we have yet to heal (or make whole) in ourselves.

Through decades of working with couples in therapy, workshops, and relationship intensives – what I call Heartwork – I have found a number of tools that are useful in healing relationships. Before I describe them in detail, though, I'd like to say a few things about romantic relationships, generally.

First, relationships are a matter of multiplication, not addition. Two "half people" (i.e., people divided in themselves), make "one-quarter" of a relationship when joined – not a "whole" one. Only two healthy and mature people coming together in true Love can make a whole relationship. Since very few people are whole in themselves, it is rare for romantic relationships to achieve true Love. However, if both people in the relationship Love each other and are willing to do their own work in and through the relationship, they stand a good chance of moving through their internal barriers to sharing Love. In fact, I can guarantee that two loving partners who have the right tool set can have a most intimate, loving relationship.

For this to happen, a few prerequisites exist. First, both people must be willing to take full responsibility for what they have created and are going to create in the relationship. Relationships are not a 50:50 deal; they are a 100:100 affair. Both people are equally and totally responsible for creating the relationship. It must be so.

Just think about it for a minute. When a fight ensues, for example, it takes two people to perpetuate the fight. If one person stops arguing, the argument ends. If the other person tries to continue the argument, it's like he or she is "spitting straight up in the air!" Each party has the power to end an argument at any moment.

If you really think about this, you realize that we are each, in every moment, creating our own reality. Reality is simply what is happening! But each of us makes something out of that reality, according to our beliefs. As Anaïs Nin said, "We don't believe what we see; we see what we believe." Cultural and familial conditioning, wants, desires, aversions, etc., all shape our reality.

There's also an old *Talmudic* saying on point: "We do not see things as they are, we see things as we are." In other words, we project our beliefs onto reality and then think that it is real. Mostly, our reality is just our ideas about who we are, who other people are, and how we view the world. For example, what is real in this moment is a bunch of black lines of different shapes on a white piece of paper. You are, in this moment, visually taking in these shapes and creating a reality in your mind based on black squiggles. Each person reading this paragraph is interpreting it differently – however slightly – from everyone else reading it. We are all creating our own reality every moment of our lives, believing it is the truth.

Acknowledging the relative nature of reality opens the door to a new possibility – the possibility of wanting to know the absolute truth of any given situation, to be more committed to the truth than protecting our own cherished ideas, opinions, and beliefs about what is real. Openness of this magnitude allows a couple to share their understandings and look at issues that arise in their relationship together, from the same side. No longer is it important that someone be right and someone else be wrong, that one wins and the other loses. All that matters is that they arrive at a joint truth that can bridge the gap which is keeping them from sharing their Love. In this way, Love is the force that unites. Two become one in Love.

One last thing – the real secret: Love is stronger than fear! If the partners in the relationship lovingly commit to face their fears and the derivative emotions – anger, betrayal, pettiness, etc. – all these fear-based emotions will transform into Love.

What follows are some of the tools I've used in my work to help couples build deeper, stronger, more intimate relationships.

THE Relationship Commitment

When I work with couples, either individually or in seminars, I first have them connect in the Love they have for each other. After all, Love is always present, but we aren't always present to Love. We open to the presence of Love in and through a connection to our beloved, even when the relationship is under stress. Once established, I suggest that couples be watchful of this connection and that when they feel it is being lost, they should stop whatever they're doing and get reconnected. Fear, in particular, can quickly spiral out of control, so it is wise to pause when needed to reestablish a Love connection during healing work.

Then, I invite them to honor something I call THE Relationship Commitment, which is a pledge: *We commit to being honest and kind in all our communications with each other and to helping each other honor this commitment.*

Honesty means knowing what you are thinking and feeling, as well as sharing every thought and feeling that might create distance if it were withheld – even if that thought or feeling is difficult to share. Withholding thoughts and feelings creates separation in the relationship. By being committed to seeing and sharing our truth, as opposed to protecting our own position, belief, or self-image, we create trust in a relationship. And kindness promotes openness and vulnerability. It also creates a safe space for compassionate speaking and listening – the ability to hear and be heard.

Additionally, THE Relationship Commitment fosters presence by allowing each member of the couple to see what is getting in the way of giving and receiving Love and how to move through these barriers. It also helps each partner take full responsibility for what he or she creates in the relationship. It opens the possibility of working together to resolve conflict in a non-adversarial manner, working from the same side instead of opposing sides. These are essential ingredients in creating an emotionally and spiritually intimate relationship.

THE Relationship Formula

I believe that 95% of all conflicts in relationships are due to both people being unconsciously needy at the same time and colliding at the "needy intersection." If couples accept this simple yet profound formula, they will absolutely transform their relationship. THE Relationship Formula has four simple (but not necessarily easy) steps:

✣ Ask yourself: *What am I feeling right now?*
✣ Ask yourself: *What do I need right now?*
✣ Ask for what you need.
✣ Deal with the consequences.

I often suggest to couples that at the end of each day they look back at any incidents that occurred that day during which they were anything other than loving towards the other, and view the incident through the lens of THE Relationship Formula. This helps them understand what they were feeling and needing and didn't ask for. By replaying the incident as if they had been aware of these things and acted accordingly, they can see how they could have created a more loving relationship at the time and have a much better chance of being aware of their needs in the future.

If a partner holds back, he or she creates a gap that will widen over time until the inevitable separation occurs (whether emotional and/or physical). For this reason, it's especially important not to hold back the things that are difficult to share. I am a huge believer in impeccable honesty. An excellent book that describes this process in detail is *Nonviolent Communication* by Marshall B. Rosenberg.

Time Out

When things get heated – as they do in any living relationship between two people – taking a time out, a temporary cessation to the fighting, is often a good idea. To be effective, the couple agrees beforehand that whenever one of them says or signals that he or she wants a time out, the two will go separate ways with the sole purpose of seeing how and why, if possible, they created the fight. When either party is ready to share what he or she has discovered, that person offers to reconvene the discussion. When both parties are ready, the conversation continues, with each party sharing what he or she has seen and helping the other one understand his or her role in the creation of the conflict. I place one condition on this tool: Whoever calls the time out should come back to discuss the issue within twenty-four hours (or whatever time limit the couple agrees upon as the maximum time tolerable).

Freeze Frame

Freeze Frame is a wonderful tool that allows partners to use the material of their daily life to access the deeper issues that keep them from having what they really, really want. To do this effectively, the couple should set aside a period of time each day (usually in the evening) to review the events of the day and see what happened that created some level of dis-ease in their relationship. Usually, it is best to begin with the issue that prompted the most intense reaction.

In any conflict between two or more people, each person involved is 100% responsible for the creation of the problem. Freeze Frame creates the possibility for a couple to look together – from the same side – at an incident that caused a painful rift in the relationship. It helps both to take full responsibility for creating the problem and ending the blame game. It also lets each person see how and why he or she created the issue to begin with. Both parties need to commit to discovering the truth in themselves, as opposed to taking, holding, and defending a position. Here's how it works:

Partner A relates an incident needing healing to Partner B in as much detail as possible, paying close attention to what he or she was feeling at the moment that person felt hurt by Partner B. Then, Partner A replays the moments immediately before the hurt, this time in very slow motion, paying even closer attention to what he or she was feeling.

When Partner A gets to the precise moment when Partner B dealt the blow, Partner A "freezes the frame." Partner A keeps his or her awareness on this awe-full moment in time and then drops all defenses: he or she stays totally open, "takes the hit" again, so to speak, and feels what it touches in his or her consciousness.

That pain – if Partner A allows it to take him or her where the pain wants to – will eventually take the person back to an even earlier pain (usually much earlier), that needs healing. Partner A will see how he or she co-created the pain in order to open the door to an old wound. Have you ever noticed how we recreate the same pain over and over in our lives until we finally stop running away and turn around to see what it is trying to tell us? This exercise is all about exposing that original pain and healing it once and for all.

Once Partner A recognizes the source of the pain, he or she will possess the awareness to look at Partner B in precisely the same "freeze the frame" moment and see and feel where Partner B was coming from. At this point, both partners come to the underlying truth about the conflict and, by sharing it in this manner, their hearts fill with compassion, understanding, and forgiveness.

Legal Dump

Sometimes when one partner is very upset, he or she may simply need to unload the feelings on the other person to become fully conscious of the content. In such a situation, that partner may ask for permission to do a Legal Dump. If the other person is open to receiving the dump, the first partner may then go ahead and "blow it all out" at his or her partner. It is best for the partner receiving the dump to be sitting in a chair, open and vulnerable as possible. And the dumping partner should be standing and just let it fly, totally uncensored.

Following the dump, a moment of rest is encouraged. And then another tool is employed to hash out what has been dumped, such as Freeze Frame. In this way, the dumper will get help accessing where the anger was really coming from.

Just Listening

Perhaps the greatest, most healing gift we can give another is the gift of unconditional presence. To work through the emotional material that is released during the previous exercises, I recommend a tool called Just Listening. This exercise creates a spiritual and emotional environment wherein one person can unburden his or her soul in the sacred space provided by the other's Love and compassionate listening. It is one of the best tools for opening to and moving through the deep emotional murkiness that often prevents us from having what we really, really want. If used regularly (at least weekly), it will transform romantic relationships.

As with the previous exercises, Just Listening is fundamentally a very simple tool. The goal is to explore as deeply as possible the feelings surrounding whatever issue is rising to the surface. While the technique is very straightforward, it is easy to get lost in thoughts about the issue instead of the feelings. Consequently, partners need to try the exercise a number of times before they master it. These are instructions for Just Listening with a partner:

✤ Create a physical "sacred space" and set aside at least four hours where the two of you can be completely undisturbed.

✤ Partner A lies down in a comfortable position and Partner B sits next to Partner A, without touching or looking at Partner A unless Partner A requests it.

✤ Partner A allows any and all feelings to be expressed that need to come out, regardless of content or intensity. Partner A continues releasing until he or she feels absolutely finished.

✤ During this process, Partner B just listens. Just Listening means more than hearing the words, it means empathy and compassion– feeling the feelings with Partner A. Compassion literally means "to have passion with" another. If Partner A is expressing difficult feelings toward or about Partner B, Partner B listens as if Partner A were talking about someone else. Partner B does not prepare a defense or rebuttal to Partner A's expression of feelings. This exercise is not about being right – it is about getting to the heart of the matter. Partner B provides the safety of a compassionate external witness to allow Partner A to explore uncharted and oftentimes frightening internal territory. The only time Partner B may say anything is to remind Partner A to explore his or her feelings. To accomplish this, Partner B may gently say to Partner A, "That sounds like a thought, not a feeling. What are you feeling?"

✢ When Partner A is done, the partners switch roles. Partner B now has an opportunity to explore and express any and all feelings he or she wants.

✢ When Partner B feels complete, Partner A may have another opportunity to further explore his or her feelings. And when Partner A is done, Partner B may have another turn.

✢ The partners continue going back and forth until each feels satisfied that they have done everything possible to explore their feelings and feel compassion for the other.

Please remember as you approach this Heartwork that it is a process and not an event. These exercises, which open our hearts to the Love that is us and that flows through us, should be done on a regular basis if you want to continue to feel connected to that Love. Some days and some issues are easier than others, so be kind to yourself and your partner on this journey of the heart.

Remember also that we progress a little as we open to Love, and then retreat a bit as we step back from it. Hopefully, you will take two steps forward as you gain confidence in yourself and your partner and only one step back as an old fear surfaces and is dealt with. True Love creates this rhythm – a unique dance that is beautiful exactly as it is.

Only by accepting our whole selves – what we perceive to be "bad" as well as "good"– may we be fully present to Love. Such balance allows us to see ourselves and our lives from a higher perspective, one that sets our fears aside and gives us the chance to heal. I've had the great honor and privilege of witnessing this magnificent unfolding countless times with my clients and students. It is my greatest hope and desire that this essay will help you to transform your romantic relationship as well.

⋙◆⋘

It would be ridiculous to think that even true soulmates never clash. We are human, which means we have a multitude of human needs. Consequently, it is inevitable that couples will collide at the "needy intersection" so aptly described by Dale. The issue, then, is whether we have the intention and the tool set to meet the needs of our beloved.

And in some cases, we better be prepared for even greater challenges if we want to live happily ever after …

LET ME COUNT THE WAYS

By Pat

Of all the Love stories deserving of continued celebration, the romantic odyssey of Elizabeth Barrett and Robert Browning remains alluring and fresh to this day. And why not? It has everything a good romantic Love story should have: an intriguing plot with two beautiful, successful poets, one a shut-away invalid and the other a persistent, passionate suitor; an autocratic, unyielding father; a secret engagement; a kidnapped dog; and finally, a wedding and heart-stopping escape!

Moreover, to add first-person luster to their story, Elizabeth and Robert wrote three- to four-page letters to each other almost every day (often twice a day), for nearly two years, starting with the moment they first established contact and ending with their elopement. Because their personal letters were carefully preserved, we may follow this incredible romance as it unfolded – literally, day by day. Not only are we privy to their moments of anguish and ecstasy, we also vicariously live through and feel every emotional element that flows through the timeless, eternal dance of romantic mating.

Elizabeth Barrett Moulton-Barrett (1806–1861) was born into the well-to-do Barrett family in Durham, England, the eldest of twelve children who were all provided excellent, home-schooled, classical educations by Mr. Barrett, who had made a considerable fortune in Jamaican sugar plantations. Always an eager learner and precocious from an early age, Elizabeth was just eight years old when she began writing poetry. As a young teenager, although in fragile health (some say due to a fall from a horse), Elizabeth easily mastered history, classic literature, Greek, Latin, and Hebrew. At the age of twenty, she was publishing mature poetry.

By the time the family moved to the now famous 50 Wimpole Street address in London in 1837, Elizabeth was an internationally celebrated poet. Unfortunately, her health continued to decline, and by 1840, she became a reclusive, bed-ridden invalid. She spent the next six years writing in her bedroom, seeing only one or two close family friends besides her immediate family. Her most important contact from the outside world was a wealthy lover of the arts, John Kenyon, with whom she consulted about her writings. In 1844, Elizabeth's newly published work, *Poems*, drew Robert Browning into her life ... which was then changed forever.

Robert Browning (1812–1889), who had been born into a literature and music-loving family, also had been classically educated and was fluent in Italian, Greek, Latin, and French. In contrast to Elizabeth, however, he was vigorous, adventurous, and well-traveled. He, too, was a published poet and dramatist, although he had not, by the time of their first contact, reached Elizabeth's level of fame. Upon returning from a trip in 1845, Browning read her latest book of poems and was excited by them. As fate would have it, he also happened to know Mr. Kenyon, Elizabeth's close friend, who urged Browning to write and tell her of his admiration for her work. The rest, as they say, is romantic history.

> *R.B. to E.B.B.*   *January 10, 1845*
>
> *I Love your verses with all my heart, dear Miss Barrett – and this is no off-hand complimentary letter that I shall write ... in this addressing myself to you – your own self, and for the first time, my feeling rises altogether. I do, as I say, Love these books with all my heart – and I Love you too. Do you know I was once not very far from seeing – really seeing you? ...*
>
> *Well, these Poems were to be, and this true thankful joy and pride with which I feel myself,*
>
> *Yours ever faithfully,*
> *Robert Browning*

This first contact thrilled Elizabeth, but it scared her too, especially when Robert immediately proclaimed his Love – not only Love for her poetry, but for her very self! However, his sincere flattery was irresistible, and they immediately embarked upon daily correspondence. Robert pressed for a meeting, but Elizabeth declined, citing her invalid status, and countered by proposing a meeting later in the spring if her health improved.

Their letters clearly indicate that Elizabeth and Robert found in each other literary and intellectual equals. However, the thrust of their correspondence was the furthering of their mutual emotional attachment – which occurred in spite of Elizabeth's growing misgivings. Due to her mixed feelings, Elizabeth managed to delay their first meeting until the middle of May.

> *E.B.B. to R.B.*   *May 16, 1845*
>
> *[A]s to the how and when ... you must choose whether you would like best to come with Mr. Kenyon or to come alone – and if you would come alone, you must tell me on what day .... And my sister will bring*

> *you up-stairs to me; and we will talk; or you will talk; and you will be*
> *indulgent, and like me as well as you can. ...*
> *Remember that the how and the when rest with you ....*
>
> *Always your friend, E.B.B.*

By the time of their first meeting, Elizabeth already matched Robert's ideal of an intellectual equal – he considered her to be one of the greatest living poets. But the physical woman he met that fateful Tuesday in May made an equally powerful impression. She hit him like a thunderbolt. Elizabeth looked much younger than her thirty-nine years, she was very small and delicate, and she had ropes of thick dark curls that fell down her cheeks to frame her large, beautiful, expressive eyes.

Elizabeth, too, was obviously struck by Robert's presence. However, in her case, seeing him and being physically attracted to him only increased her grave misgivings. From the very beginning, Elizabeth struggled with demons which, in her mind, closed the door to romance. She had been an invalid for years and lived in her father's home, a virtual prisoner. Mr. Barrett was extremely domineering and autocratic, forbidding all twelve of his children, sons as well as daughters, from marrying, and he disinherited the three who dared. Escaping this stranglehold would have been difficult enough, but Elizabeth faced an even greater barrier to a Love affair with Robert: Elizabeth viewed herself as too old for romantic passion – like "an out-of-tune worn viol," as she described herself in one of her poems. To make matters worse, Robert was healthy and worldly. He also was six years younger than she – simply too much for her to reconcile.

Elizabeth's ongoing struggle with these issues makes for fascinating reading, both in her letters as well as her poetry. In particular, she wrote a collection of poems, *Sonnets from the Portuguese* ("Portuguese" being Robert's pet name for her). These poems chronicle her deep angst and read like diary entries.

> *If thou must Love me, let it be for nought*
> *Except for Love's sake only. Do not say*
> *"I Love her for her smile – her look – her way*
> *Of speaking gently, for a trick of thought*
> *That falls in well with mine, and certes brought*
> *A sense of pleasant ease on such a day" –*
> *For these things in themselves, Beloved, may*
> *Be changed, or change for thee, and Love, so wrought*
> *May be unwrought so. Neither Love me for*
> *Thine own dear pity's wiping my cheeks dry –*
> *A creature might forget to weep, who bore*

Thy comfort long, and lose their Love thereby!
But Love me for Love's sake, that evermore
Thou may'st Love on, through Love's eternity.

Elizabeth Barrett Browning,
Sonnets from the Portuguese, Poem 16

Elizabeth presented this collection of poems to Robert in 1850, after they moved to Italy. He thought they were extraordinary and immediately had them published for her. They are, perhaps, her most famous work. But, 1850 is jumping ahead in this Love story …

From May 1845 until the next spring, Elizabeth continued to agonize over her perceived obstacles and raised them constantly, advising Robert that the Love affair could never work. Nevertheless, Robert patiently endured her constant attempts to sabotage the relationship. He was steadfast and unshakeable in his Love for her, single-minded in his pursuit of her, and relentless in his attempts to make her feel comfortable and secure enough to accept his Love.

R.B. to E.B.B.   *August 30, 1845*

I Loved you from my soul, and gave you my life, so much of it as you would take, and all that is done, not to be altered now: it was, in the nature of the proceeding, wholly independent of any return on your part … while, as to you, your goodness and understanding will always see to the bottom of involuntary or ignorant faults – help me to correct them …

Yours – God bless you – R.B.

R.B. to E.B.B.   *September 13, 1845*

I never dreamed of winning your Love. … I began to look into my own life … and I know, if one may know anything, that to make that life yours and increase it by union with yours, would render me supremely happy …

I beseech you, dearest – all you shall say will be best – I am yours – Yes, Yours ever. God bless you for all you have been, and are, and will certainly be to me, come what He shall please!

R.B

By January 1846, Robert's persistence finally was rewarded when Elizabeth stopped denying their Love. However, she now began worrying about the danger of other people (i.e., her father) finding out about their Love letters, intercepting them, and destroying them before she could read them. Though still fearful, Elizabeth accepted Robert's proposal of marriage.

E.B.B. to R.B.   *February 24, 1846*

> *At first and when I did not believe that you really loved me, when I thought you deceived yourself, then, it was different. But now ... now ... when I see and believe your attachment for me, do you think that any cause in the world (except what diminished it) could render it less a source of joy to me? ...*

> *BA.* [pet name]

Now secretly engaged, Elizabeth and Robert continued with their romantic meetings aided by Mr. Kenyon and Elizabeth's sisters. By March of 1846, they were even trading jokes about escaping to Italy on a tramp steamer. On the serious side, however, Elizabeth and Robert schemed to keep their engagement a secret, not just for their own sakes, but to protect those who were helping them.

Unfortunately, Elizabeth's precarious health continued to be an issue, and it could not be ignored. As she now was determined to leave, Elizabeth bravely struggled to get stronger. By summer, she not only managed several forays out of her bedroom to the downstairs of the house, she also took several short carriage trips with her faithful maid, Wilson. Matters came to a head when Elizabeth's doctor, looking ahead to the coming winter, strongly recommended that she be taken south for her health. To everyone's astonishment, Mr. Barrett refused to let her go, even if accompanied by one of her brothers. At that point, the lovers' hands were forced. They planned an immediate elopement.

E.B.B. to R.B.   *September 1, 1846*

> *I told you in so many words in July ... if September shall be possible, let it be September. ... and I told you how out of the question it was, for me to leave the house early. I could not, without involving my sisters. Arabel sleeps in my room, on the sofa, and is seldom out of the room before nine in the morning ....*

> *Being too much your own, very own BA.*

As luck would have it, the lovers had no sooner made their plans than Elizabeth's little dog, Flush, was stolen and held for ransom by "the archfiend, Taylor," as Elizabeth called the dog-napper. When her father refused to pay the ransom, Elizabeth was furious. Being sick at the time, Robert was unable to help her, so Elizabeth pulled her strength together and went into the bowels of the London slums to rescue Flush herself! Her bravery was rewarded and the archfiend Taylor returned little Flush for six guineas.

The lovers then quickly planned their elopement for the following Saturday. Early on September 12, 1846, accompanied by her faithful Wilson, Elizabeth managed to successfully leave the house and take a cab to St. Marylebone Church in London, where Robert was waiting. The two were finally – and secretly – married.

> First time he kissed me, he but only kissed
> The fingers of this hand wherewith I write;
> And ever since, it grew more clean and white.
> Slow to world-greetings, quick with its "O, list,"
> When the angels speak. A ring of Amethyst
> I could not wear here, plainer to my sight,
> Than that first kiss. The second passed in height
> The first, and sought the forehead, and half missed,
> Half falling on the hair. O beyond meed!
> That was the chrism of Love, which Love's own crown,
> With sanctifying sweetness, did precede
> The third upon my lips was folded down
> In perfect, purple state; since when, indeed,
> I have been proud and said, "My Love, my own."

Elizabeth Barrett Browning,
Sonnets from the Portuguese, Poem 38

But their difficulties still were not over. For the next six days, they returned to live in their respective homes, both to give Elizabeth time to recuperate from the adventure to the church, and to wait for the ship's departure date. They were so nervous during this period that Robert, who refused to call upon her using her maiden name, chose not to risk visiting her before their escape. Finally, it was departure day.

On September 19, Wilson helped Elizabeth and Flush stealthily tiptoe from her bedroom, down the staircase of the house, and past the dining room where the family was having dinner. It is reported that Elizabeth whispered to the dog, "O Flush, if you make a sound, I am lost." Once safely outside the house, Elizabeth, Flush, and Wilson hopped into a waiting carriage to rendezvous with Robert. The group quickly made their way to the harbor where they boarded a boat for Paris. Their ultimate destination was Florence, Italy, where Elizabeth and Robert embarked upon a new life together.

The resulting uproar was as expected; both families were furious. Robert's family was horrified because they believed he had risked Elizabeth's health – perhaps her very life – by the elopement. And as threatened, Mr. Barrett promptly disinherited Elizabeth and declared that he would never speak to her again. Despite these recriminations, the couple never looked back. They happily settled into their new home called Casa Guidi, and, while her health continued to be precarious, overall, Elizabeth thrived. In fact, her health improved to such an extent that at the age of forty-three, she gave birth on June 29, 1849, to a robust baby boy – Robert Barrett Browning, whom they called "Pen."

The marriage, from all accounts, was a very happy one. Pen was adored by his parents and all who met him. Robert continued to be attentive, watching over Elizabeth's health and bearing the brunt of the outside world for them both. Additionally, the couple developed a unique social life, entertaining world-renowned literary and artistic friends, such as author Harriet Beecher Stowe and American sculptor Hiram Powers.

The Brownings wrote prodigiously and produced some of their most famous works while married. Among these were Elizabeth's *Casa Guidi Windows II* and *Aurora Leigh,* and Robert's *Men and Women,* which he dedicated to his wife. While Elizabeth had already established herself as a great poet, Robert's new works greatly increased his fame. It was also during this period that Elizabeth shyly gave Robert her diary-like collection of poems, *Sonnets from the Portuguese,* which he promptly published for her. This collection contains Elizabeth's ultimate surrender to Love's embrace, as captured in her most famous poem: *How Do I Love Thee? Let Me Count the Ways.*

How do I Love thee? Let me count the ways.
I Love thee to the depth and breadth and height
My soul can reach, when feeling out of sight
For the ends of Being and ideal Grace.
I Love thee to the level of everyday's
Most quiet need, by sun and candlelight.
I Love thee freely, as men strive for Right;
I Love thee purely, as they turn from Praise.
I Love thee with the passion put to use
In my old griefs, and with my childhood's faith.
I Love thee with a Love I seemed to lose
With my lost saints, I Love thee with the breath,
Smiles, tears, of all my life! And, if God choose,
I shall but Love thee better after death.

Elizabeth Barrett Browning,
Sonnets from the Portuguese, Poem 43

The two lovers continued to live what Robert later described as "my real life – before and after nothing at all," until Elizabeth began yet another slow, final decline in the fall of 1860. The curtain to this beautiful Love story closed on June 29, 1861 in their bedroom in Casa Guidi, when at the age of fifty-five, Elizabeth died in Robert's arms.

⋙＞◆＜⋘

The Brownings' story of Love "against all odds" is rare, but not so rare that we can't relate to it – if not personally, then vicariously through our favorite romantic novel, movie, or episodic Love story of a dear friend. Thus, I would venture to guess that every person reading this book has a Love story to tell that would make us laugh, cry, gasp, tingle, and cringe. Such is the very nature of romantic Love.

My own life has been a romantic roller-coaster at times – a mirror of my adventurous life. But now, at age forty-seven, I believe I have found my soul-mate. His name is Steve, and while it will be immensely embarrassing if after the publication of this book he should depart from my life, I am compelled to sing his glory right now, our glory. Indeed, how can I *not* think of the man I Love at the conclusion of this chapter?

I knew Steve when I was fifteen and he was seventeen – exactly thirty years ago. We had two dates during high school, the limited number of which I chalked up to my gangly body, pimply face, and complete inability to speak in his presence. He left my sphere of existence in 1977, when he graduated from our high school. I bumped into him one more time during a college break in Ocean City. I would have been eighteen at the time, he twenty. And then I never saw him again. Over the years, I forgot about him, as I continued on to law school, married my college sweetheart, and started my "adult" life.

Then, two years ago, Steve and I met again, not at a high school reunion, but as a result of what lodge-leader Pete would call Great Mystery. I had just ended a relationship, and I was convinced that I would never Love again. I had finished my first book, *The Truth*, and I was engrossed in the mission of The Oracle Institute. In fact, it was my spiritual work that so bothered my last boyfriend. Consequently, I thought no man would ever understand me, accept my obsessive focus on the Institute, or be able to handle the kooky collection of characters who now felt at liberty to drop by my home at any hour of the day or night to discuss God. I consoled myself with the knowledge that my new friends better understood and supported me, and that my work was more important than another distracting romance.

Yet, despite the richness of the company of my new friends, I was lonely. I dreamed of having someone who would share the excitement of my "new life." So I was curious. Would I ever experience romantic Love again? I put the question to the Universe one day in meditation and, after a few moments of silence, the answer came back: "Steve." I opened my eyes in astonishment and then had a good chuckle. How absurd!

Within a half hour I was at work, having completely forgotten the message about Steve. When I sat down at my computer, the first email that appeared was from Classmates.com, a solicitation to join and an offer to find anyone from my high school as an enticement. Steve popped back into my head. Was this another sign? I wrote one sentence asking the company to locate and send Steve a short message, in which I included my phone number. I hit the send button and, again, let the random reference to Steve drift from my mind ...

Not ten minutes later, the phone rang. It was Steve! And the caller ID was showing a Virginia area code.

"Are you in Virginia?" I wondered out loud.

"Yes," he replied in a deep, soulful voice.

"So you never left the area?" I asked, referring to the fact that we grew up just over the border in Maryland.

"No, I've been in Texas for the last twenty-five years and I just got back in the area."

"Why are you back?" I cautiously queried.

"Well," he started with a strange apprehension in his voice, "I'm going through a divorce and I decided to come home to start a new life."

New life ...

I later learned that he had asked the Universe for the same thing: a new Love to go with his new life. Somehow, the matrix aligned, granting us both a most glorious gift. Of course, I am no longer a mute and Steve has gained a few pounds. No matter. For the past two years he has been by my side, covered my back, and taken me to new heights of ecstasy. Not only that, we are weird in wonderfully complementary ways – just as the Greys prescribed. He understands who I am at my essence and he Loves me for it. On a sub-atomic level (almost), this man gets me! And I get him. Today, tonight, forever, I hope.

I Love you, Steven, and I thank God for you.

CHAPTER

LOVE OF LEARNING

EPISTEME

But it is not lawful to join the gods without having pursued philosophy, without departing absolutely pure. Only the lover of learning may go there. ...
True philosophers abstain from all the lusts of the body and, instead of surrendering themselves, exercise willpower. ...

The lovers of learning find that philosophy ... encourages the soul to gather itself up into itself, all alone, and to put trust in nothing but itself – to trust only such realities as it may discern in their essential nature by its own essential nature.

Plato (427–347 B.C.E.), *Phaedo*

As early as the 4th Century B.C.E., indeed, since the beginning of recorded history, mankind has recognized the essential truth that the rigorous pursuit of knowledge – *episteme* in Greek – is a necessary component of the spiritual journey. Conversely, the greatest barrier to self-actualization is ignorance, in all forms.

Today, the masses have the power to be more than mere pawns for the ruling class, since education is no longer the province of the elite. Consequently, there is no excuse for intellectual laziness, social apathy, or blind faith in ancient man-made religions, broken political institutions, or failed financial systems. Such self-imposed ignorance not only poses a dire threat to the core values of a free society, it prevents us from building the utopia prescribed by God's messengers.

To master the final stages of Love, we must first acquire the ability to discern truth for ourselves. Only then will we be able to reject hypocritical religious and political leaders and accept the grave responsibilities of the 21st Century. Thus, let us use our intellect as an instrument of reason, enhanced by the moral and ethical application of the other Divine gifts so lovingly granted to us by our Creator.

FUN FOR ONE

By Cowboy Bob

As a boy I did play
In a place oh so far away
Run boy run on a summer day
Over the hill to the creek
Where you play

Pull from the willow
A whip you can pop
Eat fresh mulberries
Climb a tree to the top

Good guys and outlaws
You can see them from here
Or face a gunslinger
And stand without fear
The sheriff is the hero
He wears the white hat
Good always wins
And that is that

Ride with the Indians
On your pony bareback
Or sit with their council
And plan your attack
Against the white man
Whose greed you will never
Understand

Wade in the shallows
Catch a tadpole
Go skinny dippin'
In that old swimming hole
Watch the dragon fly
Suspended in flight
Fill a jar with fireflies
To brighten your night

Fly past the white clouds
Into blue sky
Now see the world
With an eagle's eye
There are no boundaries
Here you can find
And there are no limits
To a young child's mind

—◆—

Sadly, most adults have forgotten how children learn about themselves and their world. But Cowboy Bob remembers. It is called play. In this day and age, where we routinize, scrutinize, analyze, and monopolize our children, something precious has been lost. Play.

Today, educators admit that our children are in trouble. They are stressed out and restless. Some blame diet, some blame teachers, some blame bad parenting, but the fact is undeniable that our children are exhibiting more and more psychological and physiological disorders: anorexia, depression, hyperactivity, and autism rates are all rising. And what has been our primary response? Medication.

While playtime is not the total answer, it is pretty clear that the disconnect from nature readily observed in adults has filtered down to our children, who now spend countless hours playing video games and interacting with each other, if at all, through technology, as opposed to face-to-face. Moreover, even when they are outside, children are being micro-managed by parents who dutifully shepherd them from one structured activity to the next. As a result, many children are growing up uninspired, uncreative, and lacking initiative.

When I was a child, there was a hollowed out tree in a park near our home. It had been struck by lightning and I could fit inside with room to spare. Without question, I was odd from the start. I spent hours in that tree, singing, dancing, and pretending all sorts of things. Had an adult been present or if there had been some frenetic schedule to keep, I surely would have grown up self-conscious, inhibited, or even neurotic.

Recently, I went to my old neighborhood to see if the tree was still there. It was! I managed to crawl inside and then spent about an hour meditating inside the tree, *my* tree. Out of the blue, the strangest memory drifted back. I remembered how I used to cross my arms and blink really hard, like in *I Dream of Jeannie*. Funny, I am still trying to do magic ...

TRUE EDUCATION: A LOVE AFFAIR OF THE HEART AND MIND

By Chris Mercogliano

Of course the Love of learning is one of learning's essential components, and it is there that I will begin. The profound role that Love plays in the educational process becomes even more paramount when we extend our focus beyond the scope of the individual student. Learning in the context of others depends on the presence of Love on many levels in order for learning to flow with the ease and the limitlessness that nature intends. It is on this process of "schooling" that I will direct the lion's share of my attention.

That said, we must first recognize that over the course of a lifetime, most of our learning is accomplished primarily on our own. In fact, according to Joseph Chilton Pearce and Michael Mendizza in *Magical Parent, Magical Child,* we acquire only about 5% of our knowledge through formal instruction, and of that 5%, only 3 to 5% remains readily available for any significant length of time. The remaining 95% of all learning occurs independently, through play, exploration, and experimentation. My own life is a testament to this truth. With my formal education amounting to only a single year of college, I went on to a highly satisfying and successful teaching career. I also have found the wherewithal along the way to produce four solo books, each representing a Ph.D.'s worth of research and analysis. Currently I am in the midst of writing my fifth book. I also have contributed to a half-dozen anthologies like this one.

But having spent my entire adult life as a teacher of children, I feel particularly moved to probe the learning that is catalyzed by the relationship between teacher and student. And because so much – but by no means all – of the teaching/learning dynamic tends to locate itself under the aegis of a "school," I will zoom the lens out still further in order to view the critical role Love must play at the macro level we commonly refer to as "education." If there is to be any hope of education becoming the transformative process that I, and no doubt many of you, believe it should be, then Love has to become a far more common denominator than is presently the case.

Born to Learn

Babies greet the world with an instinctive Love of learning. Literally, Webster's definition of Love – "to like or desire actively" – matches recent discoveries in neuroscience that show that the attentional network in the newborn brain is hard-wired to seek out interesting phenomena. In neuroscientific terms, "a novel stimulus triggers nonspecific cortical arousal," arousal referring to the brain's general level of activation. In a sense, Love provides the energy necessary for learning to occur.

Novelty, however, isn't the only ingredient. Arousal will dissipate quickly unless the stimulus is meaningful and exciting and the infant feels some kind of emotional connection to it. As long as there remains a desire to watch, listen to, taste, or touch the stimulus, the brain will remain alert and focused. Then, according to Self-Determination Theory, a model of child development devised by psychologists Edward Deci and Richard Ryan at the University of Rochester, a baby will continue to explore a new situation until he or she has gained a satisfactory level of understanding and mastery. It's not something we teach little ones; it is simply their nature to pursue what fascinates them and to be "persistent in their attempts to make it familiar." This is because mastery or competence is one of the three innate, primary needs that drive the developmental process. The other two are the need for autonomy/self-determination and the need for relatedness, which once again involves Love.

The Love Affair Begins

But we are already getting ahead of ourselves. As Joseph Chilton Pearce describes in glorious detail in *Evolution's End*, all of the developmental processes that support learning are first triggered and nourished by the baby's relationship with the mother. What Pearce calls the "unfolding of intelligence" starts in utero, where the baby is soothed by the rhythmic cadence of the mother's heartbeat and bathed in her emotional experience. Language learning, for example, begins in pregnancy's seventh month. Then, right before the onset of labor, the infant's body releases powerful birth hormones that bring about a neural growth spurt in preparation for the enormous transition ahead. Pearce believes each of us is born with a fully formed intelligence just waiting to be encouraged by the right cues from the environment.

Immediately following birth, the mother will invariably place her infant at her left breast (and will continue to do so for the next several months). There are several critical reasons for this instinctive behavior. Foremost, the familiar sound of the mother's heart continually reinforces the outside-of-the-womb bonding that is crucial to the brain's full neural development, and it also signals the potentially toxic stress hormones that accompanied the birth process to switch off. Then the multi-modal contact between mother and newborn assures the activation of all the senses that weren't yet functional in utero and provides a confirmation of those that were. For instance, the neonate has only one genetically encoded visual circuit: the ability to respond to a human face at a distance of six to twelve inches. This means that upon leaving the womb, the only object a baby can see clearly is mama's face, and the mere act of doing so provides the stimulus for awakening the entire visual apparatus. Then over the following eighteen months, the mutual exchange of loving gazes between mother and infant will serve as the primary stimulus for the maturation of the brain centers responsible for self-awareness and the child's ability to regulate his or her own bodily functions, impulses, and emotions. Breastfeeding instantly activates the sense of taste and provides the hormones critical to the establishment of a resilient immune system. Likewise, the mother's touch and smell jump-start these two remaining senses.

The bottom line is that the deeper and more uninterrupted the bond between mother and infant, the more quickly and easily the baby will be able to fulfill the inborn directive to become a confident and competent learner. And the core ingredient of that bond, of course, is Love.

However, there is one catch to the successful unfolding of intelligence, according to Pearce: "No intelligence or ability will progress unless given the appropriate model." This model imperative means that children develop only those capacities that are modeled for them by the surrounding adult culture. A normal infant born to a deaf-mute mother, for example, cannot develop speech without close and prolonged contact with a speaking person.

When It Takes Two

The model imperative brings us to the teacher's role in learning. It defines from the outset the true parameters of the teaching process by reminding us that it is neither the motivation nor the content that the learner needs the teacher to provide, but rather the embodied example of the skill or information the learner is seeking. Such a notion is embedded in the etymology of the term "educate," which comes from the Latin *educere*, meaning "to lead out." And the English word "lead" means "to guide on a way, especially by going in advance."

So we have the image of teacher as guide, someone who has gone farther than the students and therefore can lead them toward knowledge, rather than trying to make daily deposits into the private information vaults inside their students' skulls – what educator Paolo Freire called the "banking method" of education. Early in his career, Freire was hired by the Brazilian government to launch a literacy campaign among disenfranchised peasants in his local district. He soon found himself at the center of a distressing Catch-22. On the one hand, his aim was to empower his students with tools that would enable them to climb out of poverty – the ability to read and write effectively. But on the other hand, Freire gradually came to realize that the traditional lecture/memorize/test style of teaching was profoundly disempowering. His relationship with his students was based on hierarchy, separation, and passivity: the teacher chooses, the students comply; the teacher is the subject, the students are the objects; the teacher teaches, the students are taught. Finally, Freire concluded:

> *The more students work at storing the deposits entrusted to them, the less they develop the critical consciousness which would result from their intervention in the world as transformers of that world. The more completely they accept the passive role imposed on them, the more they tend simply to adapt to the world as it is and to the fragmented view of reality deposited in them.*

Paolo Freire, *Pedagogy of the Oppressed*

Freire's experience in those remote rural classrooms taught him that true education is interactive and relational. It is a partnership based on what Freire refers to as "mutual humanization," where teacher and student "become jointly responsible for a process in which all grow," and where students, "no longer docile listeners – are now critical co-investigators in dialogue with the teacher." Dialogue, according to Freire, only occurs in a horizontal relationship based on mutual trust wherein students explore their world and "name it." He explains, "The naming of the world, which is an act of creation and re-creation, is not possible if it is not infused with love."

Freire also discovered that his students learned exponentially better when he stopped lecturing, threw out the grammar textbooks, and instead centered classes on the students' own original essays about meaningful aspects of their daily lives, which they then read aloud and critiqued together. This far more personal and interactive approach goes beyond technique and content, which involves mainly the head. It includes exploring feelings and one's reason for being, meaning that true education is equally a Love affair of the heart.

The Heart/Brain

Some of the latest and most exciting work in neuroscience involves newly discovered dimensions of the human heart, which is turning out to be far more than the muscular pump Western thought previously considered it to be. We now know, for instance, that up to 65% of the heart's cells are neurons, and that those neurons are in constant conversation with neural networks throughout the brain. Likewise, when the muscle walls of the heart contract, they produce Atrial Natriuretic Factor, a potent neurohormone that communicates directly with the immune system and also with the brain centers that influence emotion, memory, and cognition. Heart transplant expert and author Paul Pearsall has concluded that the heart generates – through the aforementioned neurotransmitters and hormones, as well as through subtle quantum energies – an electromagnetic field that is 5,000 times stronger than the brain's, extends up to ten feet beyond the body, and exerts at least as much influence over the brain as the other way around. Thus, Pearsall and other researchers in the emerging field of neurocardiology are now referring to the heart as a "heart/brain."

The implications of this paradigm-shifting idea – that the heart maintains an equal, if not dominant, neurobiological connection with the brain – are staggering. Of particular relevance to the subject at hand are the pronounced effects the feedback loops between the heart, our emotional states, and the cognitive centers in the brain surely have on the learning process. To understand these connections it is important to realize that the human organism consists of a set of interacting rhythmic processes: heartbeat, respiration, digestion, sleep, brain waves, and so on. The heart that is the conductor of the orchestra, as it were: its electromagnetic force is so compelling that the other players tend to fall in step with its tempo. With every beat, the heart transmits to the brain and the body complex patterns of neurological, hormonal, and electromagnetic information that, together with the brain and the nervous and hormonal systems, form the backdrop for our emotional selves.

Thus, the heart plays an actual and not just a metaphorical role in our emotional makeup. The prevailing notion that emotions are purely mental expressions produced by the brain alone is no longer valid. When all is well, the heart helps to maintain a proper working relationship between all of the body's oscillatory systems – circulatory, respiratory, nervous, sensorimotor, endocrine, hormonal, and immune. A harmonious rhythm will induce a state of "coherence," a term borrowed from physics to describe when two or more of the body's systems, such as respiration and heartbeat, become entrained and oscillate at the same frequency. Not surprisingly, positive emotional states such as Love, care, and appreciation create coherent electrical patterns in the heart's beat-to-beat signals.

It is important to note here that the number of times per minute a heart beats is relatively inconsequential. Rather, the strength and the amount of variation between beats over a given period of time is what counts. According to Mimi Guarneri, a leading cardiologist and founder of the Scripps Center for Integrative Medicine, our Heart Rate Variability (HRV) "is the most dynamic and reflective indicator of our inner states of stress and emotion." The bottom line is that the heart is very emotionally sensitive.

With regard to learning, research shows that coherent HRV patterns generated by positive emotions entrain brainwaves into alpha patterns that are most conducive to the mental operations which support learning, like memory and attention. Coherent HRV also promotes increased cognitive flexibility and creativity, open-ended thinking, and innovative problem solving, as well as cooperation and sociability.

Conversely, negative emotional states such as fear, anger, frustration, anxiety, and depression – often lumped together in the catchall term "stress" – provoke jagged, incoherent HRV patterns. When these patterns are communicated from the heart to the brain, they have a debilitating effect on the neural underpinnings of thinking and learning. For example, one recent study shows that both intense fear and chronic stress cause actual neuron death in certain of the brain's cognitive centers, as well as a significant reduction in the production and deployment of new neurons to support the brain's ongoing growth. Common sense has always dictated that happy, loved, and relaxed children learn faster and more easily, and now we know why.

The HRV discovery is part of a growing body of research demonstrating how stress undermines children's ability to learn. And while the neural mechanisms involved are highly complex, the underlying reason why emotion has so much influence over the development of a child's brain is really quite simple: The neural networks that frame emotional experience are fully mature at birth, whereas the infant's thinking brain is a virtual sea of undifferentiated and disconnected neurons which take an entire childhood to reach maturity. Neurologically speaking, this means young children are fundamentally emotional beings guided primarily by their hearts, and that the early imprinting of their emotional brains will have a tremendous impact on the rapidly developing neural networks in the thinking brain.

The bad news is that emotional patterns eventually become hard-wired into the young brain's neural pathways, and when those patterns are negative they become the source of all kinds of dysfunctional development that impede learning. The good news is that the repeated experience of positive emotion has the power to repattern the brain. If the heart and brain can establish and sustain a new baseline of positive coherence, the child will gradually release the maladaptive stress responses caused by unhappiness and adopt a healthy coherence.

All of which brings us back to Love. When caring, and connection, and Love are sufficiently present in children's daily lives, the full unfolding of intelligence is all but a foregone conclusion.

A School Must Have a Heart

My thirty-five years of teaching – at an unusual, extremely diverse little school that places kids' emotional and social well-being first and attaches a high value to the relational dimensions of learning – absolutely confirms the conclusions neuroscience is reaching about the forces that enable learning and those that disable it. Indeed, I can testify to the fact that nature has marvelously equipped children to be voracious, lifelong learners. But the design is not foolproof. As we have seen, the growth (or lack thereof) that occurs in the cognitive centers of a child's brain depends heavily on conditions in the emotional brain and in the heart, which in turn are dependent on conditions in the child's world.

The dominant educational approach today remains tragically oblivious to students as emotional and social beings. More than ever, our schools engage children only from the neck up, as though they are disembodied brains whose only purpose is data storage and retrieval. And since schools mirror the surrounding culture, our education system is fraught with anxiety and stress. I don't need to drag you through the particulars; we're all aware of how pressurized schooling has become. It's a trend that can be traced back three and a half decades to the publication *A Nation at Risk*. This federal report unleashed a panic over the education system that, unlike radioactive isotopes, appears to have no half-life.

So, given that modern neuroscience informs us that anxiety and stress literally kill the brain's capacity to learn, and given that our children spend a full quarter of their waking lives inside the four walls of a school, the question becomes: *What would an education system look like if we finally recognized the nexus between learning and Love?*

It is my belief, based on both theory and long-term experience, that in order for a school to be a place where children thrive, it must behave as a living organism. It must have a pulse and a metabolism that provide a steady, self-renewing flow of energy. It must have the ability to breathe in creativity and imagination. In Latin, *inspirare* means "to inspire," which in turn means "to exert an animating, enlivening, or exalting influence on." All these organic functions depend on a healthy school environment, just as every cell in the human body depends on a semi-permeable membrane which allows for constant exchange with the outside world but which filters out toxins. To be alive, a school needs to welcome parents and community leaders to share their skills and knowledge with the kids – and not just a token number of times a year. Additionally, students should be encouraged to pursue learning opportunities in the marketplace, working alongside adults who can provide valuable modeling and mentorship.

In order for a school to sustain its vitality, it must be able to adapt and evolve according to the needs of the changing cast of child and adult participants. The "one-size-fits-all" approach to education has never worked and it never will, because human beings are simply too different from one another and the world is changing at too fast a pace. Greater standardization is not called for; higher levels of improvisation and flexibility are what's needed.

Yes, a school must have a head, because thinking is essential to the learning process and creative thinking is essential to a satisfying life. But at its center must be a heart. I am speaking metaphorically of course, but if a "school-as-organism" approach is to foster the kind of learning that enables children to become the competent, autonomous, and related selves that are their birthrights, then the school must sustain an inner state of coherence. And as neurocardiology now shows, positive emotional states help the heart to coordinate all these tasks. Or, in common everyday parlance, the key to a school's coherence is happiness.

Dr. Nel Noddings worked seventeen years as a school teacher and administrator and raised ten kids before earning her Ph.D. in educational philosophy. She has written numerous books on the subject of healthy school environments and has concluded:

The best homes and schools are happy places. The adults in them
recognize that the highest aim of education – and life – is happiness. …
Happy children growing in their understanding of what happiness is,
will seize their educational opportunities with delight, and they will
contribute to the happiness of others.

Nel Noddings, Ph.D., *Happiness and Education*

Noddings believes that in order for schools to be happy places, teachers must focus on their students' emotional well-being and maintain their classrooms as miniature communities in which everyone is included and respected. Teachers should be free to establish give-and-take relationships with their students and get to know them as people. Only then can a charged and fresh energy exchange take place between teacher and student.

Noddings is suggesting that in a school-as-organism, the heart function is shared. It can't be left to a single leader; all teachers should be sensitively attuned to the school on a heart level. Teachers, students, parents, and grandparents all should have input into the daily life of the school, and students should be empowered to share in decision making at age-appropriate levels, and also in resolving conflicts with each other.

For Noddings, human relationships are the single most important ingredient in happiness. She recommends that teachers spend more than a single year with their students because the ingredients to happiness – friendship, commitment, Love – all spring forth from intimacy, and intimacy takes time to achieve. She also advocates for smaller schools and for teachers specializing less and teaching more than one subject, so that they can have closer contact with fewer students.

Caring, says Noddings, is the next most important ingredient. Schools should enhance caring because kids have a deep-seated need to receive it from all the significant adults in their lives. Teaching is a caring relationship, not a role. Consequently, teachers should be encouraged to be themselves and to hold their students' whole beings in their awareness, not just their academic performance.

To this wisdom I would add a caution from psychiatrist Dr. N. Michael Murphy: teachers can only care for their students to the extent they know how to care for themselves. Only when teachers are able to nourish and replenish themselves can they meet their students' innermost needs. Unfortunately, self-care is rarely, if ever, a part of teacher education. As a result, most of our schools suffer today from a "crisis of caring," laments Nodding.

Educational researchers David Aspy and Flora Roebuck confirmed Noddings' insights over three decades ago with a landmark study involving over five hundred public school teachers who had received special training in emotional awareness and interpersonal communication. Aspy and Roebuck found without exception that student learning is enhanced when teachers provide high levels of the "Big-3": empathy, congruence/authenticity, and unconditional regard.

In one study, Aspy and Roebuck compared two groups of third graders, matched for gender, socioeconomic status, and IQ. The kids who received high levels of the Big-3 had significantly higher attendance. In another study with third graders, the group who received high levels of the Big-3 scored significantly better on a series of academic achievement tests. Then, with two randomly selected groups of first graders, they administered the Stanford-Binet Intelligence Test at the beginning and end of the school year. The group that received high levels of the Big-3 made an average gain of nine points; whereas, the low Big-3 group showed no significant change. This outcome is especially significant because IQ is considered to be a fixed attribute, determined by nature and not nurture.

It is noteworthy that the same results occurred when teachers at a beleaguered inner-city elementary school in Shreveport, Louisiana, attended Aspy and Roebuck's summer training. The school enjoyed its highest attendance rates in its forty-five year history, its reading test score ranking increased nine places within its district, and its students made even larger gains in math performance. Moreover, vandalism and fighting decreased significantly, teacher turnover dropped from 80% to 0%, and teachers from other schools asked to be transferred to the school. Even more impressive, these results held up in subsequent years.

The Proof Is In

Intelligence fully unfolds when schools are structured around genuine relationships rather than task-driven roles and routines. Teachers and students interact meaningfully with one another when the basis of the relationship is personhood, as opposed to mental performance and left-brain academic skills. Only when schools nurture learning in all its myriad forms, can they be places where each and every student shares in a generous harvest of wholeness and maturity.

Undoubtedly, there are some rare students who are born with gifts and privileges that guarantee success regardless of the school's influence. But for the vast majority of students, decades of studies clearly show that the school's environment is the key to success. Today, leading experts and researchers in the fields of psychology, neuroscience, philosophy, and education all point to the same conclusion: Children flourish in schools which provide caring environments and which fully embrace an emotional and social core of Love.

—◆—

In rereading Chris' essay, I was struck by the research that shows children benefit from having the same teacher for more than one year because friendship, commitment, and Love may develop, thereby enhancing learning. From firsthand experience, I can attest to the truth of this, since I had the same teacher for three years when I was little and the bond I formed with him still supports me to this day.

Mr. Telford taught 4th, 5th, and 6th grade at my small public elementary school, which was often used as an incubator for experimental educational programs. He moved up with my class each year, so we got to know each other very well. He knew my sister, my parents, and all about my extracurricular activities, many of which he sponsored. For example, he taught guitar after school, and he organized the school play every year – a musical that included everyone. He was an amazing man, a teacher who loved his work and his students.

About ten years ago, my mom saw a notice in the paper that Mr. Telford was retiring. Although I had not seen him in more than thirty years, I snuck into his retirement party with a gift. It was my first screenplay (it never sold), but I had dedicated it to Mr. Telford and I wanted him to know that. I wanted him to know that I was still grateful for the Love he gave me when I was a little girl.

Clearly, I was lucky. He could have been a horrible teacher and then I would have been saddled with him for three formative years. But when educators understand the important role they play and that care and compassion are the very foundation of a safe and productive learning environment, children flourish. Thereafter, the desire to learn is imprinted and education becomes a life-long process.

THE FELLOWSHIP OF BOOKS

By Edgar Guest
(1881–1959)

I care not who the man may be,
   Nor how his tasks may fret him,
Nor where he fares, nor how his cares
   And troubles may beset him,
If books have won the Love of him,
   Whatever fortune hands him,
He'll always own, when he's alone,
   A friend who understands him.

Though other friends may come and go,
   And some may stoop to treason,
His books remain, through loss or gain,
   And season after season
The faithful friends for every mood,
   His joy and sorrow sharing,
For old time's sake, they'll lighter make
   The burdens he is bearing.

Oh, he has counsel at his side,
   And wisdom for his duty,
And laughter gay for hours of play,
   And tenderness and beauty,
And fellowship divinely rare,
   True friends who never doubt him,
Unchanging Love, and God above,
   Who keeps good books about him.

LOVING WISDOM

By Margaret Starbird

The first man never finished comprehending Wisdom,
nor will the last succeed in fathoming Her.
For deeper than the sea are Her thoughts;
Her counsels, than the great abyss.

Sirach, Chapter 24:26-27

In ancient times, information was imparted by word of mouth long before it was committed to writing. Sages and shamans cultivated a connection with their inner wisdom, mining the treasures of their unconscious to share with the community. Before there was a Love of learning – books to study and people who could read them – there was a passionate Love for Sophia, the Holy Wisdom, the Beloved. She was encountered in the deep silence of dream, meditation, and trance, as well as in appreciation and contemplation of the beauty and order manifested in physical creation.

The Hebrew Bible contains profound passages extolling Holy Wisdom, the "first-born" of the Divine: "Before all ages, in the beginning, he created me, and throughout all ages I shall not cease to be." (*Sirach* 24:9). "From of old I was poured forth, when there was no earth. When there were no depths I was poured forth, when there were no fountains or springs of water. Before the mountains were settled, before the hills, I was brought forth." (*Proverbs* 8:22-24).

We are told in the sacred texts of Judaism that from his youth, King Solomon sought Wisdom as his Bride and was enamored of her beauty. (*Wisdom* 8:2). She is the "spotless mirror of the power of God, the image of his goodness." (*Wisdom* 7:26). "Resplendent and unfading is Wisdom, and she is readily perceived by those who Love her and found by those who seek her." (*Wisdom* 6:12). Wisdom was Solomon's mentor and teacher, who instructed him in the workings of the Universe, the paths of the stars and the cycles of the seasons, the natures of animals, and the uses of plants and roots. For in her he found "a spirit intelligent, holy, unique, manifold, subtle, agile, clear, unstained, certain, loving the good, keen, unhampered, beneficent, kindly, firm, secure, tranquil, all-powerful, all-seeing, and pervading all spirits ... she penetrates and pervades all things ... she is an aura of the might of God and a pure effusion of the glory of the Almighty." (*Wisdom* 7:21-25).

In reading of Wisdom's amazing attributes, one is reminded of Hildegard von Bingen and the books of natural history she wrote based on revelations received during her meditations.

The Hebrew Bible tells us that Wisdom has built a house with seven pillars, an image that became the foundation for Western education in the seven liberal arts. But Wisdom is not just the result of book learning and memorization of multitudes of facts. Wisdom is the spirit of revelation emanating from the Divine. She was the Sophia, passionately sought by the learned men of old.

The Greek derivation of the word "philosopher" – literally, the "lover of Sophia" – springs from her name. Her sacred number is seven, "whole unto itself," because alone of the first ten numbers of the Greek *tetractys*, it can neither generate nor be generated by any other number. And She is likened to a mist that covers the Earth or a fountain or spring of pure, refreshing water. The Greek *gematria* for the phrase "Fountain of Sophia" is 1080, the same as for the phrase "Holy Spirit." It is a feminine/lunar value, reflecting the radius of the Moon in the ancient canon of sacred numbers. In the *Song of Songs,* one of the metaphors for the Bride is a "fountain sealed."

Like other concepts articulated by human beings attempting to describe and understand reality, Sophia evolved over many centuries. Sophia was clearly feminine. She was God's delight day by day, ever playing before him, and eventually finding her dwelling place in the Holy City Jerusalem and her people. (*Sirach* 24). She set a banquet for her guests and sent her maidens out into the streets to invite them. (*Wisdom* 9). Her instruction was sweeter than honey in the honeycomb and her gifts manifold: "I bud forth delights like the vine and my blossoms become fruit, fair and rich." (*Sirach* 24:17). "By me, kings rule and lawgivers establish justice." (*Proverbs* 8:15). Wisdom-Sophia sings her own praise: "I am the mother of fair Love, and of fear, and of knowledge, and of holy hope. In me is all grace of the way and of the truth; in me is all hope of life and of virtue." (*Sirach* 24:24-25, *Douay-Rheims* translation). Her ways are pleasant and peaceful, and no possession can compare to her. For She is worth more than coral or precious gems; She is more valuable than silver or gold. *Who is She?* She is, beyond doubt, the feminine face of the Divine, the Holy Spirit personified as benefactress and mediatrix. One has only to ask for her, to seek her companionship, for "how much more will your heavenly Father give the Holy Spirit to those who ask him?" (*Luke* 11:13).

In contemplating these passages from the depths of our Judeo-Christian traditions, we encounter a profound appreciation for the esteem in which Jewish scholars and mystics held Sophia. She was a manifestation or effusion of the Divine expressed in creation. Like Cinderella, one of her many daughters in Western literature, Sophia is dressed in many gowns and rainbow colors, just as the cycles of the seasons array the Earth in many colors. She is styled as the manifestation of the glory of God – the first "aura" of the Divine power and the refulgence of eternal light. Obviously, all of these attributes are mere words attempting to describe the indescribable and ineffable Holy Sophia – Beloved of God. She bears many similarities with the Shekinah, the feminine Bride of God vested in the people of Israel, whose bridal chamber was the Temple in Jerusalem.

We can tell from the sacred literature of the Jews that Sophia was honored and sought as the greatest of all gifts of God to his people. And very often, She is sought through dream and divination. She speaks through the prophets and those who interpret dreams and visions, as in the story found in *Genesis*, the oft-told tale of Joseph who receives this gift and is able to interpret Pharaoh's dream of the seven fat and seven emaciated cows. In Jewish lore, the essence of Wisdom is clean and righteous living, avoiding pride and excesses, behaving with propriety and good judgment, and obeying the cosmic laws of God and nature that dictate order and balance in all things. This gift is not found in books or in memorized creeds, but rather comes through obedience to the *Torah* and to revelations of the elders. But Wisdom is apparently also directly accessible through *gnosis* or personal experience of the Divine – the experience of the visionary or psychic dreamer and of a person on the street. In modern pop terms: WWJD (i.e., "What would Jesus do?").

Many ancient peoples honored the experience of the shaman and the wisdom mined through access to unconscious realms by this mediator between the worlds of the seen and the unseen. In temples of the Greek god Apollo, people rested in a secluded alcove and incubated the Sophia by deliberately entering into deep meditation and trance, often staying in this altered state of consciousness for days or even weeks. A priest, trained in his art, approached the "seeker," periodically interrupting his meditation to give him water, preventing death by dehydration. On his return to normal consciousness, the dreamer often shared the wisdom he had received through trance or vision during his period of seclusion.

In his book *In the Dark Places of Wisdom,* Peter Kingsley discusses this practice of incubation among the ancestors of Western civilization, sometimes in caves and grottos, often in temples. These "lovers of Sophia" cultivated a deep interior life and *gnosis* connected with the rich contents of their unconscious. They honored the "body wisdom" mined in this altered state – through intuition and vision.

We remember stories of Greek heroes visiting one or another of the Oracles. The most famous was the Oracle at Delphi in the Temple of Apollo, where the prophetess imparted cryptic messages and warnings about the future. Ancient societies took such utterances very seriously, as direct communication with the Divine. As a culture, they honored their connection with the realm of the unseen, accessing it through meditative arts, staying connected with the Source and the rhythms of the natural world.

I am reminded now of the radical disconnect with these values in the 21st Century, so visible during the 2005 Tsunami that hit the coastlines of Southeast Asia. While the animals sensed danger and all ran for higher ground, thousands of tourists – curious about the phenomenon of the suddenly dry beaches – ran out to look at the mammoth wave. Our heads are apparently so far removed from our bodies that we cannot perceive dangerous vibrations which are obvious to elephants and monkeys.

What happened? How did the Western mind become so separated from its innate and native intelligence, its deepest intuitive knowing, instincts gained through experience and connection with the natural world?

In some part, Plato (427–348 B.C.E.) and his immediate circle of followers bear responsibility for the great divorce of Western civilization from its body wisdom. In the 4th Century B.C.E., Plato and his philosopher friends apparently took a ninety degree turn to the right and headed off in search of masculine modes of logic and rational thought, promoting scientific inquiry and discovery and gradually giving up time-honored practices of incubating the Sophia through dream and trance. They became the "lovers of Logos" and in effect, they abandoned the Sophia. At the same time, and possibly as a corollary of this shift, the Sacred Feminine was systematically devalued in Greek culture, relegated to "second class" status by Logos-oriented thinkers. Aristotle (384–322 B.C.E.), the acknowledged "father of science," stated his considered opinion: "A female is female by virtue of certain lack of qualities – a natural defectiveness." His mentor, Plato, had held that females were degenerated males: "It is only males who are created directly by the gods and are given souls."

These and other blatantly unscientific misogynist views were rampant among Greek philosophers, who no longer were servants and devotees of Sophia – the personification of feminine consciousness. Aristotle taught his students that women were infertile males, deficient because of their inability to create semen: "[H]er only contribution to the embryo is its matter, and a 'field' in which it can grow." Only the male is a complete human being, according to Aristotle, noted for his scientific method: "The relationship between the male and the female is by nature such that the male is higher, the female lower, that the male rules and the female is ruled."

At the time when Aristotle was making these pronouncements, his student Alexander, now called "the Great," was preparing to conquer the entire known world, from the Mediterranean basin all the way to India – a feat he accomplished in 330 B.C.E. For the next three hundred years, Greek hegemony was established throughout the region, subsequently subsumed into the Roman Empire in the 1st Century B.C.E. Since the Roman nobility had Greek tutors, the culture is rightly dubbed "Greco-Roman." It later was inherited by the fathers of the Christian Church whose misogynist pronouncements are legion. "Among all savage beasts, none is more harmful than woman," was the stated opinion of St. John Chrysostom (d. 407 C.E.), the 4th Century Bishop of Constantinople. Another Church father, Irenaeus (d. 202 C.E.) insisted that, "Both nature and the law place the woman in a subordinate condition to the man." St. Augustine of Hippo (d. 430 C.E.) stated without hesitation, "It is the natural order among people that women serve their husbands. ... This is the natural Justice, that the weaker brain serve the stronger." And of course, many of the Church fathers denigrated women based on the story of Adam and Eve. "Do you not realize that each of you women is an Eve? You are the gate of Hell ... you are the first deserter of Divine Law," according to Tertullian (d. 220 C.E.).

Bound by the shackles of gross misogyny and spurious science, it has taken women nearly two thousand years to excavate themselves from the 2nd Century Greco-Roman worldview and to reclaim their voices in Western society. We assert ourselves now, ready to reclaim our heritage of partnership, bequeathed to us in the Gospels but later stolen by those who could not yet accept the idea that God might have a feminine face. It is the saddest story ever told – the story of the Great Divorce, perpetrated (most ironically) by a religious institution that proclaims its abhorrence of divorce. In the words of Jesus, "What God has joined together, let no man separate." (*Matthew* 19:6).

For more than twenty years, my life's work has focused on reclaiming the voice of the Bride, an embodiment of the Holy Sophia at the heart of the Christian gospels. We recognize the woman who sat with Jesus, drinking in his teachings, unable to tear her eyes from him. She is the model for the contemplative soul and for the Bride of the Church. She is Mary of Bethany, better known as Mary Magdalene, the sister of Martha and Lazarus. This is the same Mary who so passionately anointed the feet of Jesus as he was reclining at a banquet in her home and then wiped his feet with her hair. Later, she went to his tomb to anoint him again, but instead met him resurrected in the garden.

This is a re-enactment of ancient rites indigenous to the Near East, where the Bride of the sacrificed god-king goes to the tomb to mourn the death of her Beloved and is reunited with him. Every pagan convert to Christianity would have recognized Mary Magdalene cast in the role of the bereaved Bride at the tomb, embracing her resurrected Lord. Since Neolithic times, these rites of the "sacred marriage" were celebrated at the Spring Equinox. They honored the eternal return of the Life Force, personified as masculine and feminine deities and incarnated in the archetypal Bride and Bridegroom. It is the image of the Divine as Beloved Complements, as in the Hebrew liturgical poem *The Song of Solomon,* also called *The Song of Songs.*

Over the years I have become more and more convinced that Jesus deliberately embraced the Sacred Feminine principle in an attempt to restore her honor, so long devalued under Greco-Roman influence in the Israel of his day. We can see in the Christian gospels that Jesus openly accepted and encouraged women followers. His parables included stories about women and the routines of their daily lives, and he often healed women during his ministry. It has been noted by scholars that Jesus' treatment of women was radically different from the standards of his cultural milieu, where women were considered to be property of their fathers and, later, their husbands, and where women had virtually no voice or influence. Consistently we are reminded in the gospels that women are devoted followers of Jesus, supporters and friends of his ministry. In a period when women's testimony was in most cases not allowed in court, Jesus chose a woman, Mary Magdalene, to carry the first report of his resurrection, making her the messenger to the others – the "Apostle to the Apostles."

There is little doubt that Jesus and Mary Magdalene modeled a sacred partnership for their community and that she was recognized as "First Lady." In the gospel narratives, she is mentioned first on all but one of the eight lists of women who walked with Jesus. The gospels do not say whether or not Jesus was married, but chances are that Mary was his wife. Judaism at that time did not even have a word for "bachelor." Moreover, marriage to 1st Century Jews was a cultural imperative, based on the *Book of Genesis:* "It is not good for the man to be alone. I will make a partner for him." Based on this passage from *Genesis*, Jesus further explains:

> *Have you not read that from the beginning the Creator "made them male and female" and ... for this reason a man shall leave his father and mother and be joined to his wife, and the two shall become one flesh?*

Gospel of Matthew, Chapter 19:4

Saint Paul's epistles are the earliest testimony about the practices of the first generation of Christians. In his *First Letter to the Corinthians*, Paul says that the brothers of Jesus, Cephas (a/k/a Peter), and the other apostles are all traveling with their "sister-wives." He is talking about missionary couples traveling in pairs, carrying the "Good News" of the Resurrection throughout the Roman Empire. Paul was unmarried, and when he suggests that the Jewish mandate for marriage can be waived in light of the coming "kingdom of God," he cites himself, rather than Jesus, as the model for celibacy (1st *Corinthians* 7:7-8).

The Gnostic Christians of a later period had an interesting myth of the "Fallen Sophia," whom they equated with Mary Magdalene. They wrote that Sophia was a "prodigal daughter" who left her father's celestial house and descended to Earth to partake of the pleasures of the flesh. After a period of dissipation and dissolution, Sophia became so disgusted with her immoral lifestyle that She cried out in desperation for salvation, and her "Brother Bridegroom, the Logos" was sent down to reunite with her and lead her back to the celestial bridal chamber.

Based on this Gnostic Christian tale, it is clear that Mary Magdalene was styled as the dissolute, desperate Sophia, and that Jesus was the Logos/Bridegroom dispatched to save her from her sins. It is this view of Mary Magdalene that later took hold and became the established tradition in orthodox Christianity. She was then easily conflated with the "penitent sinner" described in the *Gospel of Luke,* who anointed Jesus at a banquet and cried over his feet, drying them with her hair. Luke stated of the Mary called Magdalene that she was cured of possession by demons, another slur on her memory which gave further impetus to the myth of her sinful past. Mary is clearly the incarnation of Sophia, called "sister" and "Bride" in various passages of the Hebrew *Bible*. She represents feminine consciousness and all females who are saved and restored by their hero-Lord, who purifies her, enlightens her, and embraces her in the Christian myth of salvation.

But, as in many human constructions, there is a flaw in the story of the Fallen Sophia. Sophia did not voluntarily leave her father's house and become corrupted "in the flesh." Sophia – the personification of the Sacred Feminine half of God and of feminine ways of thinking and being – was deliberately abandoned and desecrated by Plato and his friends who, in a master stroke of deception and duplicity, continued to call themselves "philosophers," long after they had ceased to be lovers of Sophia.

In short, Sophia did not fall from grace; She was kicked out of heaven ... and along with her went generations of her daughters. Sophia did not fall into disrepute; She was deliberately set aside ... her gifts devalued, her promises ignored. Jesus came to reclaim her, embracing her in the person of Mary "the Magdal-eder" – the representative of her land and people, Daughter of Zion, Bride of God. (*Micah* 4:8).

A similar legend is found in the prologue of Chretien de Troyes' 12th Century poem *Le Conte del Graal*. It tells of a Celtic realm where the inner and outer worlds are intertwined. The realm has nine sacred wells, each attended by a beautiful and virtuous maiden who offers travelers refreshing waters from a golden cup. But the evil ruler of the domain, King Armangons (a/k/a "man of stones" or, better yet, "testosterone-driven monarch"), lusts after one of the maidens and rapes her, takes her prisoner, and steals her golden cup. Continuing this horrific act of violence and desecration, he similarly defiles the other maidens of the sacred wells, and the peace and tranquility of the realm are utterly destroyed. Wasteland ensued. And the impoverished land is ever the mark of the loss of "Eros-relatedness" which, according to Carl Jung, becomes embodied in the feminine principle of Sophia. Thus, when not properly partnered, the Sacred Masculine embraces materialism, violence, and hedonism – so very obvious in the excesses of the Roman Empire and its Caesars. In the words of historian Tacitus, "Rome ravages and burns the lands and calls it 'peace.'"

My work reclaiming Mary Magdalene as Bride of the Christ is not about the ordinary coupling of a woman and a man. It is about reuniting Sophia and Logos, often called the primary emanations of the unseen Source, gender specific personifications of right and left-brain modalities, and incarnations of feminine/lunar with masculine/solar principles – the Divine Complements. In losing the voice of the Bride – the incarnation of Sophia or the feminine face of God – we also lost the color red, our passion for life. We lost our connection with flesh and blood, with our own body's innate wisdom, and with the rest of the created cosmos. Sadly, we lost the "way of the heart," the Eros-relatedness of all that lives, and our direct experience or *gnosis* of the Divine.

In reclaiming Mary Magdalene as Bride and Beloved, we restore the ancient balance inherent in Sophia and Logos, the archetypal Bride and Bridegroom at the heart of early Christian teachings. Ultimately, their union presents us an image of the Sacred Marriage between the Human and the Divine, the marriage of flesh and soul that occurs in each of us, for if the truth be told, we are each an earthen vessel, filled with consciousness – the Spirit incarnate. Seen this way, the marriage of the Beloveds is an image of the enlightened or integrated self, an image of wholeness and Divine potential of the perfected human being.

> *In the beginning was not only the Logos, but also the Sophia. Together they were in the beginning with God and without Them was made nothing that has been made. In Them was life, and the life was the Light of the human race.*
>
> *Gospel of John,* Chapter 1:1-4 (reinterpreted)

Jesus came to restore and embrace Sophia, so long denigrated under Greco-Roman hegemony over Israel. I believe that his sacred partnership with Mary was at the very heart of the early Christian community, the principle cornerstone later rejected by the architects of the institutional Church. It is time for Christians and all people of faith to reclaim this Sophian heritage, to become once again lovers of Holy Wisdom, and to celebrate the sacred union of the masculine and feminine Divine.

Mary Hath Chosen by Stephan Adam
Kilmore Church, Dervaig, Scotland

Once again, we encounter Sophia, mistress of the Second Spiritual Paradigm. She is the personification of the feminine half of God and represents Wisdom. Margaret's research provides a telling *his*-tory of how we "lost" Sophia. In truth, the male dominated cultures that sprang up during the Third and Fourth Spiritual Paradigms purposely subjugated her in a vain attempt to claim the Godhead for themselves.

Truth, however, is not so easily undermined. Truth has a funny way of surviving and resurfacing. Not surprisingly, the ideal of Truth, when personified, also takes the feminine gender. Consider this section of Thomas Jefferson's *An Act for the Establishment of Religious Freedom*, upon which The Oracle Institute patterned its formal mission statement.

> *Truth is great and will prevail, if left to herself; that she is the proper and sufficient antagonist to error, and has nothing to fear from the conflict, unless by human interposition disarmed of her natural weapons, free argument and debate; errors ceasing to be dangerous when it is permitted freely to contradict them.*

Interestingly, the ideal of Justice also is depicted in the feminine – sitting blindfolded with the scales of justice in her hand.

Using biology to underscore the point, we now know that the left hemisphere of the brain is responsible for analytical thinking (i.e., masculine energy), and the right hemisphere of the brain is the seat of imagination and abstract thinking (i.e., feminine energy). Consequently, the mystics *rightfully* ascribed the ideals of Wisdom, Truth, and Justice to the feminine half of the Godhead (no pun intended).

To correct the injustice done to Sophia during the patriarchal paradigms, we would not wish to overcompensate with feminine energy. Rather, the Fifth Spiritual Paradigm will be an era of "whole brain" thinking and feeling. When such temporal balance is achieved, the results are spectacular! Our most revered scientists, statesmen, and even warriors are whole brain thinkers.

We therefore honor the resurrection of Sophia as the personification of Wisdom, Truth, and Justice. These feminine aspects of God have been veiled during the patriarchal paradigms. We need these faculties now – we will need all our masculine and feminine faculties – if we wish to one day understand and fully express our Divine nature.

TRUTH IS GOD

By Mahatma Gandhi
(1869–1948)

Truth ever more has been the Love
Of holy saints and God above,
And he whose lips are truthful here
Wins after death the highest sphere.
As from a serpent's deadly tooth,
We shrink from him who scorns the truth.

The Ramayana (circa 400 B.C.E.)

In my early youth, I was taught to repeat what in Hindu scriptures are known as the one thousand names of God. But these thousand names of God were by no means exhaustive. We believe, and I think it is the truth, that God has as many names as there are creatures. Therefore, we also say that God is nameless, and since God has many forms, we consider God formless, and since God speaks through many tongues, we consider God to be speechless, and so on. ...

I would say for those who say "God is Love," God is Love. But deep down in me I say though God may be Love, God is Truth above all. If it is possible for the human tongue to give the fullest description of God, I have come to the conclusion that God is Truth. But two years ago, I went a step further and said Truth is God. You will see the fine distinction between the two statements: "God is Truth" and "Truth is God." I came to that conclusion after a continuous and relentless search after Truth which began fifty years ago.

I found that the nearest approach to Truth is through Love. But I found also that Love has many meanings, in the English language at least, and human Love in the sense of passion could become a degrading thing. I found too that Love in the sense of *ahimsa* [non-violence] has only a limited number of votaries in the world. But I never found a double meaning in connection with Truth and not even atheists have denied the necessity or power of Truth. ...

For these and many other reasons, I have come to the conclusion that the definition "Truth is God" gives me the greatest satisfaction. And when you want to find Truth as God, the only inevitable means is Love, that is, nonviolence, and since I believe that ultimately the means and ends are convertible terms, I should not hesitate to say that God is Love.

✣

The word *satya* [truth] is derived from *sat*, which means "being." Nothing is or exists in reality except Truth. That is why *sat* or *satya* is the right name for God. In fact it is more correct to say that Truth is God than to say that God is Truth. ...

Devotion to this Truth is the sole justification for our existence. All our activities should be centered in Truth. Truth should be the very breath of our life. When once this stage in the pilgrim's progress is reached, all other rules of correct living will come without effort, and obedience to them will be instinctive. But without Truth it is impossible to observe any principles or rules in life.

Generally speaking, observance of the law of Truth is understood merely to mean that we must speak the Truth. But we in the Ashram should understand the word *satya* or truth in a much wider sense. There should be Truth in thought, Truth in speech, and Truth in action. To the man who has realized this Truth in its fullness, nothing else remains to be known, because, as we have seen above, all knowledge is necessarily included in it. ...

Therefore the pursuit of Truth is true *bhakti* [devotion]. Such *bhakti* is "a bargain in which one risks one's very life." It is the path that leads to God. There is no place in it for cowardice, no place for defeat. It is the talisman by which death itself becomes the portal to life eternal.

✣

I claim no perfection for myself. But I do claim to be a passionate seeker after Truth, which is but another name for God. In the course of that search, the discovery of nonviolence came to me. Its spread is my life mission. I have no interest in living except for the prosecution of that mission.

━━━▷◆◁━━━

As a dedicated truth seeker, I appreciate the above passages at a deep level. In fact, I am tempted to accept the definition that truth is God, and I came close to doing so in my first book, *The Truth*. But I have come to a different space during the three years it has taken to produce this anthology. My readings on Love and the selections in this book have changed me. Thus to me, God is Truth, Love, and Light, which explains, I suppose, why I feel compelled to write one more book entitled *The Light*.

To hold truth supreme is to sublimate other primordial forces, like Love. Taken to an extreme, the pursuit of knowledge can lead to unintended consequences, such as the dystopia of the Great Cusp, explained in our next essay.

SLEEPWALKING THROUGH THE APOCALYPSE

By William Van Dusen Wishard

For some time now, we appear to have come to the "end of the world" as we have known it. Nukes in North Korea. Jihad vs. McWorld. A potential India-Pakistan nuclear shoot-out. The events of 9/11 and "the war on terror." The merger of human and artificial intelligence which scientists say will create the "post-human" epoch. Increasingly, the next three decades loom as the most decisive thirty-year period in history. Within this context, I want to offer some thoughts on the larger implications of such rapid change.

I will start by offering the view of one of the world's most experienced observers of global events. In 1957, Peter Drucker wrote, "No one born after the turn of the 20th Century has ever known anything but a world uprooting its foundations, overturning its values and toppling its idols." If Drucker's right, and I personally think he is, despite all the political, social, and technical advances of the past century, the underlying story of the 20th Century was about a world where the historic social arrangements, spiritual underpinnings, and psychological moorings that had anchored nations for centuries, have been in a transition of epochal proportions. The tectonic plates of life as we've known it are shifting.

To illustrate Drucker's comments, I briefly offer six trends that suggest how the entire context of human existence is changing. Then I'll focus more in depth on what I see as the underlying dynamic of our particular moment in history.

First, science is in the process of redefining our understanding of terms first given to us at the dawn of human consciousness, such as "nature," "human," and "life." Increasingly, scientists are subordinating humans to technology. The faster computers go, the faster our whole tempo of life goes just to keep up. In essence, we may be abdicating our own psychological center of being and handing it over to the computer. Within the next three decades, we'll have reached the point where the question will be: *What are humans for in a world of completely independent, self-replicating technological capability?*

Second, for the first time in history, the Caucasian race is no longer reproducing itself. No European country is reproducing its population; nor are Caucasians in North America reproducing themselves. The implications of this are so far-reaching that it's difficult even to speculate what they might be.

Third, future ages may view man's seeing the Earth from the Moon as the defining event of all subsequent history. Joseph Campbell clearly considered it the most significant psychological event of the past several thousand years. Seeing Earth from the Moon vastly accelerated the collapse of all the boundaries that provide identity for nation, race, religion, class, and gender. Thus everyone, to some degree or other, faces a crisis of identity. This also profoundly affects the underpinnings of all religions, as every religion includes some cosmological concept of how the Universe was first created. But space exploration has given us new and different information and perspective.

Fourth, for the first time in history, what constitutes a family is being redefined. This has acute implications for government, education, social cohesion, and what we broadly term "civil society."

Fifth, the ability to create change, as well as the attitude that change is desirable, is now a global possession. Throughout history, in all civilizations, continuity rather than abrupt change has been the normal state of affairs. No society on the planet knows how to live with constant, radical change. Thus, for the first time in history, every nation is, concurrently with all other nations, in a state of profound crisis as we try to adjust to an ever-accelerating pace of change. Hence, there is no global center of stability and order such as Britain provided in the 19th Century and which America supplied in the second half of the 20th Century.

Sixth, our whole symbolic language has been devalued. For example, "heaven" used to carry a sacred meaning. It was the dwelling place of the gods, a place people hoped to go when they died, our link with eternity. Now we speak simply of "space," an endless void. Similarly, we used to speak of "Mother Earth," which gives the Earth a creative, nurturing implication. Now we speak only of "matter," an abstract, lifeless substance. In this way, our symbolic language has been diminished. The function of symbolic language is to infuse into our conscious life some of the transcendent meaning that emanates from the unconscious realm, from the depths of our inner being. That connection has been weakened, so there's far less transcendent vitality brought into our conscious life.

These trends – and many others – will be shaping the global context for the rest of our lives. And these trends portend, as I suggest, that we've come to the end of the world, as we've known it.

Let's focus now on what I believe is the underlying dynamic of our time. For perspective, I want to offer the insights of three well-known Americans.

Adlai Stevenson had the unfortunate luck of twice being the Democratic presidential candidate chosen to oppose Dwight Eisenhower. In 1954, Stevenson asked in a speech at Columbia University, "Are America's problems but surface symptoms of something even deeper, of a moral and human crisis in the Western world which might even be compared to the 4th, 5th, and 6th Century crisis where the Roman Empire was transformed into feudalism and primitive Christianity?" Stevenson continued his query, "Are Americans passing through one of the great crises of history when man must make another mighty choice?"

In 1961, Dr. Edward Edinger, considered by many to be the dean of Jungian analysts until his death in 1998, began a talk in New York on symbols and the meaning of life with these words:

> Modern man is passing through a major psychological reorientation equivalent in magnitude to the emergence of Christianity from the ruins of the Roman Empire. Accompanying the decline of traditional religion, there is increasing evidence of a general psychic disorientation. We have lost our bearings. Our relation to life has become ambiguous. The great symbol system which is organized Christianity seems no longer able to command the full commitment of men or to fulfill their ultimate needs. The result is a pervasive feeling of meaninglessness and alienation from life.

Five years later, Joseph Campbell, possibly the world's foremost authority on the symbolic and psychological meaning of myths, noted that every one of the world's "great spiritual traditions is in profound disorder. What has been taught as their basic truths seem no longer to hold." The world, he concluded, "is passing through perhaps the greatest spiritual metamorphosis in the history of the human race."

Stevenson, Edinger, and Campbell – three of the most thoughtful Americans of the mid-20th Century – all compared the condition of America and the Western world to that of Rome during its decline and the emergence of Christianity. I want to explore the ramifications of their remarks a bit, for this issue has become a dominant driving force not only in America's spiritual and psychological life, but also in our culture, our politics, and international affairs. What actually happened when the Greco-Roman world was transformed into early Christianity?

The history books tell only part of the story. We know of: the corruption of Rome; the severe decline of population; the neglect and even abandonment of farms; the collapse of the Roman system of aqueducts and roads; the high taxes and the trade imbalance; and, perhaps most importantly, the rise of what Arnold Toynbee termed the "internal proletariat" – those who no longer shared the traditional ethical and spiritual belief in the ancient religion that had provided inner cohesion and meaning to Rome's outward achievements. All of this set the stage for invasion by the "barbarians" – the "external proletariat" – that overran Rome from the north. That's all on record.

Those were the outer manifestations, but what happened to the inner life of the people? We get some sense from the Roman poet Lucretius, who summed up the temper of his times when he wrote of "aching hearts in every home, racked incessantly by pangs the mind was powerless to assuage." There was a loss of collective meaning; a disappearance of what had represented life's highest value. The old gods no longer resonated in the depths of the soul, especially in the leadership class. Belief atrophied. The cry "Great Pan is dead!" was heard throughout the empire. The God-image that had informed the inner life and the culture of the Greco-Roman world for a thousand years lost its compelling force. There was a breakdown of the historic psychic structures that had been the source and container of Greco-Roman morals and beliefs. This ushered in the collapse of the ethical and social guidelines underlying civilized order. New religions and sects arose and vied for popular allegiance. All in all, it was an extended, earth-shattering social and psychic upheaval.

The history books speak of the "decline" of Rome. But at its heart, it was a long-term – at least four or five centuries – psychological shift of the prevailing God-image from the multiple gods of the Greco-Roman period, to a new spiritual dispensation. A new God-image emerged for a new phase of psychological maturation and human experience. From Ireland to Italy, Europe went through a prolonged period of the transformation of underlying principles and symbols. What emerged we now know as Christendom.

What Stevenson, Edinger, Campbell, and others have suggested is that America and the West are experiencing a similar – and perhaps even greater – reorientation. This is what Drucker was referring to when he talked about a world uprooting its foundations, overturning its values, and toppling its idols. If this is so, it means that for some time now we have been living through the "Apocalypse." Let me emphasize that in talking about the Apocalypse, I'm not making any metaphysical statements about God or the Unknown Immensity that created the Universe. This is strictly commentary on the psychological significance of the Apocalypse on us as human beings.

Generally speaking, the Apocalypse as presented in *The Revelation to John* is misunderstood – a misunderstanding arising from two different methods of interpretation. One is the literal interpretation, which is the fundamentalist view. The other is a symbolic interpretation, which was St. Augustine's belief. Thus, the fundamentalists see the Apocalypse as the literal end of the world (and some 48 million Americans believe this will happen in their lifetime); whereas, the symbolic interpretation views the Apocalypse as the end of the Christian eon – a protracted time when a new spiritual dispensation will come into being.

When we speak of the end of the Christian eon, what we're suggesting is that the spiritual impulse that gave highest value and meaning to Western civilization is no longer the inner dynamic of the collective Western psyche. It is no longer the informing force in the soul of America and Europe's "creative minority" who give us our literature, theater, science, technology, education, cinema, and music. In this sense, the character of our culture is the best indication of what is emanating from the depths of the Western soul. For culture is to a nation what dreams are to the individual – an indication of what's going on in the depths of the inner life.

When a shift takes place on the scale we're suggesting – when the God-image changes – that is an epochal experience. For what is happening is that part of the unconscious within us is seeking to become conscious. Such a process has happened before. It's clearly seen in the differences between the rather imprecise polytheism of *The Iliad* and the purposeful and morally inclined monotheism of *Exodus*. Indeed, the differences between the *Old* and *New Testaments* suggest another such change in the God-image. Such developments represent a significant evolution of consciousness. The underlying continuity of that process must be taken into account as we evaluate our own era.

If we are in the midst of such a reorientation, when did it start and how has it been expressing itself? Part of the answer lies in the 16th Century when the earliest harbinger of this reorientation emerged. That omen was the appearance of the Faust legend around the 1540s.

Faust made a pact with the devil in order to gain knowledge, power, and pleasure. During the second half of the 16th Century, over fifty versions of the Faust myth spread across Europe – an age with no internet, TV, or even newspapers. So the European collective psyche was beginning to express something that was clearly the antithesis of Christianity. The Antichrist was manifesting itself. The reorientation had begun.

By the time of the Enlightenment and French Revolution, reason had replaced Christian belief as life's highest authority, at least for the creative minority. And so Notre Dame, one of Christendom's most hallowed cathedrals, was turned into a temple honoring the Goddess of Reason.

In the 19th Century, the reorientation/Apocalypse gained momentum, despite the Romantic Movement's reaction against reason. The great German philosopher Hegel wrote in 1827, "God has died – God is dead – this is the most frightful of all thoughts, that everything eternal and true is not, that negation itself is found in God." In 1850, English poet Matthew Arnold wrote *Dover Beach*, lamenting the "retreating sea of faith." At the same time, Lord Tennyson, England's Poet Laureate, warned of "the secular abyss that is to come." In France, Baudelaire urged his readers to study "the rhetorical methods of Satan," proclaiming, "The true saint is the person who whips and kills the people for the good of the people" – an attitude that later was given concrete expression in Fascism and Communism. And in Russia, Dostoyevsky's Ivan announced that if God is dead, then, "Everything is permitted."

So when Nietzsche proclaimed in 1883 that "God is dead," he was not announcing a new thought; he was expressing a psychological reality for most of Europe's creative minority. Thus it was not at all surprising that as the 20th Century opened, Thomas Hardy should write *God's Funeral*, a poem noting "our myth's oblivion," and asking "who or what shall fill his place?" W.B. Yeats echoed Hardy in his 1920 poem *The Second Coming:* "And what rough beast, its hour come round at last, slouches towards Bethlehem to be born?"

America was not immune to these influences working on the European soul, although there was a certain lag-time. In 1925, when America was creating the "consumer society" with new technologies and a booming stock market, F. Scott Fitzgerald published America's first celebrated expression of the loss of transcendent meaning. Said Daisy in *The Great Gatsby*, "I'm pretty cynical about everything. I think everything's terrible anyhow. Everybody thinks so – the most sophisticated people." Fitzgerald's biographer André Le Vot later wrote about the meaning of *The Great Gatsby*, saying, it is "not men who have abandoned God, but God who has deserted men in an uninhabitable, absurd material Universe." This theme of the absurdity and meaninglessness of life became a core premise of American culture: Arthur Miller's *Death of a Salesman*; J.D. Salinger's *Catcher in the Rye*; James Dean in *Rebel Without a Cause*; Allen Ginsberg's *Howl*; Jack Kerouac's *On the Road*; Joseph Heller's *Catch-22*; and John Updike's *Rabbit Angstrom* series – all reflective of Camus, Beckett, Sartre, and the "school of the absurd."

Similar disquiet showed itself throughout other areas of society. Paul Samuelson, America's first recipient of the Nobel Prize for Economics, wrote in the mid 1970s, "More isn't enough. People are better housed, fed and educated than twenty-five years ago, but that isn't producing satisfaction. There's a spiritual element missing." *The Wall Street Journal* echoed Samuelson. *The Journal* noted that it is "not only religious belief that has declined; so has the powerful secular faith that sprang from the Enlightenment. The power of reason, the power of science, the belief in progress – all are coming under increasing doubt."

What this darker side of two centuries of Western culture represents is an erosion of the structures and values which historically have been the architecture of the collective Western psyche, and which are no longer expressed by an operative religious myth. This breakdown of collective psychic structures has led to the increasing dysfunction of our social arrangements such as family, education, culture, government, and, inevitably, the church. In 1980, Robert Nisbet, one of America's foremost historians and social theorists, provided a remarkable assessment in his book *The History of Progress*:

> *What was present in very substantial measure in the basic works of the founders of political democracy was a respect for such social institutions as property, family, local community, religion, and voluntary association, and for such cultural and social values as objective reason, the discipline of language, self-restraint, the work ethic, and, far from the least, the culture that had taken root in classical civilization and grown, with rare interruptions, ever since. ... The architects of Western democracy were all students of history, and they had every intellectual right to suppose that moral values and social structures which had survived as many vicissitudes and environmental changes as these had over two and a half millennia of their existence in Western society would go on for at least a few more centuries.*

Then, in a stark conclusion, Nisbet wrote, "But in fact they have not [gone on]." Similar expressions of the Apocalypse – or loss of life's highest meaning – have continued to the present day.

Walter Russell Mead is a senior fellow at the Council on Foreign Relations. In February 2003, he wrote an article for *The Washington Post* that carried the headline, "It's the Dawning Age of the Apocalypse." After surveying what he considered to be the retreat of progress, Mead noted that "apocalypse anxiety has moved into the mainstream of American politics and culture ... a line has been crossed. This is Oppenheimer country. The Age of Progress is in the past and this is the era of Shiva, destroyer of worlds." The Council on Foreign Relations and *The Washington Post* – you don't get more "establishment" than that.

We see expressions of this loss of collective meaning in the regression to earlier forms of political, ethnic, nationalistic, and religious ways of thinking. All nations seem to be in the midst of some form of crisis of identity. None of the categories of the past – social status, religion, ethnicity, culture, heritage, region, nation – is an adequate context of thought and action in an era which is seeking some new spiritual and psychological foundation.

A further sign of reorientation is the massive spiritual search under way. Look in any bookstore and you'll see hundreds of books on religion, spirituality, mysticism, addiction, and the meaning of life. Forty years ago, no major bookstore carried such an inventory of "New Age" books. Today, new religions and sects are emerging literally every day. There are over 1,500 so-called religions in America, including some anomaly called "Catholic-Buddhists." Look at the popularity of TV shows such as *Touched by an Angel* and books like the *Chicken Soup* series, with sales of over ninety million books. And the internet offers endless virtual prayer chapels and spiritual blog-sites. Some people even see the internet as a new metaphor for God.

The reorientation also is expressing itself through power. When the psychic energy behind life's highest value is no longer projected into a God-image, it doesn't simply evaporate. That psychic energy is often projected into some other value – usually pleasure or power. Thus for many people, power is substituted as life's highest value. But power needs to be held in creative tension with its opposite – restraint. Colin Powell has a plaque on his desk that reads, "Of all the manifestation of power, restraint impresses men the most."

Many powerful people lack Powell's understanding. Think of the countless corporate mergers that have taken place since the 1980s. Many of these mergers resulted from the power complex of CEOs who didn't have power in a creative tension with restraint. Psychologically, power served as their god, their supreme value. So stockholders, employees, and communities have lost trillions of dollars simply because of individual CEOs' ego-inflation. That's not an argument against mergers; it's an observation about why some mergers have taken place.

Here's another example of ego-inflation that is even more serious – from the scientific community. *The Washington Post* quoted Microsoft researcher Steven Shafer, formerly a professor of computer science at Carnegie Mellon

University, as saying, "Teaching steals from research time." At Microsoft, however, Shafer seemed happier: "To me, this corporation is my power tool. It's the tool I wield to allow my ideas to shape the world." My "power tool" – a classic expression of what appears to be the inflated power drive, or what the great theoretical physicist Freeman Dyson described as "the technical arrogance that overcomes people when they see what they can do with their minds."

Most Americans are totally unaware of the extent to which scientists are fascinated with what they can "do with their minds." This mind-set is now driving our scientific research and the constantly accelerating pace of technology development. Indeed, scientists themselves are unaware of it, which is the prime reason why it's so dangerous. Scientists are so mesmerized by the power of technology, they simply don't realize (or don't care) whether it is improving the human condition. As Francis Bacon put it in the 17th Century, the "true and lawful end of the sciences is that human life be enriched by new discoveries and powers." The question today is: *Are new technologies improving the human condition, or replacing human meaning and significance altogether?*

The futures research staff at British Telecom predicts that as a result of the human genome project, scientists "will be able to identify the genes needed to produce a people of any chosen characteristics." Someone, somewhere, we're told, "will produce an elite race of people – smart, agile, and disease resistant." MIT's Sherry Turkel sees the "reconfiguration of machines as psychological objects and the reconfiguration of people as living machines." Ray Kurzweil suggests, "When machines are derived from human intelligence but are a million times more capable, there won't be a clear distinction between human and machine intelligence – there's going to be a merger." And another tech visionary predicts that the wiring of human and artificial minds into one planetary soul will ultimately mean "the disappearance of the self altogether, right into the collective organism of the mind." No Socialist or Communist could imagine a more stark vision of the collectivized society.

Perhaps Jaron Lanier, who coined the term "virtual reality" and started the world's first virtual reality company, is best situated to assess what is happening:

> Medical science, neuroscience, computer science, genetics, biology – separately and together – seem to be on the verge of abandoning the human realm altogether. ... It grows harder to imagine human beings remaining at the center of the process of science. Instead, science appears to be in charge of its own process, probing and changing people in order to further its own course, independent of human agency.

And Gregory Stock carries Lanier's thought to its ultimate conclusion. Stock envisions a time soon emerging, "when humans no longer exist ... Progressive self-transformation could change our descendents into something sufficiently different from our present selves to not be human in the sense we use the term now." Thus, shall we reach what some scientific intellectuals herald as the "Post Human" or the "Post Species" age.

Albert Einstein was concerned about such frightening possibilities. Speaking at Cal Tech, Einstein warned, "Concern for man himself and his fate must form the chief interest of all technical endeavors." Ignoring Einstein's warning, some scientists are, in effect, proposing the cancellation of the five thousand year quest to create a moral order for human existence. Instead, they foresee the potential self-destruction of humanity as we've known it – all under the guise of something some scientists say is our "evolutionary path." In a very real sense, many scientists have abdicated responsibility for the possible consequences of their research and invention.

What's the likely outcome? No one really knows. But England's Martin Rees, possibly the finest theoretical physicist today, looks at current scientific and technological experiments and estimates there's "a 50% chance of a catastrophic setback to civilization." He maps out numerous ways new technologies could destroy our species by the end of the 21st Century, and he concludes that this is simply something we have to risk "as the downside for our intellectual exhilaration." Rees's use of the phrase "intellectual exhilaration" is a telling expression. For it represents the enthrallment that grips some scientists when they see what they can do with the raw power of mind. The power of mind becomes life's ultimate principle. It becomes a god.

And so scientific power, when not held in a creative tension with restraint, becomes potentially suicidal in a world of planet-destroying technologies. This is all part of the end of the world as we've known it ... the end of the Christian eon ... the Apocalypse.

What is the meaning of all this for us as individuals? Unanswered questions abound. Do we understand yet what drove Mohamed Atta and others to fly into the World Trade Center? Why do we Americans tend to see ourselves as primarily "good" and many other people as largely "bad" – whether we're talking about Muslims, Russians, Chinese, or French? What does it signify that both sides in the so-called "war on terrorism" are driven by archetypal images of good vs. evil? Are we aware of how much we project our shadow side to the rest of the world? Do we understand the Muslim fear that the secular Western model of globalization may mean the eventual end of Islam? What does our blithe dismissal of other nations' views indicate about us?

More immediately, how do we respond in practical terms to the reorientation shaping Western society? To some extent, America already is responding – with the most sweeping redefinition of civilization in human history. Our institutions are being restructured. Corporations are redefining their mission, structure, and *modus operandi*. In education, countless new experiments are underway – from vouchers to charter schools to home schooling. The legal system is trying alternative dispute resolution. Numerous steps have been taken to redress the severe environmental imbalance we've created. Functions formerly executed by local governments are now undertaken by civic and charitable organizations. In fact, it's estimated that well over 50% of all adult Americans donate a portion of their time to non-profit social efforts. Perhaps most importantly, we're integrating a global perspective into the fabric of our education, culture, and international relations. So on many levels, we're already grappling with some of the manifestations of the reorientation that engulfs us.

But the personal level is the heart of the matter. To consider this core, we need draw on the work of C.G. Jung and Edward Edinger. Jung was trained as a psychiatrist; however, psychiatry was the instrument of his work, not the main work itself. In my view, Jung will be remembered for centuries to come because he introduced a new worldview and initiated a new cultural epoch. Jung's worldview enables contemporary man to develop a consciousness that can give each person metaphysical and cosmic significance. There is a sacred continuity to life that has been disrupted in our scientific age. As Edinger said in 1961, our relation to life has become confusing. Future generations may see Jung as having discovered the key to reestablishing that relationship to life. In this sense, I see Jung as one of those historical figures who only comes along every five hundred years or so, which probably explains why he is so misunderstood.

Jung uncovered the foundational layer of the unconscious that is common to humankind. He also discovered the psychological dynamics of spiritual experience. As Edinger notes, we now are able to scientifically understand the psychological processes that create religions. Prior to Jung, scientists had no data or language with which to explore the unconscious. Thus, Jung revealed the most basic dynamic at work in the world today – the realm of the soul. If we don't comprehend what's happening on the soul level, the level of the psyche, we won't be able to understand what's happening to our world. For in the end, it's the individual that makes history; it's the individual psyche that produces our philosophy, art, economic and educational theories, and technology. The psyche is the engine of history, and right now the greatest change in the world is taking place in our collective unconscious.

Epochal changes such as the Apocalypse don't take place out in the cosmos somewhere. They take place in our collective psyche which is, by definition, unconscious. Jung coined the term "archetype," which is an unconscious representation of a living pattern, a spontaneous phenomenon, completely independent of our will. In this sense, an archetype is a pattern of behavior common to all humanity. Jung discovered that an archetype is not an inert psychic pattern as Plato thought, but a dynamic agency with autonomy, spontaneity, and intention. Jung once described an archetype as "an overwhelming force comparable to nothing I know." Taken as a whole, archetypes determine our every-day activity at least as much, if not more, than does ego-consciousness. We have only begun to understand archetypes and their relevance to the totality of all life forms, including their potential cosmic significance.

In the course of his work, Jung explored the psychological meaning of the Apocalypse. The Greek word *apokalypsis* means "revelation, an uncovering of what has been hidden." But *The Revelation to John* has four features: revelation, judgment, destruction, and renewal. Revelation discloses new truth about how life and the Universe function. Judgment assesses the state of contemporary conditions in light of this new truth. Destruction is the collapse of old institutions and relationships that are no longer effective within the context of the new truth. Renewal is the recreation of civilization according to the requirements of the new truth. If one carefully considers the last century, all four of these trends are visible.

The archetype of the Apocalypse becomes activated at certain points in a culture's history. We're usually unaware of the inner psychological dynamics of this change, even though we see its outward manifestations in both culture and contemporary events. When set in motion, its function is to bring about a transition from one spiritual paradigm to a new one. That's what happened two thousand years ago in the Greco-Roman world, which was rife with Jewish apocalyptic writing such as *The Revelation to John*.

Psychologically, every worldview or spiritual paradigm revolves around Jung's concept of the "Self," which is quite different than the usual definition of self (i.e., the ego's awareness of itself and its surroundings). Jung's Self is the central archetype of order, and the unifying center of the psyche. As such, the Self functions as the God-image and expresses psychic wholeness or totality. Like all archetypes, the Self is composed of opposites: spirit and matter, Love and hate, good and evil. The Self also appears to contain the psyche's transpersonal capacity.

During an Apocalypse, such as the shift from the Greco-Roman world to Christianity, the Self becomes highly activated. It then manifests the four apocalyptic features of revelation, judgment, destruction, and rebirth. Eventually, a new spiritual expression emerges, a new God-image. The new paradigm gradually manifests a new form by assimilating the spiritual and cultural expressions that have preceded it. The Christian image of a benevolent God of Love may evolve into a God-image in which there's a union of opposites. Thus, the new God-image would include male and female, spirit and earth, good and evil. The old God-image seeks perfection through separation of the shadow: "Be ye perfect even as your father in heaven is perfect." But the new God-image seeks completeness through assimilation of the shadow.

Such completeness is "the destiny of mankind," according to historian Lewis Mumford, who further described wholeness of the psyche as:

> The creation of unified personalities, at home with every part of themselves, and so equally at home with the whole family of man, in all its magnificent diversity. ... A concept of the whole man – and of man achieving a consciousness of the cosmic and historic whole – is capable of doing justice to every type of personality, every mode of culture, every human potential.

Completeness on this order would be a manifestation, in Jung's words, of the "original oneness of the unconscious," but this time on the level of consciousness. Such a spiritual dispensation would be in keeping with the psychological reality of the Self. It goes without saying that a development of this magnitude is a prolonged process.

Because the activation of the Self takes place in our unconscious, one of two outcomes is possible: The activation of the Self may be experienced consciously and integrated into the totality of our lives – this is the preferable outcome. Or, the activated Self may manifest collectively in terms of external events. We already see countless examples of this external manifestation in terrorism, in the Arab-Israeli madness, in the degraded themes of our culture, and in the growing dysfunction of many of our social structures.

Our future may depend on how each of us studies the archetype of the Apocalypse and what it means in our era. This takes time and work, for it's not just an intellectual exercise. It's something to be assimilated over time at the soul level. If enough people internalize the psychological meaning of the Apocalypse, then the destructive phase might be minimized and rebirth encouraged. Thus, individual awareness is critically important as the spiritual shift unfolds in our collective psyche. The more conscious we are of what's happening, the greater our chance of making a positive contribution by integrating our activated Self. One way to do this is by becoming conscious of what Jung calls the "shadow" – the rougher elements of our character that social convention has caused us to reject and submerge in our unconscious. If you want to know what your shadow looks like, just list the characteristics you most dislike in other people ... and there you will see your shadow.

The shadow is the source of evil in life, as well as the source of many creative but undeveloped qualities. Other people are aware of our shadow, since we express it daily. Certainly, other nations are keenly aware of America's collective shadow. The potential danger of the scientists we mentioned earlier is that they are not aware of their own shadow, of their unconscious motivation. Most of us don't seriously confront our shadow because it takes concentrated and continued focus. Jung once remarked, "One does not become enlightened by imagining figures of light, but by making the darkness [the shadow] conscious."

Once a part of unconscious shadow is recognized, we become conscious of the need for change. In this manner, greater consciousness is achieved, which as Jung suggests, is the purpose of life. If we do this, we not only become a more unified personality, but we also leave a creative deposit in the collective soul of humanity and thereby help create the new era that is to come. As Edinger wrote, we then "become seeds sown in the collective psyche which can promote the unification of the collective psyche as a whole." In my view, this is the most vital challenge facing any individual, for it's our personal contribution to the future of humanity.

But then there's the question of how we as a nation see our collective shadow. As suggested earlier, we now worship power, whether military, technological, corporate, political, or personal. Yet one of Jung's most profound insights was that the opposite of Love is not hate, but power. "Where Love stops," he wrote in *The Atlantic Monthly* in 1957, "power begins, and violence and horror." What are the implications of Jung's observation for us as a nation and as individuals?

Part of the answer lies in another question: *What is my highest value in life?* Each of us must come to know the answer to that question. Historically for the Western world, "God" was the answer. For millions of people, that's still true. For others, they might like it to be true, but it doesn't have the ring of authenticity about it. It's a backward reach for a lost emotional feeling. For still others, it's a totally meaningless salute to an old God-image.

For myself, because I believe Jung discovered the key to interpreting the deepest truth of our spiritual and psychological life, I would say that my highest value is "the fullest possible degree of individual psychological maturity and completeness." My answer is based on the original meaning of the word "psychology" – the study of the soul. So my highest value would be "the greatest possible maturity and wholeness of the soul," which would include a relationship with that transpersonal dimension of life that's beyond all human comprehension, and a continuing awareness and integration of my shadow.

One sign of psychological wholeness might be to hold two diametrically opposite views in balance without becoming emotionally attached to either view. Other signs would be sensitivity to the sacred mystery of all life and, above all, the qualities of compassion and Love. In psychological terms, what we're talking about is seeking a complementary relationship between the ego and the Self, developing a dialogue between the two. Such a relationship has historically been one of the functions of religion. Christianity provided the basic psychological superstructure of the Western psyche, and it's that psychological architecture that's been changing over the last hundred years. In my view, the decline of Christianity is at the heart of the current paradigm shift – the end of the world as we've known it.

To sum up, I will quote Richard Tarnas, professor of psychology and author of *Cosmos and Psyche*:

> As we look at the world today, we cannot escape the fact that something epochal is dying. We daily watch and experience it in our institutions, in world events and in the ethos of destruction that has become such a cultural and social motif. What we're experiencing is a sign of the unconscious collective psyche passing through the throes of a reorientation, a death and rebirth. The great challenge is, can each of us – on an individual level – go through the reorientation that's being experienced collectively by our civilization? Can we individually recognize the great spiritual, archetypal nature of that reorientation, and engage it on that level so that civilized life finds rebirth? Or, will we be unconscious of it, blind to the deeper reality and personal implications, and consequently collectively act out the reorientation self-destructively as contemporary history?

What we're talking about involves awareness of the unconscious impulses that are inside each of us individually and in our civilization collectively – an acknowledgment that our collective soul is seeking fresh expression in a greater consciousness. That's the meaning of an Apocalyptic Age. It's more than intellectual. It's a psychological and spiritual maturation that is seeking new form. So for me, the term "psychological completeness" includes the ethical grounding and symbolic significance of our spiritual heritage, and the understanding to reinterpret the passing epoch and advance it in a fresh manner consistent with the evolution of contemporary consciousness.

Some eternal, infinite power is at work in each of us, as well as in the Universe. This power is the source of our most vital and creative energies. With all our problems and possibilities, the future depends on how each of us – in our own unique way – taps into that eternal renewing dynamic that dwells in the deepest reaches of our souls. As Jung wrote in 1957, "We must now climb to a higher moral level; to a higher plane of consciousness in order to be equal to the superhuman powers science and technology have placed in our hands. In reality, nothing else matters at this point."

We have a duty to learn from the past, delve inward, and meet this apocalyptic challenge. If we Americans engage this task, not only will we create a new foundation for liberty at home, we also will be in a position to offer the world fresh hope of a future based on wholeness, completeness, and Love.

⇒◆◆⇐

Van quotes a source who gives us only a 50% chance of surviving the Great Cusp. Why? Because when the raw power of the intellect is unchecked by wisdom, we lose our balance and our connection to the Divine. This is the true meaning of the Apocalypse.

Van also foreshadows the Fifth Spiritual Paradigm, during which we will experience a union of opposites due to a greater understanding of duality. Once we make it through the Great Cusp (a/k/a the Apocalypse), we will view Deity from a higher perspective, from a vantage point of non-polarity and non-judgement. We will reembrace the feminine half of God and even the paradox that God encompasses both good and evil. Then, we will begin to view God as a middle principle – a more accessible and integrated force that remains transcendental and yet reflects the shadow of humanity.

The current tension between the Fourth and Fifth Paradigm theosophies indicates that the paradigm shift is near. In the remaining chapters, we shall learn more about how to prepare ourselves for this change in consciousness.

LYBOV K ESKUSTVA

*Art is a human activity consisting in this: that one man consciously, by means of certain external signs, hands on to others feelings he has lived through, and that others are infected by these feelings and also experience them. ...
If people lacked this capacity to receive the thoughts conceived by the men who preceded them and to pass on to others their own thoughts, men would be like wild beasts ....*

*Art is not a pleasure, a solace, or an amusement; art is a great matter. ....
The task for art to accomplish is to make that feeling of brotherhood and Love of one's neighbor, now attained only by the best members of society, the customary feeling and the instinct of all men. ...*

The destiny of art in our time is to transmit from the realm of reason to the realm of feeling the truth that well-being for men consists in being united together, and to set up, in place of the existing reign of force, that the Kingdom of God, i.e., of Love, is the highest aim of human life.

Leo Nikolayevich Tolstoy (1828–1910), *What is Art?*

U niversal art – *lybov k eskustva* in Russian – is an expression of Love that is capable of uniting disparate and desperate people who otherwise might not experience the joy of communion. When we encounter such a masterpiece, the force of it is both cleansing and encouraging. Great art first invokes us to feel and then provokes us to act. Thus, while it takes a master to create a true work of art, his or her Divine creation is shared by us all.

For art contains the power to end our separation, educate our children, and illuminate our common goals – which far outnumber our differences. So, too, does art help us to recognize the best within ourselves and others, by inspiring us to follow our dreams, nurture our hopes for the future, and manifest our never-ending visions of Love.

THE SEER

By Alex Grey

From the caves of Altimira
to a New York studio,
the Seer has inspired the Artist
with vision's unceasing flow.

The Seer is the soul of the Artist,
Magus through ages untold,
transmuting the lead of matter
into bullets of spiritual gold.

The ego picks up the weapon of art,
childlike, it plays with the trigger.
Blowing the head off its contracted self,
awareness is suddenly bigger.

By slaying the ego and stunning
the chatter of thoughts as they rise,
great art shuts out distractions,
delighting the heart through the eyes.

The Seer is the soul of the Artist,
revealing the Mystery as form,
advancing our civilization
by inventing and destroying the norm.

The redemptive Sorceress, Art
can heal the nausea of being,
opening vistas of hope and beauty,
revealing deep patterns of meaning.

The function of art is to stop us
and take us out of our skin,
unveiling the spirit's pure nakedness
without beginning or end.

The Seer is the soul of the Artist,
gaze fixed on primordial perfection.
Radiance emerges from emptiness,
each point of light etched with affection.

The boundless Void, open and formless
is the basis of all creation.
Visions appear and then dissolve,
reinforcing this realization.

From beyond the vision descends,
from within the vision arises,
coalescing in the divine imagination,
Source of continual surprises.

The Seer is the soul of the Artist,
the Maker is the Artist's hand.
In the studio their conversations
translate a timeless command.

These dialogues of Maker and Seer
weave together matter and soul,
consecrating the practice of art,
as speech of the ineffable.

Art making transforms the Artist,
and to any hearts truly under
creation's intoxicating spell,
the Seer transmits holy wonder.

———◆———

    The first thing I did when I stopped practicing law in 2002 was rent an art studio. Not a studio, really, just one corner of a room where three other "real" artists worked. Intuitively, I knew that I was over-weighted in masculine energy. I had spent my adult life in business school, in law school, and then practicing law – all left brain activities. It was high time to give the right hemisphere of my brain a chance to express itself.

    Almost immediately, my meditations soared in a new direction. The act of painting, the music I was listening to while I painted, and the stunning visual work that surrounded me in that room took me to new dimensions. In fact, I was so inspired by the mere act of creation that within six months of painting, I started writing my first book. (Incidentally, not one of my paintings sold.)

    If possible, get some paints, a box of crayons, some magic markers, or a pencil and start creating. Despite what you may have been told when you were little, there is an artist inside of you!

ART, PLEASURE, AND LOVE

By Christopher L.C.E. Witcombe, Ph.D.

We live in two realities. One is the external world of objective reality, and the other is an internal perceptual replica of that external world. We are aware of the external world through our five primary senses, which pick up information about it and pass it on to the brain. This flow of information, however, is one-way; it moves in one direction only. Our conscious awareness of the external world, therefore, is only indirect. Although we may believe that the things we see, hear, taste, touch, and smell are outside of us, our actual perception of them occurs inside our head. Thus, the only way we can perceive the external world is by its effects on our internal conscious experience.

The ancient Greek philosopher Aristippus of Cyrene (*circa* 435–356 B.C.E.) and his followers, the Cyrenaics, taught that we are aware of external forces because they have an effect upon us. From these effects, we learn that some things cause us pleasure while others cause us pain. The Cyrenaics argued, therefore, that the only sensible course of action in life is to seek out that which produces a pleasurable effect and avoid that which is unpleasant or painful.

By prehistoric times, humans already had discovered that by making changes and adjustments or by adding to objects and features in the external world, they could make things that produced a more satisfying internal experience. In this pursuit of a more pleasurable experience, humans created art.

Love of the arts begins with the senses. As a result, art can take many forms – usually in direct relation to one or more of the senses to which it is most naturally allied. In ancient Greece, the poetic arts and the visual arts were referred to jointly as the "mimetic arts."

In *Poetics*, Aristotle explained that the mimetic arts employ either singly or in various combinations five media: language, rhythm, melody, colors, and shapes (forms). Expanding a little on Aristotle's formulation, it can be observed that the mimetic arts involve the two senses of hearing and vision, ranging from music and poetry, which are purely auditory, to sculpture and painting, which are purely visual. Drama and dance lie in-between, as they combine both the auditory and the visual. In this respect, drama and dance serve to link poetry and music on the one side with sculpture and painting on the other.

In 18th Century Europe, the visual arts and poetic arts became known collectively as the "Fine Arts" – a term derived from the French *Beaux Arts*, which is a translation of the Italian phrase *Belle Arti*, meaning "Beautiful Arts." It is the beauty of art that is the chief source of our pleasure in it. But what is this beauty, and why does it engender a Love of the arts?

I now shall focus on the visual arts for which the dominant sense is, of course, sight. For most of us, it is through our eyes that we discover beauty. An explanation of the nature and source of this beauty requires a brief examination of the eye, brain, and body.

The optical system of the human eye functions in response to two classes of stimuli: light and a person's mental or emotional state. The eye's response to light is easily measured. More difficult to measure is the eye's response to mental and emotional states. When you see something that you like or that is of special interest to you, your body's sympathetic nervous system causes the pupil to dilate in order to focus visual attention on it. Other experiences can also cause the pupil to dilate, such as sudden loud noises, fear, or pain. This sort of stimulation is accompanied by the sensation of pleasure, which is the result of chemical reactions in the brain. When the level of pleasure is intense, these reactions can induce a number of associated physical responses. The sympathetic nervous system also governs other organs, such as the heart and lungs, as well as the salivary and sweat glands. Thus, when we see something interesting, beautiful, or attractive, not only do our pupils dilate, but our heart also beats faster, our blood pressure rises, and our breathing, salivation, and perspiration levels change.

But the experience of art is more than one of visual pleasure; it also is psychological, since it provokes thought and imagination via associations. Associations are the mental connections we formulate between what we see and what we know. The process of association is extremely dynamic and escalates by degrees from simple pattern recognition to more complex levels of identification. It triggers thoughts about other things, people, places, and events in a ramified pattern of associated images and sensations drawn from memory. A work of art actively involves the imagination. The imagination literally turns sensation into an image, which then becomes the basis for thought. The act of thinking enhances the imagination because it draws in additional images from the memory through associative connections. It is this combination of visual experience and imaginative, thought-filled, associative connections that determines our response to a work of art and gives it a quality of meaningfulness.

Aristotle regarded imagination as part of the functional processes of the mind and body. Imagination provokes movements and changes, giving rise to desire, which in turn gives rise to the "affections" (*pathe* in Greek). Affections are the things we feel, such as anger, gentleness, fear, pity, courage, and joy, as well as Love and hate. Thus, viewing a work of art sets off a chain of responses – beginning with sensation through the sense of sight, which affects perception through associations and memory, which stimulates the imagination, which may excite the affections ... such as Love.

In *On the Soul*, Aristotle explained that the affections can and do produce various kinds of responses in the organic or physical parts of the body. When gazing at a beautiful work of art, for example, we may experience muscle relaxation and smiling (in addition to pupil dilation mentioned above). Thus, our psychological responses to art are often accompanied by changes in our physical body.

In *Nicomachean Ethics*, Aristotle observed further that our emotions, desires, and passions not only alter the state of the body, but in some cases even cause "madness." For Plato, madness was a kind of possession. He declared in *Phaedrus* that "the greatest of blessings come to us through madness," which he believed was sent as a gift from the gods. He divided this divine madness into four types, each ascribed to a different god or goddess: prophecy was inspired by Apollo, mystic madness by Dionysus, poetic madness by the Muses, and the madness of Love by Aphrodite and Eros. It was this last madness – the madness of Love – that Plato declared to be the best, as it produced an altered mental and physical state in the beholder of beauty. Such madness, Plato explained, "is given by the gods for our greatest happiness."

Arguably, it is the body's biological mechanism of response to visual stimulation and psychological associations that contributes the most to how we react to works of art. Indeed, it is the intensity of our physiological response that serves as the primary indicator or measure of what we see. If we experience a high level of pleasure when viewing something, we are inclined to use a word like "beautiful" to describe both our pleasurable feelings and (through transference) the object that produced them. In other words, the term "beautiful" is ascribed to the sensitive and imaginative feelings provoked in us by certain objects. If the pleasure-inducing object is a painting or a piece of sculpture, we single it out as special and use the term "art" to describe it.

The Italian Renaissance polymath Leone Battista Alberti (1404–1472), in his treatise *On Painting*, enjoined painters to produce beautiful works of art.

The creation of beauty was the goal. Alberti believed that the key to the nature of beauty was proportions, which, when correctly manipulated, not only produce something beautiful, but also give access to the harmony of the Universe and the perfection of God. For Neoplatonic philosopher Marsilio Ficino (1433–1499), beauty engendered Love. A beautiful work of art not only causes you to Love art, but it also has the effect of inserting you into what Ficino called the *circuitus spiritualis* – a mystical or spiritual circuit, a continuous self-reverting flow of Love from you to God and from God back to you.

In the 16th and 17th Centuries, beauty was central to the question of the nature and purpose of art. In the 18th Century, beauty became the basis for the study of "aesthetics." Beginning with Immanuel Kant (1724–1804), the philosophical approach to aesthetics focused on matters of taste and treated the question of pleasure as a purely intellectual experience. In the middle of the 19th Century, however, the German psychologist and founder of psychophysics, Gustav Fechner (1801–1887), initiated experiments in which he sought to identify, by actual measurement, which lines and shapes produced the most aesthetic pleasure. His investigations showed that simple figures are most pleasing when divided symmetrically in the proportion 1:1 or in a proportion corresponding to the "Golden Section." The Golden Section – also termed the "Golden Mean," "Golden Ratio," or "Divine Proportion" and expressed as a mathematical constant denoted by the Greek letter *Phi* (1.6180339887498 ...) – has been shown to occur throughout nature, in plants, animals, and humans, and in many human-made objects. Often the things we perceive as beautiful embody the Golden Section. In the visual arts, it frequently occurs in the form of the "Golden Rectangle," the side lengths of which have a ratio of approximately 1:1.618. For reasons we do not understand, this particular ratio causes us to feel pleasure, which we describe as beautiful.

Pleasure is a familiar criterion of judgment; we use it every day. We try to surround ourselves with things that we like because they give us more pleasure than things we do not like. Judgments based on pleasure guide everything we do: from how we dress in the morning, to the furniture and other items we purchase, how we decorate our living and work spaces, the food we eat, the car we drive, the house or district where we live, the places where we spend vacations, the friends we make, the companion with whom we live or marry, etc. Pleasure is a state of satisfaction. It can be generally equated with feelings of delight, enjoyment, gratification, fulfillment, and happiness. It can, and often does, engender Love.

Pleasure is fundamental both to the artist who makes the art and to us, the viewers of art. The experience of pleasure guides the artist as she or he seeks satisfaction in the process of creation. An artist continues to work at a project until a level of satisfaction is reached. Indeed, it is only when a certain level of satisfaction is achieved that the artist knows the work is finished. The artist is fortunate if we, the viewers, also find pleasure in the work. Consequently, pleasure is the measure of the work's success for both the artist and the viewer. And again, that pleasure may be so intense that Love is generated.

The seeds of Love are sown through the senses. The sight, sound, touch, taste, and scent of things can introduce you to pleasures which, if they persist, can turn into Love. But there are degrees of Love, and these may be measured according to the extent of your sensual and psychological involvement in its source. When all five senses are stimulated and the brain is overwhelmed with pleasure, a type of "madness" ensues. A stranger you *see* across a crowded room catches your interest (your pupils dilate as you focus your attention on that person). You introduce yourself, and the *sound* of that person's voice is delightful to your ear. You take that person's hand in yours, and the *touch* of his or her skin is immensely satisfying. The *taste* of that person's kiss, the *scent* of that person's skin and hair add further to your pleasure. The pleasure you feel when you are with this person becomes so sweet, so enjoyable, and so intense that you do not want to be separated from its source. It is at this point that pleasure is transformed into the longing and desire of Love.

Love is exhilarating. We see Love as representing everything that is good and wonderful in humans. When you Love, it is a pleasure you want everyone to be able to enjoy. Because of this condition, Love is boundless and inclusive and reaches out to everyone and everything around you. The value of art is the way it helps us to Love the world.

⇒◆⇐

Beauty may be in the eye of the beholder, but Christopher reminds us that once our eyes, ears, nose, fingers, or mouth touches beauty, we all react in the same way – with soulful ecstasy.

I was fortunate to have several painters in my family. My grandmother Ruby likes to paint her dreams – ethereal images of angels and stargates. And my Uncle Dick's work leaves me breathless – I merge with his paintings every time I gaze at them.

Our next artist, Patrick, is a composer whose spiritual symphonies and hymns serenade me while I write. To all the artists in the world, we send our gratitude and Love.

MUSIC AND THE WAY

By Patrick Bernard

Since early mystics first attempted to describe their aching need for Cosmic union, Love has been expressed in song.

> You came down from Your throne and stood at my cottage door. I was singing all alone in a corner, and the melody caught Your ear. You came down and stood at my cottage door.
>
> Masters are many in Your hall, and songs are sung there at all hours. But the simple carol of this novice struck at Your Love. One plaintive little strain mingled with the great music of the world, and with a flower for a prize You came down and stopped at my cottage door.

Rabindranath Tagore (1861–1941), Gitanjali

Often, however, artists write about Love without speaking of pure Love. Something is, of necessity, missing. "These beings who Love too much" we sometimes see in books or hear in songs. Yet no one can really Love "too much." We can Love badly, but we cannot Love too much. If we Love too much, it means that it is not Love itself. It is something other than Love. Why is that? Because Love is autonomous, it suffices unto itself. It is not something that can be bought or exchanged. Jealousy and possessiveness are two toxic emotions very far removed from true Love. When we Love through Love, we Love even in moments of rejection. We continue to Love without thinking about it, even if the person we Love does not Love us. At some point, everyone experiences this type of Love – a miracle that occurs in the interior. This loving state is integrated into a harmony of the absolute.

Yet, asking ourselves "What is Love?" is like asking "What is infinity?" or "What is God?" When we look up at the stars in the night sky, we have an impression of what infinity might be. By contemplating life, by meditating on what is happening to our spirit and how our thoughts are able to create our reality, artists gain an impression of what Love is.

Nevertheless, contemplating life and Love is not an easy thing to do. It requires sincerity, a strong desire for interior peace, an ardent desire for knowledge, as well as integrity and perseverance. To do this we have to slow down, put a brake on our madcap existence, breathe a little, appreciate the smallest of small things and learn to marvel at them. The energy of gratitude toward life transmits a lover's vision to us directly from our own interior. A loving thought which springs spontaneously from my conscience will ensure that this loving vibration will be returned to me sooner or later.

Many of us do not realize all the wealth that is within our reach. Often it is just a question of starting to appreciate the infinite mystery of our own body in order to feel a first wave of Love in the depths of our heart. The pain of existence may still be there, but it becomes tolerable; we accept it as being part of a balance that surpasses our understanding, and we admit that it exists in order for us to grow.

I have two eyes, two hands, two legs, a brain equipped with two hemispheres, various organs, millions of intelligent neurotransmitters, and a subtle body with which I can dream. I can read, write, sing, share my music with the world, and communicate in so many ways other than just crying out. It is magnificent ... a loving miracle ... I honor life ... Love.

Whoever succeeds in making this Universal force of Love spring from their hearts will fall in Love with Love itself and rise up on the scale of human consciousness. Outside this experience, life can easily seem an absurd continuum of more or less sterile labors. Love is life itself and represents the source of all beauty.

> Ever in my life have I sought Thee with my songs. It was they that led me from door to door, and with them have I felt about me, searching and touching my world.
>
> It was my songs that taught me all the lessons I ever learnt; They showed me secret paths, they brought before my sight many a star on the horizon of my heart.
>
> They guided me all the day long to the mysteries of the country of pleasure and pain; And, at last, to what palace gate have they brought me in the evening at the end of my journey?

Rabindranath Tagore, *Gitanjali*

This Love we are speaking about does not let itself be conditioned. It is something like a container that is filled right to the top and then starts to overflow ... we cannot stop it. One day the heart opens and is overflowing with Love. This has nothing to do with romanticism. This is a Universal Law that controls all molecular movement, which is the basis of life and harmony.

Music expresses Love when it helps us to raise the lid on our conscience. Tears spring forth spontaneously. And such tears are tears of pure joy, liberating, purifying. These are tears which can heal. They have no identity, no flag, no religion, no established medical order, no favoritism. They spring forth freely from the quantum Universe whenever intelligence becomes enlightened by Love's subatomic particles. All is then potentially attainable.

This Love has very little to do with being attracted to others of the opposite sex or of the same sex. Love is much more than an act. It is a state of being that must be cultivated and is nourished by thousands of tiny signs in everyday life. The best way of receiving is to give. The smile you send out will come back to you, undoubtedly, inexorably, untiringly. The Love you project will come back to you, many times over.

There is a twofold problem, however: on the one hand, individual hearts are locked; and on the other hand, we have a world imagining that Love is some sort of act. Love is above all a state of being. As genuine peace is not simply a truce in between conflict, Love is not simply the absence of hate between two challengers. Just as genuine pleasure is not a cessation of suffering, Love is not just a pause in a war.

Healing our spirit body is akin to an alchemical marriage where we welcome the transforming properties of Love into our life. Then do we find ourselves in a purely artistic realm. The loving state we find there exists permanently, without having to depend on any particular circumstance or condition. Nothing determines the fact of loving. Love is nourished of itself and its source of nourishment is infinite because it is the origin of supreme Cosmic beauty. In this way, music has the capacity to lift man above his human self to reach Divine union.

> When Thou commandest me to sing it seems that my heart would break with pride; I look to Thy face, and tears come to my eyes. All that is harsh and dissonant in my life melts into one sweet harmony – and my adoration spreads wings like a glad bird on its flight across the sea.
>
> I know Thou takest pleasure in my singing. I know that only as a singer I come before Thy presence. I touch by the edge of the far spreading wing of my song Thy feet which I could never aspire to reach.
>
> Drunk with the joy of singing I forget myself and call Thee friend Who art my Lord.

Rabindranath Tagore, *Gitanjali*

The Universe is Love and its Love is different from sentimentality. The great art of Love is at once eternally feminine and eternally masculine. It is not limited to just the physical or emotional body. It represents the essence of the evolution of human consciousness. While Love is "The Way," music is one path.

The Masters who practice this alchemical, shamanic, and mystical art emanate Love. They comprehend infinity. They meet with God. And through their art, they help save humanity. They are voyagers of The Way.

AN ARTIST'S ODE TO KATRINA

By Alice Lovelace

In this day of parable and hymn, there is no room for poets,
all doors remain locked by politicians who hold advance reservations
on the day of earthly destruction.
So no, they would not fund the levy, not the schools, nor the teachers,
there were no buses, and no, they did not care for the elder or ill.
Not even the writers were saved,
for art was jettisoned to make room for false idols and temples to gold.

In this age of lent and sacrifice, you are the manna on their altar.
It is your words, your images, your truths they burn.
Words that do not please those who take all pleasure unto themselves
leave the artist drunk on fumes of oil fed funeral pyres.

In this millennium of empires on earth, heavenly dynasties in the sky,
the global rulers stalk any writer who dares write truths that belie the lie
told long and sure by the power brokers land to land.
They insist: Let them eat the bloated bodies,
the fouled reputations of the poor,
the stagnant air of a sickening senseless selfishness
floating in a brew of flood water and oil.

No cries of art can reach the empire seeking soul, the imperialist heart;
to Halliburton go the spoils,
while writers toil to lay bare the plan of the elite
to escape at the Rapture then outsource the Earth.
In the face of shattered levies, we witnessed suffering and shame,
but not of the moment's making.

How many people died of starvation before the hurricane?
How many homeless slept under our bridges, below our sight line?
How many children, elders died for want of medical care?
Whose situation went unattended by bright lights and news reporters?
Whose cries cannot be heard in the den of the holy trinity
where prayers of one world global control are offered at altars
of oil, information, and land?
The voice and pen of art are moot in the land of media
where the people are not invited to partake of the banquet.

Pass me my pens and my pencils.
Pass me my paints and canvas.
Let me sing you a new Blues,
for a new day is here and a new art is rising.
In the face of the flood we stand naked,
exposing a deep persistent poverty in the heart of America;
Bear witness to the crucifixion of art, of memory –
this cultural starving of America.

We have stopped swallowing excuses –
Every day on this planet is filled with disaster.
Every nation shoulders its share of the pain.
Every people pays homage to stale old masters,
headmasters, grandmasters
who for every reason drain us of our laughter.
This is their feeding season.
It is a time for art to stake its claim to the human psyche
for any key to these days of man-made catastrophes.

Let us salvage every pain, every death, and every slander.
Let us render of this pain all the dreams that were slain.
Let us make of this a prescription –
to remedy the ills of our soul and suffocate past shame and suffering.

Let us give rise to a new art –
stunningly simple, simply prophetic,
prophecy imprinted on the face of the old.

⟫⟫◦◦⟪⟪

Alice is one of the amazing people I met at the *Building a New World* conference in Radford, Virginia. I actually had the honor of hearing her deliver this poem live on stage – what a performance! Like most other artists, Alice's work has a central theme, and here it is: *If you're not pissed off, you're not paying attention!*

Through her art, Alice changes lives. Indeed, I am not the same person after hearing and reading her poetry. She helped motivate me to speak more courageously about my dreams for the Independence, Virginia project. She strengthened my warrior spirit by modeling for me what this energy looks like in female form. And she encouraged me to manifest change *now*, since we are running out of time. This is what great art does for the soul. It provides us with a Divine spark so that we may contribute – in whatever way feels right and with whatever talents we possess – to building a new paradigm for humanity.

ART AND SHIFTING SPIRITUAL PARADIGMS

By Adelheid M. Gealt, Ph.D.

Introduction to Past Paradigms

Art, religion, and Love have been intertwined throughout history. The ancient Greeks and Romans personified various aspects of nature (both physical and human) into multiple divinities. Venus, for example, represented Love, and Mars represented war, his rages quelled by acts of Love from Venus. This was the era of polytheism, a distinct spiritual paradigm.

By the 1st Century, when Christ, a prophetic figure, was preaching about a single God, the Creator of all things, he was speaking from the Jewish tradition based on the *Old Testament* – a spiritual paradigm based on male monotheism. In the mythology of that religion, the book of *Genesis* assigned Eve a fatal role in human destiny. Interestingly, though, Jesus expressed great sympathy for women, if the four gospels in the *New Testament* are any indication. He thereby foreshadowed a spiritual paradigm yet to come.

Unfortunately, however, through a mixture of creative interpretation and the play of legend, Mary Magdalene was turned into a reformed harlot. She was Jesus' most devoted female acolyte after his own mother Mary, who dogma declared was a virgin. Jesus also was sympathetic to a fairly loose-living woman of Samaria whom he met at the well, and he saved an adulteress from being stoned to death by declaring: "Let he who is without sin cast the first stone." Maternal Love and personal loyalty also were present in the final stages of Christ's story: his mother Mary and the Magdalene were famously present at Christ's crucifixion, and Mary Magdalene was the first person to see the resurrected Jesus according to the gospels. Peter, who denied Jesus and then repented, is another character whose tale is rich with personal conflict – loyalty and Love on the one hand, doubt, fear, and human frailty on the other.

Western Art in Early Christianity

But these aspects of the Christian story, which stress Jesus' Love and compassion, did not inform the early Christian pictorial tradition. From what little survives of early Christian art – 1st Century through the fall of the Roman Empire in the 5th Century and the Dark Age that followed – an abstract pictorial language was dominant. It rendered Christ into a cipher, a cross, a schematic divinity upon the cross. And as late as the 8th Century, the magnificent *Book of Kells* demonstrates this same theme, with an insistent, magical, and mystical abstract language of repeated patterns that can be seen as visual counterparts to the chanted prayers that issued with regularity from the lips of the Celtic priests who created this masterpiece about the "Word of God."

There is a theory to which I ascribe, that the actual horrors of a real crucifixion were much too terrible for early Christians to want to see depicted in their art. Only after a millennium, when that form of execution and the gruesome bloody violence associated with the condemnation of the lowest of Roman criminals was no longer routine, did artists begin to show Jesus on the cross. When they finally did so, Jesus was shown alive and triumphant over death.

When did this change occur in Western art? More than a thousand years after Jesus actually died. We see the change by the 13th Century, when Saint Francis of Assisi (*circa* 1181–1226), the son of a rich merchant, rejected his family's wealth, took a vow of poverty, and began to preach. He preached a living, human Jesus, and Francis himself was so loving that he also cared about the animals and even preached to the birds. Francis, who loved Jesus so much that he miraculously bore the wounds of Christ (the stigmata), was canonized in 1228, soon after his death. Thereafter, his impact on Christian art was incalculable. By personalizing and humanizing Jesus, Francis inspired the Pisano family of sculptors working in 13th Century Tuscany and, later on, the great revolutionary Florentine painter Giotto di Bondone (1267–1337), who changed the direction of art by giving Jesus and other holy characters a human (if not monumental) presence. For example, Giotto's *Santa Maria Novella Cross* and his frescoes in the Arena Chapel of Padua are testimony to an artist who injected not only a new physical reality but a psychological depth into his renderings of holy beings.

The 14th Century saw the growing veneration of the Virgin Mary as the embodiment of the loving intercessor on behalf of humankind. The emergence of the *Madonna della Misericorida*, whose massive cloak shelters the huddling masses, became a standard image and remained popular for centuries. Later examples include the work of Piero della Francesca, a 15th Century master. Whole cities, Siena for example, were dedicated to the

Virgin Mary, and countless images stressed the Virgin's Love of Jesus by depicting Mary clasping Jesus to her and the two embracing cheek to cheek to express their Love. Though derived from abstract Byzantine icons, these intimate images became fictive flesh and, more importantly for this topic, expressions of the heart in the hands of such 14th Century masters as Ambrogio Lorenzetti (*circa* 1290–1348), Pietro Lorenzetti (*circa* 1280–1348), and many others.

The 15th Century produced a most innocent, devout, and loving personality, Saint Fra Angelico (*circa* 1395–1455). Angelico was a Dominican friar in Florence and the patron saint of artists who reportedly wept as he painted such scenes as *The Deposition of Christ* (Uffizi Gallery, Florence). Angelico spent much of his life decorating each of the cells of the San Marco Monastery with holy scenes. One of his finest surviving works is a panel entitled *The Last Judgment*, which imagines paradise as a place where he and his fellow monks will see each other again in a lovely, flower strewn garden wherein the monks embrace with happiness and Love.

The Deposition of Christ by Fra Angelico

The Religious Art of the Renaissance

By the 16th Century, the Renaissance was in full flower and a variety of historic individuals lived and acted boldly. The artists of this era gave a larger than life impression and shaped their own destinies, not so much under God's protection but as though in partnership with the Divine. After all, this was the era when Michelangelo (1475–1564) carved his gigantic *David*, subsequently placed in front of town hall as the defender of Florence. Pope Julius II had the ambition to create the greatest church in Christendom (a rebuilt Saint Peter's in Rome). This church would have housed a magnificent multi-figured marble tomb for Julius, designed and carved by Michelangelo. The tomb was never assembled, but it created such a need for ready cash that Julius' solution was to invoke Indulgences for money, among many other abuses. Such papal greed and immorality pushed Martin Luther over the edge, and the Protestant Reformation movement was born.

Paradigms of all kinds shifted during the Renaissance. In this same century, English King Henry VIII, who was bigger and taller than nearly all his contemporaries and the competitor of the Holy Roman Emperor Charles V, decided to rid himself of a barren but loving Catholic wife, Catherine of Aragon (who also happened to be Charles' aunt). Henry took his cue from Martin Luther and broke with the Catholic Church in Rome. He declared himself the supreme head of the newly established Church of England and, through these actions, managed thereafter to marry and behead two wives, divorce two others, and finally die in 1547, in the arms of his last spouse, the carefully obedient Catherine Parr.

Where do faith and Love fit into such a world? One simple and not entirely incorrect answer would be – in old age. Here are just a few notable examples: Charles V retired to a monastery in 1556 to meditate and pray. Michelangelo, whose marble *David* was a celebration of human potential, had a change of heart as he grew older. He wrote poems and exchanged letters with his good and pious friend Vittoria Colonna (1490–1547) about issues of faith, in which he contemplated over and over again the mystery of the crucifixion. Michelangelo sent Vittoria one of his drawings of the crucifixion as a special gift. And his final work, fittingly enough intended for his own tomb, was a *Pieta* – the image of the dead Christ being mourned by his mother. The unfinished *Rondanini Pieta* simultaneously deals with the essentials of faith, Love in the form of mourning, and art. Michelangelo worked on it until he drew his last breath, smashing it when it was nearly finished to achieve a different vision, and thereby creating an elemental, profoundly moving masterwork that has influenced how future artists view the idea of finish. Michelangelo's great Venetian competitor, Titian (1485–1576), likewise chose for his final subject and his tomb the *Pieta*. Titian's surviving painting, with its scumbled surface, refracted light, and broken surfaces, becomes a hallucination about grief, sacrifice, and death and not a literal description of it. It is one of the most moving works of art found at the Accademia in Venice.

Neither Catholicism nor the newly formed Protestant movement triumphed in 17th Century art. Catholic art devoted itself to stressing the mystical, miraculous, and emotional dimensions of faith, leading to deliberately visionary, irrational, and theatrical masterpieces. One of the finest is by Gianlorenzo Bernini (1598–1680). His *Ecstasy of Saint Theresa* for the Cornaro Chapel in Rome captures the rare visionary experience of the famous nun Saint Teresa of Avila (1515–1582), the leader of the discalced Carmelites. In Protestant regions throughout this century, faith, age, and the painful realities of human existence led to the creation of images based on sacred themes, the greatest of them relating to redemption and Love.

The most famous example comes from the Dutch master Rembrandt van Rijn (1606–1669). Toward the end of his life, Rembrandt lost his common law wife, Hendrijcke Stoffels, and his son Titus. Bankrupt and no longer the leading painter of Amsterdam, Rembrandt turned to a biblical theme and created his greatest masterpiece – *The Return of the Prodigal Son*. Now in the Hermitage Museum of St. Petersburg, Rembrandt's *Prodigal Son* is unquestionably the most thoughtful, deeply moving interpretation of this famous theme. An icon of simplicity and grace, and glowing with the mysterious light of Love, this work emanates the message of repentance and forgiveness.

Faith and Art During the Age of Enlightenment

It would be wrong to assume that the 18th Century Age of Enlightenment was without religious sentiment or concerns. True, it was a period when atheism was freely avowed and science, rationality, and information offered exciting developments. After all, this was the era of the encylopedists (Denis Diderot among them), the great naturalists (Georges-Louis Leclerc, Comte de Buffon), and many marvelous discoveries, including Benjamin Franklin's experiments with lightning and electricity. This also was the century when the great scientist Antoine-Laurent de Lavoisier discovered the properties of water, had his portrait painted by Jacques-Louis David (1748–1825), only to lose his head in 1793 during the French Revolution. But what about faith? Did artists shape its course? If not directly, I still would argue that art impacted culture and religion in some unusual ways.

On the one hand, religion was associated with the established monarchies. Hence, all rulers ascribed to some religion, punctiliously carried out their acts of piety, and sometimes commissioned sacred works that turned out to be important art historically, despite the fact that some rulers commissioned art more out of political expediency than faithful sincerity. But for those artists whose religion had become a personal matter, when patronage and religion coincided, the results could be stunning. A case in point is the work of the

Venetian master Giambattista Tiepolo (1696–1770), who died working for Charles III of Spain. Among his final works are a series of moving, evocative, and personal interpretations of sacred stories, which are appreciated by today's scholars as surprisingly sincere expressions of piety.

In 1797, Giambattista's son, Domenico Tiepolo (1727–1804), witnessed the fall of his native city Venice to Napoleon – an event which ended a thousand years of Venetian independence and threatened to destroy the beloved and much revered ecclesiastical infrastructure that acted as one of the strong threads holding the fabric of Venetian society together. After all, wherever Napoleon went, he seized church property, closed convents and monasteries, and looted much of Europe of its greatest artistic treasures. In a single campaign of plunder, Napoleon managed to dislodge and dislocate thousands of altarpieces and separate the Catholic devout from the images they had relied upon to carry out their devotions. Pope Pius VI, whom he put under house arrest, later died in exile (as would Napoleon himself). Napoleon's actions, undertaken in a spirit of reform and secularism, amounted to an anti-clerical campaign which, not surprisingly, spawned reaction and resistance.

I believe this anti-religious climate was well underway throughout Europe as early as the 1780s and may have prompted Domenico Tiepolo to commence a uniquely personal and stunning project – one that was nearly lost and forgotten. But in 2006, Professor George Knox and I pieced together the story of Domenico Tiepolo and, after ten years of research, published our findings in a book entitled *Domenico Tiepolo: A New Testament.*

Jesus in the Garden of Gethsemane: The Second Prayer by Domenico Tiepolo

Domenico's work involved a pictorial history of early Christianity, tracing the ancestry of Jesus from his grandparents (Joachim and Anna), through to the establishment of the early church via the actions of two of its principal leaders (Saint Peter and Saint Paul). Drawing on 316 uncut sheets of paper,

Domenico privately worked in his own home located in Mirano, Italy, to secretly create a vast Christian narrative (possibly more than 316 pages in length). Domenico culled this visual narrative not only from an unusually careful reading of the *New Testament*, but also from extensive research into rare apocryphal and medieval literature. This massive body of drawings was still in his studio when he died in 1804.

We surmise that Domenico's wife sold the collection to a Venetian art dealer who split up the series. A large portion of the work was sold to a collector named Fayet, who donated his 138 sheets to the Louvre in the 19th Century. The rest were likely bought by a collector named Luzarches; this group of drawings eventually was scattered to the winds. What the world lost was a rare and unique visual testament – personal and historical – to an artist's faith.

Why did he do it? We're not certain, but at least one motivation was to rehearse and remember – with an accent on eye witness – the pictorial and literary traditions that made up the Christian story. Another was to stress the pictorial monuments that connected to that story, be they relics or pictures. Another motivation was to study the gospel texts closely; he placed a new emphasis on the *Gospel of Mark*, anticipating what 19th Century theologians would later discover – that *Mark*, not *Mathew*, is the oldest gospel. Domenico had a vast body of material from which to work and he must have labored, entirely voluntarily, for years on the project. His was an act of great Love – a Love for his heritage, his faith, and his art, as they came together in a remarkable way in the creation of a unique monument in art history which is now, thankfully, taking its rightful place among the artistic achievements of the period.

Domenico's pictorial cycle was probably the last of its kind, based so carefully and inventively on earlier pictorial models. By the time he died in 1804, Europe was in the wake of bloody revolution and returning to religion as a source of comfort. The limits of reason had been reached, as demonstrated by the bloody violence of the 1790s and a new emerging artistic expression – the so-called Romantic Movement.

A "Natural" Shift Occurs

During the 19th Century, the vehicle for sacred expression was found most often through the landscape and not through the repetition of old narrative models. Two artists stand out for the purity of their vision and their correlation of nature and Love: German painters Caspar David Friedrich (1774–1840) and Philipp Otto Runge (1777–1810). Both of these artists were pioneers in the use of nature for sacred expression. Friedrich's views of mountains and the sea with crosses or other shrines contained within them, or of monks carrying a coffin through the snow, are captivating images of nature and the purity of nature as a manifestation of the Divine. Runge, who died prematurely, likewise found a language of symbols through nature which had at its heart his belief that Love is the wellspring of all life and that the source of Love is the Divine.

This body of work had a powerful impact on later groups of artists, most notably the English Pre-Raphaelites, among whom William Holman Hunt (1827–1910) probably produced the most consistently religious subjects. His initial attempt to travel to the Holy Land was cut short, stranding him in Florence and leaving him widowed with a son he barely knew how to care for. But his commitment to re-envisioning the old sacred stories in new, highly realistic ways never faltered, and he ultimately produced some stunning masterpieces, of which *The Shadow of Death* in the Manchester City Galleries is probably the most famous. This painting shows the young Jesus, his arms stretched as though already crucified, turning his back to his mother as he stands in the doorway of his father's carpenter's shop.

In the 20th Century, nature herself, either directly or indirectly, remained the preferred metaphor for artists to express God's presence in the world – and it arguably remains the dominant theme to the present day. One need only consider the works of Thomas Cole (1801–1848), whose *Voyage of Life* series at the National Gallery of Art in Washington, DC, utilizes landscape to trace human development from childhood through death and delivery into God's eternity. While religious expression became more individual – not to mention sporadic – one can find unique and moving works from the hands of notable

The Shadow of Death
by William Holman Hunt

Resurrexit by Anselm Kiefer

artists like: Giacomo Manzu (1908–1991), who ranks among the best of the Italians and whose friendship with Pope John XXIII led to a number of Vatican commissions; and Salvador Dali (1904–1989), whose *Christ of Saint John of the Cross* at the Kelvingow Art Museum in Glasgow is one of the most original images of the crucifixion created in modern times.

A strong spiritual current also runs through the landscapes of German painter Anselm Kiefer (b. 1945), whose work deals with the aftermath of WWII, as well as broader issues of human existence. Keifer's interest in faith and religion is a factor that shapes his vision, as proven by a recent exhibition in 2007 of his work at the Louvre, which included a self-selected display of master drawings depicting sacred themes. Among his choices was an album containing 138 of Domenico Tiepolo's *New Testament* drawings which George Knox and I had reconstructed. Recently, numerous contemporary artists have started speaking in diverse visual voices, motivated by a deep spirituality. For some, the sacred is expressed in landscape, for some through abstraction, and for others in very literal expressions of a specific belief.

Art in the New Millennium

For most artists today, as for most individuals, expression of faith is a matter of personal choice. Indeed, contemporary art is moving in numerous directions all at the same time. Within the context of post-modern art, there appears to be little faith in the heroic potential of individual human beings, but a great faith and hope in our collective potential for righting wrongs.

Is the latest art indicative of another paradigm shift? A paradigm of spiritual unity as opposed to separateness and duality? This is difficult to say, since we are seeing so many branching currents and no single, powerful stream. What is fascinating, however, is that many artists today hold a fundamental belief in the good found in two very human and essential places: heart and spirit.

Having contemplated the meaning of life as expressed through art, I was touched to receive a letter last week from a friend who quoted John Keats. My friend wrote that nothing else matters except the "holiness of the heart's affections." For myself, I profoundly believe in that holiness. As I marvel at the miracle of existence each morning and my great fortune to be part of the art community, the abiding conclusion I reach is that creation – in some mystical and only partially understandable way – must be the product of a great act of Love. That is the anchor of my personal belief system; both logic and faith tell me that there is a Creator of all things and that Love itself is a product of that creation. Humanity's ability to create sacred art and explore the nature of God is a product of that perfect Love.

———◆———

In her essay, Heidi gives us a powerful glimpse into how art helps mold cultural and spiritual beliefs. She chose to focus on Christian art, but she could have written about Buddhist inspired art instead. The message remains the same: *Art reflects, impacts, and shapes spiritual paradigms.*

Almost without exception, artists are visionary. They access their own anxiety, hopes, and fears. Then, they tap into those same change agents that exist within their culture. In other words, they don't hide from the changes they see coming, they embrace the looming change – no matter how scary or unpredictable. As a result, artists are usually ahead of the curve, which means they foreshadow for us what is arising within the collective unconscious by depicting it in their literature, poetry, songs, dance, plays, movies, sculpture, paintings, and photography.

It will be interesting to observe the art produced during the remainder of the Great Cusp. I am no art historian or critic, but the art I have seen lately is far from depressing – it is exhilarating! Consider the work of Alex Grey (two paintings of his are included in this anthology). Consider also the spectacular artwork at Damanhur in Italy (a sample is included in Chapter X). If art intrinsically foresees and foretells shifts in the collective unconsciousness, then I am heartened by what I see. Already, great numbers of artists are preparing the way for the Love of the Fifth Spiritual Paradigm.

And now, it is time to get personal: *How are you handling the chaos and confusion of this Great Cusp?*

SADDHA

*Life of my life, I shall ever try to keep my body pure,
knowing thy living touch is upon all my limbs.*

*I shall ever try to keep all untruths out of my thoughts,
knowing thou art that truth which has kindled
the light of reason in my mind.*

*I shall ever try to drive all evils away from my heart
and keep my Love in flower,
knowing thou hast thy seat in the innermost shrine of my heart.*

*And it shall be my endeavor to reveal thee in my actions,
knowing it is thy power that gives me strength to act.*

Rabindranath Tagore (1861–1941), *Gitanjali*

In Eastern traditions, there exists a Sanskrit word which means inner faith or Love of oneself – *saddha* – a word for which there is no Western equivalent. Often, saddha is translated as "faith," but the word means so much more, as it connotes trustful confidence in oneself. *Saddha* also represents the first stage of a faith devotee or "stream-entry," since at this level of spiritual awareness the soul starts to transgress the illusions of the material plane.

Thus, to Love oneself is a critical step in the assumption of the highest experience and expression of Love. More to the point, one cannot consistently practice compassion nor realistically serve God until one has met and mastered the self – a graduation that is exceedingly difficult.

Hence, it is common at this juncture for the soul to get stuck, as the ego fervently clings to its former state. The ego senses its extinguishment and fights for survival by seeking a narcissistic plateau over true clarity. Yet, to proceed further yields the next prize: spiritual liberation.

EIGHT LESSONS ON THE ART OF SELF LOVE

By First Lady Elena Moreno

Self Love is an art. A visual artist begins the process of making a painting by stretching a canvas, preparing it with gesso, and sketching an image. Then, the artist applies under-layers and mid-layers of color, texture, and line before adding the final details which complete the work. Likewise, as a teacher of consciousness, I help my students build foundations that are strong enough to support a lifetime of creative choices and actions, a careful and strategic layering of Love. When my students begin this learning process, we start by creating a clean canvas of the heart and mind. The process requires the student to be open and free of preconceived notions.

If we look in a dictionary, what does it tell us about Love? Love is defined as "an intense feeling of deep affection." This definition is informative, but it doesn't actually help us to comprehend the full meaning of Love. Understanding Love requires us to find its fullest meaning and truth within ourselves. Like art, Love is the process and product of creative skill. No one can find Love for you. All a teacher can do is help a student chart a path that will lead to personal realizations. It is in the doing that you will know. Therefore, my contribution to Love is as a teacher to a student, like an artist to the canvas, building layers of color and texture on a canvas of human consciousness.

Many people tend to focus on romantic Love when, in fact, we Love in many unromantic ways: our Love of country, family, pets, and beliefs. In order to know Love, we have to explore it on all levels. It is not enough to look only at physical Love or the feelings of Love. We also must be prepared to reach Divine Love if we want to have a complete experience. Only by first understanding self and then reaching for the Divine are we able to discover the depth, breadth, nuance, and direct experience of Love.

The following essay is based on an eight-week course that I offer called *The Artful Process of Love*. I encourage the reader to make this more than an intellectual exercise. I invite you to participate as a student by completing the assignments provided at the end of each section. To begin, I suggest that you read the manuscript through once completely. Then, reread each section and complete each assignment. If possible, read and complete one section per week, just as if you were taking an eight-week course.

1. Love Is Gravity: The Power of Attraction

Love is gravity. In physics, gravity is defined as the force that attracts one body to another body having physical mass. At this mundane level, Love is attraction; it calls us to unite or bond with someone or something. For instance, a bee is attracted to a sweet smelling flower. Is that Love? In a strictly physical sense, it is. We experience this attraction all the time in varying degrees and on many levels: affection, desire, caring, agreement. Truly, Love takes on the guise of many forms.

In the beginning, we experience attraction quite innocently. A child prefers carrots to squash, or the red ball instead of the green one. Attraction manifests as the urge to play in water, to wear the strawberry colored dress, or to sleep only with the purple teddy bear. Thus, Love begins with small attractions that make us want to comb our hair in one way, arrange our room just so, and explore one career over another. Love opens with simple little preferences, but it ends up building an entire life. Each one of your choices becomes another contour that forms and ultimately defines your sculpture of self.

For most people, it is simple to choose Love but difficult to choose the *right* Love. It is fun to choose the most scrumptious dessert on the tray, but if you are trying to lose weight, the best choice may be no choice at all. Similarly, wanting too many things is as damaging as eating too much food. Material and emotional obesity can easily overwhelm the quality of our life and diminish our freedom. Consequently, attraction is the easy part, but mature Love requires discipline to choose appropriately. Our choices ultimately reveal who and what we are. Only experience will teach us about limits and show us how to handle the various personal attractions that we encounter throughout life.

Love is derived from the Sanskrit word *lubhyati*, which means "desire," and the Latin words *libet* (it is pleasing) and *libido* (desire). So, the original idea was that we Love something that gives us pleasure. The word *libido* also refers to sexual energy, although we now consider Love to be much more than the sex drive. Even so, Love is a force, a magnetic field. We succumb to that force field when we allow ourselves to move or be pulled toward the person or object of our attraction. We want to bond with it, make it a part of us, or become a part of it.

In this way, the nature of Love is both co-dependent and inter-dependent. Think about this: Does a bee take honey from a flower, or does the flower draw the bee so it can be pollinated? Does a man pursue a woman because he wants sex, or does a woman attract a man because she wants a baby? Indeed, Love is an inter-connected need that keeps us moving and producing to fulfill our various appetites.

It is said, "Love makes the world go around." Truly, it is *the* primary motivator. Consider that we do not eat exclusively to live and sustain ourselves. We also do not buy clothes merely to protect our bodies. We build elaborate houses and fill them with complex appliances, furnishings, and all sorts of "things" that supposedly give us pleasure and comfort. We live in a consumer society and our appetites are huge. But how many pairs of shoes do you need? How many tools and toys do you own? Do you feel good when you walk out of the store with the latest computer? Do you want the most exciting car? Do you possess your stuff or does your stuff possess you?

Assignment 1: *Take a good look at some of the things you "Love." Pay attention to what attracts you. Why do you buy one particular item over another? What types of items beckon you? Are you able to resist temptation or must you possess what you desire? Are you materially or emotionally obese? Write a poem about your desire for tangible objects.*

2. Love Defines: The Importance of Choice

Love defines, limits, prefers, excludes, and measures against itself. Love pulls us toward and at the same time moves us away from that which we seek. This is because any measurable form exists as a continuum between two opposite poles. For example, light and dark are opposite poles, and in between these polarities are varying degrees and shades of color. Just think of a thermometer that measures the ascending or descending degrees between cold and hot.

Ironically, Love and hate are essentially the same thing, only opposite extremes. Love's maximum expression is Divine Love. From this positive extreme, we gradually move by degrees toward its polar opposite – hate. In the middle, we find a neutral point with little force of attraction. However, as we pass the neutral midpoint and move toward the negative pole, Love gradually becomes less and less distinct until it finally devolves completely into hate.

Thus, if you know Love, you also know hate. Similarly, if you know what you Love, you also will be able to define what you hate. In essence, your poison and pleasure are one and the same. For example, the person you Love so ardently also has the power to generate hatred in you in direct proportion to the Love which they generate, discomfort in relation to comfort, and pain in relation to ecstasy. You have only to ask someone going through a divorce about this bi-polar phenomenon. Is Love the satisfaction you experience when you unite with your beloved, or is Love the pain you feel when denied the object of your Love? On this plane of existence, nature is expressed through duality. Everything has its opposite form, its opposite mate. When you see something manifest, you should be able to recognize its polar expression.

When we are born, we are undefined and free. Slowly, our preferences, attractions, and antipathies begin to characterize who we are. When we choose to embrace something, we are rejecting something else. Before long, a personal package of the "self" begins to emerge. For example, I worked with a woman named Susan who is the marketing director of a computer company and the mother of three children in Montessori school. Susan is Episcopalian, wears a size 8 dress, is semi-hip, lives in Manhattan, and boasts about her husband, who graduated from the Massachusetts Institute of Technology. Unfortunately, thirty-four year old Susan is no longer free. Her attachments now define her, even as they make her feel secure. Identifying labels now delineate her so thoroughly that she came to me in danger of losing her core self. She worried, "What would happen if I lose my job, balloon to a size 14, or divorce my husband?"

Like Susan, you may wish to break free or even destroy your packaging in order to evolve into a more authentic definition of your self. To do this, you must have a clear sense of who you are beneath and beyond all the style and hype. You must Love your self more than the labels and possessions which feed your ego. And you must be in a position to evaluate your past choices and identify which of them still serve your true values and principles.

What are your core values and principles? They are the organizing factors of your life. They help form who and what you are. One of the biggest self-deceptions is to say one thing and do another. The Native Americans have a saying: "Let your walk be your talk and your talk be your walk." For example, if you value thriftiness, you shouldn't buy a car you can't afford. If you care about the environment, you should live in a way that does not pollute or damage your community. If your choices fail to reflect your fundamental beliefs, you will be out of alignment with your core truth and you will experience psychological dissonance. Conversely, you become free when your values are clear and you take responsibility for your actions.

It takes courage to Love your self enough to make choices that are congruent with your core values and beliefs. Think about your standards. What are your core principles? Do your actions reflect your personal philosophy? Do you walk your talk? Remember, attraction is blind; it merely pulls. Just because something calls, you don't have to answer.

Assignment 2: *Meditate on your belief system. List the most important rules by which you live. What do you see when you remove all your attachments and labels ... is anyone there?*

3. Emotional Love: Love That Cares and Love That Desires

Attraction is physical, but if you pay attention, you will notice that the intensity of the attraction becomes charged with a different energy once your emotions are engaged. When attraction combines with emotions, Love moves to a different level, since emotions add complexity to attraction. Take a moment to think about what causes you to experience the following:

adoration	affection	appeal	attachment
caring	desire	devotion	egotism
envy	fascination	fear	fondness
friendship	gluttony	greed	jealousy
lust	passion	pride	sharing

All these feelings are generated by the ever-vigilant ego. The ego seeks to embrace those circumstances and objects that increase personal stature, and moves us away from those that decrease or diminish it. This is the primary function of ego. On the other hand, emotions also warn us of danger and alert us to opportunities that may lead to personal development and a heightened sense of self.

We can chart the extremes of emotional Love by placing self-less, compassionate Love at one end of our scale and self-serving, possessive Love at the other. This is the duality of emotional Love. Self-less Love is affection that is tender, sentimental, and generous. It Loves beauty and invites others to share. It shows appreciation and concern for the object of the affection. Such deep caring often motivates us to protect and defend the object of our affection, even at our own expense. The focus is not on taking but on giving and sharing.

By way of contrast, self-ish Love is about taking for the benefit of oneself. It covets and craves to fulfill its own needs. It strives to possess beauty and may take advantage of others to realize its objectives. Such desire-based Love comes in packages both large and small. It may take the form of Ben and Jerry's ice cream or a million dollar house. It also compels us to risk and fight for the object of our yearning. Attraction combined with narcissistic emotions is not a simple matter of being drawn toward something or someone; instead, it is a revved-up machine with an engine fueled by passion. This is when desire may compel us to buy something we cannot afford or to feel jealous of others. Appetites may be sparked by advertising, style, or the politics of the moment. The media also pressures us to conform. If everyone has "it," I must Love "it" too. Additionally, cravings are stirred when our instinctive fight, flight, or sexual antennae are activated. And if our appetites go unsatisfied, we may feel anger, anxiety, envy, or resentment.

Desire, just like positive attraction, does not think. On the contrary, the ego demands immediate satisfaction. So, how do you overcome such base feelings? By establishing a connection to the rational mind and spirit. Take time to think and make a plan of action. Avoid rash action. Do something physical or creative to pull yourself away from your emotions, such as exercising or going to the movies. Also, take positive steps to reinforce those things that make you feel good about your self. Most importantly, find ways to avoid situations that make you feel uncomfortable or threatened. Let your values be the litmus test for your actions. If what you want doesn't measure up to what you believe is right, change your course of action.

Assignment 3: *Think about what causes you to experience particularly strong emotional states. Ask yourself, "What is my ego trying to accomplish?" Do pleasant emotions encourage you to move toward an experience or person? Do unpleasant feelings make you cautious or cause you to avoid some situations or people? Look at your life and try to make some distinctions between incidences of attraction, appetite, affection, and desire. Observe how you reacted to these very different experiences of Love.*

4. Higher Love: Spiritual Love of Family, Friends, and Self

The Love that we have discussed so far is connected to our physical and emotional self – our ego and personality. Yet, there is another level of Love that surpasses personal attractions and emotions. This is the spiritual Love that we often feel for our friends and family. Usually, we feel detached from strangers, but with family and friends we are able to develop an authenticity that precludes masks, judgments, and fear. Our familiarity, common backgrounds, shared experiences, and mutual beliefs with friends and family help us to form intimate bonds and reciprocal life models. Love at this level leads to intimacy.

Even so, there are two sides to Love relationships with family and friends. In my case, I feel a deep and unalterable affection for my loved ones that is beyond measure, unconditional. This Love is deep within my soul and I would sacrifice my life for them. On the other hand, in my everyday relationship with them, I have expectations. Consequently, my family may disappoint, infuriate, amaze, or frustrate me. Sometimes I do not even like my children! I also can get angry with my siblings and friends. Yet, no matter how much my friends and family hurt me or how angry I get with them, deep inside my heart I maintain a spiritual Love for them.

Surprisingly, this Love is not sentimental in nature. Rather, it is connected, intimate, safe, and self-affirming. Loving this way always makes one feel like a larger human being. It also gives others permission to express their Love for you. It is a powerful blessing to share your self with others and show unconditional Love for them. Such Love is like the wind – an invisible force that we perceive in dancing leaves and billowing clouds. We see it in a tender smile, a warm embrace, a passionate kiss, and a farewell tribute for a loved one who has died. Love is an energy that must flow if it is to unite with others; only then does it truly become manifest.

Moreover, everyone needs to know that they are lovable. Unfortunately, we often wait for a sign from the other person before we show our Love. We do this because we are afraid of not getting a mutual response. But we should not wait for the other person to act first. I encourage you to overcome your fears and make the first move because the corresponding rewards of Love exceed any risk.

Just as importantly, you need to feel unconditional Love for your self. When you Love your self, you are both the lover and the beloved. Self Love insists that your behavior be impeccable, that your work be excellent, and that you live with integrity. Love of self does not allow violence in its name, nor does it abuse others. To develop a culture of personal Love, one must be respectful of self and others. And stop being so hard on yourself! Accept compliments. Do not contaminate your personal perception of who you are by surrendering to the pessimism of self-doubt, insecurity, or fear. One of the key elements of self Love is forgiving your mistakes and learning the lessons of life. Everything you need to know about Love is already within you. You just need to trust your self enough to listen to the voice of your heart.

Assignment 4: *We not only forget to Love our self, we also forget to tell our family and friends how much they mean to us. Be a good spouse, parent,* *son or daughter, sibling, and friend. Reconnect with the people you Love. Be affectionate and tell them you Love them. Express your gratitude for the special things they have done for you, the sacrifices they have made on your behalf. Also, be loving with your self. Do something special that will reinforce your sense of self worth. Learn to accept compliments with a simple "thank you," and learn to listen to criticism with an honest ear and optimistic heart.*

5. Romantic Love/Erotic Love

Now, let us look at romantic Love and erotic relationships. So far, we have explored four levels of Love: material Love, emotional Love, spiritual Love of our intimates, and Love of self. So, you may wonder: Where do romantic Love and erotic Love fit in? Actually, they can impact all levels. Up to this point, we have been talking about Love from a singular perspective – yours. But when we look at a romantic relationship, there are two points of view and sets of expectations. The other person may be approaching Love on a different level and may have a completely different perspective on how to Love.

Let us imagine that a woman meets a man at a party. He is good looking, but what really attracts her is his humor and apparent sensitivity. He finds her sexy, so he tries to make her feel comfortable. They decide to go on a date. So, what is the magnetic pull? Are we talking about physical appetites, emotional needs, or spiritual union?

Let's assume that the woman wants a light evening of conversation, while the man is entertaining erotic fantasies. In such a case, each person has a different agenda: she is attracted on the emotional level but he is attracted on the physical. Although these two people are not exactly polarized, it will be hard for them to make a strong connection because at this point in the relationship, they share no common ground. So what happens when they go on their date? Let's assume that she begins to find him sexually attractive and he begins to see her as more than a conquest. Now, they will start to connect. If they pursue the relationship further, they may eventually experience a deep spiritual union and develop a profound Love for one another.

I have observed that partners who do not share at least two mutual points of attraction rarely stay together. It is even worse when two people miss all points of connection, as in our earlier scenario, where the woman approached the relationship from a point of emotional need, and the man acted on the point of physical attraction.

Let us put this into a formula: Point 1 is a physical connection; Point 2 is an emotional connection; and Point 3 is a spiritual connection. A relationship that is purely physical will connect two people on Point 1. Likewise, a purely emotional relationship will connect two people on Point 2. And a spiritual connection will connect them on Point 3. However, people often are attracted to each other for different reasons. In the previous example, the woman was an emotional Point 2 trying to connect to a man who was a physical Point 1. Even if they share intercourse, their interior realities are separate – no real connection will take place. It's like two people on an elevator: one person gets off at the 1st floor and the other gets off at the 2nd floor. They're in the same building, but they won't find each other. But you may ask, "they slept together – how could they not be intimates?" My answer is that intercourse does happen between strangers, as in mercenary transactions with prostitutes, the misfortune of date rapes, and fleeting one-night stands.

It is possible, however, to establish a robust emotional and spiritual two-point connection without a physical connection. A couple might also establish a two-point connection on the physical and spiritual levels. Both of these relationships are "working" but they are not complete. It takes a full three-point connection – on the physical, emotional, and spiritual levels – for true union to take place. Only then does the possibility of true romantic Love exist.

When we partner with another human being, we are making energetic contact. When we are in relationship with more than one person at one time, the energies become very confusing, especially if one or both partners are having sex with others. This sexual mingling is particularly disconcerting for a woman because when she has sex, the male deposits energy within her. When you sleep with someone, you share energy with his or her prior sexual partners. Think about it! Take personal responsibility for your life and be careful not to mix energies unknowingly. And it is not just a question of the prevention and spread of communicable diseases. Emotions also can contaminate. Emotions are energy and come in all flavors – dark to light, painful to joyful, active to passive. Each of us, in fact, is a collage of emotions. When we have sex with someone, we not only leave physical residue, we exchange particles of emotion and leave our psychic imprints on our partner. Unfortunately, that imprint can be toxic. I strongly suggest that you avoid the confusion generated by having sex with more than one person at a time.

If you are having a relationship with someone other than your primary partner, it is best to separate while you explore this other union; otherwise, you will never have clarity about either partner or your self … neither will you find or know true Love. Take time to understand your relationship and your true goals. My Mother used to tell me, "If you are buying apples and he is selling oranges, don't settle for oranges, expecting that he will suddenly start selling apples." In sum, you need to understand the significance of shared objectives, needs, and expectations. Relationships need connection, common ground, and the dimension that comes from developing a holistic partnership at all levels.

Assignment 5: *Take time to reflect on your romantic relationship. How can you make your union more complete? Think about how you and your partner connect with each other. Review your connections on the three points and think of ways to better balance your relationship.*

6. Rebuilding Love: Searching for Gravity

How do we rebuild a relationship that is in conflict or struggling? Even good partnerships can become problematic and stale. The physical and emotional components of Love are part of the physical reality, so they are subject to change. The good news, though, is that you can build something new out of the old. All is in flux, so you can vibrate from bad to good. It also is important not to hold onto a passing reality. If you allow for growth and evolution, relationships can expand, transform, and become stronger – especially if the spiritual component has remained viable. Spiritual Love is the exception to the rule: It is not subject to conditions. It just is.

A new study by the Japanese National Institute for Psychological Sciences has found that compliments stimulate the same pleasure centers in the brain as do financial rewards. Praise is particularly seductive if you are feeling unappreciated. We all thrive on attention. If your partner seems distant and disinterested and the bond between you becomes weak, you may be tempted to insist that your partner change his or her behavior. The reality is that only you can control how you feel. You cannot depend on anyone else to make you happy or solve your problems. If you see a problem, you need to fix it.

Perhaps your partner does not realize that there is a problem. So, where do you begin? You begin at the beginning. Go back and find the original "gravity" in your relationship, and reconnect with what attracted you to your partner in the first place. Second, both you and your partner need to give the relationship time and attention. Third, both of you have to put focused energy into an agreed-upon plan of action. For whatever reason, one or both of you closed down or dimmed your attraction to the other. You have to reopen what is now closed. To be successful, you must explore why it happened. Do you know why? Can you talk about it with your partner?

Once you identify the problem, you need to deal with it on the appropriate level. A physical problem requires a physical solution, an emotional problem requires an emotional solution, and a spiritual problem requires a spiritual solution. For example, if you need your partner to give you more quality time, his gift to you of a diamond tennis bracelet will not help. What you need is an intimate weekend trip that will inspire conversation and closeness. A crisis that cuts across all levels of the relationship, such as infidelity, requires an attack on all levels. I do not mean to suggest that every problem can be solved. Nevertheless, if you work with the best in your self and the best in your partner and you also bring forth solutions for change, then each day will be better and, with time, a new rapport will emerge.

Any plan that you formulate must include attention, availability, and communication. You may have to slow down other areas of your life and make the partnership your priority. Pay attention to your partner and give each other positive and encouraging signals. Tell each other what you want so that you can satisfy each other's needs. And tell your partner how much you miss not being close. Most importantly, let your partner know how much you enjoy the physical and sexual part of the relationship. Find ways to play and laugh with each other again. Be a good friend. Be openly erotic. Be a sacred companion.

A spiritual Love is beyond the whims of change. Even so, sometimes ego can dominate the Love you feel for your partner. Maybe your ego feels threatened, so it needs to reestablish its individuality. It is all about your sense of self. You may storm around doing things to show that you are your own person. You may proclaim, "I'll do it my self, thank you!" I asked one of my students how she and her partner acted out their anger. She told me, "He goes into his cave and I freeze him out. I stop doing little things for him. We withdraw from each other but, eventually, we miss each other. We become so unhappy not being together that we finally overcome our egos and make up." So, be aware when ego enters the relationship.

One last thing: Try using intuition to work out bumps in your relationship. I have observed that when people have been together a long time and are sexually active, not only do they exchange energy on physical and emotional levels, their spirits also become entwined. It is as though each partner's inner wisdom is connected. Take advantage of this special awareness. Put yourself in your partner's place and intuit what your partner wants or needs. This requires quiet time, thought, meditation, and prayer. Then, you will see your relationship from a different perspective, get the bigger picture. When there is a problem, do not blame your partner; instead, seek the grace to change yourself. You may be surprised to see your partner change as well.

Assignment 6: *Look for ways to renew your relationship and put into practice some of the suggestions in this section. Reflect on your relationship at the different levels, using meditation and prayer. Write a Love letter, story, or poem to illustrate what your partner means to you.*

7. Unconditional Love

Earlier, we talked about the spiritual Love that we feel for friends and family. Let us take some time to examine the roots of this deep communion. In order for us to understand true unconditional Love, we need to gain insight into the fundamental composition of the spirit body. Consequently, I find it helpful to look at our perceptions of God, as spiritual belief systems highlight the differences between the human and the Divine. Our spiritual beliefs also help us to connect with and share many extraordinary features of the Divine with others.

Different religions and philosophic schools refer to God as Allah, the Creator, the Absolute, the Supreme Force, the All. However, no matter what name you wish to use, the reality is that God is unknowable. We cannot say with certainty who, how, or what God is or is not. Even if we could know God, our attempts to use our finite language to explain the Infinite would surely fail. Personally, I do not think humans can fathom the vastness of God; however, we may infer some of God's attributes. Three words, in particular, come to my mind: omnipotent, omniscient, and omnipresent. *God can do anything. God knows everything. God is everywhere.* These are what I call the three "omnis." Additionally, I think there are four relevant attributes that we can acknowledge. God is immortal, eternal, absolute, and unchangeable. This means that God was not born and will never die. God is timeless. God is complete. And God will never change.

How do these Divine attributes compare to how we behave on this plane? We are mortal, so we are born and we will die. We have bodies, so we face physical limitations. We are still evolving and, therefore, we are incomplete and subject to error. And our Universe is subject to change. In sum, we need specific conditions to sustain ourselves: food, shelter, water, sun, air. But God does not depend on anything because God is everything. There is nothing that is not God.

The essence of my point is this: When we experience unconditional Love, it too is immortal, eternal, absolute, and unchanging. Unconditional Love expresses Divine qualities. On the other hand, mundane Love is connected with ego and expressions of separateness. It is the car you desire or the cute puppy you adore. These are the kinds of fluid, material, emotional attractions and infatuations that we experience in daily life. Such ordinary attraction is very different than spiritual Love because true unconditional Love takes place on a higher plane of consciousness.

The expression of this Love is beyond the petty emotions of daily life. Our human side is always present, but unconditional Love is connected to the Divine. And it flows from a union with the divinity in the other person. When you Love someone at this level, you place no conditions on him or her. You have no need to conquer or possess the beloved. This very special Love does not restrict, limit, or require anything from the other person. This Love is pure.

At this point, let us do a little review. Do you see the distinctions between personality and spirit? Do you understand that ego and self-condemnation change how we Love? Do you see how unconditional Love is independent of changing circumstances? Is it fair to say that the affection which stems from the physical and emotional levels is fluid, while the Love which is played out on the spiritual level is steadfast and true?

Assignment 7: *I encourage you to think about the people you Love unconditionally. Pay attention to how unique and precious these relationships are. Respond to this question: Are you capable of extending unconditional Love to a complete stranger?*

8. Divine Love

In the last segment, I asked if you could Love a stranger unconditionally. Recently, I put the same question to a student who gave me the following response:

> *Your question about unconditional Love for a stranger caused me to really pause and think. I thought about people risking their lives in war and natural disasters. I wondered what is this all about? How can they be so heroic? What compels a soldier to give his life to save his buddies, or Mother Teresa devoting her whole life to the poor people of India? Then, I thought of Christ and how he sacrificed himself for others and I wondered, "Is this what Divine Love is all about? Is this that higher Love? Is Love for a stranger that kind of thing?"*

Earlier, we discussed how Love can be based on attraction, desire, affection, or sentimental feelings related to personal fulfillment. After that, we discussed the special or spiritual Love sometimes called *agape*, which is completely self-less. Unconditional Love is the giving over of the personal self in favor of the God self. It is a heroic Love that loves everyone deeply – even a stranger. Love is about coming together, uniting, dissolving boundaries. I believe that deep within we have an intrinsic understanding that we are one with everyone and everything. If true, it means that if I save you, I also save myself. When we have that powerful realization of "Oneness," we overcome the interest of ego. Our heart conquers the rationality of intellect. This profound Love gives without thought of self. Divine Love is ours once we defeat the ego, practice unconditional Love, and unite with the All.

The sacrifice of the self is the cornerstone of Divine Love. The word "sacrifice" comes from the Latin word *sacer*, which literally means to make holy or sacred. When we offer ourselves to others, it is a holy or sacred act. Have you ever done something for someone without expectation of reward? Have you ever given service or made a sacrifice for a stranger? Sentimental Love is about your feelings, your satisfaction, and your ego. But when you Love on a Divine level, it is impersonal and unsentimental. In fact, you surrender the self for the beloved. As a result, there is a coming together – a communion. This is the poetry of the purest Love. Truly, ethereal Love is beyond words.

Before our Universe was created, all matter, all energy, everything that exists today was joined together in one unfathomably dense mass. Then, the Big Bang occurred ... the mass exploded ... and our astounding and expanding Universe was created. There is a shared memory of that original state of unity. When we collectively come together, we go back to our roots – Eden, our Divine commonality.

Thus, Divine Love is spacious and encompassing because it is no longer about you. It is about all of nature. We connect with everything – from the most beautiful to the most horrid manifestations of life. We are the Universe and the Universe is us. We are in God and God is within each of us. This is unequivocal Love and it opens us to the endless possibilities of life.

In this way, Divine Love changes our very perception of self, of being. I cannot help but wonder: If unity is our natural state, why is it so difficult to stay connected to Divine Love? Perhaps it is because we have become accustomed to being separate. We have become so used to protecting our individual self that we hold onto the defensive limits of our ego. I think it requires a deliberate act of will to dissolve the boundaries of our personality and allow Spirit to come through. It is difficult to know this kind of Love. You cannot detect it through your senses. You will only know it with your heart and your soul.

When I am in church, at temple, or in meditation, I experience a yearning, a painful state of longing. It is not "religious" in nature, but a deep need within my soul to connect with the Great Mystery of God. Meditation and prayer bring relief. The pettiness of my life fades into the background and, at the same time, everything seems clearer to me. I feel limitless, free, and full. My Spirit connects with the Spirit of God and the Divine fills and transforms every particle of my being. This Love is rooted deep within my heart, but it is not hidden. Like a flowering plant, I bloom with the beauty of Divine color, fragrance, and form. I connect with God. I hope that you have experienced this state of being as well.

Assignment 8: *Now, for your final assignment. Review your answers to the previous seven lessons and write down why you should fall in Love with life itself. A dear friend once told me, "Love is the question and Love is the answer." Contemplate this statement and explain to your self why you are a perfect manifestation of Love.*

So, there you have it: The Artful Process of Love in one essay! I have tried to build a foundation of solid ground for you to stand on after stripping away the layers – peeling the onion of the self. I hope it has helped you to acknowledge Love, experience the gratitude of Love, and validate your Love of self and others. It is now up to you to accept the qualities of Love in your self and acknowledge the value of higher states of spiritual Love. It is up to you whether to explore Love on your own.

Please remember that Love is always within you. Love births self and self births Love. It does not depend on anyone else. In all ways and at all times, become Love.

In this chapter, we will explore ourselves in more detail. The Love lens will focus inward. Elena's essay is a wonderful start, as it identifies the various ways in which we Love, guiding us upward on the Love continuum. As we shall see, proper Love of self is a necessary precursor to the more advanced stages of Love.

With chaos and change in the air, it will be more important than ever to practice introspection. Ask yourself: *How am I doing so far in handling the Great Cusp?* This chapter will help you access your higher self. Such self-inquiry, self-discipline, and self-acceptance will be necessary if you wish to meaningfully participate in the Fifth Spiritual Paradigm.

AIN'T I A WOMAN?

By Sojourner Truth
(1797–1883)

I want to say a few words about this matter. I am a [sic] woman's rights. I have as much muscle as any man, and can do as much work as any man. I have plowed and reaped and husked and chopped and mowed, and can any man do more than that?

I have heard much about the sexes being equal. I can carry as much as any man and can eat as much too, if I can get it. I am as strong as any man that is now. As for intellect, all I can say is, if a woman have a pint, and a man a quart – why can't she have her little pint full? You need not be afraid to give us our rights for fear we will take too much – for we can't take more than our pint'll hold.

The poor men seems to be all in confusion, and don't know what to do. Why children, if you have woman's rights, give it to her and you will feel better. You will have your own rights, and they won't be so much trouble.

I can't read, but I can hear. I have heard the *Bible* and have learned that Eve caused man to sin. Well, if woman upset the world, do give her a chance to set it right side up again. The lady has spoken about Jesus, how he never spurned woman from him, and she was right. When Lazarus died, Mary and Martha came to him with faith and Love and besought him to raise their brother. And Jesus wept and Lazarus came forth. And how came Jesus into the world? Through God who created him and the woman who bore him. Man, where was your part?

But the women are coming up, blessed be God, and a few of the men are coming up with them. But man is in a tight place: the poor slave is on him, woman is coming on him. He is surely between a hawk and a buzzard.

This speech was given by Sojourner Truth in May 1851 at the Women's Rights Convention in Akron, Ohio. It was recorded by Marcus Robinson, who attended the meeting and worked with Truth. Robinson published this version of the speech in the *Anti-Slavery Bugle* on June 21, 1851, just one month after Truth spoke.

However, the above rendition is not the same as the legendary "Ain't I a Woman?" speech recorded by suffragette Frances Gage and recited in most history books. Gage was the organizer of the convention and embellished Truth's speech by, among other things, adding a crude Southern dialect, even though Truth spoke with a Dutch accent (she didn't learn English until she was ten years old). Gage's speech also has Truth lamenting her thirteen children who were sold into slavery; however, Truth had five children.

Gage's erroneous version of the speech first appeared in the *New York Independent* on April 23, 1863 (twelve years after Truth spoke). And in 1881, Gage published her version again in *The History of Woman Suffrage*, which she co-authored with Susan B. Anthony. Here is a small sample of the more famous, but false, oratory:

> *Wall, chilern, whar dar is so much racket dar must be somethin' out o' kilter. I tink dat 'twixt de niggers of de Souf and de womin at de Nork, all talkin' 'bout rights, de white men will be in a fix pretty soon. But what's all dis here talkin 'bout?*

Truth's real name was Isabella Bomefree. She and her youngest daughter, Sophia, escaped their owner in 1826, just one year before slavery was abolished in their home state of New York. In 1843, she changed her name to Sojourner Truth because she said God had given her a mission: to travel the land speaking the truth. In 1864, while the Civil War still raged, Truth met with President Abraham Lincoln to discuss her life's work: abolition, women's rights, prison reform, and the end of capital punishment. Once, Truth was threatened with imprisonment herself, to which she reportedly declared that if put in jail, she would "make this nation rock like a cradle."

Sojourner Truth attained a level of self-awareness and self-confidence that is truly amazing, especially considering the limitations of her era due to her skin color and her gender. She is a testament to the soul's innate, fierce drive toward self-determination and self-expression. Let us follow Truth's example and learn Love of self – a state of acceptance and being to which we all may aspire. And like Truth, may each of us find our life mission.

Sojourner Truth

FINDING YOUR LIFE MISSION

By Henry Reed, Ph.D.

Do you remember when the popular media started to write about angels? Maybe you saw a book on angels or an announcement about a TV special. If you can remember, what was your reaction to the growing popularity of angels?

For me, the recognition struck when I was in the checkout line of the grocery store and I saw a picture of an angel on a weekly news magazine. Angels were the cover story that week. To see angels appearing in the popular media, I rejoiced. It wasn't just that I was pleased that the rest of the world was getting savvy. And it wasn't so much that I was applauding the miracle of angels, although in a way, I suppose I was. My focus was on angels as perfect messengers – the idea that angels can take us somewhere that others have tried but failed to do.

One thing that makes angels perfect messengers of intuitive reality is that they have the advantage of familiarity. There is a tradition for them: *They exist in all religious cultures.* Another thing going for angels is that they have a face, a personality. So angels put a friendly face on the invisible realm. Whereas many "New Age" concepts are frightening to some people, full of mystery and potential unknown danger, angels are familiar and friendly. They are not diabolical, they are not alien, and they are not pervasive invisibilities – like force fields – that are hard for the average mind to comprehend.

The idea of the existence of angels takes us into the realm of intuition because they provide a way for us to have a relationship with intuitive reality. They give us a handle on another dimension that we cannot otherwise touch. And they provide a bridge to a place we cannot otherwise go. As such, they are messengers of knowledge that we cannot otherwise understand.

The Intuitive Popularity of Finding Your Mission in Life

In a similar way, I am pleased to see the interest in the notion of "life mission." More and more people are pondering their soul's purpose. Even corporations, the current arbiters of shared social reality, compose "mission statements." I bet you have thought about your mission in life. Do you remember when this thought first occurred to you: *I wonder if my life has a special purpose?*

Like focusing on angels, paying attention to one's mission in life is another way in which intuitional reality is finally being embraced by our culture. There is something about the concept of "mission in life" that now is acceptable to us. It's pretty obvious, on the face of it, why we would ponder our life mission. Yet, it still is not obvious to some people, due to the materialistic culture that promotes logical, cause-and-effect reasoning, instead of intuitive linkages.

Our standard cultural model of the human being holds that each person is endowed with certain talents or potential skills and that these abilities should be actualized in accordance with society's needs – thereby matching what you have to offer to what the marketplace wants. Perhaps a series of tests, combined with a market analysis, could yield a statistically favorable match-up between your talents and current market trends. Certainly, that concept of life mission would be acceptable, even laudable, to our mechanistic culture.

Yet, the idea that we each came here with a purpose – a mission that is something inborn and which seeks fulfillment – goes beyond our typical thinking. It is becoming a popular idea because it speaks to people in a fundamental way. And like an angel, the concept of life mission becomes a vanguard, a diplomat, a messenger, that helps us form a relationship with something that might otherwise go unnoticed.

The Practical Side of Intuition

These days, the practical side of intuition is receiving a lot of attention. In fact, the source for much of the intuition research has come from the business world. Although the world of corporations and high finance may seem quite removed from the fluid world of New Age metaphysics, big business invests substantial resources and time into perfecting intuition. They don't want to make trusting intuition a matter of luck. They want to know what they are doing!

Consequently, to the businessperson, intuition is a practical matter. As the world becomes more complex and change is the only constant, planning and decision making become even more difficult. Rational analysis often fails. By the time a business analyzes all the pertinent facts, the world has moved and the facts have changed. As I heard one businessperson lament, "How do you keep your eye on the ball when it is moving at the speed of light?"

At the first international convention of the Global Intuition Network, held in Hawaii a few years back, a representative from the International Institute of Management in Geneva, Switzerland, presented the results of that prestigious think tank's analysis of the role of intuition in business. Through interviews and other case-study methods, they concluded that intuition has three major roles in business: The first is to get a vision; the second is to determine a starting point to achieve that vision; and the third is to make decisions at choice points along the way to manifest the vision.

For the purpose of identifying a life mission, these three questions can be translated as follows: What mountain shall I climb? Where shall I begin my journey? And when I reach a crossroad, which path shall I take? Even more to the point, this model begs the intuitive questions: What kind of life is worth living? How can I get started? And what choices do I make along the way to bring harmony to my life?

Therefore, intuition plays a huge role in discovering and enjoying a life mission. Intuition is that special ingredient that gives a mission its extraordinary appeal, its inspirational focus, and its promise of something transcendent. Identifying a life mission is more than crafting a job description. It has something to do with the nature of the soul, and it requires intuition to be realized.

Finding Your Magic Elephant

When I was a youth, I used to enjoy watching a TV show about a boy who lived in the jungle in India. I don't remember the name of the show anymore, nor the name of the boy, but let's call him "Jungle Boy." I remember that the show's sponsor was Buster Brown Shoes, and at breaks in the show, they ran shoe commercials. The ads featured a special X-ray device that revealed how your toes fit within the shoes when you were trying them on. Several times when my Mom took me to Buster Brown's, I got to try out that machine and see my toes through the shoes.

The reason I liked the show so much was that it showed how Jungle Boy lived. He was orphaned and had no parents, so he was a free agent within the jungle. He had an elephant for a companion. I don't remember the elephant's name either, so let's call him "Rama." Rama was the key to Jungle Boy's ability to thrive in the jungle without adult support. Jungle Boy would ride around on top of Rama and, whenever there was a problem, Rama would save the day. If Jungle Boy got into a life-threatening predicament, such as being cornered by a wild beast, Rama would come to the rescue. If Jungle Boy encountered bad guys, again, Rama would emerge to protect Jungle Boy. Rama also guided Jungle Boy to treasures, helped him find food, and generally acted as an ambassador to the jungle, making Jungle Boy perfectly safe and at home in the wilds like no other human in the show.

In contrast to that pleasant fantasy life, reality gradually imposed itself upon my world. Do you remember the first time you thought about what you would do when you "grew up?" I remember. It was a rude awakening that came one day in junior high school. The teacher got out a chart that listed professions and careers. We were to choose one. What did we want to be when we grew up? A doctor, a lawyer, a baker, a fireman? You get the idea.

The list was long and I studied it for a long time. I couldn't find a listing for cowboy. I couldn't find anything that seemed like fun – certainly nothing like the life Jungle Boy led. So as I went over the list from top to bottom, searching for something that I would like, panic began to rise: *What was I to do?* Nothing on the list appealed to me. What would become of me if I did not fit into what society had available? Would I be left out?

In college things went well for a couple of years, and then I ran into some trouble. I became obsessed with what I would do after college. I was a math major, and although I enjoyed my schoolwork, the idea of making a living at math was not attractive. For a summer job, I went to the East Coast to work as an actuary in a large insurance company. I hated it! I returned to college in the fall in a real predicament. What was I to do? My work in math began to suffer, and I fell into a mid-life crisis at the tender age of twenty!

One of my teachers noticed that I wasn't my usual self and referred me to the college counselor. The counselor gave me tests to determine what I'd be good at and would enjoy. The tests indicated that I should pursue a professional career of some sort. He wondered, based upon my scores, "Had I ever considered being a psychologist?"

Have you ever received a suggestion that really clicked inside – the click that happens when you realize the idea was inside you all along, just waiting to be noticed? When my counselor said the word "psychologist" I heard bells ringing ... literally! I heard a cascade of bells ringing and felt a flash of happiness. Later that summer, I experienced my first psychological "self-insight." I began to gobble psychology books with ease, and my mind filled and thrilled with the various concepts I was learning.

Have you ever experienced a moment when you felt really at home with yourself? Have you ever noticed when you were naturally "following your bliss?" Have you ever found yourself so connected with what you were doing in the moment that you felt you were doing what you were meant to do?

These peak experiences are what researchers recognize as moments of intrinsic meaning. We do something for the joy of doing it, not for the reward it may bring, because doing it is reward in itself. These tasks are intrinsically inspirational. When we do them, we slip into our "flow," where everything seems to work out on its own, naturally, and without effort. There is a "meant to be" quality about such experiences, and we sense the "meaning in life" by doing them. At these moments, something deep within us has a chance to come out and participate with what is going on around us. Intuition and external reality melt into a combined experience of meaning and significance. Think about how many of these moments you have had in your life. Your own intuitive wisdom was responsible for those remarkable synchronistic moments.

Now that I had found my flow, I started exploring consciousness, meditation, and dreams. It was my dream studies that would eventually make a difference in my life, although I didn't know it at the time. Also, a friend inspired me with his dreams. His dreams were different from the kind we were learning about in graduate school. At that time, during the late 1960s, dreams were viewed as something like medical samples – something best viewed by experts in a lab, not something the public could comprehend. But my friend used his dreams to guide his life, without the aid of a professional's diagnosis. I was impressed, and asked him where he learned to dream like that. He told me about a psychic named Edgar Cayce, and he suggested that I create a dream diary.

Like your first encounter with angels, do you remember the first time you thought dreams might have value? What image have you formed about the power of your dreams? Do you think your dreams can help you zero in on your life mission?

My Life Mission Begins

When I graduated from UCLA with my Ph.D., I became a psychology professor at Princeton University. Yet, I was leading a dual life. On the one hand, I was learning how to play the university game and finding security in the academic world. But I also was studying my dreams and learning how to find messages from my higher self. I began to view my dreams as a compass, a pair of infra-red glasses, a super telescope, a crystal ball.

Isn't that what a lot of us do? On the outside, we try to appear "normal," but on the inside, in our private moments, we live a secret life of the crazy "real" person that we are. Is there any way to bring these two lives together? And how do you balance security vs. creativity? People talk about having a secure job, but such security can be a prison. People are wistful about having a creative life, but creativity involves exploring the unknown and having a relationship with uncertainty. It takes real courage to follow your bliss.

I spent a sabbatical semester away from Princeton at the C. G. Jung Institute's Sleep and Dream Laboratory in Zurich, Switzerland. While there, I helped design new types of lab experiments involving humanistic interactions with research subjects. And I made the acquaintance of Charles Thomas Cayce, Edgar Cayce's grandson. I become a member of the research advisory board for the Association for Research and Enlightenment in Virginia Beach (ARE), and I later taught a youth program on dreams at the ARE summer camp. At camp, I developed a "dream tent" to help kids have special dreams. It was a great success. The kids were having inspirational dreams, healing dreams, out-of-body experiences, and past life recall in the dreams.

When I returned to Princeton, I wrote up my research in the form of a scholarly article and submitted it for publication to the *Journal of Humanistic Psychology*. It was immediately accepted by the editor with no revision required – a rare honor. But when I showed the article to the chairman of the psychology department, he was upset that I had used no hard numbers in my research. Instead, I had advocated the use of symbolic ritual to tap into deep, spiritual levels of the dreaming mind. I thought I was opening an entirely new approach to science, but instead I was accused of not being "scientific." As a result, my contract at Princeton was not renewed.

Shaken but undaunted, I continued to work with ARE by creating a home-study dream project for its membership. This dream project led to the development of a publication devoted to my dream work. Moreover, my own dreams were taking me into an exploration of the meaning of "community." The concept had external meaning for me, in terms of getting along with others, cooperation in getting things done, and collaboration in the creative process. However, the concept of community also had internal meaning, in terms of finding ways for the various parts of myself to work together, such as merging my intuition with my burgeoning expertise in the relevance of dreams.

For example, I started having dreams about "Sundance" as a way of enhancing creativity in community. I knew nothing about this term, and was intrigued to discover that there was a Native American ceremony called the

Sun Dance. How did this come to me in my dreams? The Sun Dance is a community ritual designed to meet the needs of the tribe. The theme of the ceremony is integrating the "many and the one" – *mitakuye oyasin* in the language of the Lakota. Edgar Cayce would express it by saying that each individual is unique yet one with the whole. So I incorporated the word in a new dream periodical: *Sundance: The Community Dream Journal*. The creation of this magazine sparked the national "Dreamwork Movement" that brought dreams to the attention of the public, removed their stigma as mere medical samples, and helped dreams become accepted as a natural personal resource.

Thus, it seemed that my inner and outer lives were coming together. Maybe the secret was that I was working within a spiritual community, a place where people accept you just as you are. During that time, I also was invited to address young people about career development. It was at this juncture of my life that my childhood Love of Jungle Boy came flooding back to me. I realized that Jungle Boy and his elephant provided a vehicle that enabled me to venture into the unknown and go where my parents could not guide nor accompany me. My dreams, quite literally, led me to found the Dreamwork Movement – my life mission.

I had found a match between my gifts and society's needs. I was good at nurturing creativity in others and well suited to editing a journal on dreams. I fulfilled my own vision about dreams and I was helping others gain confidence in their own dreamwork skills ... which would, in turn, help others identify their own mission in life.

Mission Making: Matching the Individual to the Whole

The idea of a fit between inner and outer worlds is a universal theme important to the intuitive reality of finding your life mission. It's a theme that is closely related to the cult of Asclepius, who was the god of healing arts in Greek mythology and the son of Apollo. Specifically, Asclepius performed healings during the dream state. Sleep sanctuaries were created in his name, such as at Epidaurus. People with illnesses would sleep in these temples and have dreams that healed their afflictions – the dream experience itself was the curative factor. The mystery of this homeopathic principle was declared by the Oracle of Apollo at Delphi, "the wound heals." It is the notion that an illness itself spawns a cure. In other words, there is something in an illness that heals – but only if you incorporate it into your life.

The history of dream incubation appeals to me, as it confirms my own feeling that dreams can unlock our intuition and, thereby, heal us naturally. Asclepius was regarded as the archetypal "wounded healer" because his power of healing was said to originate from a wound. This intuitive vision of reality – mythic and full of meaning – is very different from the mechanistic and materialistic view we carry with us in our waking hours. In this way, dreams have the power to merge our inner and outer worlds.

I used to tease my students that what we all want is simply to be ourselves and make a living at it. Have you ever had that wish yourself? We sometimes laugh at the idea because the joke relieves some tension – the tension of having to suppress a bit of ourselves in order to fit in with everyone else. Sigmund Freud had an important insight into human nature in this regard. His insight was that society is important for human survival and progress but it exacts a high price: it requires each individual to surrender some of his or her natural pleasure seeking in favor of a higher order of adaptation.

Beneath Freud's insight lies an archetypal, mythical memory of what The Oracle Institute calls the First Spiritual Paradigm. It is a soul memory of a time when we did not have to suppress our natural spontaneity in order to fit in. We fit in naturally, without effort. This memory is reflected in the Paradise myths, like the Garden of Eden. In Paradise, there was a synchronicity to all life. No one had jobs, no one had to work, and there were no laws. People acted spontaneously, yet everything flowed harmoniously. People and animals were in telepathic rapport. All of creation functioned as a whole.

Of course, Paradise didn't last. In most of the Paradise myths, humans did something that destroyed the harmony. In the Garden of Eden parable, Adam and Eve disobeyed God by eating from the Tree of Knowledge. As punishment, Adam and Eve were kicked out of Paradise and forced to earn their bread by the sweat of their brows – that is, to get jobs!

When we look at this myth, its demise, and its consequences, we see that in Paradise, natural intuition reigned. When we are spontaneous, we are acting on the basis of inborn intuition. We improvise every step of the way. Telepathic rapport with the other creatures also suggests an intuitive level of awareness. Everything was in harmony because every creature and nature itself were connected. A natural synchronization of creation, action, and reaction existed, and the world flourished.

However, when intuition was supplanted by thinking – by the birth of the rational, conscious mind – we began to view experiences as separate from our-

selves. We started to think of ourselves as "experiencers," and our
natural intuitive belongingness fell
away. Next, we began to wonder:
How do I fit in? Since there was no
longer a natural spontaneity to our
actions, we started to invent rules,
customs, laws, and religions to maintain order. And the concept of work
evolved into having to do what you
would not ordinarily do on your
own to support the culture. Paradise
fell and "civilization" was born.

The Love of the Dove
by Henry Reed

The concept of life mission reflects our memory of Paradise. On a primordial level, we know it is possible to match our deepest joys with what the world
most needs from us. We can rediscover the spiritual ecology that creates a perfect fit between what comes naturally to us and what the world needs.

How do we get back to this awareness and spontaneity? Through intuition. Only through intuition will we be in harmony with the mystery of life
that Lao Tzu described in *The Tao* (a/k/a "The Way"). The Way is the essence
or flow of life. It is the "just so" integration of all the moving parts, so harmonious that there really are no parts, only energy transformations which we
experience as events.

> *The Spirit of the valley is immortal;*
> *She is called the Mysterious One.*
> *The Mysterious One is the source of Heaven and Earth.*
> *Her power is continuous and endless;*
> *Flowing and without effort.*

Lao Tzu, *Tao Te Ching*, Verse VI

Dream work is a similar vehicle – like Jungle Boy's magic elephant – that
can steer us through the jungle of life to a higher consciousness that is our
guiding awareness. And intuition – just like the Buster Brown X-ray device –
is a kind of vision that enables us to see beyond outer appearances into our
inner reality … our mission in life.

Incidentally, in dreams, shoes symbolize our "standpoint." And our standpoint is the attitude that we bring to a situation or the understanding that
enables us either to progress gracefully and sure-footedly, or to stumble and
fall. In other words, shoes represent our intuition!

Now, you won't find your shoes in a store. But if you're lucky, angels may present you with a custom-made pair while you sleep. And once you start walking in your shoes, you will help others find their perfect pair of shoes, as well. Because when you find your mission in life, you set a wondrous example for everyone around you. You become a model of wholeness.

⟢◦⟣

An important aspect of knowing and loving yourself is taking the time to explore why you are here. What special gift do you possess that you can share with the world? As Henry suggests in his essay, a good school counselor or friend can help you uncover your "life assignment." In the final analysis, though, only you will know what you are meant to do with your life.

I struggled with this issue for many years. My father wanted me to be a lawyer, and I questioned this career path too late – after I graduated and my student loans were due. So I worked as a lawyer in a big law firm while having babies. Those were miserable years, and I often woke up in the middle of the night wailing, "There is something else I'm supposed to be doing!"

Gratefully, the Universe presented me with a second chance, another period of time in which to explore myself and discover my life mission. Due to my ex-husband's generosity, I was able to stay home with our children and reevaluate my life. Because of him, I was able to form The Oracle Institute and write. Today, I am energized because I know what I came here to do.

I recognize that many people are not so fortunate. Most of us get force-fit into jobs that we hate and lifestyles that are stifling. Matters have gotten even worse during the Great Cusp, as global financial markets buckle and unemployment rates skyrocket. Not surprisingly, many people are feeling hopeless and lost. Truly, it is a dark time for most people on this planet.

On the other hand, light shines the brightest when brought into a dark room. In fact, when our eyes are accustomed to the dark, a single candle is blinding! Likewise, when the Fifth Spiritual Paradigm begins to emerge, we will be shocked at first. But then we will fixate on it! This prophesied time of peace and harmony will be so alluring that we will pour our heart and soul into helping it manifest. Then poof! The Great Cusp, the darkness will be gone ...

It is now time to prepare ourselves for this new age of enlightenment, the same way that good parents prepare for the birth of a child. Our next selection speaks to the inner work that is required from each of us. Please, partake of the immense wisdom of Tau Malachi.

PRIMORDIAL MEDITATION:
THE WAY OF THE SACRED HEART

By Tau Malachi

The foundation of authentic spirituality and Self realization is the generation of Love and compassion. Such Love opens our eyes to the sacred unity underlying all creation, and it reveals our dynamic interdependence and interconnection with everyone and everything. Many people in the New Age movement seek psychic and spiritual gifts, and some claim higher levels of consciousness, such as Cosmic Consciousness or Enlightenment. Yet, until one learns about Self and how to generate the Sacred Heart of Love and compassion, it is impossible to attain the Light presence.

According to Gnostic Christianity, generating Love and compassion cultivates our true humanity. The first step is the development of the "presence of awareness," which is accomplished through such practices as Primordial Meditation. Once awareness is present, the second step is the generation of the Sacred Heart of compassion. All intermediate and advanced spiritual practices in the Sophian Way stem from this foundation.

What sets Gnostic Christianity apart from orthodox forms of Christianity is the view that we do not merely believe in Yeshua Messiah, but that we are able to directly experience the living Yeshua – the risen Christ. The Sophian tradition teaches that we are meant to consciously work on ourselves and evolve to embody the Light presence. Hence, it is our destiny to attain Christhood, just as Lord Yeshua and the Holy Bride Mary Magdalene did.

There are many different states of meditation, all reflecting different levels of *kavvanah* (concentration) and *devekut* (cleaving). But on a fundamental level, meditation is a state of mindfulness and alertness in which one is completely aware of what is transpiring in one's consciousness and environment. Essentially, meditation is a state in which one is fully alert, yet also fully relaxed and receptive to peaceful spaciousness.

In the Sophian Way, the practice of mindfulness is not limited to formal sessions of meditation practice in which one is seated; it is integrated into one's daily activities. Thus, the Sophian Gnostic seeks to cultivate mindfulness throughout the day, ultimately seeking a seamless union of spiritual practice and daily living. It is this path which leads to the development of higher states of consciousness and actual Self realization. Through Primordial Meditation, the goodness within oneself will naturally shine forth.

In our ordinary condition, our consciousness tends to be fragmented and our mind scattered. Likewise, our desire energy tends to be unfocused and, consequently, our manifesting power is sorely limited. The practice of mindfulness naturally gathers up the fragments of consciousness into an integral whole and brings about a state of focused awareness that allows us to consciously direct our energy. This brings about an experience of greater peace and joy, makes us more effective in whatever we might be doing, brings a state of clarity, and empowers us to consciously direct our manifesting power. Hence, it supports our prosperity, success, health, and happiness.

Generally speaking, the Self tends to identify with the various moods and mental states that arise in our consciousness. We grasp at one fragment of thought after another, thinking, "this is me" or "this is who I am." Through the practice of mindfulness, however, we learn to cultivate a more spacious and panoramic view. We become aware of the Light and the Dark within us, and realize our transcendence into the sacred unity of our true being. Essentially, we become an authentic individual and experience the *tikkune* (healing) of our soul.

If you consider times when you have acted badly and caused harm to others, you will find that you were not acting as your Self, but rather that you were compelled by negativity – an inclination to violence and turbulent emotions. Basically, in such moments, you have identified your Self with the mood and mental state of your surface consciousness and lost touch with the deeper part of your Self – your innate goodness. Through the practice of Primordial Meditation, we learn to diffuse the negativity, aggression, and tumultuous emotions. Instead of identifying with such emotions or repressing or indulging them, we learn to bring them into the Light of awareness, thereby liberating the energy bound up in them. Essentially, the Self wakes up and comes to life, more open and sensitive to Spirit.

This practice is called Primordial Meditation because it unveils and reveals your bornless being and innate goodness – your primordial nature, the very essence of Enlightenment. In the *Kabbalah*, the highest name of God is *Eheieh*, which means "I Am" or "I Shall Be." When Lord Yeshua spoke "I am" statements, he was speaking from the inmost part of the Self, which is pure or primordial being. The nature of this Divine being is pure radiant awareness, and it is this state which Gnostic Christians speak of as the "Christos" or our Enlightened nature.

In this Light presence, there is understanding and wisdom, for it is a state of *gnosis* (spiritual knowing). While in this state, the Self experiences Love and compassion, life and freedom, all the good things. It is the source of all power and all blessing in us, and it is the true Holy Grail of the sacred quest. It is this Master Yeshua was speaking about when he said, "I am the Way, Truth, and Life."

About this state, one Holy Apostle wrote: "Without father, without mother, without genealogy, having neither beginning of days nor end of life, but resembling the Son of God, he remains a priest forever." (*Hebrews* 7:3) This text glorifies Melchizedek who, according to the masters of the Sophian tradition, represents bornless being or primordial Enlightenment – one who reintegrates him or herself into the state of pure being in the Light continuum. This is the truth of our inmost Self. Primordial Meditation is the most essential way to reach this Self realization of our bornless nature ... and eternal life.

In preparation for the various types of Primordial Meditation, let us join in the affirmation Master Yeshua has given to us: *I am the Way, Truth, and Life.*

Primordial Meditation with Breath

This method is most ancient and is found in many esoteric schools. Essentially, you allow your body to find its own natural rhythm of breath and rest your attention gently on the breath, using inhalation and exhalation as the vehicle of awareness.

According to *Genesis*, God breathed a living soul into the first human, who was both male and female. In the *Kabbalah*, all words for the parts of the soul mean "air," "wind," or "breath," with the exception of *Yechidah*, which means "Divine Spark." Thus, there is an intimate connection between the breath and the power of our soul. Through our breath, we are connected to all that lives and to the spirit of God. In many Christian Gnostic practices, the breath becomes the vehicle of the Light presence and the direct expression of the power of our supernal soul. Thus, using the breath as our focus can facilitate the Enlightenment experience, as well as activate the powers of the soul of Light – psychic and spiritual gifts – within us.

When you meditate using this method, breathe naturally, with even inhalations and exhalations. Focus your awareness very gently on the out-breath, and when you exhale just flow out with the breath. Every time you breathe in, let go and let be, and imagine that at the end of the out-breath your breath dissolves into the infinite spaciousness of Truth. At the end of every exhalation but before the next inhalation, you will find there is a "gap" – let go and enter into it. The gap is the place of pure and primordial being, also referred to as perfect repose.

Do not focus too tightly upon breath, but focus upon it lightly. Basically, you want to place about one-fourth your awareness on breath and leave the remainder free, abiding in a quiet and spacious state of relaxed awareness. In this state, you remain aware of your Self, what is happening in your consciousness, and what is happening in your environment. Progressively allow your Self to identify with your breath, as though you are becoming your breath. Gradually, merge in a natural way with your breath.

Adding the Silent Witness

Becoming a Silent Witness means merely observing your mental and emotional states and all of the thoughts and feelings that arise, without any judgment or attachment. One simply watches what is happening – inwardly and outwardly – without identifying the Self with anything that is transpiring.

Whatever thoughts or emotions arise, neither grasp at them nor push them away. Just let them be, and let them naturally arise and pass away, without entertaining any judgment. If you become distracted or identify with arising thoughts and emotions, or if you find your Self daydreaming, merely restore your focus to your breath. Ideally, your mind will enter the gap, then let go and just calmly abide. It is that simple.

So long as we remain identified with what is arising in consciousness, we are powerless to make any real change. But if we can remove our Self identification with thoughts, emotions, and even events in life, we become empowered to make changes. Likewise, we discover that often by merely letting go of Self identification, with mental and emotional phenomena and events of life, we can bring what is happening into the Light of awareness, at which point most problems naturally and spontaneously dissolve. Basically, the Silent Witness is an exercise in Self knowledge and the cultivation of Self awareness – the presence of awareness.

As your presence of awareness grows, you will experience the mind becoming more and more silent and the vital emotional Self becoming more and more quiet. It is as though you are shedding your skin and putting on a body of clear, transparent Light. In this way, you are set free!

Primordial Meditation with an Object

This method is also very ancient and simple. Instead of focusing your awareness upon the breath, gently rest your mind on an object. You can use any object that has a natural beauty and that inspires you: a flower, crystal, or flame. Sacred objects are even more powerful: Divine images of the Holy Mother, Lord Yeshua, Lady Mary, John the Baptist, or images of the Archangels, such as Raphael, Gabriel, Michael, or Uriel. If you have a living *Tzaddik* (Teacher), this can be the most powerful image of all, because of your direct and personal connection to the Elder or Tau who is serving you. Merely seeing her or his face invokes the remembrance of the Light within you and thus generates confidence in the bornless nature of your true Self.

In this method, merely rest your mind upon the chosen object or person, and let your Self merge with it – the same way as with breath – but use the object for focus instead. If you become distracted, restore your Self to the practice. If the natural state of Spirit dawns, let go of the practice and abide in it. It is that simple.

Primordial Meditation with Sound or Chant

Another ancient and universal method of meditation is with chant and sound. Essentially, by taking up a chant, you merge your mind with the sound of your voice. In the prologue to the *Gospel of John*, it is written: "In the beginning was the Word, and the Word was with God, and the Word was God. He was in the beginning with God. All things came into being through him, and without him not one thing came into being." The Word or *Logos* is sound vibration, and in advanced practice, initiates discover that all things are sound vibration and Light. In the *Kabbalah*, there is an art of vibrating Divine names and words of power through which initiates learn to facilitate shifts in consciousness and are able to cause corresponding changes in external phenomena (i.e., work wonders). Primordial Meditation using sound and chant is part of this sacred art and, like the practice with breath, can lead to Enlightenment.

The simple sound "Ah" can be used. Or, for more advanced practice, any of the Divine names may be used. In particular, the blessed name Yeshua is very powerful, or you can use the corresponding chant, "Adonai Yeshua, Yeshua Messiah." The name of the Holy Bride is just as powerful, or you can use Mary Magdalene's chant, "Kallah Messiah." Simply take up the chant and gradually merge the mind with the sounds. If the natural state dawns, let go and abide in the silence of pure being.

Primordial Equipoise

These are the basic methods of Primordial Meditation. You might wish to try each of these methods and find which one works best for you, or you may wish to consult a Sophian Elder or Tau to receive guidance and further teachings on the practice. Primordial Meditation is the foundation of all other practices in our Tradition, as it provides an effective method for generating the Sacred Heart of the true Self. Many have experienced liberation and Enlightenment through this practice.

May the eyes of all beings open to see the Kingdom of Heaven spread out upon the Earth, and the World of Supernal Light within and all around them!

Amen

———✦———

I have had the immense honor of studying the Christian *Kabbalah* with Tau Malachi. I also have studied with a priest in the Order of Melchizedek. Both of these traditions teach that the Godhead contains masculine and feminine energies. Thus, although ancient, the Sophians and Melchizedeks should not be confused with Second, Third, or Fourth Paradigm religions. Rather, they represent esoteric schools of thought that, until recently, have been purposely veiled from the public.

For *The Truth*, I researched the five primary religions, and I ended up rejecting all five belief systems due to the patriarchal dogma embedded in each. While compiling *The Love*, however, I stumbled onto the Sophian and Melchizedek traditions, which are different for two important reasons: First, both of these mystical paths acknowledge and celebrate the feminine half of God. Second, both practices believe that the prophesied New Millennium is dependent upon the emergence of unconditional Love. To the extent that I have found a spiritual home, it is with these esoteric teachings.

I encourage those of you who are ready to explore a more comprehensive view of Deity to examine the Sophian and Melchizedek traditions. Furthermore, for those of you who are Christian, these practices will ring true at a deep level, since both schools revere Jesus as an enlightened master, along with his sacred partner Mary Magdalene. As more and more Christians – particularly women – realize the difficulty involved in attempting to self-actualize under the burden of a male-dominated religion, the fertile *gnostic* approaches to Christianity will be a breath of fresh air. Indeed, all energetically balanced spiritual paths will bloom during the Fifth Paradigm.

THE SAINTS TERESA: FROM DARKNESS TO DAWN

By Laurel

The spiritual journey toward union with God has distinct stages, with proper Love of self presenting the greatest challenge to the completion of the journey. In other words, it is at the Love of self stage that most spiritual quests come to a grinding halt. The good news, though, is that the path to enlightenment has been well-documented by masters of the wisdom traditions – whether it be the Jains of Hinduism, the Kabbalists of Judaism, the Arhats of Buddhism, the Gnostics of Christianity, or the Sufis of Islam. Any one of these esoteric traditions, if devoutly studied and practiced, will help a soul achieve Divine union or Love of God.

However, it is highly unlikely that mere adherence to the orthodox teachings of any of the five primary religions will result in Ethereal plane transcendence. The Oracle Institute in its premiere publication, *The Truth: About the Five Primary Religions*, makes this point in great detail. But to summarize: Many mainstream religious sects operate in a divisive, intolerant, and political manner. Indeed, religion has become the new racism. Rather than preaching the Universal law of Love and helping their laity reach new spiritual vistas, many orthodox religious leaders are obscuring the path to the kingdom of God.

> *Woe to you scribes and Pharisees, you hypocrites! You lock the kingdom of heaven before human beings. You do not enter yourselves, nor do you allow entrance to those trying to enter.*

Jesus, *Gospel of Matthew*, Chapter 23:13

But of all the ancient religions still practiced by humanity, probably the most detrimental to the enlightenment experience is orthodox Christianity, for the story of Jesus that was crafted by the early Catholic Church bears little resemblance to the esoteric path which this ascended master came to the Earth plane to explain. Indeed, the Catholic Church almost succeeded in destroying Jesus' holy mission though suppression and destruction of his original teachings. Moreover, the Catholic Inquisition, which raged for eight hundred years, was a brutal force that purposely scrambled and systematically obliterated those Christian sects that attempted to preserve Jesus' teachings on enlightenment. Thankfully, the *Gnostic Gospels* and the *Dead Sea Scrolls* – both discovered in the 1940s and untouched by man for nearly two thousand years –

provide us with a glimpse into the journey that Jesus himself made to achieve reunion with God.

> Whoever finds the interpretations of these sayings will not experience
> death. ... Let him who seeks continue seeking until he finds. When he
> finds, he will become troubled. When he becomes troubled, he will be
> astonished, and he will rule over all. ... When you come to know
> yourselves, then you will become known, and you will realize that it is
> you who are the sons of the living father. ... We came from the light, the
> place where the light came into being on its own accord and established
> itself and became manifest through their image.

Jesus, Gospel of Thomas, Verses 1-3, 50

Why is orthodox Christianity such a barrier to enlightenment? Because standard Christian doctrine contains numerous spiritual errors that prevent the soul from attaining true Love of self, and by that I mean a proper sense of the soul's relationship to God.

To start, Christian dogma contains the mind- and heart-numbing lie that we humans are born with the stain of "Original Sin" and, therefore, are innately sinful. From this cardinal error, even more self-loathing principles follow, such as the belief that we need a "Savior" because we cannot attain an Ethereal existence on our own. No other faith promotes such a self-destructive and helpless belief system. Rather, the other faiths acknowledge that humanity was created in the image of the Divine and, therefore, has the potential to achieve perfection. Thus, in one form or another, the other religions teach the principle of *karma* – that our actions on the Earth plane affect our spiritual progress toward Ethereal plane enlightenment.

As a result of this sad start, most Christians now believe that "blind faith" as opposed to "good works" is the formula for salvation. According to Saint Paul, a man who never met Jesus and who defied the chosen Apostles in Jerusalem, faith in the divinity of Jesus is more important than performing good works and adhering to God's laws (i.e., pursuing enlightenment).

> But now the righteousness of God has been manifested apart from the
> law ... the righteousness of God through faith in Jesus Christ for all
> who believe. For there is no distinction; all have sinned and are deprived
> of the glory of God. ... What occasion is there for boasting? It is ruled
> out. On what principle, that of works? No, rather on the principle of
> faith. For we consider that a person is justified by faith apart from
> works of the law.

Saint Paul, Letter to the Romans, Chapter 3:21, 27

It is important to realize that the Catholic Church enjoyed exclusive dominion over the teachings of Jesus for almost a thousand years. Not until the Great Schism of 1054, when the Eastern Orthodox Church split from the Catholic Church, was the seed of dissent firmly planted. This rebellious seed later split again into the Protestant Reformation movements of the 1500s, led by Martin Luther, John Calvin, and King Henry VIII. The point is that *all* later Christian denominations inherited faulty theology. Indeed, even though Luther rightly objected to the excesses and obscenities of the Catholic popes, he nevertheless retained the erroneous concept of salvation through faith, thereby cementing the notion of innate sinfulness to this very day.

And then there is the purposeful subjugation of women – the most soul crushing propaganda of all. By assigning Eve the blame for Original Sin, relegating Jesus' most devout follower, Mary Magdalene, to prostitute status, designing the Vatican as a male bastion, and mandating celibacy for priests, the historical treatment of women by Christian men has created even more barriers to enlightenment.

Despite these and other spiritual barricades, there have been Christian mystics who managed to ignore the detrimental dogma, attain Love of self, and proceed on the path toward union with the Almighty. And to make the point that even in a wasteland, some flowers bloom, we shall look at three Catholic nuns, all of whom struggled with the concept of self during their spiritual journeys home. We also shall ponder the bleak sub-stage known as the "Dark Night of the Soul," since during the Love of self stage, all mystics encounter this dreaded transition which requires the penultimate self examination.

Mother Teresa (1910–1997) was born Gonxha Agnes Bojaxhiu to Albanian parents in a region of the Ottoman Empire that is now Macedonia. She joined the Institute of the Blessed Virgin Mary in Ireland at the age of eighteen and took her final vows as one of the Loreto Sisters in 1937. By that time, she already was working with the poor in India. But her official marching orders from God came on September 10, 1946, during her annual spiritual retreat.

It was on this day in 1946 in the train to Darjeeling that God gave me the "call within the call" to satiate the thirst of Jesus by serving Him in the poorest of the poor.

Mother Teresa, *Mother Teresa: Come Be My Light*

In 1950, after sharing her mystical vision with her confessor and making repeated overtures to the Vatican, Mother Teresa was granted formal permission to commence a new order called the Missionaries of Charity, dedicated to serving the poorest members of Indian society. Her success in this endeavor is legendary. In 1979, she received the Nobel Peace Prize for her humanitarian work, and today her order operates 610 charitable offices in 123 countries. Following her death in 1997, the Vatican immediately began the process of canonization for Mother Teresa, who undoubtedly will soon be known as Saint Teresa of Calcutta.

Despite the amazing scope of her missionary work, Mother Teresa had a very dark secret. From her private letters to her confessors, we now know that Mother Teresa never again had direct contact with God – at least that is how she reported her fifty years of spiritual anguish – the longest Dark Night of the Soul ever recorded.

> *Lord, my God, who am I that You should forsake me? The child of your Love – and now become as the most hated one – the one You have thrown away as unwanted – unloved. ... The darkness is so dark – and I am alone. Unwanted, forsaken. The loneliness of the heart that wants Love is unbearable. Where is my faith? ... I have no faith. ... If there be God, please forgive me. ... Love – the word – it brings nothing. I am told God Loves me – and yet the reality of darkness & coldness & emptiness is so great that nothing touches my soul. Before the work started – there was so much union – Love – faith – trust – prayer – sacrifice. Did I make the mistake in surrendering blindly to the call of the Sacred Heart?*

Mother Teresa, *Mother Teresa: Come Be My Light*

This soul-scarred passage is painful even to read. It illustrates the depths of her self-doubt and her longing for union with God. Based on her letters, she never again achieved the bliss of one-on-one communion with the Almighty. In fact, atheists have jumped on her letters, using them as evidence that she concocted her mission and that there is no God. But I disagree. Clearly, this woman was on a Divine mission and received help from the "other side." Her problem was not a lack of Love for her fellow man or Love of God. Her problem was lack of Love for her self – the result of insidious indoctrination by Catholic teachings which state that we are inherently unworthy of spiritual ascension. In other words, her lack of self Love prevented her from achieving permanent union with God, what we now call enlightenment.

Compare now the story of Saint Thérèse of Lisieux (1873–1897), also known as the "Little Flower." Saint Thérèse was born in France and entered the order of the Carmelite nuns in 1888, when she was just fifteen years old.

At that tender age, she had already set the goal of becoming a saint. The question was: *How?*

> You know it has ever been my desire to become a Saint, but I have always felt, in comparing myself with the Saints, that I am as far removed from them as the grain of sand, which the passer-by tramples under foot, is remote from the mountain whose summit is lost in the clouds.
>
> Instead of being discouraged, I concluded that God would not inspire desires which could not be realized, and that I may aspire to sanctity in spite of my littleness. For me to become great is impossible. I must bear with myself and my many imperfections; but I will seek out a means of getting to Heaven by a little way – very short and very straight, a little way that is wholly new. We live in an age of invention; nowadays the rich need not trouble to climb the stairs, they have lifts instead. Well, I mean to try and find a lift by which I may be raised unto God, for I am too tiny to climb the steep stairway of perfection.

Saint Thérèse of Lisieux, *The Story of a Soul*

What is so interesting about the Little Flower is her dogged determination to attain sainthood, despite her self-perceived limitations. Hers is a soul that has accepted, on one level, the Catholic dogma about perpetual imperfection; yet, she still believes she can attain some measure of worthiness – enough to achieve union with God. Could it be her strong work ethic? No lack of good works here. In fact, the Little Flower took on the most menial and filthy chores on her quest to serve others and the Lord, which is precisely how she attained sainthood and the rare distinction of being one of three female Doctors of the Catholic Church.

> How can a soul so imperfect as mine aspire to the plentitude of Love? What is the key of this mystery? O my only Friend, why dost Thou not reserve these infinite longings to lofty souls, to the eagles that soar in the heights? Alas! I am but a poor little unfledged bird. I am not an eagle, I have but the eagle's eyes and heart! Yet, notwithstanding my exceeding littleness, I dare to gaze upon the Divine Sun of Love, and I burn to dart upwards unto Him. I would fly, I would imitate the eagles; but all that I can do is to lift up my little wings – it is beyond my feeble power to soar. What is to become of me? Must I die of sorrow because of my helplessness? Oh, no! I will not even grieve. With daring self-abandonment there will I remain until death, my gaze fixed upon that Divine Sun. Nothing shall affright me, not wind nor rain. And should impenetrable clouds conceal the Orb of Love, and should I seem to believe that beyond this life there is darkness only, that would be the hour of perfect joy, the hour in which to push my confidence to its uttermost bounds.

Saint Thérèse of Lisieux, *The Story of a Soul*

Now let us compare the ebullient Saint Teresa of Avila (1515–1582), one of my heroes. Avila was born in Spain at a time when the Spanish Inquisition was terrorizing the populace. After a fairly boisterous youth, reportedly involving adventure, intrigue, and even romance, Avila joined the Discalced Carmelite order at the age of twenty ... and never looked back. She is credited with restoring the piety of the discalced (shoeless) order and opening seventeen convents. Along with Saint Catherine of Sienna, she was pronounced a Doctor of the Church in 1970.

One might assume that a nun would be safe from charges of heresy – not so. Once the Church learned that Avila's grandfather was Jewish and that she was experiencing ecstatic raptures during her meditations, her "superiors" decided that she might be talking to the devil, as opposed to the Divine. As a result, she was accused of lying about her intimate spiritual encounters. She was then sequestered by a panel of priests who ordered her to write about her experiences and thereby convince them that her visions were sacred and not sacrilegious. Consequently, we have the Inquisition to thank for the recordation of her holy communions. Here is Avila's account of how to conquer the ego and attain proper Love of self.

> *Oh, that His Majesty would be gracious unto me, and enable me to give a clear account of the matter; for many are the souls who attain to this state, and few are they who go farther. ...*
>
> *And it is of great importance for the soul that has advanced so far as this to understand the great dignity of its state, the great grace given it by our Lord, and how in all reason it should not belong to earth; because He, of His goodness, seems to make it here a denizen of heaven, unless it be itself in fault. And miserable will that soul be if it turns back; it will go down, I think so, even to the abyss, as I was going myself, if the mercy of our Lord had not brought me back. ...*
>
> *Therefore, for the Love of our Lord, I implore those souls to whom His Majesty has given so great a grace – the attainment of this state – to know and make much of themselves, with a humble and holy presumption, in order that they may never return to the flesh-pots of Egypt.*
>
> Saint Teresa of Avila, *The Life of Saint Teresa of Jesus*

This woman knew what she was talking about! She had usurped her own sense of self and entered a higher state of consciousness. She possessed no false humility, either – although Avila was famous for addressing the needs of her audience. Frequently, she would write a passage denouncing herself in order to keep her lesser evolved interrogators mollified. Here is a sample of her feigned inferiority to the petty male egos which held earthly power over her.

It is painful to me to say more than I have said already about the graces which the Lord has granted me. Even these are so many that people will find it hard to believe they have been granted to anyone as wicked as I. But in obedience to the Lord, who has commanded me to do so, and also to your Reverences, I will describe some more events, to His greater glory.

Saint Teresa of Avila, *The Life of Saint Teresa of Jesus*

Let us end, however, on a more important note: Saint Teresa of Avila made it all the way to the finish line – she met God face-to-face and repeatedly. Her descriptions of "locutions" (direct messages from the unseen world), her revelations of "rapture" (semi-sexual climaxes of *kundalini* energy), and her airborne levitations (witnessed and attested to by her sisters), all point to Avila having reached the sublime state of enlightenment.

How did she achieve such spiritual heights? Through meditation.

Ecstasy of Saint Teresa
by Giovanni Bernini

The prayer of quiet, then, is a little spark of the true Love of Himself, which our Lord begins to enkindle in the soul; and His will is, that the soul should understand what this Love is by the joy it brings. ...

This spark, then, given of God, however slight it may be, causes a great crackling; and if men do not quench it by their faults, it is the beginning of the great fire, which sends forth – I shall speak of it in the proper place – the flames of that most vehement Love of God which His Majesty will have perfect souls to possess. ...

In these persons, thus far advanced, Love is already grown, and Love is that which does this work. But as to beginners, to them it is of the utmost importance, and they must not regard this consideration as unbecoming, for the blessings to be gained are great – and that is why I recommend it so much to them; for they will have need of it – even those who have attained to great heights of prayer.

Saint Teresa of Avila, *The Life of Saint Teresa of Jesus*

Although Saint Teresa of Avila called her communion with God "quiet prayer," she actually was describing the Eastern practice of meditation. Prayer is more akin to supplication – a beseeching to God or worship. On the other hand, meditation, when perfected, is a direct dialogue with God – an actual exchange with the Supreme Being or with other spiritual entities. Once the soul feels worthy of such intimate interaction, the stage is set for higher levels of communication.

Thus it is that proper Love and acceptance of self precedes perfection of the soul and union with God. One must thoroughly examine the self and conquer the Dark Night of the Soul if one wishes to proceed with the spiritual journey. The Dark Night is regarded by mystics as the most difficult stage of the enlightenment experience, because it is a testing phase during which God appears to abandon the initiate. As a result, the soul feels an inconsolable loss, since previously union was readily achieved. There also is a dread that reverberates throughout the soul, since a person at this stage of the spiritual quest has attained the gifts of an empath – someone who feels the pain of the world. Truly, it is a most frightening and painful stage of the journey back to God.

After the Dark Night subsides, the soul starts to awaken to its true or higher self. This can be a fearful phase as well, as the silence of the purified self can be deafening. Eventually, a steadfast and dedicated soul will attain union with God once again. However, it is not the same type of exuberant union experienced during the earlier stages of the enlightenment process. Rather, mystics report that the next stage of the quest brings a detachment from the Earth plane – a temporary peace to regroup, reenergize, and reemerge a true servant of God capable of sharing unconditional Love. It is not ultimate union. Instead, it is a plateau which permits the soul to gather strength before the next challenge: the actual work of an enlightened master.

To proceed this far in the enlightenment process is very difficult and, therefore, a great spiritual accomplishment. To proceed further is quite rare. As Saint Teresa of Avila attests, "for many are the souls who attain to this state, and few are they who go further."

May those who achieve this elevated awareness of self
continue their quest for God.
And may all of us be blessed with the
courage of conviction and the purity of intention
to reach ultimate enlightenment.

SISYPHUS AND THE SUDDEN LIGHTNESS

By Stephen Dunn

It was as if he had wings, and the wind
behind him. Even uphill the rock
seemed to move of its own accord.

Every road felt like a shortcut.

Sisyphus, of course, was worried;
he'd come to depend on his burden,
wasn't sure who he was without it.

His hands free, he peeled an orange.
He stopped to pet a dog.
Yet he kept going forward, afraid
of the consequences of standing still.

He no longer felt inclined to smile.

It was then that Sisyphus realized
the gods must be gone, that his wings
were nothing more than a perception
of their absence.

He dared to raise his fist to the sky.
Nothing, gloriously, happened.

Then a different terror overtook him.

Stephen's poem provides a glimpse into how it feels to survive the Dark Night of the Soul. A spiritual hiatus follows, which at first is a great relief. However, the silence is accompanied by a dawning dread of what may be asked next by God, and the soul quickly realizes that new challenges are coming.

As we shall see in the next chapter, a final release of material realm illusions is required before the soul may attain true freedom. This includes detachment from fear, from ego, and from man-made belief systems. Only at the end of this stage does the soul achieve freedom ... and perhaps a last chance to turn back before the most difficult work begins.

LIEFDE VAN VRIJHEID

Whereas, God did not create the people slaves to their prince ....
This is what the law of nature dictates for the defense of liberty, which
we ought to transmit to posterity, even at the hazard of our lives. ...

The King of Spain ... sought by all means possible to reduce
this country ... to slavery ... under the mask of religion ....
He would have introduced the Spanish Inquisition ....
He did not only seek to tyrannize over their persons and estates,
but also over their consciences, for which they believed
themselves accountable to God only. ...

So, having no hope of reconciliation and finding no other remedy,
we have, agreeable to the law of nature in our own defense ...
been constrained to renounce allegiance to the King of Spain,
and pursue such methods as appear to us most likely
to secure our ancient freedoms and privileges.

Oath of Abjuration, Republic of the Seven United Netherlands (July 26, 1581)

Love of liberty – *liefde van vrijheid* in Dutch – is an innate gift from the Creator which becomes a passion once a soul renounces materialism, usurps self, and glimpses God. However, due to the continued oppression of greedy and prideful souls (capitalistic, political, and ecclesiastical), actual freedom, even in the 21st Century, is hard won and hard kept.

Even so, once a soul reaches such lofty heights, enslavement is no longer a possibility, and any man-made institution which threatens freedom (business, government, or church) will fall – it is only a matter of time. Conversely, any monument founded on Truth, Love, and Light will rise.

We therefore honor The Hague, the birthplace of modern democracy, and the Peace Palace, the seat of the International Court of Justice. And we wish all of you true liberation of the soul.

FREEDOM FROM FEAR

By Aung San Suu Kyi, Ph.D.

It is not power that corrupts but fear. Fear of losing power corrupts those who wield it and fear of the scourge of power corrupts those who are subject to it. Most Burmese are familiar with the four *a-gati*, the four kinds of corruption. *Chanda-gati*, corruption induced by desire, is deviation from the right path in pursuit of bribes or for the sake of those one Loves. *Dosa-gati* is taking the wrong path to spite those against whom one bears ill will, and *moga-gati* is aberration due to ignorance. But perhaps the worst of the four is *bhaya-gati*, for not only does *bhaya*, fear, stifle and slowly destroy all sense of right and wrong, it so often lies at the root of the other three kinds of corruption.

Just as *chanda-gati*, when not the result of sheer avarice, can be caused by fear of want or fear of losing the goodwill of those one Loves, so fear of being surpassed, humiliated, or injured in some way can provide the impetus for ill will. And it would be difficult to dispel ignorance unless there is freedom to pursue the truth unfettered by fear. With so close a relationship between fear and corruption, it is little wonder that in any society where fear is rife, corruption in all forms becomes deeply entrenched.

Public dissatisfaction with economic hardships has been seen as the chief cause of the movement for democracy in Burma, sparked off by the student demonstrations of 1988. It is true that years of incoherent policies, inept official measures, burgeoning inflation, and falling real income had turned the country into an economic shambles. But it was more than the difficulties of eking out a barely acceptable standard of living that had eroded the patience of a traditionally good-natured, quiescent people – it was also the humiliation of a way of life disfigured by corruption and fear.

The students were protesting not just against the death of their comrades but against the denial of their right to life by a totalitarian regime which deprived the present of meaningfulness and held out no hope for the future. And because the students' protests articulated the frustrations of the people at large, the demonstrations quickly grew into a nationwide movement. Some of its keenest supporters were businessmen who had developed the skills and the contacts necessary not only to survive but to prosper within the system. But their affluence offered them no genuine sense of security or fulfillment, and they could not but see that if they and their fellow citizens, regardless of economic status, were to achieve a worthwhile existence, an accountable administration was at least a necessary if not a sufficient condition. The people of Burma had wearied of a precarious state of passive apprehension where they were "as water in the cupped hands" of the powers that be.

Emerald cool we may be
As water in cupped hands
But oh that we might be
As splinters of glass
In cupped hands.

Glass splinters, the smallest with its sharp, glinting power to defend itself against hands that try to crush, could be seen as a vivid symbol of the spark of courage that is an essential attribute of those who would free themselves from the grip of oppression. Bogyoke Aung San regarded himself as a revolutionary and searched tirelessly for answers to the problems that beset Burma during her times of trial. He exhorted the people to develop courage: "Don't just depend on the courage and intrepidity of others. Each and every one of you must make sacrifices to become a hero possessed of courage and intrepidity. Then only shall we all be able to enjoy true freedom."

The effort necessary to remain uncorrupted in an environment where fear is an integral part of everyday existence is not immediately apparent to those fortunate enough to live in states governed by the rule of law. Just laws do not merely prevent corruption by meting out impartial punishment to offenders. They also help to create a society in which people can fulfill the basic requirements necessary for the preservation of human dignity without recourse to corrupt practices. Where there are no such laws, the burden of upholding the principles of justice and common decency falls on the ordinary people. It is the cumulative effect of their sustained effort and steady endurance which will change a nation where reason and conscience are warped by fear into one where legal rules exist to promote man's desire for harmony and justice while restraining the less desirable destructive traits in his nature.

In an age when immense technological advances have created lethal weapons which could be, and are, used by the powerful and the unprincipled to dominate the weak and the helpless, there is a compelling need for a closer relationship between politics and ethics at both the national and international levels. *The Universal Declaration of Human Rights* of the United Nations proclaims that "every individual and every organ of society" should strive to promote the basic rights and freedoms to which all human beings regardless of race, nationality, or religion are entitled. But as long as there are governments whose authority is founded on coercion rather than on the mandate of the people, and interest groups which place short-term profits above long-term peace and prosperity, concerted international action to protect and promote human rights will remain at best a partially realized ideal. There will continue to be arenas of struggle where victims of oppression have to draw on their own inner resources to defend their inalienable rights as members of the human family.

The quintessential revolution is that of the spirit, born of an intellectual conviction of the need for change in those mental attitudes and values which shape the course of a nation's development. A revolution which aims merely at changing official policies and institutions with a view to an improvement in material conditions has little chance of genuine success. Without a revolution of the spirit, the forces which produced the iniquities of the old order would continue to be operative, posing a constant threat to the process of reform and regeneration. It is not enough merely to call for freedom, democracy, and human rights. There has to be a united determination to persevere in the struggle, to make sacrifices in the name of enduring truths, to resist the corrupting influences of desire, ill will, ignorance, and fear.

Saints, it has been said, are the sinners who go on trying. So free men are the oppressed who go on trying and who in the process make themselves fit to bear the responsibilities and to uphold the disciplines which will maintain a free society. Among the basic freedoms to which men aspire that their lives might be full and uncramped, freedom from fear stands out as both a means and an end. A people who would build a nation in which strong, democratic institutions are firmly established as a guarantee against state-induced power must first learn to liberate their own minds from apathy and fear.

Always one to practice what he preached, Aung San himself constantly demonstrated courage – not just the physical sort but the kind that enabled him to speak the truth, to stand by his word, to accept criticism, to admit his faults, to correct his mistakes, to respect the opposition, to parley with the enemy, and to let people be the judge of his worthiness as a leader. It is for such moral courage that he will always be loved and respected in Burma – not merely as a warrior hero but as the inspiration and conscience of the nation. The words used by Jawaharlal Nehru to describe Mahatma Gandhi could well be applied to Aung San: "The essence of his teaching was fearlessness and truth, and action allied to these, always keeping the welfare of the masses in view."

Gandhi, that great apostle of non-violence, and Aung San, the founder of a national army, were very different personalities, but as there is an inevitable sameness about the challenges of authoritarian rule anywhere at any time, so there is a similarity in the intrinsic qualities of those who rise up to meet the challenge. Nehru, who considered the instillation of courage in the people of India one of Gandhi's greatest achievements, was a political modernist, but as he assessed the needs for a 20th Century movement for independence, he found himself looking back to the philosophy of ancient India: "The greatest gift for an individual or a nation ... was *abhaya*, fearlessness, not merely bodily courage but absence of fear from the mind."

Fearlessness may be a gift but perhaps more precious is the courage acquired through endeavor, courage that comes from cultivating the habit of refusing to let fear dictate one's actions, courage that could be described as "grace under pressure" – grace which is renewed repeatedly in the face of harsh, unremitting pressure.

Within a system which denies the existence of basic human rights, fear tends to be the order of the day. Fear of imprisonment, fear of torture, fear of death, fear of losing friends, family, property or means of livelihood, fear of poverty, fear of isolation, fear of failure. A most insidious form of fear is that which masquerades as common sense or even wisdom, condemning as foolish, reckless, insignificant or futile the small, daily acts of courage which help to preserve man's self-respect and inherent human dignity. It is not easy for a people conditioned by the iron rule of the principle that "might is right" to free themselves from the enervating miasma of fear. Yet even under the most crushing state machinery, courage rises up again and again, for fear is not the natural state of civilized man.

The wellspring of courage and endurance in the face of unbridled power is generally a firm belief in the sanctity of ethical principles combined with a historical sense that despite all setbacks, the condition of man is set on an ultimate course for both spiritual and material advancement. It is his capacity for self-improvement and self-redemption which most distinguishes man from the mere brute. At the root of human responsibility is the concept of perfection, the urge to achieve it, the intelligence to find a path toward it, and the will to follow that path if not to the end at least the distance needed to rise above individual limitations and environmental impediments. It is man's vision of a world fit for rational, civilized humanity which leads him to dare and to suffer to build societies free from want and fear. Concepts such as truth, justice, and compassion cannot be dismissed as trite when these are often the only bulwarks which stand against ruthless power.

—◆—

Daw Aung San is the daughter of a Burmese revolutionary, General Aung San, who is considered the father of modern Burma, now known as Myanmar. General Aung San fought for and helped win his country's independence from the United Kingdom in 1948, but tragically, he was assassinated just before the country obtained its freedom. Even more tragic was the military coup that took place in 1962, which effectively ended democracy in Myanmar to this day.

Daw Aung San has steadfastly opposed the military junta that controls her country. She participated in the famous "8888 Uprising" (August 8, 1988) against the dictatorship, during which thousands of civilians and monks were slaughtered. Thereafter, Daw Aung San founded the National League for Democracy, in response to which the military dictatorship quickly placed her under arrest in 1989. With Daw Aung San removed from the public eye, the military allowed an election in 1990, which Daw Aung San's party handily won, thereby entitling her to be Prime Minister of Myanmar. However, the dictatorship negated the election results. The international outcry was swift, and in 1991 she was awarded the Nobel Peace Prize *in absentia*.

To characterize this woman's sacrifice as substantial does not do her justice. She has been under arrest and in isolation for most of the past twenty years. Indeed, she has suffered not only the loss of her freedom, but also the loss of her family, friends, and supporters. As of this writing, she still is under house arrest.

The Institute decided to cameo her life as a freedom fighter because Daw Aung San is a symbol for the type of courage and commitment needed by those souls who desire to be free. Americans often take freedom for granted. Yet, loss of liberty takes only a nanosecond. As an attorney, I have been greatly disturbed by the loss of freedoms in the United States over the past decade. Sadly, many Americans have been asleep during the Great Cusp. But it is time to awaken. We must be vigilant if we wish to remain free, really free.

ESSAY ON SLAVERY

By Robert Eisenman

Slavery is the adherence to a system.
Slavery weakens the individual.
There is only one freedom in this world,
That is, independence in mind as well as body.
The Lord is the only foundation –
Naked as you came into this world,
Naked you shall go out of it.

The only man who is capable of enjoying
All the pleasures of this world
Is the man who is not bound to it.
There is a new slavery in the world,
The slavery of men to goods,
The slavery of men to ideologies,
The slavery of man to systems beyond himself.
There should be only one slavery in the world –
The slavery of man to Justice.

No man is capable of enjoying all the happinesses
Of this world, though he say he be,
If he is blind, fettered, or in chains
Either physically, morally, or intellectually.
There are two kinds of beings in the world –
There are the enslaved and the free.
The heroes are the free;
The vast majority are the enslaved.
The men of courage, though poor-sighted,
Are struggling to achieve freedom.

The slavery of men to systems beyond each other:
Corporations, manners, style –
These unseen networks stemming
From the basest emotions of man –
This is the problem in the world today,
Not the slavery of men to each other.
The latter was simple and could be fought;
The former are far more complicated
And infect even the strongest of men,
Tying them in the end to their own basest emotions.

It is a constant struggle – there is no end to it.
Your enemies are your closest friends,
The people you have grown up with,
Your parents, who are all worshipping it.
It is a subtle beast and waits to ensnare you
At any moment your guard is down.
Such is the world today and in such a world,
With men no longer in control, but unseen deities –
Secret mysteries in control of all,
There can be only destruction.

I tell you, if you rebel,
If you free yourselves,
Though you earn the enmity and spite
Of all those sickly creatures around you,
You in the end earn their respect
And undying Love, for you are going
A long way towards freeing them.

The revolution cannot occur at the class level
Or at the national or even the international level.
It must occur at the personal level with every man
Throwing off his chains and becoming free –
With even the poor in spirit, the weak,
The infected, throwing away their crutches
And walking as free men and becoming free.

This sickness is impervious to class, to rich or poor.
It cuts across all monetary distinctions.
The rich are as enslaved as the poor, even more –
In this case, "blessed be the poor."
There is war in the world, a constant never-ending war,
No longer between nations, but between those who are slaves
And those who would be free.

It cuts across all borders and international boundaries,
It takes no heed of countries or political doctrines,
It takes no heed of class distinctions or of color or of race.
Its weapons are those of shame, poverty, and convention.
Its fruits are the fruits of all the ancient struggles –
Strength, power, women, and freedom from enslavement.
The battlefield is the college classroom,
The job section of the local newspaper –
The living room. It cuts across families.

It takes place at cocktail parties
And the spoils are another man's wife.

It is an age-old and perennial war
Between the conquered and the conqueror.
There is war in the world,
War between the weak and poor in spirit,
Between the short-sighted and the long-sighted,
Between the half-men and the slaves
And the perfect – the complete.

All things are at stake in this war,
All the age-old superhuman virtues:
Hospitality, honor, justice, pride.
It is a war between man's nature and himself,
Between the small in him and the big,
His power and his emotions,
The courageous and the weak,
The cringing and the strong,
The will to adventure and the will to convention.
On its outcome depends the fate of the world,
On its end, the end of the human tradition –
Not on the end of the world's politics and governments,
On its end, the bigness or smallness of man –
For man will either destroy himself,
In all the senses of that word, or go on.

Bombay, India
June, 1962

———⟫◆⟪———

This poem by Robert, another of my heroes (he was responsible for rescuing the *Dead Sea Scrolls* from the clutches of the Catholic Church), speaks of a different type of oppression. Here, he is addressing people who are free – physically, technically – yet who voluntarily bow to an unseen despot: a sickened culture. Even with shackles removed, some prefer to be slaves.

I am reminded of a video I recently received from a friend over the Internet. The video was entitled *Free Range Serfs,* and it presented a tantalizing yet credible comparison between free-range farm animals and the plight of middle-class laborers. In the Fifth Spiritual Paradigm, the illusion of freedom will not suffice. It is true liberation that souls will seek.

ADDRESS TO A CHRISTIAN MISSIONARY

By Seneca Chief Sagoyewatha "Red Jacket"
(1750–1830)

Friend and brother, it was the will of the Great Spirit that we should meet together this day. He orders all things, and he has given us a fine day for our council. He has taken his garment from before the Sun and caused it to shine with brightness upon us. Our eyes are opened, that we see clearly; our ears are unstopped, that we have been able to hear distinctly the words that you have spoken. For all these favors, we thank the Great Spirit, and him only.

Brother, this council fire was kindled by you; it was at your request that we came together at this time. We have listened with attention to what you have said. You requested us to speak our minds freely. This gives us great joy, for we now consider that we stand upright before you and can speak what we think. All have heard your voice, and all speak to you as one man. Our minds are agreed.

Brother, you say you want an answer to your talk before you leave this place. It is right you should have one, as you are a great distance from home and we do not wish to detain you; but we will first look back a little, and tell you what our fathers have told us, and what we have heard from the white people.

Brother, listen to what we say. There was a time when our forefathers owned this great island. Their seats extended from the rising to the setting Sun. The Great Spirit had made it for the use of Indians. He had created the buffalo, the deer, and other animals for food. He made the bear and the beaver, and their skins served us for clothing. He had scattered them over the country, and taught us how to take them. He had caused the Earth to produce corn for bread. All this he had done for his red children because he loved them. If we had any disputes about hunting grounds, they were generally settled without the shedding of much blood.

But an evil day came upon us; your forefathers crossed the great waters and landed on this island. Their numbers were small; they found friends and not enemies. They told us they had fled from their own country for fear of wicked men, and come here to enjoy their religion. They asked for a small seat; we took pity on them, granted their request, and they sat down among us. We gave them corn and meat; they gave us poison in return. The white people had now found our country; tidings were carried back and more came among us. Yet we did not fear them; we took them to be friends. They called us brothers; we believed them and gave them a larger seat. At length, their numbers had greatly increased; they wanted more land; they wanted our country. Our eyes were opened and our minds became uneasy. Wars took place; Indians were hired to fight against Indians, and many of our people were destroyed. They also brought strong liquor among us; it was strong and powerful and has slain thousands.

Brother, our seats were once large, and yours were very small. You have now become a great people, and we have scarcely a place left to spread our blankets. You have got our country but are not satisfied. You want to force your religion upon us.

Brother, continue to listen. You say that you are sent to instruct us how to worship the Great Spirit agreeably to his mind, and if we do not take hold of the religion which you white people teach, we shall be unhappy hereafter. You say that you are right and we are lost; how do we know this to be true? We understand that your religion is written in a book; if it was intended for us as well as you, why has not the Great Spirit given it to us, and not only to us, but why did he not give to our forefathers the knowledge of that book, with the means of understanding it rightly? We only know what you tell us about it. How shall we know when to believe, being so often deceived by the white people?

Brother, you say there is but one way to worship and serve the Great Spirit. If there is but one religion, why do you white people differ so much about it? Why not all agree, as you can all read the book?

Brother, we do not understand these things. We are told that your religion was given to your forefathers and has been handed down from father to son. We also have a religion which was given to our forefathers and has been handed down to us their children. We worship that way. It teaches us to be thankful for all the favors we receive, to Love each other, and to be united. We never quarrel about religion.

Brother, the Great Spirit has made us all; but he has made a great difference between his white and red children. He has given us a different complexion and different customs; to you he has given the arts; to these he has not opened our eyes; we know these things to be true. Since he has made so great a difference between us in other things, why may we not conclude that he has given us a different religion according to our understanding? The Great Spirit does right; he knows what is best for his children. We are satisfied.

Brother, we do not wish to destroy your religion or take it from you; we only want to enjoy our own.

Brother, you say you have not come to get our land or our money, but to enlighten our minds. I will now tell you that I have been at your meetings, and saw you collecting money from the meeting. I cannot tell what this money was intended for, but suppose it was for your minister; and if we should conform to your way of thinking, perhaps you may want some from us.

Brother, we are told that you have been preaching to the white people in this place. These people are our neighbors; we are acquainted with them. We will wait a little while and see what effect your preaching has upon them. If we find it does them good, makes them honest and less disposed to cheat Indians, we will then consider again what you have said.

Brother, you have now heard our answer to your talk, and this is all we have to say at present. As we are going to part, we will come and take you by the hand, and hope the Great Spirit will protect you on your journey, and return you safe to your friends.

The freedom to craft our own spiritual belief system is the most fundamental power we humans possess, which explains why this right is protected under the United States Constitution. It is reported that after Chief Sagoyewatha ("Keeper Awake") delivered this speech in 1805, the Christian missionaries would not shake his hand and that their leader pronounced, "There can be no fellowship between the religion of God and the works of the devil." So much for the First Amendment, which by that time had been in force for fourteen years!

The frequent hypocrisy of orthodox Christianity is well-documented. Throughout history, conversion by force has been its favored tool; rarely has tolerance been practiced, let alone true acceptance or Love. Now, some followers of Judaism and Islam have embraced aggressive tactics to justify their religious zealotry. Clearly, lethal force is anathema to spiritual freedom – that which Jesus, Muhammad, and the later Jewish prophets prescribed ... seemingly in vain.

> *They shall beat their swords into plowshares*
> *and their spears into pruning hooks;*
> *One nation shall not raise the sword against another,*
> *nor shall they train for war again.*

Isaiah, Chapter 2:4

THE THREE LOST BOOKS OF PEACE

By Maxine Hong Kingston

My *Book of Peace* is gone. And my father is gone. Fatherless. And thingless. But not Idea-less.

Suddenly, I felt rushing at me – this fire movie is about to run in reverse; smoky ghosts will hurry backward into rising houses and trees, refill them, and pull them upright – I felt coming into me – oh, but here all along inside chest and stomach and all around me and out of the smoking ground – Idea. Idea has weight and life; I can feel it. Ideas are pervious to firebombs, which shoot through them without harming them. Americans own too many things. I can feel Idea because I am thingless, and because of my education, thinking, reading, meditation. I heard the monk and teacher Thich Nhat Hanh say the *Five Wonderful Precepts*, which are the moral foundation of Buddhism. Having ethics, even intentions and aspirations, turns you in the right direction, toward some lasting Idea about good. I am a manifestation of Idea, food that makes blood, bones, muscles, body, self. I stood alive in the fire, and felt Idea pour into me.

I know why this fire. God is showing us Iraq. It is wrong to kill, and refuse to look at what we've done. Count the children killed, in "sanctions": 150,000, 360,000, 750,000. "Collateral damage." The counts go up with each new report. We killed more children than soldiers. For refusing to be conscious of the suffering we caused – the camera-eye on the bomb went out as it hit the door or roof at the center of the crosshairs – no journalists allowed, no witnesses – we are given this sight of our city in ashes. God is teaching us, showing us this scene that is like war.

I'm not crazy. I'm not unpatriotic. People who've been there, who saw Hiroshima and Nagasaki after the A-bombs, the Ong Plain and Hue after the firefights, compared our fire to war. Oakland Fire Captain Ray Gatchalian, Asian American, Green Beret, Viet Nam vet, Panama vet, said:

> *When I went up in the helicopter the day after the fire, I couldn't even film, I was so stunned. You have to remember, I went to Mexico City after the earthquake where hundreds and thousands of people were displaced, but when you see your own environment, people you know, whose homes were burned to the ground, I was stunned, in total shock. That day, one house burned every five seconds. Seeing it the next morning, it brought me back to the shock and horror of Vietnam. When I looked down on the devastation that day, I thought: What an*

opportunity this would be to bring busloads of people and busloads of children and tell them when we, as a country, decide to go to war against somebody, this is what we are going to get. When we decide to send our military and our bombs into a country, this is what we're deciding to do.

My father is trying to kill me, to take me with him. At this morning's funeral fires, we burned gifts and provisions for him, but it was not enough, and he's angry. He wants more – my book, all my books, my house, and neighborhood – and is taking more – my cities, Berkeley, where I teach, Oakland, where I live. In the incinerator at the Chinese Cemetery, we burned blank paper to him, a symbol of everything, like money. He wants writing, real things. This heat that covers me and my territory from hot ground up to the sun is anger, the anger that had been one man's task to civilize. Now that my father is dead, this energy is loose.

It discharged out of his too-old body, which had no illness but time, leapt sky-high, and divebombed earthward, me-ward. My father is now part of the father-god of the Americas, who haunts his children, spears and fishes for us with his lightening yo-yo. BaBa is not focusing his terrible new death powers. He is carpet-bombing. He can't catch me, small and alone, driving and running here and there, Stockton, Oakland, back and forth across the Berkeley-Oakland border. I had taken belongings most full of manna. He wants back his spectacles, which fit my eyes, his wristwatch, his draft card, the Cross pen that I had given him, the brass spindle for spiking gambling tickets and laundry tickets, the bamboo match extender-holder he invented for lighting firecrackers. His brass ashtray from the 1939 World's Fair.

I had made an arrangement of these things on my kitchen desk, and they'd evoked him. But mostly he wants my book. "I have always wanted the life you have." My father started saying that to me when I became a published, paid writer. He was wishing to have many poems come to him, and to have readers. My mother – Brave Orchid – tried scolding him into poetry: "You used to be a poet. Where are the poems, poet?" He would wonder, "How is it that I can like poems so much, but can't write them anymore?" In China, he had written six tomes of poetry, "each one this thick." Brave Orchid held up her hand, thumb and forefinger wide apart. Poetry comes out of the country – the ground and the people – but he couldn't hear the voices so well in America as in China.

At the blanketing ceremony three weeks ago, we, his children and children-in-law, two by two, everybody married, holding a piece of printed cloth between us, walked up to the coffin and spread it over his body. We blanketed him with layers and layers of colors and flowers as in a fairy tale. I put the fountain pen my son had given me into BaBa's breast pocket. Then Earll and I pulled the coverlet up to his chin; it felt like being young parents again, tucking the baby into bed.

Heeding the rituals argued by the constantly scolding old women from China – wear hoods and sashes, black hoods; no, white hoods; no, black hoods; eat, bow, eat, bow; no, not toward the chicken, you stupid *ho jee* boy, toward your father; buy yellow candy; no, not lemon drops, you stupid *ho jee* girl, Brach's butterscotch – turning in the directions that you're pushed and pulled – you infer Heaven. Its distance from Earth is a month's walk away. Kneeling in the grass, my kind cousin-in-law from China instructed us, who were standing, "Say bye-bye to BaBa, *la*."

The movements of ceremonies indicate the direction and timing for escorting BaBa on his journey away from us to another, farthest-away home. For twenty-seven days and nights, he has been climbing and clambering up a steep mountain, the back of a dragon. He scrabbles forward, turns about and walks backward, and sees us again, eats with us, and looks down at the Earth and the trees that he planted. He is lonely, missing his body and us. Our every wish against his leaving makes it hard on him. We have to persuade him on and on. Climb the mountain, go through the double door into the sky, all the great nothing.

The last words I said to him were, "Okay, okay. You rest now BaBa. Rest. You have been a good BaBa." Too late to discuss any bad fathering. Norman also said, "Rest, BaBa." We didn't know the Chinese word for "relax." Maybe there isn't one. I considered "I Love you," but that would be an American sentiment unnatural for me to express, and for him to hear. I should have said: "Thank you, BaBa, for working hard for us. *We* Love you."

These thoughts – that the fire is to make us know Iraq, and that my father caused the fire – came to me when I stood still in the center of devastation.

My mother most approves of sons sending things to fathers and grandfathers. Women's offerings seem to get routed to in-laws. She scolded me and my sisters for participating in the burning of the gold-and-orange leis that we had origamied and strung. "You shouldn't have burned the paper. It's not your business to burn paper." Behind Brave Orchid's back, Corrine, who is a lawyer, and I passed the spangly train hand-to-hand into the fire. The boxes of air whiffed into flames.

It was a mistake to have the red ceremony today – too early. We did it just because Sunday is convenient. We shouldn't have hurried our father. BaBa had three more days on this side of the sky door, and so he set fire to Oakland and Berkeley. We burned paper in a small fire in the walkway in front of his house, and jumped over it; he was not to have followed us. The Berkeley-Oakland fire will burn for three days.

It can't be too late. All I want is a minute inside the house – run to the far end of the living room, to the alcove where my book is in a wine box, take one more breath, and run upstairs for the gold and jade that my ancestress had been able to keep safe through wars in China and World Wars and journeys across oceans and continents.

I stopped at the curb plotting how I was going to fade past the police. While the policemen – the Oakland cops aren't as big during the Vietnam demonstrations – were busy, I walked through the barricades into the defined fire area. Householders were staying, hosing down roofs and dry lawns. I ran on. I felt afraid when there was not a person in sight. I ran up the center of the street, between the houses, locked up tight. I wanted to run faster, through and out of this deserted place. But I was trying to breathe shallowly. The car radio had said that poison-oak was burning; I coughed, thinking of breathing poison-oak smoke, which must blister lungs. The air smelled poisonous – toxic polymers, space-age plastics, petrochemicals, refrigerants, freon, radon. I am breathing carcinogens, I will die of lung cancer. I held my long white hair as a filter over my nose and mouth and ran at a pace that allowed me to control my wind.

"Do you want a ride on my bike? May I give you a ride?" I reached for the Coke cup attached to a handlebar. He said that the water was dirty and proffered me a wet facecloth, and again a ride. I covered and wiped my face, wanted to suck on the cloth but did not. I got up sidesaddle on the crossbar; we did not wobble and topple like kids pump-riding.

Now that I am on the move, the bicycle moving, the wind and the scene moving, is Idea still there? I'd forgotten to keep noticing Idea. Yes, it's still here, I can feel it, a solidarity at the center. But would it exist if I were killed? What if Idea were just my life, me feeling my life? Can Ideas really exist as cloudsouls, hovering, waiting to be breathed in? I'm the only one who knows about and works on the *Book of Peace*. Its Idea depends on me – small, slow, forgetful. Things gone, Idea remains. The bicycle wheels went round and round, birds were circling, and my thoughts were going around. "No things but in Ideas; no Ideas but in things." Things – red wheelbarrows, white chickens, rainwater – all gone. Idea remains. Ideas cause things. I am alive because of Idea. A book exists before its words. Remember.

Here I come – Samantabhadra, bodhisattva of contemplated action, charging on her flying elephant, bicycling out of the smoke – out of dreams and thoughts into action. Right action is effortless. See? No pedaling. You get help. Samantabhadra crosses the wide boundary from imagination to deeds.

The fire had reached from the foot to the armpits of the phone poles; crossbars were hanging by a burning arm. Atop its white metal flagpole, higher than the utility poles and away from the trees, on a mound in a clearing, was the American flag, limp and singed, but still there. I have ambivalence about the flag. It is a battle flag, a war flag, and I don't like being patriotically roused and led to war. The Red, White, and Blue stands for competition and nationalism. I want it to stand for peace and cooperation. I get scared of my fellow Americans going crazy as it waves.

I did not have a sudden moment of knowing that my house and all that was in it were no more. I stood there reasoning. If I can see that flag from here, then I am also looking through the place where my house was. I was laying eyes on it without registering which piece of blackened land amidst all this blackened land was exactly my piece. The landscape was utterly changed. I had come to the ash Moon of a planet that passes through the Sun.

I had flown a flag, too, a white dove on a sky-blue silk field. UN colors plus orange beak, green leaves, brown branch, brown eye. I appliquéd and embroidered two peace flags at the beginning of my country's continuing war against Iraq, and hung one out the upstairs front window, the other out the side, toward the peaceful neighbor, to hearten her. Christina Simoni was the only other neighbor who put up peace signs, made on her home computer, across the top of her picture window: "Every Soldier is Somebody's Son," and across the bottom "Or Daughter." She was answering President Bush, who made a speech. On another day of our country's mad fit, Christina hand-lettered a new poster: "War is Not an Energy Policy." We were two households with such Ideas, amidst neighbors who tied the trees and poles and gates with yellow ribbons.

I called my mother. I couldn't call my husband; I didn't have Earll's current number memorized. He was in Virginia doing Chekhov, playing Sorin in *The Seagull*. Typical: he's playing; I'm working. I shouldn't call MaMa with bad news; but upon hearing her say, "What's wrong?" I blurted out, "MaMa, my house burned away. My house is all gone."

She reacted the same as when I woke her and told her BaBa had passed on. (I heard a man's voice announce in my sleep, "Your father has passed on." Just before Carmen phoned and said, "BaBa has died.") MaMa had sat bolt upright, held her body, hands, face tight, big eyes wide, and said, "I am so glad. I am glad." All is as she wills it. "He is a lucky, lucky man. He suffered for only two and a half days and nights. He didn't suffer. He was entirely healthy. His every drop of spit was clean. There was nothing wrong with him. Then he went unconscious. No use my accompanying him to the hospital." She hadn't seen him for his last two and a half days. He was already gone; he wasn't himself. "He did not die of an illness. He died of age. He died of time." She talked on and on, leaving me no room to say how I felt. "I am glad. I'm so very glad he didn't live to worry about you in the fire."

"The entire house, MaMa, and everything in it. Burned away. All gone. My writing too. My book that took years of work." I yelled into the phone and her ear; her sight and hearing were fading. She's going deaf because she really doesn't care to hear me, or anyone. She likes to talk, not listen, even to music or books on tape. "Oakland and Berkeley are on fire, thousands of houses, cities, burning right now, MaMa, and the firemen can't stop it. People have been killed."

"I'm glad. I'm glad," she kept saying. "I'm so glad it wasn't you. The house doesn't matter. Things don't matter. Don't *hun* things." *Hun* is the very sound and word for pain at loss. "Hunger" must come from that same groan from the guts.

"I almost got there in time, MaMa. I tried to save everything. The books. My book. The jewelry, your jade bracelet, the one with the brown flecks." Like the age spots on her hands. "And the three jade bracelets Joseph brought from China." They cost pennies, but my son, her grandson, had bought them. "And the gold necklaces."

"Don't *hun* things."

"I had a plan, MaMa. My plan was: first, run for my work, run into the front room, save my book, then run upstairs for your jewelry. I couldn't accomplish any part of the plan. I took too long reaching the house, and it was all burned when I got to it. I drove and ran as fast as I could. But. It was too late." I said "but" in English. Chinese do not have such a strong adversative, or it's rude to use one.

"Your BaBa saved you!" she yelled. "He kept you busy and safe here. If not for him, his funeral, keeping you home in Stockton, you – I know you –

you would have been in a cloud of reading or a cloud of writing. The house burns, the city burns, you wouldn't notice. Sirens go off, you don't hear, you don't wake up. Smoke and gas fill the air, you don't smell it."

"I was going to run inside the house."

"*Wey*! It might have fallen on you. And exploded. Your BaBa saved your life."

Now, that's the right way of seeing my father, not the father-god of the Americas who haunts his children and burns things with his anger, but BaBa, who used his funeral to save my life.

The first thing in the morning, Monday, I went back to the burn. I wanted to see for myself that my book was actually completely burned. There might be remains; at the center of the thick stack of paper, pages might be readable. Earll phoned me, he said, "I can't believe that you tried to get through the fire." He doesn't know me. We'd been married for twenty-eight years. If I'd asked or told him to, he would've left the play and come home.

There was more to my house than I had seen yesterday. The stone archway for the front door remained; it stood upright, and its dusty-rose color had not much changed. On top of the lintel sat the bathtub, nakedly up in the air for all to see. I stood under the arch, under the bathtub, and looked down at the footprint of the house. It looked like the low ruins of pueblos and heiaus. From the brick-and-stone threshold, I stepped down inside the foundation, a pit of ashes. My feet were touching down beneath where the floor had been, down in the crawl space. I walked inside the footprint, and thought out which rooms had been where, which top-story room had fallen on which bottom-story room. The upstairs ashes were a middle layer, and the roof ashes the top layer.

I then found for myself and laid eyes on and touched the ashes of my *Book of Peace*. The unroofed Sun shone extra brightly on a book-shaped pile of white ash in the middle of the alcove. I had been working at the table with the hand-stenciled flowers; the pages had been to the right of the computer. The ashes of my *Book of Peace* were purely white, paper and words gone entirely white. The temperature here in the middle of the alcove had been hotter than by the wall. I held in my hands the edges of pages, like silvery vanes of feathers, like white eyelashes. Each vane fanned out into infinitely tinier vanes. Paper had returned to wood grain. I touched the lines, and they smeared into powder. I placed my palm on this ghost of my book, and my hand sank through it. Feathers floated into the air, became air, airy nothing.

Supposedly, a long time ago in China, there existed *Books of Peace*. They were *Three Lost Books of Peace*, lost in deliberate fires. Ch'in Shih Huang, who built the Great Wall, a military achievement, burned books. Book-burnings go on to this day and age – the Cultural Revolution, the destruction of 6,000 temples in Tibet – 6,000 libraries. As kingdoms rise and fall, the new king would cut out the historians' tongues. Writers had to set fire to their own books and be burned to death in the book fire.

A thousand years ago, on the Silk Road in western China, the mayor of Dunhuang ordered books burned to keep them out of the hands of the invading Xiaxian tribe. Heroic readers saved twenty horseloads of books. I have heard that it is possible that a *Lost Book of Peace* was among the books taken away on horseback. A *Book of Peace* existed then, until the 11th Century, in the Sung period. Diana T. Wu, professor in the business school at St. Mary's College in Moraga, pooled these facts at a dinner party. A miracle – at the end of this millennium in capitalist America, a conversation turned to locating the Chinese *Books of Peace*. I am not the only one who knows of them.

Tibetan refugees had a choice whether to carry food or to carry books. Some of those who carried books died. Some of those who carried food also died. A lama in Berkeley started the Dharma Publishing Company, which is finding and reproducing destroyed Buddhist texts. Every year, more books are presented to readers at the Ceremony of Peace in Dharamsala.

Everybody I met who was traveling to China – tourists, students, and teachers on exchange programs, people on business – I asked to do me the favor of looking for the *Three Lost Books of Peace*. They would keep their eyes and ears open, and be able to see China better. Listen for any whisper of *Three Lost Books of Peace* – a line, a reference, allusions, words such as "peace," "pacific," *ping, wo, wo ping, ping ho, ho ping. Ho* is pronounced with the sound of an exhalation of breath. Listen to talkstory all the way through. And should you hear what might be a quote, a phrase, a stanza from the *Three Lost Books of Peace*, take note of it and the circumstances of your discovering it. Was it in a classroom, in a work camp, in the city, the countryside, at a private gathering of family and friends, a public assembly, in a viable temple, in the north, the south, Beijing, Tibet, Taiwan? And who said the line? What was his or her character and relationship to you and others? Then we will know how the book lives. That it lived through the Cultural Revolution and the Tiananmen Square massacre.

I asked Wang Tao, called Xio Wang, Little Wang, our translator twice in China, whom I remet in Great Britain after the Tiananmen Square massacre, "Xiao Wang, have you ever heard of *Three Lost Books of Peace?*"

He exclaimed, "Oracle bones!" Working on his Ph.D., he found 500 Oracle bones in the basement of the British Museum. "The bones have 'war' and 'peace' cut into them, and the paint in the grooves is still bright." The Chinese read "war" and "peace" in the colors of clouds and in bones, which are clouds solidified. Little Wang and I conjectured: Had the ancients thrown the bones like dice, to make decisions, to divine? When a bone came up Peace, what efforts did they make toward peace? When it came up War, did they attack peremptorily, or did they take time to think and plan?

Writing on bones, turtle shells, pottery, sticks, and jade began at the start of history, the Shang Dynasty, also called the Yin Dynasty. The first king of the first period was Hong, the same Hong as our name, as we Americans from the village of a thousand Hongs pronounce and spell it. Hong had an epithet – Hong the Completer.

Two learned men – Wang Meng and Mr. Yang – conscientiously questioned me about the *Three Lost Books of Peace*. "Where did you first hear of them?" I tried to remember. I've known about them always. They must have been in my mother's talkstory. Mr. Yang, great translator of *Red Chamber Dream*, asked, "Which word are you translating as 'peace'? There are many words for 'peace,' many ways of saying 'peace.'" He is a tall old wiseman with bright-white hair.

"Of course," I said. To show that I was not entirely illiterate, I said some words for "peace": *ping, p'ing, ho ping, an* (as in Tiananmen), *t'ai ping*. No, it can't be *T'ai Ping*, which is the name of a war – two wars, one in the 2nd Century A.D. and one in the 19th Century A.D. Wars for peace.

Wang Meng, the ex-minister of culture (he was deposed after Tiananmen), has jet-black hair. The hair of musicians and poets, people who have galvanizing thoughts, halos all around their heads. Wang Meng gave his voluminous smile, "You yourself imagined *Books of Peace*. And since you made them up, you are free to write whatever you like. You write them yourself."

Oh.

I have been mandated by the ex-cultural minister of China to write *Books of Peace*. I made it up, I write it. And he said I was "free." I first heard Wang Meng say "Freedom!" a decade ago. He opened the conference of Chinese American writers with one word: "Freedom!"

The Peace hexagram is number 11 of the *I Ching*, which also began during Shang. There isn't a War hexagram. I did not get the Peace hexagram on a throw of coins. I had to turn the pages to it. Hexagram 11 – Peace – *T'ai* – is beautifully balanced: three firm, bright masculine lines on the bottom; three dark, feminine lines resting on them.

I chant my *Woman Warrior* chant. I learned it from Black Orchid. It is about Fa Mook Lan, who disguised herself as a man and fought a war against the Tatars. I have told her story as a women's liberation story. Fa Mook Lan leads her army home from war. She shows the troops herself changing back from a man to a woman, and gives them a vision of the Feminine. It is possible for a soldier to become feminine.

Jik jik jik. Jik jik jik.

Fa Mook Lan is weaving the shuttle through the loom when news of the draft comes. Each family must provide one man to be a soldier in the army. Sparing her dear father the wretched life of a soldier, she disguises herself as a man, and goes in his stead to war.

With a horse, heavy armor, and her hand-fitting sword, she fights wars. She is away long years, and many battles, so long a time that her father and mother grow old and die.

At the head of her army, giving chase, and being chased, she suffers wounds; blood drips red from the openings of her armor. Her army, chasing and being chased, passes her home village six times, back and forth past her home, but she cannot stop to place offerings on the graves.

At last, the invaders flee the country, the war is done. Fa Mook Lan leads her army to her home village, and orders them to wait for her in the square.

Indoors, she takes off man's armor. She bathes, dresses herself in pretty silks, and reddens her cheeks and lips. She upsweeps her long black hair, and adorns it with flowers.

Presenting herself to the army, she says, "I was the general who led you. Now, go home." By her voice, the men recognize their general – a beautiful woman.

"You were our general? A woman! Our general was a woman. A beautiful woman. A woman led us through the war. A woman has led us home."

Fa Mook Lan disbands the army. "Return home. Farewell." Beholding – and becoming – Yin, the Feminine, come home from war.

Jik jik jik. Jik jik jik.

The *Fourth Book of Peace*, the book I was working on – 156 good rewritten pages that burned in the fire – was fiction. I was making up characters who use peace tactics. It had to be fiction, because Peace has to be supposed, imagined, divined, dreamed. Peace's language, its sounds and rhythms, when read aloud, when read silently, should pacify breath and tongue, make ears and brain be tranquil.

After the fire, I could not re-enter fiction. Writing had become a treat for my own personal self, as it was when I was a kid and it first came to me, for nobody to read but me. Say any manner of thing. For my own benefit. Retreat into the Yin mother darkness. Oh, the necessity and comfort of writing, "I ... I ... I ... I ... I ..." the selfish first person, author, narrator, protagonist, one. Freedom.

My friend the Quaker poet Phyllis Hoge Thompson called me to say, "If a woman is going to write a *Book of Peace*, it's given her to know devastation." Oh, say that again. "If a woman is going to write a *Book of Peace*, it's given her to know devastation." I've got to hang up and write that down. Goodbye, Phyllis. She just gave me the first line to the *Fifth Book of Peace*. I'd lost the *Fourth* in the fire; this will have to be the *Fifth*. And the fire's aftermath also gave me the method of how to write it – with others, in community.

Carl Jung had a dream at the age of three that he remembered and worked on into his eighties. It fueled him all his life: God sat on the church and shat; his turd fell through the roof. My recurring dream from the smallkidtime is that bombers and missiles fill the sky, steadily moving, like words on a page. I can prevent the bombing by finding the *Three Lost Books of Peace*. *Three Books of Peace* came into existence, it's said, when Chinese civilization began, and were somehow lost. We must find them. We need them. Now.

⤜⟐⤛

Maxine wrote *The Fifth Book of Peace* after her manuscript *The Fourth Book of Peace* was destroyed in the Oakland Firestorm of 1991. Her essay about the legendary *Three Books of Peace* provides us with much to ponder, not the least of which is how we should be utilizing our freedom to build a better world for others. Consider also the description of the Peace hexagram (three feminine lines on top of three masculine lines) and the tale about the spiritual warrior Fa Mook Lan (she accesses her masculine side to make war and her feminine side to make peace). This theme – that masculine and feminine energies must be in balance for us to attain our highest ideal of freedom – is universal. Let us now look at the interplay of some other dualistic energies.

REMEMBERING FREEDOM

By Thomas Hansen, Ph.D.

Sometimes I am thoroughly convinced that we are powerful spiritual creators who have been "turned loose" to create what we want. I like this idea. I see myself awakening to being a wonderful nurturer, a planter of seeds of new thought, a spiritual being who can actually create new life forms. I see myself as being an individual.

At other times I don't want to be independent at all. I just want to be enveloped in the pure energy of my Creator. I have had experiences of being flooded with light, like floating in the Aurora Borealis, which have given me some sense of the magnificent energy of our Creator, and of our oneness with that energy. At these times I've had feelings of total security, joy, harmony, and peace. There are times when that feeling is all I want. I see myself as not needing to be an individual at all. I don't care about my individual identity. I see that together we are the same loving consciousness, without the need for individuality.

Those seem to be the two extremes of my perception of myself: independent individual or dissolved into oneness with my Creator and all of life. While I imagine these two extremes occasionally, most of the time I imagine myself somewhere between those two extremes, on a continuum of independence versus dependence. Perhaps the correct word for this middle ground is "interdependence." In this middle ground I see myself as an individualized member of a community of spiritual beings. I am in a community of co-creators who are forever committed to helping each other and serving the creative function our Creator gave us. At times this circle includes just my guides, angels, and past-life parts of my soul. At other times, this circle includes all of humanity, joined together as individualized aspects of the same divine consciousness. We share the consciousness, but we each have our own particular individualized frequency of vibrations as well. In this model, I am balanced between being one with the circle and being an individual.

Thus, my thoughts of who I really am spiritually range on a continuum from:

> *A freely creating individual, but aware of my Creator, having only my*
> *own individual consciousness, creating in Love, and thus multiplying the*
> *pure energy of my Creator; to*

An individualized aspect of a common consciousness, sharing a common loving consciousness with others and my Creator as a community, multiplying the energy of each other and our Creator, but reaching out individually from that consciousness as the rays of the Sun from the central light; to

Total oneness with the thoughts and actions of my Creator, living totally within the pure Love energy of my Creator, serving as needed, sustained completely by the thoughts of my Creator, and desiring no individuality.

My fluctuation along this continuum, from independence to interdependence to dependence, influences how I look at my actions in the physical world, how I view my spiritual experiences, what I want to awaken to, and what could be the process for awakening. For example, I sometimes view myself as a powerful spiritual being who can create whatever he wants, when acting from Love. Thus, when I ask for spiritual help, I am asking only my True Self. While I recognize and appreciate the help of guides and angels, I see that my goal is to be independent – to be able to create a loving reality here through reliance on my True Self. I do not deny my Creator nor my spiritual helpers, but my goal is to be a freely creating individual True Self.

At other times I ask help only from my angels and guides, or from Jesus or Mary. I am overjoyed to receive this help from my spiritual helpers, and marvel at the way coincidences line up perfectly to bring me what I need to awaken, even though the process seems so slow at times. I accept this help the way a member of a family of friends accepts help. I see myself as representing that family here on Earth, as we jointly try to raise the consciousness of all humanity. But in this process, I do not see myself as independent and free, as when I rely on only my True Self for the creating.

At other times, I pray to my Creator for everything I need. While I realize that spiritual helpers may be used by my Creator in the process, I rely completely on the grace of my Creator. I am content to let my Creator take over and give me whatever is necessary for my spiritual and physical health. I surrender my own thoughts, asking only for the thoughts of my Creator to fill my mind.

I can identify with all of these points on the continuum at different times. Sometimes this fluctuation bothers me. Sometimes I feel deeply uncomfortable when I think of oneness with my Creator, because it may mean the loss of my individuality. At other times, this thought brings me peace. Have I identified myself with my ego in the first case and with my True Self in the second? Which is the correct approach?

Perhaps both approaches are correct, if they both are based on the premise that we are the gift of our Creator. Perhaps there is a place for some of the independent flavor of the ego, if the goal is still to create only Love. Perhaps my movement along the continuum now, in this physical plane, indicates the movement we experience in spiritual dimensions. Perhaps we can lose our identity from time to time in the energy of our Creator, and at other times branch out in individuality to create what we wish. Or, perhaps we can choose to stay eternally in one place on the continuum of Love, if we wish. Maybe my wavering from one end of the continuum to the other is really just a symptom of the gift our Creator has given us – the freedom to choose.

As long as my goal is to produce Love energy, I believe that any point I choose on the continuum is fine. It is acceptable to envelop myself totally in my Creator for a while, to be a person who doesn't affect the pure Love energy of the universe in any way. There is a role for me. Thank goodness there are those who choose that role. Perhaps they are the guides who help us constantly.

If on the other hand I decide to be an adventurer, to be more independent of my Creator, to be an expander of the creation, that is an acceptable role, too. I can choose to be an adventurer who acts independently, or one who works on a team. Of course, when I am awakened I will always realize that I am sustained by the same pure Love energy as everyone else, whether I act freely and independently or not.

I'm wondering if this idea of different roles might be what Jesus meant when he said that there are many mansions in our Creator's house. The mansions, or modes of acting, are all equally acceptable, even if the adventurers sometimes get carried away a little, as we have done in our Earth experience. Maybe that risk just "comes with the territory," and everyone, including our Creator, knows that is the chance we take. There is no judgment of us by our Creator, just help for us to correct our mistake.

The person who desires to be one with our Creator, denying individual power, is not wrong for surrendering personal individuality. That can be a point of loving service on the continuum, and it is a pathway to awakening which will succeed. This person chooses to look for the security, safety, and Love found in total reliance on the Creator, or on the messengers of the Creator, and is willing to give up all individuality.

The person who thinks that he or she should consciously take charge of the spiritual awakening by visualizing light being sent to people, searching for the unlimited freedom of creative Love inside, or acknowledging the divinity in each person, also chooses a path that is helpful for our awakening. That person explores, investigates, and questions, while at the same time keeping in mind the goal of awakening to loving service.

The person who is somewhere between these two ends of the continuum, being an individualized aspect of the one community of Spirit, also aids our awakening. That person is an adventurer who knows the value of a community of support here on Earth and spiritually; that person branches out, then comes back to the community for support, like a bird that darts out from the flock in flight, and then moves back to be part of the group again.

Freedom is a gift from our Creator. We can freely choose where we want to be on the continuum now and after we are fully awakened to who we are. We can move about from one end to the other with ease, enjoying the benefits of any of the infinite positions. The desire for freedom seems to be ingrained in each and every person, whether it be political, economic, or religious freedom. Maybe this desire is a direct reflection of the gift of freedom which our Creator gave to us. This gift was never meant to be seen as separation, as we sometimes perceive it to be. This gift of freedom was and is given to us in Love, so that we may have a full experience of the Love that we are, always.

⟫⟦⟪

In this essay, Tom explores the interchange between a number of complex dualities: independence versus dependence; individuality versus oneness; and free will versus Divine will. By viewing these extremes as mere points on a continuum (as opposed to opposites), we can begin to fathom the full breadth of the Godhead. We also can begin to comprehend the difficulty in achieving true enlightenment.

Mystics report that once they are able to routinely surrender to the cosmic consciousness, they merge with God. They no longer feel independent, as God is their source. They no longer crave individuality because they are one with God. And their free will has evaporated, since they are completely aligned with Divine will. At this stage, the ego is gone, the self is lost, and the soul resides in pure union with the Supreme Being. When the soul reaches this level of bliss, there is no more polarity because the soul is able to see what God sees – everything all at once.

As our next author, Cliff, explains further, the path back to God is full of such paradoxes.

THE TAO OF LOVE

By W. Cliff Kayser, III

There are many ways to It;
Tao cannot be packaged, defined, or described by one.
There are many names for It;
Tao cannot be given to one.

It is always real, true, and evident – deep within the heart.
It is like a beautiful secret – waiting for discovery.
True discovery can start,
when one is not attached to what the outcome will be.

People who are unattached,
can hold the secret and see It.
People beset by attachment,
can hold only desire for It.

Secrets and discoveries together tap It – the Source that:
brings new to old, and old to new;
connects above to below, and below to above;
shines light through dark, and reveals what is true.

Experience It – It is Love.

Tao Te Ching, Poem 1 (reinterpretation)

The *Tao Te Ching* is a Chinese classic of eighty-one poems written by Lao Tzu around 600 B.C.E. In this work, Lao Tzu discusses the essential unity of the Universe, of reversion, polarization (yin and yang), the leveling of all differences, and the return to the Source of all things.

Lao Tzu claims the path of *Tao* or "The Way" is an embodiment of all truths, unlimited and always available. The *Tao* is transcendent and includes all things. Lao Tzu states that the true *Tao* cannot be named or described, which is why I prefer "*It*" as a descriptor of the *Tao*.

One can point to *It*, until one begins to see the finger which points. *It* precedes forgiveness. *It* is manifested as experience of the real and true – like the most wonderful secret waiting to be discovered. *Its* discovery begins when motivations, expectations, and outcomes are absent.

When discovery occurs, *It* has been tapped. *It* is a feeling of perfection and wholeness. *It* can be felt when one sees the stars in the eyes of a child, and the eyes of a child in the stars; when one sees a tree in a seed, and the seed in a tree. This manner of "seeing" is the essence of fulfillment from the Source. *It* is the experience of Presence of the highest order and of consciousness in its purest state. *It* is Love.

I HAVE NO RELATIONS

By Mirabai
(1498–1547)

I have Krishna and no other.
He is my spouse on whose head is a crown of peacock feathers,
Who carrieth a shell, discus, mace and lotus, and
Who weareth a necklace.

I have forfeited the respect of the world by ever sitting near holy men.
The matter is now public;
Everybody knoweth it.
Having felt supreme devotion, I die as I behold the world.
I have no father, son, or relation with me.

I laugh when I behold my Beloved.
People think I weep.
I have planted the vine of Love and irrigated it again and again
With the water of tears.

I have cast away my fear of the world.
What can anybody do to me?
Mira's Love for her God is fixed,
Come what may …

———＞◆＜———

Mirabai was a Hindu princess who notoriously abandoned her family to be with God. Her devotion to Lord Krishna was so great that she dedicated herself exclusively to writing poetry and singing songs in his praise. We included this poem because of its beauty, but also to underscore the point that some souls who achieve Divine union never really return to Earth. Instead, they choose to stay in a mystical embrace with their one true Love – God.

Undoubtedly, those who "hold" the light of God fulfill an important function. However, those who "teach" the word of God are even greater masters, in my opinion. While it is true that Mirabai's devotion to God has inspired millions, in times of great peril, we need teachers who can share their wisdom in a more direct manner. May this next essay help those who seek liberation of the soul attain their freedom and then return to assist others.

LIBERATION OF THE SOUL

By Andrew Cohen

If you want to be free, if you want to be a liberated human being, then it is essential that you become interested in what it means to be simple – terrifyingly simple, frighteningly simple, shockingly simple. For simplicity is where our salvation starts.

The movement from bondage to liberation is the movement from complexity to simplicity. It will demand the willingness to transcend all that is superficial and irrelevant. It will reveal the insidious need to always see "self" as separate. And in the end, this movement will require the renunciation of all that is false, wrong, and untrue.

After a lifetime of exploration and teaching, I have come to believe in five basic tenets that define the path to enlightenment. They describe simply and clearly how to live what is discovered in the process of spiritual revelation – how to embody the absolute nature of that revelation in the life that we are living here and now. If we are truly sincere in our desire to manifest the precious jewel of liberation in this life, then these five tenets must be lived without conditions, at all times, in all places, and though all circumstances.

The Principle of Clarity

If we want to be free, then instead of wanting many things, as most of us do, we have to come to a point where we want only one thing – *liberation.* If we want only one thing and that is liberation alone, then our vision becomes clear and distinct and our attention becomes very focused. Wanting to be free more than anything else not only liberates us from the endless burden of having so many choices, it also releases us from the often compelling attraction to all that is false, wrong, and untrue.

If we are truly seeking liberation, our relationship to the whole world and everything in it changes and all things become possible. Why? Because inwardly our attention is one-pointed. It is now focused upon a mystery in which there exists no sense of limitation whatsoever. This mystery is immeasurable, indescribable, and unknowable. But when our attention is primarily focused on the material world – on what we want from it or how we think about it – all things are no longer possible because we have given our attention to that which is inherently limited. And when our attention has been given entirely to what is limited, very little is possible.

Now it's important to understand that those who have come to this place that I just described – those who cannot be swayed from their one-pointed interest in liberating themselves from fear and ignorance in this life – have a lot in common with one who has actually succeeded. If you want to be free more than anything else, and if you're willing to make any sacrifice in order to succeed in winning the prize of liberation, then from a certain point of view you've already won.

Of course, we don't know how many of us are actually going to succeed in becoming enlightened in this life. We can never predict these things. But from a certain point of view, whether or not we actually succeed in becoming fully enlightened doesn't really matter. What matters is whether we have the passion to seek liberation now, and whether we recognize that the power to go that far lies in our very own hands.

You see, this kind of passion, this intensity of interest cannot be taken for granted. In this world, where there is so much distraction and where attention is usually and painfully focused upon a self-centered and deeply materialistic relationship to life, the delicacy and preciousness of this kind of passion is almost completely unknown. Indeed, in this world, the passion for freedom will not survive within us unless we are deadly serious, unusually vigilant, and extremely careful. That's just the way it is.

It's so easy to deceive ourselves. In fact, it's the easiest thing to do. Most people do it all the time. What is ignorance? Ignorance is a state of constant self-deception. It is so rare that a human being actually wakes up for more than a few moments. And it is because of the intensity of this habit – of living in a self-deceived way – that it is essential to be absolutely one-pointed about liberation. Unless we become focused, we are not going to make it.

In fact, spiritual practice, in any context other than that of liberation alone, may even become the enemy. Why? Because it will in all likelihood enable the ego to feel better about itself. Then there is the great danger that we may lose touch with the overwhelming sense of urgency that is so essential if anything is really going to change. Consequently, for spiritual practice to lead to extraordinary transformation, we must be deeply grounded in an unshakable desire to become liberated. Unless we are, there is going to be a return, which means we are going to come back.

To understand clarity of intention for oneself is to understand the meaning and the significance of simplicity. And when you experientially get in touch with what simplicity actually means, you can then begin to look into its opposite, which is complexity. Then, everything will be revealed to you. All will become clear – the difference between wisdom and ignorance, freedom and bondage, heaven and hell.

The Law of Volitionality

If we want to be free, we have to be willing to assume absolute responsibility for everything we do. And although we live in a world where most of us believe that we couldn't possibly be responsible for everything we do, on a deep level we all know exactly what we are doing. Everything is volitional, including our relationship to liberation from fear, ignorance, and selfishness.

Often when spiritual seekers speak about their internal experience, they have an interesting habit – they refer to different "parts" of themselves. Some even report that there are different "voices" speaking to them inside their own heads – one voice expressing a passionate desire for freedom and the other voice very much opposed to the idea.

The reason there appear to be different parts of ourselves is that we are in the habit of making choices that follow these extremely contradictory impulses. Indeed, when we choose freedom, when we choose liberation from ignorance and selfishness, we experience a sense of self that is so positive that it shatters all the concepts we ever had about what the word "positive" means. And when we choose that which is negative, we instantly experience a sense of self that is inherently separate and ambitious because we are driven by fear.

There is only one self – one "experiencer" – who is either experiencing that which is positive or that which is negative due to the choice that one self has made. So, therefore, what self are we choosing to manifest? What self are we choosing to be?

The reason that we suffer incessantly, the reason that the painful experience of isolation and separation is so common, is that we don't make the right choices. Why don't we make the right choices? The traditional answer is that due to our state of ignorance, we don't know any better. But after we make the conscious decision to be liberated in this life, ignorance will never again be a reasonable excuse for making wrong choices because from that moment on, deep in our hearts, we will always know exactly what we are doing.

The most difficult choice for us to make is the choice to be responsible for everything that we do. Most of us do not want to get anywhere near that relationship to life. Most of us don't want to assume this degree of responsibility. Why? Because it's just too big. Sadly, most of us are far more committed to maintaining the freedom to be separate, the freedom to not be fully responsible for ourselves, than we are to attaining liberation here and now.

But for those who seek liberation in this life, we have to ask ourselves difficult questions: What choice am I making in every moment? Do the choices that I make express a Love for the truth and a preference for that which is sacred? When we look into such questions, everything becomes simple and obvious – as a matter of fact, everything becomes shockingly simple and terrifyingly obvious. That's when we discover the enormous burden that must be carried by any man or woman who is awake, any man or woman who is truly conscious of the fact that he or she is alive.

When we make the wrong choices over and over again, a *karmic* momentum is created. And the *karmic* force of this momentum can gain so much energy that it actually seems as if we can't help it. It literally appears to be happening by itself, but only because of all the momentum behind it that has been accumulated over time. However, when we no longer make the wrong choices, we have finally been purified of the desire to choose ego and separation. It is then that we begin to see directly for ourselves how the law of *karma* actually works.

To succeed, we must be convinced beyond any doubt that liberation is a living possibility – that it is real – and start making the right choices over and over again until a new momentum is born. That new *karma* is the energy of liberation itself. If pursued, that energy also becomes self-generating and will, eventually, overtake the ego. That is liberation – when the Absolute reveals itself through us in this world.

The Importance of Facing Everything and Avoiding Nothing

Without being aware of it, most of us are in the grip of a fear-driven habit – a habit of avoidance and denial. That habit is the movement of ego, which is a compulsive need to remain separate at all times, in all places, though all circumstances. For the individual lost in the nightmare of ignorance, the survival of that separate sense of self always appears to be more important than anything else.

But if we have made up our minds that we want to be free, then the whole picture changes. Now the primary object of our attention is the desire for freedom, not the survival of the ego. In the startling shift of perspective experienced in revelation, our attention is temporarily liberated from ego fixation and, as a result, it literally expands in all directions. In that expansion, we discover something extraordinary and profound – the true and right relationship of all things.

In the spiritual experience, this third tenet of evolutionary enlightenment is recognized as being the natural expression of a liberated state of consciousness. Why? Because in the liberated state there is no longer any desire to avoid anything and there is no longer any motivation to deny anything. In this state, there is no motivation to see things other than as they actually are.

So what does it mean to face everything and avoid nothing? It means we have to ceaselessly inquire into the true nature of what it is that is motivating us to make the choices that we make. Do we have the humility to face the aggressive and frighteningly selfish nature of our actions? Do we have that kind of courage? Because if we refuse to face the darkest parts of ourselves, we will never be able to transcend them. And if we deny the overwhelming brightness of our own unexplored heights, the inevitable result can only be mediocrity.

When consciousness is liberated from the veil of ego, it's thrilling. It's thrilling because instantly there is infinite depth, extraordinary vastness, and the recognition of a profound connectedness within a context that is limitless. Facing everything means daring to face the infinite depth of our own self, a depth that reveals a mystery so awe-inspiring that it simply cannot be imagined – our own infinite potential.

The Truth of Impersonality

If we want to be free, it is essential that we find a way to understand our personal experience from a perspective that is inherently objective. Conversely, it is in the subjective or personal domain of our experience that we so easily become lost and confused. Unless we sincerely want to be free, it's going to be very difficult, if not impossible, to even begin to become aware of the impersonal nature of our own experience. Impersonality points to the fact that ultimately all human experience is one and the true nature of that experience is not unique.

For example, when you experience fear, when I experience fear, when anyone experiences fear, what is felt is exactly the same. There may be some difference in the degree of intensity with which the feeling is experienced, but the presence of fear, the feeling of fear itself, is one and the same.

The arena of spiritual experience is no different. A yearning for transcendence, a longing for liberation, is a manifestation of an *impersonal* evolutionary impulse. Many people experience the movement of this impulse at different times in their lives. But the awakening of the desire for transcendence within the individual is an expression of the evolutionary impulse in the race as a whole.

For most people, there is an enormous amount of momentum that has been generated through a blind and compulsive drive to see oneself as being separate. This is the drive of the ego. The most significant component of this compulsion is the need to see our own personal experience as somehow different, special, and unique. Simply put, the need to personalize is ego. And the destruction of ego occurs when the need to personalize falls away.

To move from a very personal relationship with our own experience to one that is deeply impersonal requires an enormous leap. In order to actually accomplish this very challenging task, we have to be willing to die to the way things have been. But we live in a world where we are so invested in the idea of being unique that it's a heroic task to even begin to consider what it could mean to give that up.

Clear perception cannot reveal itself as long as we are invested in seeing ourselves as being unique. Only the individual who sincerely wants to be free will know the enormity of renunciation that is required for the mind to become liberated from the pull of ego. In order to directly experience that extraordinary quality of mind, all attachment to the personal must burn away. Very few succeed in liberating themselves from the overwhelming temptation that the illusion of the personal creates. To be victorious, one has to have enough strength to stand alone in one's own experience without needing to personalize it.

Many mistakenly assume that a perspective that is impersonal is inherently cold and devoid of human qualities. But nothing could be further from the truth. Impersonal does not mean inhuman. Impersonal means free from the distortion that is always created by that which is personal. When the true self is able to freely express itself, only then will the depth of our humanity reveal itself in all its fullness and glory. For an individual who has been freed from the distortion of the ego can be instantly recognized as having fearless clarity, flawless spontaneity, and overwhelming compassion.

The Revelation of Oneness

Most seekers are interested in enlightenment only for their own sake, only for their own personal liberation. But there comes a time when some seekers begin to recognize that the spiritual experience is not only for their own welfare. Because they have gone deeply into the spiritual experience, they have discovered something sacred – the revelation of oneness. It is the recognition of an obligation, an obligation that literally commands them to cease to live for themselves alone and, instead, to live for the sake of the whole.

This last tenet of enlightenment tells us that to become liberated only for our own sake is selfish. What is of the greatest importance is that our passion for liberation be not only for our own sake but for the sake of the whole – which means liberation for everyone else. True liberation can be found only when this life is lived not for our own happiness, but in the service of a cause that is always greater than ourselves.

But relatively few get to this point because most seekers are only looking for a way to be happy. They want to find a way to alleviate their own suffering. They want to personally be able to experience a permanent state of peace, joy, and Love. Consequently, the ego hates the revelation of oneness because it recognizes, in a way that is unequivocal, that in that passionate, impersonal care for the whole, it has absolutely nothing to gain and everything to lose.

If we cease to live for our own sake, we will indeed experience relief, but not the kind of relief we bargained for. You see, in ceasing to live for ourselves alone, we assume a great burden. And that burden is the evolution of the whole. When it no longer makes any sense to you to live only for yourself, something mysterious and utterly liberating will occur. You will discover that this life, your life – with your own memory, lived in your own body, with your very own thoughts and your very own emotions – suddenly makes perfect sense! And the "you" who you are right now will be recognized as being perfect "as is." It will become obvious that you are in exactly the right place, at the right time, for the right reasons, doing the right thing – just as you are.

In the beginning there was nothing. Then, for no apparent reason, from nothing suddenly everything was born. From pure emptiness the whole universe of life sprang into being. In that instant there was a big "YES!" When you give everything that you have and everything that you are to everyone else, there will be nothing left for you. And that nothing that is left is your liberation. At that moment, you will realize that you are not separate from the Source of life itself.

When you cease to live for yourself, when you give everything you have and everything you are for the sake of the whole, that's the end of it. It's the end of you as you've known yourself to be. It's the end of becoming. It's the end of having a problem that you need to overcome. It's even the end of striving for enlightenment. And it is the beginning of an unconditional response to life that says "YES" and that only gives. Then a new passion emerges. This passion wants order where there is disorder, wholeness where there is division, truth where there is falsehood, and Love where there is hate.

Spiritual liberation that has the power to transform gives nothing to us; it only takes everything away. The overwhelming austerity of this simple truth, when we recognize it for ourselves, brings us to the very edge of the known. And what we discover out there at the edge is that the power of absolute Love to affect this world – so overcome with self-created pain and misery – is entirely dependent upon us.

In many ways, this essay challenges us. For those who seek enlightenment, Andrew's essay provides a plausible checklist of what the soul needs to accomplish before it may both reach Divine union and return to Earth as a master teacher. Discipline, practice, meditation, and humility are required. Most critically, the soul must make a firm commitment if it wishes to be a conduit for the evolutionary force of God.

Let us review the significance of the last two chapters. First, the soul must have the confidence to explore its inherited spiritual belief system and the outer-reaches of its imagination. Such Love of self, or *Saddha*, is not arrogant, but simply curious. Thus, we need an ego strong enough to propel us into the unknown, yet humble enough to undergo serious introspection. Inevitably, the soul encounters the Dark Night, and if it manages to conquer the fears attendant with releasing the ego, the ground for true liberation is sown.

Second, for the soul to flourish, it must be free to fully probe and adjust its belief system; otherwise, its religion is no better than a cult. I believe the patriarchal Fourth Paradigm religions are in crisis because their leaders know that they cannot keep their laity blindly obedient much longer. We all crave freedom, whether from a restrictive family, a repressive government, or an oppressive religion. True liberation also requires acceptance of ultimate responsibility. Only then may the soul attain an elevated understanding of the Creator and its own innate power to co-create.

Third, the now free soul has a choice: whether to remain in bliss with the Creator or return to assist other sentient beings. Andrew's "Revelation of Oneness" refers to the compulsion which enlightened masters feel to return to the physical plane and help those of us who still need comfort and guidance. In the next chapter, we will explore this evolved state and the practice of unconditional Love.

MITAKUYE OYASIN

Then I was standing on the highest mountain of them all,
and round about beneath me was the whole hoop of the world.
And while I stood there I saw more than I can tell
and I understood more than I saw;
for I was seeing in a sacred manner the shapes of all things in the spirit,
and the shape of all shapes as they must live together like one being.

And I saw that the sacred hoop of my people was one of the many hoops
that made one circle, wide as daylight and as starlight,
and in the center grew one mighty flowering tree to shelter
all the children of one mother and one father.
And I saw that it was holy. ...

But anywhere is the center of the world.

Black Elk, Medicine Man of the Oglala Sioux (1863–1950),
Black Elk Speaks

In this chapter, we ascend to the realm of the sages, saints, brahmins, bodhisattvas, masters, mystics, and medicine men and women who have assimilated their *karmic* lessons and reached a heightened state of awareness and existence. Such souls are at peace. Such souls never judge. Such souls practice acceptance and spread Love throughout the world.

For those who have reached this level of consciousness, it is obvious that the entire Universe is connected. Consequently, these evolved men and women know that to harm anyone or anything is to harm oneself. Once the soul completely comprehends both brotherhood and sisterhood, there simply is no other way to express or experience life.

Thereafter, unconditional Love becomes the spontaneous response to any given stimulus, even the destructive acts of others. Automatically, you treat others just as you wish to be treated. The Lakota explain it thus: ***mitakuye oyasin*** – we are all One.

THE SPUTTERING BUTS:
BEAR-HUGGING THE WHOLE ENCHILADA

By Chief Michael Hull

I have times when I Love from a no-self place. This space is just delightful; there is no me to hurt or to be hurt – just an unlimited expanse of "us." Technically, I am not sure whether I am actually loving, since there is no "me" to Love and no "you" to be loved. Still, my experience of it is something like Love, so the word will have to do for now.

I also have times when I Love everyone and everything. When there is lots of me and lots of you, even the painful times somehow are cushioned by a soft pink pillow of Love. Everyone is lovable during these times.

And then there are the rest of the times. The human times. The times when I have a self and you often seem wrong, inconsiderate, and selfish. Loving everyone and everything seems very difficult in the human times when I am not graced with limitless Love. It is the rest of the times – the human times – I will write about here.

During the human times, loving you can be a wonderful experience. Loving you can also be just awful. I can be hurt, feel pain, get scared, and never want to Love again. I also may, through practice and with grace, Love you, myself, and God more often and more fully.

Several years ago, I dedicated myself to loving during the human times, to loving as a conscious choice, without the protection of the grace of no-self or the joy of "everyone is wonderful in their own way."

A side note here about "choosing" Love as a practice. The major religions seem to agree something survives the death of our physical body. They also agree that an end-point of some kind awaits us (nirvana, heaven, the happy hunting ground). The major religions each have a central figure who appeared on Earth to illustrate two points: (i) how to live in harmony with our relatives; and (ii) what to do in the present to improve what happens in the end. The differences in the major religions include method and practice; that is, what did the central character do to illustrate how to live in harmony with our relations and improve our chances of a positive end point? The prescribed practice (meditation, prayer, ritual, sacrifice) becomes institutionalized over time; the "doing" of it continues while the "why"of it is lost. In my view, religious practices tend to emphasize what-to-do-to-improve-what-happens-in-the-end at the expense of how-to-live-in-harmony-with-our-relatives. While I agree the two approaches are not exclusive (indeed, they should be complementary), in practice we have tended to give the future more consideration and deference than the present.

A "successful" spiritual practice seems to require discipline and guidance, buffered with understanding, tolerance, and compassion. I picked loving as a practice in response to my consistent discomfort over the numerous theological questions that have plagued me throughout my life. I have been tormented by various doctrines that address major common issues but which reach seemingly opposite conclusions. People with bright minds, open hearts, good intentions, and superb educations have carefully studied these matters yet disagree. How, then, am I to resolve these questions?

One grace-filled day, I was led to research whether the major religions share any consistent teachings on theology and practice. My search uncovered this nearly universal lesson: *Love God, Love Others, Love Self, Be of Service.* I decided to follow this one teaching, to strive to get really good at it, and to reserve for another day the debates, both internal and external, about other important theological matters and spiritual disciplines.

I have been graced over many years by the teachings and ceremonies shared with me by my Lakota friends. We strive for patience, perseverance, courage, generosity, and Love. Ours is a very human path: *Love now, this day this moment, this step, this person.* Ours is a service path: *How can I be helpful to you today?* The great *Wiyang Wacipi*, the Sun Dance, is an embodiment of this path. Sun Dancers pledge to dance to relieve you, us, of our suffering. "I suffer, so the people may live," we sing at the Sun Dance. My Lakota friends consistently teach that loving you and God trumps form, doctrine, theology, and other considerations.

The Love of my Lakota friends persuades me that Love is stronger than anything else. Love has no opposite. The challenge is to live as if this principle is true. How do I respond to you if Love wins in the end?

The commitment to Love during the human times has transformed my life. Yes, I remain challenged by translating into practice an abstract teaching of "Love everyone, be of service." And now that I spend less time engaged in the grand debate, I have more energy to practice this teaching.

Translating a commitment to Love into action is often difficult. My friend Bonnie Myotai Treace says, "Doing is indistinguishable from being; doing is where the question and answer meet." So, how do I "be" Love? How do I translate the lofty ideal of loving everyone into loving a particular person at a particular time? The people in my own life – my friends and family, the people I work with, those I see often and may not really click with – how do I Love them?

Doing Love, being Love, practicing Love, all raise my "sputtering buts" – a phrase which describes what happens when I am called to Love a specific someone while my too human brain is shouting, "but … but … but." Some days, truth be told, I just don't want to Love you. I may *say* I want to Love you and mean it, but then a "but" arises; as in, "but not if you want something from me" or "but not if you hurt me or someone I Love." Consequently, to practice my commitment to Love, I have to be aware of and responsible for the removal of my sputtering buts – one "but" at a time.

How do I Love through my sputtering buts? How do I live as if Love is really all that is? For me, loving fully, past my sputtering buts, is to Love all, excluding none. I want to embrace life fully and bear hug the whole enchilada. This is not an A-frame, conform-to-form hug, but a big full-body hug of all that is good and fun and right and bad and nasty and ugly, too.

I Love most fully when I embrace without discrimination. A friend tells me she Loves the "Divine spark" in all of us, tries to see and cater to that, and ignores the rest. I admire her tenacious commitment to her path. Finding the Divine spark in you is often a great starting place for me. I fundamentally accept that we all have one. We share this spark, even when I am sure we share nothing else. Finding it, though, is only a starting point. For me, to Love only your Divine spark puts me in a place of picking and choosing, of trusting my finite ability to pick which parts of you are Divine. Too often, I will identify as Divine the parts I like and reject the rest. I want to Love all your parts, not be enamored by, approve of, or endorse only ones I like. I want to Love all your parts.

In my practice of loving past my sputtering buts, I try to remember that I am a newborn to the process and that I get to practice, make mistakes, apologize, and try again. Valentine, a friend of mine who is a ski instructor, sings this teaching in his wonderful Bulgarian accent, "little by little, bit by bit." Bear hugging the whole enchilada is like that for me: loving one step at a time. I do best when I start small and pick one small "but" to focus on and eliminate. I don't have to Love that unlovable jerk right from the start, just as I don't have to summit Mt. Everest the first day on the mountain. Better to find a few easy "buts" and gain some confidence.

I also must remind myself to be realistic about loving. I want to Love with eyes as wide open as possible. To Love during human times is to risk all in order to gain everything. The nitty-gritty of loving, at least during the human times, is hard work – raw, vulnerable, heart opened-to-be-stomped-on work. Loving means that I will get hurt, taken advantage of, left out, and ignored. Loving like this is going to be painful, beyond all good reason to choose this course of action or strategy for living. This is the reality of practicing Love during the human times.

Some may worry that I am inviting negative energies. Perhaps they are right. Perhaps their brand of loving or their level of spiritual maturity enables them to Love completely and without pain. I read about those people from time to time. I even have gone to see a few who make such claims. Yet, when push comes to shove, we all seem to carry our little children with us – little children who want to be loved, noticed, recognized, and appreciated. Our inner child has been run over by the trucks of life, until we gradually withdraw inside a protective shell so that the next person or next circumstance can't flatten us on the road ... or so we hope.

If I am to be loving during the human times – little by little, bit by bit – I need help identifying my sputtering buts. Two great teachers are my emotions and thoughts. My emotions are reliable barometers of where my reservations live. If I become angry, irritated, or scared, odds are good that you have hurt my feelings, threatened me in some way, or pushed my fear button. If so, I may recoil and prepare to defend myself against the threat you represent. You might not even know you are threatening me, but you could see a friendly guy transformed into a fearful angry guy, and then you might back away from me. Hopefully, though, I'll have enough self-awareness to discover where the "but" lives. In that instant, I can choose either to Love now or to remember to come back later to work on the trigger I tripped over on my way to loving you.

My thoughts also teach me about my withholding "buts." Inside of me is a detailed picture of "the way things should be" – a picture my friend Jim Schulman calls the "infrastructure of life." I developed the basics of my picture early on, as influential people in my life told me how life "should be." I see this pattern repeating with my daughter. I will comment on a situation (a view based on my infrastructure), and days later she will replay the exact comment! She has internalized my picture, made it her truth, and repeated it back to me as if it were her original thought. The scary thing is that the comment arose from my infrastructure, my unconscious mind. I memorized my picture early in life, perhaps from my father, who learned it from his father, and so on.

When I have an infrastructure moment, if what I perceive about you is inconsistent with how things "should be," then I may experience strong feelings, judgments, or arising points of view and, more importantly to this discussion, create distance between you and me. Although the origin of my oppositional views may be hazy and I may not consciously agree with them (some of them having germinated even before my birth), I nevertheless may succumb to a sputtering but.

One of my more persistent infrastructures is an out-dated notion of what Love is. The deeper I dig, the more I find old movies – a romantic comedy where a man and a woman meet, misunderstand each other, then fall in Love during the process of resolving the misunderstanding (often after the misunderstanding fosters further conflict, all of which have to be resolved in one hundred minutes, give or take). So, Love for me sometimes resembles the tragedy of *Dr. Zhivago,* or the selfless sacrifice of Paul Newman in *Hombre,* or the nobility of Kirk Douglas in *Spartacus.* It's a Love that goes well with popcorn. Then sometimes when I dig, I hear old songs. I envision a 1960s psychedelic party where rainbows and clouds and cute young people with lollipops float around singing the Beach Boys' *Wouldn't It Be Nice.*

But loving hasn't worked out that way for me in real life. And I've made more mistakes than I care to admit. Jackson Browne's line rings true, "Don't confront me with my failures, I have not forgotten them." God has to help me understand what it means to truly Love – what it means to accept, forgive, refrain from judging, and what it means to walk the line between loving you and accepting your outrageous conduct.

These days, I find the mystery of Love deepening. The more I explore, the more I find surprising nooks and crannies where anxieties fester in the dark, and old points of view wait to spring forth with self-serving opinions that pronounce me "better" than you. I am surprised by these infrastructure views that somehow give me permission to judge you or see you as different, and which allow me to view myself as more noble or, at times, more deserving of a meritless grace that I do not, thank God, control. So for me, what it means to Love is adulterated by my infrastructure. Often, the imprinting is so deep that I can't overcome it on my own. I ask God to teach me how to Love and what it means to Love. But even this can be dangerous.

For example, I suspect that the folks who piloted the planes into the Twin Towers believed they were loving God the entire time. I presume that abortion clinic bombers also believe they are loving God by killing others. So why is my perception of Love and God superior to the view of others? It may be healthier on occasion but, then again, it may not be. I have learned that the more extreme my view or the more it corresponds to what I want to do, the more I must carefully check my understanding of Love with others – those who seem wise and who will give me an honest and candid opinion.

I also have learned that my sputtering buts about loving you are often (always?) a reflection of my own unloved places – my fear that I am somehow fatally different. I can't find a true path to loving God, you, or myself without embracing all of my parts – the ones I like and the ones that seem incompatible with how I think Love should be. If I look inside myself for the things about you I don't like, I usually will find them. We share common faults and common possibilities.

I am responsible for removing my "buts" one "but" at a time. This does not mean I can remove them all. Some I can change pretty easily; others are habits or uneducated beliefs that are subject to change only through discipline and hard work. A few, however, are stronger than I am. For those super-entrenched "buts," only Spirit can remove them. Perhaps, some "buts" never go away. For those never-going-to-leave-me-buts, I pray that Spirit will help me not act on them today – little by little, bit by bit.

Regarding the practice of unconditional Love, I would be remiss if I omitted three additional points which underscore the spiritual benefits I am experiencing. First, as a result of my loving practice, I feel room – interior spacey room – where previously I had clutter. I used to see a broad field in my mind's eye, filled with afternoon sun, a cool breeze, rustling golden grass, and colorful butterflies. But the field also contained an array of rubbish, abandoned cars, thread-worn tires, broken mattress springs, and dilapidated refrigerators. As I stood in the middle of this field, hemmed in by all the junk that needed recycling, I would start to wander around. Invariably, I would walk straight into something – a rusting Oldsmobile not two feet in front of me – and suffer an injury like a skinned shin or a bruised knee. But today the vision has changed. Now when I walk about the field, it is cleaner, less cluttered, with fewer hunks of metal. So first and foremost, my loving practice is giving me room to roam, a space to learn about myself, and a place to meet Great Mystery.

Second, my loving practice is making me tougher. The little child inside of me is less sensitive to insult or slight, whether real or imagined.

Third, my loving practice is enhancing my comprehension. I now can hear and accept perspectives broader than my own. I am open to considering that *my* truth may be something other than *the* truth.

In sum, my loving practice has helped me to see us as we are. Now, when I get upset with you, I resist the impulse to want you to be something you aren't. Loving has helped me realize that a hammer is great at pounding nails, but lousy at tightening nuts. When I expect the hammer to be something it is not designed for, then I am asking the hammer to be a wrench.

Here is my aspiration:

> God, help me to see with your eyes, hear with your ears, touch with
> your hands, and feel with your heart;
> > Help me to be of service to you, others, and myself, under the grace
> of your direction and guidance; and
> > Help me to Love as you do, without reservation.

I am comforted by knowing Love is never lost. Most everything we create in this finite world is itself finite. Semantics disguise whether we create Love, discover it, get in the flow of it, accept it, or become it. There are so many linguistic choices – choices that may not exist in Love. I sometimes picture Love as a great big ball of chewing gum. Over time, we stick more gum to the ball. One day, our gum-ball is huge … it is all of us … all our parts … all that remains of us past death. In some way, we all get to join this gum-ball of Love. As another friend likes to say, "We never lose points."

Finally, a drawback of writing instead of talking with you is that I miss the opportunity to tell you in person the gratitude I hold within my heart for you. So I want to end by speaking directly to you:

> I appreciate your interest, your talents, your focus, your dedication, and
> your time – a commodity I increasingly value. Daily, you serve as an
> example for me of a growing faith living and loving on a mysterious
> path, reaching far beyond the horizon.
> > Through it all, because of and despite our differences, you illuminate
> my faith and strengthen my hope. On occasion, when I become
> discouraged or listen too long to the demons that distract me from my
> purpose, your Love knocks at my door and brings me to my senses.
> Please forgive me when I forget to say "thank you" or when I forget
> what is most important. You are my bedrock. The foundation of all that
> we do is you.

The beauty of you is often overwhelming for me – like the radiance of God that is too bright to be seen directly. Sometimes, in a ceremony or just sitting in a chair, I see you in ways that provoke awe in me and gratitude for the One who makes such beauty possible.

Whatever circumstances of life present themselves to you at this time, I hope you will think clearly, see truly, feel with the heart of God, speak with the words of truth, listen with the ears of compassion, answer with the words of kindness, hold your tongue when harm rests on its tip, and touch all you meet with grace and healing power. The world sorely needs you. I hope you see yourselves as I do, in all your glory and Love.

We are at a changing point in history. Previously, spiritual life was encouraged by the "carrot and stick" approach, as in: follow this religion and get the carrot (heaven), or ignore this practice and get the stick (hell). I want a spiritual practice that helps both of us in the moment, that celebrates life, and that enhances the relationships we have right now.

We are born into this life – a life full of relationships with family, friends, distant peoples, animals, the Earth, and the Divine. Many spiritual practices are designed to detach us from life and return/graduate us to Source. I appreciate those practices, and I understand without judgment why some people might prefer that approach. For me, I want a practice that Loves life – this life I was gifted – inside a circle with you ... helping you, me, all of us ... now, in this moment.

Commitment to Love is the practice for me.
Thank you for loving me and for allowing me to practice loving you.

⋙✦⋘

As Mike amusingly points out, loving when we are feeling good, or when the other person is enjoyable to be around, or when it's convenient for us to be generous, really doesn't count. Not until we demonstrate Love toward those who make us fearful, angry, or jealous, are we practicing true unconditional Love. Jesus put it thus, "For if you Love those who Love you, what credit is that to you? Even sinners Love those who Love them." (*Luke* 6:32).

The hallmark of unconditional Love is the absence of judgment, prejudice, and even preference – a very high bar, indeed. That is why it is so rare for a soul to make it this far along the Love continuum. But despite Mike's self-effacing prose, I suspect he has made it that far ... he is the first white man ever to be named a chief by the Lakota Sioux.

THE *METTA SUTTA*: THE BUDDHA'S TEACHING ON LOVE

By Karen Lang, Ph.D.

The Buddha teaches that Love is the foundation for all spiritual practice. This Love, he says, should radiate out and embrace all living beings, even those who are yet to be born. Unconditional Love knows no boundaries: *May all beings be safe and well; May all beings be happy.* This abundant Love grows with patient cultivation. It takes root in a heart that cherishes everyone, with the same self-sacrificing Love that a mother feels for her child.

Those who are adept at doing good
And understand the path of peace should do this:
Let them be able, honest, and straightforward,
Easy to speak to, gentle and not proud.

Contented and easy to support,
With few obligations and a simple way of life,
With serene sense faculties, intelligent and modest,
Let them be unconcerned with society's material wealth.

They should never do the slightest thing
That other wise people would criticize.
Let them make this wish:
May all beings be safe and well,
May all beings be happy.

Whatever living beings there are,
Without exception, whether they are weak or strong,
Big, tall, or middle-sized,
Short, thin or fat,

Whether visible or invisible,
Living nearby or far away,
Already born or not yet born –
May all beings be happy.

Let no one deceive anyone else
Or despise anyone anywhere at all.
Let none through anger or animosity
Wish each other harm.

Just as a mother would protect
With her own life her child, her only child,
In the same way, for all living beings,
Cultivate a heart that knows no boundaries

And with Love for all the world
Reaching above, below, and all around, without any barriers,
Freed from hatred and hostility,
Cultivate a heart that knows no boundaries.

Whether standing or walking, seated or lying down,
As long as wakefulness persists,
Develop this mindfulness.
This is the sublime state here and now.

And after letting go of wrong views,
The virtuous, endowed with clear vision,
Conquer desire for sensual pleasures,
And never again enter any womb.

Buddhists believe that Love must be cultivated and developed by first loving oneself. Love is cultivated as an antidote to self-loathing, which threatens to sabotage our own self-worth and undermines our relationships with others. People who cannot Love themselves cannot Love others, either.

The warm and compassionate heart that develops through a practice of cultivating Love progressively reaches out to relatives, close friends, and finally to once-despised rivals and enemies. Enlightened people are those whose Love knows no limitations. They reach the sublime state of peace here and now.

<hr>

Karen's translation of *The Metta Sutta* needs little explanation, as it crystallizes for us the true meaning of unconditional Love. All the ascended masters spoke of this pure Love, no matter where they incarnated, regardless of what religion they espoused, and independent of how those in power perceived them. Without exception, their message is always the same: *Active Love is the path of righteousness.*

Why do I say "active" Love? Because, again, if Love is not concretely expressed for the benefit of others, it doesn't count. In short, it's all about good works.

GOOD NEWS FOR ALL PEOPLE

By Brian McLaren

It's a small detail that's easy to miss, but it's full of meaning for people of good will. It comes in a story that nobody has ever told better than Linus from the *Peanuts* cartoon, in the 1965 TV special *A Charlie Brown Christmas*. Linus is reading from the *Gospel of Luke* about the shepherds, who represented the bottom rung of the socio-economic ladder at the time – smelly, homeless, uneducated and unwashed (today, they'd be right down there with drug dealers, slumlords, and hedge fund managers). In Luke's narrative, a mysterious light shines around the shepherds and a messenger appears to them and says, "Do not be afraid. I bring you good news of great joy that will be for all the people."

Now obviously, the words "good," "joy," and "great" would get their attention, but the phrase "for all the people" would strike shepherds even more powerfully, I think. This good news isn't just for the rich, the educated, the powerful, or the religious ... it includes them – the left-out, left-behind, left-over, and left-alone. In fact, not only does the good news include the shepherds, they're the first to hear it! Today, we might imagine this supernatural pronouncement coming to some homeless folks in an inner-city shelter, or some refugees living under plastic sheeting in a camp, or maybe some street kids who scrape by cleaning windshields at stop lights in one of the world's poorest cities.

But the good news is even more radical and surprising than that. It's intended not just for all the Jewish shepherds, not just for all the Jewish people, but for *all the people*. Wow!

For Christians like myself, we still have to come to terms with this small but significant detail: Jesus and his message aren't simply a gift to Christians, but to all the people of every religion. And nowhere is that realization more important than when we are seeking to understand and practice the way of Love – in particular, the way of unconditional Love.

At the center of Jesus' mission is the same message announced to those shepherds: *good news of great joy*. Now Jesus called it the "good news of the kingdom of God," and the word "kingdom" is a little outdated for us. So today, we might call it the good news of the "dream of God," or the "movement of God," or maybe the "economy of God," or even the "dance of God." Whatever metaphor we use, the meaning is still profoundly important and rich.

A great place to root our understanding of unconditional Love is in Jesus' most famous speech, known to many as the *Sermon on the Mount*. I think an even better title would be: *Manifesto of the Kingdom of God*. I was formerly a college English instructor, and I'm an incurable literature nut, but no other piece of literature has enchanted me – and continued to surprise me – as long or as deeply as the 2,500 or so words that make up this epic speech.

For me, the speech crescendos from a quiet, almost whispered beginning to this dramatic climax mid-way through:

> You have heard that it was said, "Love your neighbor and hate your enemy." But I tell you: Love your enemy and pray for those who persecute you, that you may be children of your Father in heaven. God causes his sun to rise on the evil and the good, and sends rain on the just and the unjust. If you Love those who Love you, what reward will you get? Are not even the tax collectors doing that? And if you greet only your brothers, what are you doing more than others? Do not even pagans do that? Be perfect, therefore, as your heavenly Father is perfect.

Gospel of Matthew, Chapter 5:43

Love your enemies. It's a shocking moral summons. Immediately, a thousand arguments rise up against it. After all, isn't that unrealistic, naïve, even foolhardy? Couldn't that kind of thinking get you killed? Of course, you could also argue that it's even more naïve to think that hating your enemies is going to magically start delivering better results than we've gotten so far ...

But it's not just the ethical and social summons that strikes me. I'm equally struck by the reason Jesus gives for rising to his summons. He doesn't say, "Love your enemies, because it will really confuse them and drive them crazy!" Or "Love your enemies, because it's a clever diplomatic strategy." He says, "Love your enemies, so you will bear the family likeness of God." Then, he makes the absolutely staggering claim: *God Loves God's enemies too.* Consequently, those who Love God, God Loves; and those who hate God, God Loves. Those who believe in God, God Loves; and those who don't believe in God, God Loves. Those who please God by their just lives, God Loves; and those who grieve God by their unjust lives, God Loves. In sum, people may set themselves against God as enemies, but God is friend to them just the same.

God's Love, Jesus implies, is unconditional. It is not dependent on the lovability of the object, but rather, it is inherent to the subject's ability to Love. God Loves us because of who and what God is, not because of who we are or what we do. God's identity, God's essence, God's very being is Love. (See 1 *John* 4:8).

Of course, this helps explain why Jesus referred to God as "Father." By doing so, he wasn't intending an insult to mothers, nor was he intending to validate patriarchy, though sadly, his followers have done so with amazing consistency. In fact, Jesus often compared God to a woman, and his own Love to a mother's Love. (See *Matthew* 13:33, 23:37; *Luke* 15:8). By calling God Father, Jesus was giving his followers an alternative vision – something radically different from their tribal notion of God as a deity who Loves some and hates others, and who justifies exclusionary tendencies.

Instead, Jesus taught that the living God is more like a mother or father than a preferential tribal deity. A mother never forgets the baby she gives birth to from her womb or nurses at her breast. A father won't turn away when his hungry child cries out for a piece of bread, or when his rebellious teenager comes home defeated and broken. In the same way, God is full of undivided loyalty and unlimited compassion for every human being – whether just or unjust, Jew or Gentile, rich or poor. There are no insider versus outsider or us versus them qualifiers to God's Love.

Jesus explains that tax collectors (Jews who collaborated with the oppressive Roman regime) and pagans (people who worshiped multiple mini-gods rather than one ultimate creator) Love conditionally. Has anything really changed? Today, he might say that crooked politicians swap favors with friends, terrorists are committed to their warlords, and drug dealers provide for their own. People still are living on a humdrum level. What's needed now are people who transcend that norm and rise to a higher level – the level of unconditional Love.

Additionally, when Jesus says, "Be perfect as your heavenly Father is perfect," he's not saying, "You must keep every one of the Ten Commandments 100% of the time and achieve technical moral perfection." God is not as stern as a quadratic equation or as uncompromising as the IRS. Jesus is saying almost the opposite! His real meaning becomes brilliantly clear when you look at Luke's version of this same message:

> But Love your enemies, do good to them, and lend to them without expecting to get anything back. Then your reward will be great and you will be children of the Most High, because God is kind to the ungrateful and wicked. Be merciful, just as your Father is merciful.

> *Gospel of Luke,* Chapter 6:27-36

"Be perfect," Luke renders, as "Be merciful," and I think you can see why. God's perfection, Jesus says, is very different from human religious perfection.

Human religious perfection can be judgmental and unforgiving, but not God's. God's perfection is a compassionate perfection from beginning to end, because God's perfection is characterized by unconditional Love. So when Matthew uses the word "perfect," he doesn't actually mean "technically perfect," as in bowling a perfect 300 or getting a perfect par in golf. He means achieving a mature, fully formed, and inclusive Love.

Taken in this light, Jesus is issuing a challenge to all of us, whatever our religion: *You must rise above the religious norm of only loving insiders, and you must stop fearing, damning, excluding, disadvantaging, and marginalizing outsiders.* In terms of human perfection, we mirror this parental image of God when we join God in expressing unconditional Love.

When Jesus speaks of the unconditional Love of God, it truly is "good news of great joy." But it's even more impressive to watch him embody that Love in the gospel stories. Again and again, Jesus points out the social boundaries that mark "the outsider" and "the other." And again and again, he crosses those boundaries and violates those constructs, whether he encounters a woman of questionable moral status, a man who works for the Roman regime, a person from a different religious group, someone who is mentally ill, an outcast leper, or little children – who, in Jesus' day, were definitely supposed to be seen and not heard, and maybe not even seen.

Nowhere is this message of unconditional Love more dramatically embodied than during Jesus' crucifixion, when he says, "Father, forgive them, for they don't know what they're doing." Even at that moment – of torture, humiliation, rejection, and execution – he is able to express unconditional Love ... for all of us.

Of course, as a confessed Christian, I sometimes feel like a big fat hypocrite when I ponder all of this. I've demonstrated something far below unconditional Love three or four times today already, and it's not even 3 p.m. yet!

Thankfully, though, I can hearken back to the good news we began with. If Jesus was right and God indeed Loves unconditionally, then God isn't keeping score the way I am. That means that if I am willing, I can learn to look at myself with God's unconditional Love too. Therefore, whether it's in my dealings with others or myself, all I need do is remember that God's perfection is a *merciful perfection* ... which means that God's Love is an unconditional Love ... which means there is nothing in the Universe that isn't bathed and warmed and held and upheld by Love.

Can I learn this? Can I learn to see everyone – myself, my family, my friends, strangers, even critics and enemies – as bathed in that unconditional Love that precedes and pervades all of creation? Can I see unconditional Love radiating from God as surely as light from the Sun, or gravity from the Moon, or magnetism from the North Pole, or fragrance from a flower?

When I glimpse God's Love – when I believe it and when I live it – that's good news indeed ... good news of great joy for all people.

⇒◆⇐

Tragically, it appears that the further removed in time a religion gets from the messages of its founding prophet, the more dim those messages become. We see this sad truth playing out all over the world stage: Muslims have forgotten that Muhammad prohibited war against other "people of the Book," which means those who revere the *Bible* (See *Quran,* Sura V:71-72; Sura X:37; Sura IV:92-93); Jews have forgotten that God commanded them not to fight their brothers (See *Deuteronomy* 2:4, 2:9; *Isaiah* 56); and many Christians have forgotten the Eleventh Commandment – to Love their enemies. Now, compare the generous nature of the early Christians:

> *The community of believers was of one heart and mind, and no one claimed that any of his possessions was his own .... There was no needy person among them, for those who owned property or houses would sell them, bring the proceeds of the sale, and put them at the feet of the apostles, and they were distributed to each according to need.*

Acts of the Apostles, Chapter 4:32

My favorite early Christian leader was "James the Just," the natural brother of Christ. James (d. 62 C.E.) was Bishop of Jerusalem for roughly thirty years after his brother died. The *New Testament* reflects his frustration with Paul, who preached that blind faith – as opposed to good works – is the key to salvation. In this passage, James tries to set the record straight.

> *What good is it, my brothers, if someone says he has faith but does not have works? ... If a brother or sister has nothing to wear and has no food for the day, and one of you says to them, "Go in peace, keep warm, and eat well," but you do not give them the necessities of the body, what good is it? ... For just as a body without a spirit is dead, so also faith without works is dead.*

Letter of James, Chapter 2:14

I am so grateful to Brian for his essay, as his voice is well-respected by all Christian communities and interfaith organizations. He reminds all of us that Jesus died to start a new religion – the religion of Love.

THE RELIGION OF LOVE

By Barbro Karlen

One day upon this Earth, all religions will melt together into an all-embracing unity. This will be known as the religion of Love. It will not depend on tradition, dogma, or holy scripture. Some parts of all scriptures – the parts that were preserved in untainted form for posterity – will fit into this united faith that is not a religion as such, but rather a carrier of truth, completely above all laws, prohibitions, and regulations. Its purpose will not be to save man from sin or to ensure eternity in heaven, nor will it try to prove the existence of immortality. Eternity will be a reality for more and more people after the introduction of the religion of Love. Mankind will no longer fear death because we will be fully aware that our inner being is immortal. Doubting God and the sanctity of life will be as impossible as doubting your own existence.

A brilliant example of a recent prophet of wisdom is Albert Schweitzer (1875–1965), a man who practiced the "Religion of Love." Dr. Schweitzer worked in the tropical forests for no less than fifty years. He fought a never-ending battle for the weak and the sick. But humans were just part of his Love; he also loved the animals and the plants that were close to him.

Reverence for Life, a philosophy which Dr. Schweitzer wrote about and which earned him the Nobel Peace Prize in 1952, are three words that everyone should have on a sign in their home. In this passage, he explains his "religion":

> *It remains to me a painful mystery, living with reverence for life in a world in which creative will at the same time appears as will of destruction and the will of destruction appears as creative will. I have to stick to the fact that the will of life in me appears as a will to join all life forms. For me, this fact is the light that shines in the dark. My wisdom of the sanctity of life, my total knowledge of the sanctity of true Love will carry me over the far reaches of the earth. When another human being and I, in meekness and humility and in true Love to each other and to all things created, can help each other in complete understanding and forgiveness where otherwise the one will would torment the other, then the shattering of the will to live has ceased. Love has become unity, force, wisdom and health. When I save a small, frightened insect from a puddle of water, life is devoted to life and the shattering of life ceases.*

Albert Schweitzer, *Civilization and Ethics*

People in need – thousands upon thousands – wandered into Dr. Schweitzer's welcoming house in the African wilderness. They sensed the power of Love that beamed from the very core of this magnificent man. They were handed food, medicine, and advice – everything they were capable of accepting into their hearts and minds. On holy days, there was a free service in God's natural wonderland, where the prophet in the jungle preached the Master's simple faith of Love. He played on his tropical organ, the music flowed, whole and healing. There, in the small medical station in between tropical forest and water, the law of total Love reigned. Many missionaries were horrified by the mix of patients at Dr. Schweitzer's small hospital. Antelopes, monkeys, and all sorts of winged creatures formed a varied and very vivid existence, where the Reaper was often driven away empty-handed.

According to Dr. Schweitzer, there are three major supporting pillars which are significant for mankind: (i) Scientific progress; (ii) Social progress; and (iii) Spiritual progress. This last pillar is the one of greatest consequence. It represents the one true way out of all desperate situations, but it requires people to become worthy of each other's confidence. Too often, there is a state of coldness between people. People generally act according to convention, which keeps them locked in reserved orbits that block the warmth inside every individual.

Let the wisdom of the "jungle man" accompany you on your Earth journey. Let "reverence for life" be a reality in your life. You honor life when you dedicate yourself to serving others. Dr. Schweitzer used to say, "We must remain prepared for life wanting to rob us of our faith of the true and pure." Wisdom lies in our ability to walk on this Earth as unconsumed human beings. This principle shapes those who refuse to lock their souls into ready-made formulas of human invention, those who look to their inner-self to find the utmost cause of existence.

Dr. Schweitzer's last earth-wandering was rich, despite a calling without earthly rewards. Pure as gems were his deeds of Love in the feverish-hot jungle; great as gold were his efforts for the poor and weak. He lived his life in harmony with nature and the spirit of man. His confidants were the elements: the magnificent sea with its azure heart and glistening face open toward the Universe; the small, hardly noticeable jungle violet growing in the shade of impenetrable jungle vegetation. Mere words cannot describe his life work, as his wealth was elevated beyond the narrow belt of simple matter. With sorrow and sadness filling all senses, people still reminisce about the great white man with the gentle, stable hands and the loving eyes. The jungle man understood the wisdom of the Divine: everything, absolutely everything, answers to each other – life to life, truth to truth, Love to Love.

Indeed, everything – down to the smallest molecule – mirrors God's perfection. The Sun is the mother of flowers, but it does not hold itself as better than the smallest plant. For all living things, inside themselves, adhere to Universal Laws. The wind blows wherever it wants: you can hear its singing but you can't see it; you know not from whence it came or where it is going. The holy spirit of God is in the soul of the wind because it is ubiquitous. Man writes down laws and formulas, then reads and labels everything as definites. But there are no definites. That is but a construct of the limited human brain. The realm of the Sun, as well as the meaning of Life, cannot be put into formulas. Only the spirit of wisdom can come close to the truth of such ancient forces.

This prophet of unconditional Love, the human being Albert Schweitzer, was in full unity with the Lord's eternal chain of creation, without beginning and without end. He sensed the treasures of life beyond all things; he sensed the inner plane of creation. He felt the eternal soul in the smallest meadow flower where, hidden in her tiny heart's most inner chamber, resides the sanctity of the Creator's will. Peace is the legacy of this magnificent jungle man – a beautiful harmony that resonates within the Universe. He came to show us how to be honest intermediaries between the Creator and this earthly world. Let us pass on these treasures of Love and honor the sacredness of life.

> *As a note from Life itself*
> *resonates a commandment of Love from the jungle*
> *the man devoted to Love*
> *has left his spirit behind*
> *in heat, distress, and agony.*
> *A jungle man worked*
> *take wisdom from this man*
> *live in Love, be true.*
>
> *Be true to God and man*
> *be true to every little animal*
> *be true to the flower in the field*
> *be true to your soul*
> *be true to the truths you find*
> *be true to the lies as well*
> *be true in all stages of life.*
> *Everything will go your way.*

Love the little bumblebee
love all children
love the little lark
love also the snake
love all the animals
love all the people
love across all boundaries.
Be an interpreter of Love.

Be humble in everything
be secure where anxiety lives
be tolerant and expand your mind
be simple, not grand.
Give your coat to your brother
if you perhaps own two
give your last bread even
if someone wants to reject it.

Think and act only in Love
imagine yourself in the place of others
think only pure thoughts
never think ill or small
noble thoughts elevate you
as seen with the jungle man.
Learn from this wise one
who was found in the jungle.

The Religion of Love asks you to put your faith to good use. The fruits of faith shall bear the sweetness of Love in their core. The bee and the adder often collect from the same plant. One transforms the gathered material into honey, the other into poison. The force behind this transformation resides within both the bee and the adder, as it indeed resides in everything.

Prayer possesses immeasurable power. Sometimes, it is hard for us to understand the innermost nature of prayer, so we complain when we don't notice the effects straight away. But my friend, if your prayer seems to go unanswered, the reason lies solely with the prayer itself. There are many reasons you don't receive an answer. If the frequency of the prayer does not correspond to the oscillation of the treasure chamber, then the answer to your prayer shall forever be concealed. If you expect the stone to move without any effort, then you will forever pray in vain. But you do possess the power to be heard. Faith and prayer go together, as do humanity and humility. Prayer is the strongest force in the whole Universe and the true voice of the soul. Only through true prayer do we make contact with the Creator.

Always remember that you carry the image of God within you, and this is what you should show to the world. You disgrace your Creator if you disparage the Divine spark within your soul. Make a necklace out of kind thoughts and always wear this invisible rosary of Love. Never disparage yourself or blame the Lord for what you are experiencing. If you are prone to underestimation, if you proceed timidly along your path, if you feel confused and dispirited when you could go along singing to yourself, then add another pearl to your rosary. We are our own judge: if we feel false, everything is false for us; if we feel true, everything is true for us. It is unproductive to worry about others; the wise one thinks about how to improve himself.

Our present is a reflection of our past, and our future is an echo of our present. The one who doesn't know this truth is a child. The one who is searching for this truth reaches puberty. And the one who finds this truth is an old soul. These words were once said by a very wise friend of mine:

> Oh, thou who art the Father and Mother over all
> that created heaven and earth;
> open all people's hearts and let everyone hear Thy voice
> which always speaks within each human being;
> reveal thy heavenly light
> which lies hidden in human souls;
> send thy Divine Spirit's peace
> and unite all in Love.

The wise one is complete in his humanity. Immeasurable is the depth of his mind; high and wide is the extent of his being. The life of the wise one is simple yet pleasing. It is without baiting and all is handled with great purposefulness. He knows that a storm can grow out of the smallest wisp of air. He knows that climbing the mountain depends on the first staggering step in the very depths of the valley. By leading a life based upon Truth, Love, and Light, the wise one brings order and peace to the world.

Love is boundless. All things boundless are eternal. All things eternal are carried by their own power. All things carried by their own power are endless. All things endless extend in all directions. This is the complete essence of Love. Only those who have found their true self can evolve toward the total perfection of Love. Only those who have realized Love in the very depth of their soul can aspire to be true guides of humanity.

Endless Love

*Do not wander in doubt
during the span of your life;
do not forget that the Sun is shining.
Behind that which seems grey to us,
everything in life changes:
light to dark, back and forth.
He who fears the shadows of darkness
will, even so, not always stand in the Sun.*

*The Creator has shaped everything:
the given circle of endlessness,
timeless is this ring called,
each stage a spiral race
between all lives on Earth.
All souls return
when the Creator again calls "Be!"*

*Know that we must all learn the lesson
to Love everything that lives and grows.
There is no terminus;
infinity resides in us all.
Through the space of timelessness
shall we all wander thus,
that we reach a higher plane
so that we can see our life
and Love in the right way.*

Barbro has been writing poetry since her childhood. In fact, many have compared her to Anne Frank, whom she believes herself to have been in a prior incarnation. As we open ourselves to the transformative effects of unconditional Love, we open to other possibilities as well. Indeed, did not Jesus himself state that John the Baptist was Elijah? (See *Matthew* 11:14). I've also heard a rumor that President Obama was once President Lincoln ... *hmmm.*

The religion of Love opens many doors, it purifies, and it saves. Love will vanquish the Great Cusp and act as the vanguard for the Fifth Spiritual Paradigm – the peaceful epoch prophesied in all faith traditions. Therefore, we ask you to adopt Love as a fundamental principle. Once enough of us embrace Love as an over-arching belief system, a "tipping point" will be reached, after which *all of us* will pass into a glorious New Millennium, even those who may not yet comprehend unconditional Love. Who knows, maybe it is the additional weight of your soul that will create the tipping point ...

WHY ARE THERE SO MANY RELIGIONS?

By Barbara Talley

Why are there so many religions?
How do we know which one is right?
Why can't the followers of each religion Love one another?
Why must they kill and fight?

Why can't they co-exist?
Why must they seek to annihilate?
Why are the people of Haiti and Africa
Less important than those in America or Kuwait?

I think that all people should be respected
And worship God as prompted by their heart,
And that religious leaders should promote unity.
How can they preach Love and purposefully keep the people at war
and apart?

If religious people truly Love their Holy Books,
They should follow their own version of the Golden Rule.
The instruction is simple – just Love one another,
And don't be judgmental, hateful, or cruel.

And I think they should study each other's religion,
So that they will be able see:
They are meant to live together peacefully,
Even though they don't always agree.

I believe everything in God's creation represents life,
And life represents change, movement, and growth.
Right this moment two people are arguing over their religions,
Never considering that truth might be embedded in both.

Maybe if we search a little deeper,
If we open our inner eye we will see,
That it's the people who are divided and in reality,
The spiritual truths of all religions agree.

So maybe it isn't which religion is right ...
Maybe each was right for its own region and day ...
Maybe each was the Will of God for a specific reason ...
Maybe each – for a time – was the right and only way.

All the prophets brought important messages:
Moses, Buddha, Christ, Muhammad, and Bahá'u'lláh too.
But didn't Christ say there was still more to say,
And that God would send a Comforter to you?

Why are there so many religions?
Could it be that God wanted it that way?
Maybe He reveals them one after the other
Because He still has so much more to say.

———⟫◆⟪———

President Obama used the "L" word the other day ... it was music to my ears:

> Far too often, we have seen faith wielded as a tool to divide us from one another – as an excuse for prejudice and intolerance. Wars have been waged. Innocents have been slaughtered. ... But no matter what we choose to believe, let us remember that there is no religion whose central tenet is hate. ... This much we know.
> We know, too, that whatever our differences, there is one law that binds all great religions together. ... It is, of course, the Golden Rule – the call to Love one another, to understand one another, to treat with dignity and respect those with whom we share a brief moment on this Earth. It is an ancient rule, a simple rule, but also one of the most challenging.
> For it asks each of us to take some measure of responsibility for the well-being of people we may not know ... Sometimes, it asks us to reconcile with bitter enemies or resolve ancient hatreds. And that requires a living, breathing, active faith. It requires us not only to believe, but to do – to give something of ourselves for the benefit of others and the betterment of our world.

I am thinking of that boot camp drill – the one where the entire platoon has to get over a concrete wall that's about 12 feet high. If the soldiers are smart, they don't leave their slowest, smallest man behind to fend for himself. One of the bigger, taller guys gives him a leg up and then faces the wall alone. In this way, the last man is strong enough to pull himself over the wall, thereby ensuring that the entire platoon completes the drill ... and survives.

You don't get there, I don't get there, until we all get there. In our next essay, John highlights this inclusive truth.

A BETTER TOMORROW:
COMMUNITY BASED ON UNCONDITIONAL LOVE

By John Dennison, J.D.

We are each at the center of our own Universe, charged with the responsibility of creating a life that will bring us the experiences for which we came. Love of self helps us do that. However, we are not self-contained in our experience of life. The fabric of our reality is intricately interwoven with the lives of others who cross our path. While we might pretend our lives affect only us, everything we are and do is a stone dropped into the great sea of life, the consequences rippling out to affect everyone and everything else in the world.

As we learn to Love ourselves and set aside the egocentric blinders with which we go about our lives, we grow more and more aware of the interconnectedness of life within this great system of creation. This awareness is enhanced and amplified as each of us awakens to the possibilities of our inner world; it helps us move closer to our Source and to understand the oneness of all expressions of life that flow from it.

It does not take such an expansion of awareness, however, for us to realize that we affect and are affected by the people in our lives. Even the most egocentric among us recognizes that interactions with others impact how we experience life. Other people can bring us up, and just as easily bring us down.

Most of the time, we bounce from encounter to encounter like pinballs – haphazardly playing our roles in a passion play that seems scripted by an unseen hand. Nevertheless, as we awaken to the forces at work beneath the surface of these interplays and the processes they trigger within us, we become empowered to more consciously create experiences that will better serve both others and ourselves.

But this level of comprehension is far beyond where most of us are. Much of the time, we're so wrapped up in our own affairs that we're oblivious to the causes of our conditions, much less the complex roles those factors play as we touch the lives of others. Our thoughts and emotions consume us, and there is little room for anything else within the purview of our limited perspectives.

It is only through our relationships – especially those we develop with family, friends, and life partners – that we begin to raise our vision to anything beyond our own concerns. Within those relationships, we feel safe enough to drop our protective walls and open our hearts. Doing so brings mixed results.

Sometimes, the feeling of joy when hearts touch is replaced by a sense of alien-ation and even hostility when they don't. Similarly, others' peace of mind or the closeness of connection may be pushed aside by pain when judgment, per-ceived wrongdoing, or loss drives a stake deep into our hearts. While such internal reactions are central to our experience of relationships, they provide us with benefits on a far more important level – that of our personal evolu-tion. For these relationships are the testing grounds where we create the les-sons needed for our growth. Within them, we learn how to Love and be loved while living in harmony (or disharmony) with others.

Moreover, besides providing an environment where we can work within the ebb and flow of interpersonal energies, relationships expand the experiential base of even the most egocentric person. Through our relationships, we begin to vicariously experience what happens to others and how life impacts them (i.e., empathy). Just as importantly, we begin to realize how our actions impact others, and vice versa. Their joy and suffering can become ours, and ours can become theirs, since what happens to one of us bleeds over into the other.

The lessons of relationship don't stop there. Often, our concern for the well-being of others may even supplant concerns for the self, causing us to deny our own needs to serve those of the people we Love. Unfortunately, even selfless service comes at a price, especially when we give so much that there's nothing left for us. Thus, relationships challenge us to Love ourselves even while loving others, often requiring a precarious balancing act to serve the needs of all.

While family and friends are wonderful teachers in the nuances of Love, eventually our affairs bring us into contact with others with whom we *don't* share such close connections. Through these "outsiders," we gather a whole new set of experiences. And while these relationships are ostensibly to serve some common interest, like doing business or advancing a cause, they allow us to expand, refine, and apply the lessons of relationship on a far broader scale. In effect, these extended relationships plug us into the great web of human civilization, as we take our place within groups. These groups consti-tute communities, whether they call themselves that or not. Communities come in all shapes and sizes, with all sorts of reasons for being. Some are as small as the core family unit; others are entire nations of people.

Regardless of structure, communities provide an environment where we can apply the lessons of relationship on a broader scale and begin to re-learn them in a new context. For just as being part of a family allows us to be part of something greater than ourselves, participation in community pushes those boundaries even farther. Moreover, while our self-interest may remain strong, our identification with community often will cause us to subordinate our desires to the needs of the group. Thus begin our lessons in unconditional Love.

Every relationship involves the challenge of how to Love others while loving ourselves. Community allows us to test and develop that ability on a wider scale. After all, it's easy to Love family and friends; the proximity of such relationships almost mandates that we put up with each other! But in community, there often is no such closeness to paper over the clashes that inevitably occur when human beings come together. Community tests us to find a way to set aside disagreements long enough to accomplish our common intent.

Clashes are inevitable in many cases. For we each bring into community the attributes that make us who we are, including our likes and dislikes, fears and desires, and beliefs and biases. Likewise, we each have our own built-in patterns of thought, action, and response that we've developed throughout our lives. All these patterns are working beneath the surface in every human encounter, predisposing us to conflict when our goals run contrary to those of others.

It is into this cauldron that we dive when we come together in community. Only the hardiest souls are able to weather the storms of such conflicts and still press on to serve the common cause, especially if they aren't the ones whose will prevails. Is it any wonder that so many choose not to participate in group activity or give it less than their all?

At some point, though, we are either drawn or forced by necessity to work within a group environment. Only by exploring our connections with others – the issues that pull us together or drive us apart – can we hope to end the conflicts that impair our ability to work together. Community provides the setting in which we can develop the ability to look beyond surface conflicts to the causal factors that generate them. Then, we become empowered to weave our way through negative energies and, hopefully, dissipate them. Thus, it is through group activity that we begin building a new world.

Throughout history, mankind's preferred means of dealing with others has been the assertion of individual will to get our way – by whatever means necessary – restrained only by our own personal morality and societal standards. But if our vision is to create a world of peace where all our dreams can come true, then we need to evolve to a place where the use of personal will is no longer dominant. After all, will is the instrument of desire, used to advance one set of interests (yours) over another (everyone else's). In so doing, unrestrained will threatens the cohesion of community and perpetuates a "to the victor go the spoils" mentality that keeps us in a state of continual competition and conflict. Unless we learn to master our will, we are doomed; we will fight to get our way and carry the problems of today into the tomorrow we wish to create.

One way to release the use of will is to give up the object on which it is focused – usually the achievement of a desire or the avoidance of a fear. While I don't think any of us would be upset to let go of a fear once and for all, it would not make many of us happy to quit wanting what we want. While such renunciation is a core precept in many spiritual traditions, life offers a richness of experience that few of us are willing to relinquish. Besides, what good would it do to build a new world if we were forced to give up what we wanted it to bring?

There is another way to stop asserting our will; one which holds out the hope that our desires will be satisfied in the end. That way is through the situations offered by community, where our differing interests are prone to clash. It demands a level of awareness and presence that few of us now have, but it is within our reach – an awareness that begins to address the underlying conditions that unleash the energies of conflict. We hone and apply such awareness through a process known as "conscious co-creation," a form of group interaction that simultaneously serves the needs of the one, the many, and the whole.

Conscious co-creation is more than people coming together with a shared intent to achieve a desired result. It simultaneously addresses the nature of conflict and its underlying causes by shifting participants into a perspective that life is about far more than what we create. Instead, it puts the furtherance of self-interest into a greater context defined by how experiences serve the needs of the soul, regardless of whether those experiences evoke joy or pain.

Within this perspective, we no longer need to fight over what we want. We realize that desires and fears are temporary conditions through which we move, gathering what they offer to our development and then continuing on to the next situation. The benefit to our soul is not in the attainment or elimination of a particular condition. It is in what the experience offers us: that which helps us better understand ourselves and our relationship to those with whom we share this world.

Therefore, as our motivating fears and desires come into focus, they can be seen for what they are: carrots dangled to entice us into situations of learning.

In other words, when our fears or desires surface, we're confronted with a choice: we can allow them to poison our relationships and lead us into conflict, or we can somehow circumvent their influence and act in more harmonious ways that better serve us all. As our ability to make such choices grows, the influence of those fears and desires diminishes, reducing our propensity to fight and allowing unconditional Love to permeate our affairs.

So what might such an opportunity mean to us?

We begin to see the world in a new way. When we see conflict between competing extremes, we no longer feel the urge to be drawn into their battles for supremacy. Our awareness allows us to instantly recognize the opposing energies, which are just two sides of the same coin, neither of which exists without the other.

Conversely, if we witness a dispute and are compelled to jump in on one side or the other, then we will know that these extreme or opposite energies must still exist within us. And if so, that is where we'll turn our attention, instead of entering the fray. Remember, the conflicts of our outer world are simply reflections of those at work within us, inviting us to prepare our inner soil so we can consciously participate in our collective evolutionary expansion.

How, then, do we get from where we are to where we want to go?

As we embrace our connection to each other and the world around us, we will naturally come together with others of similar understanding, forming communities through which to explore our common visions. And although our communities will come in many variations and be comprised of a great diversity of individuals, those differences will quickly take a back seat to a shared sense of connection – not only to the cause that draws us together, but to the Source from which we derive life.

At first, our efforts at co-creation may feel awkward or occur in fits and starts. We who form these new communities will in a very real sense be pioneers, learning on the fly how to interact with each other in new and grander ways, as we consciously co-create the foundations which will begin to manifest in our reality. Our efforts will not be isolated to small enclaves. Rather, awakening communities will organically arise and come together with other communities, connecting through central hubs to facilitate communication and cooperative efforts, both at the community and individual levels.

But always, the focus should be on the process of co-creation, recognizing that our goal is to expand the collective consciousness by being forerunners of unconditional Love. We will strive for concrete, substantive accomplishments, but that is a secondary focus. Realistically, our effort will evolve over time with each new experience leaving behind bread crumbs so that others may follow. And we should document both our successes and failures, so those who come after us may build upon our efforts to move our world even closer to where we want it to go.

It won't only be the process, however, that will reduce our propensity for conflict. Harmony also will result from participants' release of pent-up desire, as they contribute the best they have to offer to the community. New creations will flow from participants in ever-expanding waves and without restrictive egocentric barriers to suppress inner creativity. Nor will participants feel the need to jealously guard their expressions of inspiration from others, or apply them solely for their own benefit. For they will perceive such thoughts as making no more sense than allocating blood between their head and their heart. Each soul in the community must be nurtured if the group is to function in a holistic manner.

Some will focus on building new institutions to serve these communities. Others will work to reform our systems of governance or establish new ones that are more reflective of freedom, equality and justice, and less susceptible to usurpation for the benefit of a privileged few. Still more will design and implement economic systems to allow greater opportunity for all. And many will use community to test new philosophies for social organization, like the Progressive Utilization Theory (PROUT) espoused by Prabhat R. Sarkar (presented earlier in this book). Always though, great effort must be made to smoothly interface both old and new theories out of respect for humanity's diverse experiential needs.

Anticipation of such change does not mean turning our back on the established order. Some aspects may be preserved, so long as they do not interfere with the expanding consciousness of the people or the evolution of our civilization. But some societal elements will become increasingly irrelevant to the functioning of the new world. A parallel culture will begin to form within the greater one, not due to isolationism but in furtherance of a common vision.

Eventually, more and more will awaken to the possibilities offered by this New Millenium Renaissance. As it spreads, fewer and fewer will support the money and power games played by our current world order, causing their hold over our affairs to loosen and the institutions they foster to crumble under their own weight. New organizations will naturally take their place, not by Hegelian synthesis or conflict between the old and new, but simply because the expanding consciousness of the new communities will create new methods of meeting the growing need for Love in all our affairs.

Is it possible that the established order will fight back? Certainly. But the nature of this new society will not be confrontational, nor will its members act in opposition to the existing structures. Rather, these lightworkers will operate within the current system by engaging the old guard with unconditional Love, thereby illuminating the underpinnings of a status quo that no longer serves us. Those not ready to come along should be respected for their choice – for each will awaken in his or her own time and way. We would do them a great disservice to interfere with their journey.

This is not to suggest there is anything "wrong" with our existing cultures or those who want to keep things the way they are. The old institutions have served us well, creating the conditions by which consciousness now sprouts and grows. It is just that the old ways no longer feel "good" to a growing segment of the world. As a result, people are naturally gravitating to new patterns that are more conducive to the kind of world they want to live in.

Some may want to work in opposition to the existing system to bring about reform or even revolution. This tendency, however, is best restrained. For such efforts only emphasize polarity and amount to taking sides to assert one's will. Remember, the goal of community is evolution of consciousness, and consciousness does not take sides. Moreover, the practice of unconditional Love accepts that there is value in *every* perspective, *every* desire, and *every* action in this world. To act in opposition means to refuse others the right to be as and what they are. Even worse, polarity reinforces the illusion of separation – where no one is honored and we fail to build the desired new world.

Consequently, the transition to a more perfect union will go smoother if we choose not to dwell upon that which does not match our vision. We must focus our attention, instead, on the many efforts already underway to bring Truth, Love, and Light to our world, while adding our own inspired contributions to the cause. As others see what is being offered, they will naturally join in, and a new world will result. As stated perfectly by Kevin Costner's character in the movie *Field of Dreams:* "Build it and they will come."

Community is the incubator through which this can happen. It is the means to a beautiful end ... where the Golden Rule is finally implemented and we move into the next stage of our collective spiritual journey. Let us seize today this promise of a better tomorrow.

GIFT OF LOVE, LUMINOUS CALLING: HERE I AM TO CONFUSE YOUR HEART

By Oberto "Falco" Airaudi

Translated by Elaine Baxendale
Edited by Esperide Ananas

Our species is animated by a force that allows us to desire, to want, and to achieve a real communion with ourselves and with others: This force is called Love. Love helps the completion of our inner forces. From a spiritual point of view, it allows us to become the *Androgyne* – a complete human being, in whom the masculine and feminine principles are perfectly expressed and integrated.

Opposites joined, strong in Love,
so that all obstacles can be overcome ...

The meeting, the creation,
the primordial power that nature welcomes and supports ...
All traces of Love, all dreams that nature exalts ...
Recalls, joyous calls when being meets essence ...
The signs and secrets create messages,
hidden words that the heart can read
and interpret without the tricks of the mind ...

Heart has no horizon, it dreams in flowing whirls,
like spiritual mists,
it wraps in Love that nothing asks.
The Source, the chalice-spring,
quenches the thirst of parched souls, desiring not to be alone ...

A signal that the soul reads, a call to the inner union,
and to union with whom we want to Love ...
Subtle ancestral signs tell us what to do,
with the language of the dream-sense,
with the ability of reading, once forbidden to us ...
How many am I? How many are we, inside?

To be part of our species, we need to feel loved, so that we can feel important to someone. Yet, to Love means to bare parts of ourselves that distinguish our most profound uniqueness. These two aspects contradict each other: on the one hand, we have a deep need to assert our individuality; on the other, we need to share it. If we are to understand Love, then desire and fear become two elements in apparent opposition that must be reconciled. This happens when we reach an elevated state that is the understanding of oneself joined with the offering of oneself to the other. The giving of oneself means offering what is precious within us in complete trust toward the receiver, independently of whatever they may do with it.

> Subtle communication, the scent of you,
> speaking with gestures and smells,
> telepathically knowing the pleasant depths of your soul ...
>
> It is not a barrier that boundary,
> the skin that separates our bodies,
> but a bond stronger than differences.
> One more chance of union through diversity,
> that draws us together so much ...
>
> The forces that distinguish different species,
> joined in wise alchemy,
> accelerate individual and collective evolution,
> with constant Love ...

Spiritual Love is the completion of two beings. In its fullness, spiritual Love also is made of carnal Love, independently of how sexuality is expressed. This union produces living elements. This is fundamental because we are a "bridge species" between the material and spiritual planes, and we have a Divine spark inside us. Our will and our desire for a relationship are elements that produce vitality. Thus, everything formed through the relationship creates life, even if it is not biological or lasting life.

> A cell of desire rhythmically reproduces itself,
> an inner contrast surfaces every instant,
> it is Love, it is sickness of Love ...
> Not only desire, but a sense of time unfolding,
> our strings weave together and lead to one single,
> stronger tract of time, of life together ...
> Among these signs, as on the traces of a single hand,
> a destiny drawn closer ...
>
> The traces are a call of Love, a sexual signal
> made mystic and sacred,
> shy and courageous, able to call forth the senses,
> the instincts, the personal smell that goes to your head
> and makes your limbs tremble ...
> A spiritual and carnal wrapping around, joyous and passionate,
> a bond that conjoins wanting and desires ...

Love and passion are two different aspects of this physical union, because passion implies an attraction that has limited duration in time, while Love is a force that has unlimited duration. In a relationship between two people, the fact of recognizing oneself in the other person – I am because I am loved and because I know how to Love – is a means to be able to say: *I exist.*

The centre of my Love, the essence that you represent ...
The explosions of pure light inflame the nothingness,
pre-existing non-existing, individual Love touches every form,
life comes and goes – goes and comes back,
mixes and stirs bodies till it reaches us,
our encounter which will bring more life,
more energies and attractions of great emotion ...

The idea of Love is understood by each person according to their state of mind at the moment, and often it is founded upon elements typical of the age in which they live. For these reasons, the concept of Love can manifest in a thousand different ways, from non-egotistical Love to less evolved levels.

Fusion d'Amore by Oberto Airaudi

When Love is merely an act of possession – a condition that wants to limit the expressive abilities of another individual – it transforms the other person into something in the service of our mind. Likewise, considering the other as superior to yourself or someone to adore is, of course, another error. However, if it is Love in the full sense, in the mystical sense, in the philosophical sense, there will be an equal merging, and great pleasure will be derived from the exchange with the other person. Love must be an equal sharing; otherwise, it is always purely an egotistical act.

Gift of Love, luminous calling,
here I am to confuse your heart,
to take what I feel as mine ...
In your breath I hear the soul of your voice,
the astral sense of your sparkling, blinding presence,
a rhythmic whirl spreads over my eyes,
I see you if you are not there ...

Fusion of Love, hearts spiritually transplanted,
then it is new, the heaven that shines above us,
subtle bonds, understandings,
pounding heartbeats in unison,
pulsating in our ears ...

If we do not know how to Love and we are not loved, our flow of existence is less dense, we are more opaque, and we are not sufficiently immersed in the river of existence. This philosophical theme recalls the link between Love and death, wherein one's immortality is either passed down through Love or expressed through the lack of Love (or the fear of the lack of Love). This is a symbolic, magical, and alchemical concept. In fact, in alchemy, the tale of "one's own death due to a Love that ends" is an important, classical thread because it means the ending of one world and the possible beginning of another, whose form is unknown. The ending of a Love means starting to rebuild something new. Waiting for the wounds of the heart to heal and finally close is part of recharging the energies for the new phase, the rebirth, and the hope of a new Love within a new reference.

No Love is useless. It is not true that when we abandon or are abandoned by someone we have lost years of our life. That Love is certain to have been a teaching, an element that has sculpted us so as to become what we are. Ours is an optimistic philosophy. We are committed to becoming better and better. Thus we choose to think that any experience – no matter how tragic, hard, or difficult – leads us toward a future that will be a haven of Love, a haven that we know how to reach. There we have a lighthouse, a reference point, a way of expressing and carrying our seeds further. In the economy of the Universe, moreover, how can it be possible that something we lived, which gave us a sense of duration and filled part of our existence, was of no use? The important thing is not to search for a new Love with the same points of attraction as the one before and the same flaws … as, indeed, so often happens.

> *Codes of Love, dreams to dream, mission!*
> *How do I reach completeness?*
> *I observe, act, meditate, form, the plays of light and feelings,*
> *without fear of not making it!*
> *I know how to hope …*
>
> *Hearts joined by Love for one another,*
> *able to multiply in happiness that of everyone,*
> *rendering just and rewarding the honest efforts*
> *of wanting the good and the goal …*

In the past, alchemists were able to "pass on" Love as part of the concept of eternal Love. Eternal Love is able to overcome time, old age, and anything that leads to the ending of life. We can transcend and overcome physical death through Love, since Love has a meaning beyond the duration of the body, the duration of one's life. It is even possible to meet up with a Love in the beyond. Farewell is not an absolute ending but a recall to the "after," to meeting again, without limitations and without the excessive weight of our human body, our animal self, our own limits, and those represented by things. Farewell is always an act of hope: It is not an end but it really is *an adieu, à Dieu*, to God. The meeting happens inside the realm of divinity and represents the completion of what, sometimes, has not been adequately achieved in life.

> *My Love! Appear to me in all your expressions,*
> *smile at me with convincing strength,*
> *that trust which makes everything achievable!*
> *In the journey that is life,*
> *gather and unravel synchronic alchemy, in time ...*

Thus, there are ways to follow Love from one life to another, to meet again, to look for one another, to find each other again, life after life. It is Love that travels across time and which, sometimes, cancels out time. It is Love that we rebuild in our life or that we try to recognize, lifetime after lifetime, when with our inner senses we reach and feel across the centuries, the millennia. This proves how overwhelming the force of Love can be, how far away it can carry us. Indeed, we navigate inside our feelings and our sails carry us where our hope is able to take us. At times, those anchors of Love that we truly have inside us act as reference points to create safe havens we did not even think existed. This, too, is part of the quest and of our being able to find Love again.

> *A hint of Love, a subtle sigh, things,*
> *words unspoken that suggest "I've found you!"*

Love is part of our inner senses, the senses through which the divinity contained in every human being expresses itself. It is an element arising from our instincts because it is part of our being; yet, it is also an element of our soul. Ideally, Love is the meeting point between our spirituality and our animal self. Love represents the point where these two elements meet and clash – a Divine spark – and it is upon our feelings of Love that we can turn the world around.

History, in fact, is not made with logic but with feelings and emotions. Unfortunately, until now, the coarsest feelings have dominated – the immediate, uncontrolled ones. It is hatred that creates war and conflict, and hatred arises from selfishness. Logic is employed afterwards to justify evil: It is called technology, arms, tactics, strategy ...

Captured formulas,
dreams open upon accessible worlds,
contained by magical supports of great power.

A generous people is noted for its constancy, its faith,
and above all else, its results ...
Life is history, Love, and presence.

Unconditional Love is a Love that transcends the object of Love. It confers such a high value upon those loved that they become very pure, free from alienation, equal to yourself, as it is right they should be. The Love relationship thus becomes the ultimate act of Divine expression, because the completion with the "other" encompasses an extraordinarily elevated state. It takes us in the direction of Love for Love, of Love as an element that makes us feel part of everything.

Love, spiritual union, connection with everything ...
Sensitive exchange of forces and temporal lines ...
Dream that creates, extended seed of life,
intense superhuman power,
dense with synchronic opportunities called Love,
luminous recalling ...

This heightened concept of Love is characteristic of the Divine, and when we are capable of expressing it, we pass from the animal state onto the path of realization and enlightenment. Making form Divine corresponds to transforming form into Love: Form becomes Divine when it identifies itself with the full breadth of Love. At this time, the human race is a "bridge species" between the material plane and the spiritual plane. As such, we are the bearers of a Divine seed which is realized when, on the path of discovering, recognizing, and nurturing the God contained in each one of us, we are able to express unconditional Love.

On the ideal path that leads us from evolution to enlightenment (and from there to a further successive metamorphosis), we will pass through various stages of learning and applying the concept of Love. This path inevitably involves relating to others, so the first act of Love cannot be a casual thing, but must be an act of will. How can we express Love and attend to others except by feeling Love? How can we transform ourselves, even at an organic level, into *something* able to express Divine Love, while still remaining inside the world of form?

To succeed in becoming aligned with the "other" in the realm of matter, we must first understand the complexity of the spiritual realm. We also must interpret the true value of objects, for what can be more precious than another living being? And from this point of view, what can be more precious among living beings than other sentient beings? There cannot be anything else.

> With the heart, and Love,
> and the complete force born out of pure dedication,
> real worlds are generated ...
>
> I show new roads of power, inner and yet plainly shown,
> universal, galactic,
> portals that lead to other Universes ...
>
> In the meeting of oneself, the whole of creation,
> humanity and difference,
> the completion of souls who have the courage to seek,
> to search for and find one another ...
>
> Love is also contemplation of the All ...

Now, Dear Reader, from the stimuli here given: Let there be born in you an inspiration for poetry. Let it be an expression of the Love you have within. And let it take whatever form now comes to the surface ...

At this stage in the anthology, I would imagine that much is coming to the surface ... I've read, reviewed, and relished these selections multiple times now. Yet, every time I read one, I find something novel to ponder, some new aspect that sends me into a deeper meditation on Love.

Falco is the founder of Damanhur in Italy, and he possesses the talents of a Michelangelo. He has built a community that is based on the principle that Love is a verb. Like other masters, Falco encourages us to be active participants in life. He also encourages us to follow our evolutionary impulse without inhibition. His religion is *Action*: practice, proficiency, and perfection.

Falco calls us a "bridge species." Others call our generation a precursor to the "new human." They are referring to the notion that humanity has not yet attained its full spiritual might. One day, we will be like "gods and goddesses," as foreshadowed in the Adam and Eve parable. From there, we may advance to yet a higher level of awareness by acquiring attributes that far exceed our current understanding of our own potential and the scope of the Universe.

The point is that technological advancement should no longer be our goal. Our raw intelligence already exceeds our intuition and empathy. Instead, we should be focusing on developing our right brain and allowing our feminine side to catch up to our masculine side. Only then will we make the adaptive changes required to survive the Great Cusp and express the Love of the Fifth Spiritual Paradigm – the next stage of our evolutionary journey.

O BROTHER!

By Kabir
(1398–1448)

O Brother!

When I was forgetful, my true Guru showed me the Way.
Then I left off all rites and ceremonies,
I bathed no more in the holy water.
Then I learned that it was I alone who was mad,
   and the whole world beside me was sane,
   and I had disturbed these wise people.

From that time forth,
I knew no more how to roll in the dust in obeisance.
   I do not ring the temple bell.
   I do not set the idol on its throne.
   I do not worship the image with flowers.

It is not the austerities that mortify the flesh which are
pleasing to the Lord.
When you leave off your clothes and kill your senses,
you do not please the Lord.

The man who is kind and who practices righteousness,
   who remains passive amidst the affairs of the world,
   who considers all creatures on Earth as his own self,
He attains the Immortal Being,
the true God is ever with him.

One of the most famous poets in the Middle East and India, Kabir's connection to the Divine was a natural consequence of his simple nature and inquisitive mind. What is so special about Kabir is that he reached enlightenment *without* detaching from the world – he was married, had children, worked as a weaver, and associated with the lower castes. In sum, he recognized that spiritual transformation is not achieved by following religious rules and ritual, but by performing righteous acts of Love.

In the next chapter, we will meet other souls who have managed to reach heights of spiritual ecstasy and still share themselves with the world. Like the other authors in this collection, they are true teachers whose Love of their brothers and sisters is just as great as their Love of God.

INTEGRAL SPIRITUALITY

*I think the sages are the growing tip of the secret impulse of evolution. ...
I think they are riding the edge of a light beam
racing toward a rendezvous with God.*

*And I think they point to the same depth in you, and in me, and in all of us.
I think they are plugged into the All ... and Spirit shines though their eyes.
And I think they disclose the face of tomorrow,
they open us to the heart of our own destiny ....*

*And in that startling recognition the voice of the sage becomes your voice,
the eyes of the sage become your eyes, you speak with the tongues of angels
and are alight with the fire of realization that never dawns nor ceases,
you recognize your own true Face in the mirror of the Kosmos itself:
your identity is indeed the All, and you are no longer part of that stream,
you are that stream, with the All unfolding not around you but in you.*

Ken Wilber (b. 1949), *A Brief History of Everything*

Just as there are phases to our physical, emotional, and cognitive develop-ment, so there are stages to our spiritual evolution. Today, these levels of consciousness are studied and charted by unbiased truth seekers. These teachers have left behind outdated notions about God and hold no allegiance to any of the patriarchal Fourth Paradigm religions. Instead, these gurus have painstakingly conquered all their Earth plane attachments, rejected detach-ment as yet another myopic delusion, and returned to us reborn – just like the ascended masters of old – to lead us toward God.

Love of God is not easy. Indeed, divinity was once believed to be the province of prophets alone. Yet, each of us has the potential to reach this supreme awareness, as heaven is a state of being, not an afterlife reward. Thus, may America rededicate herself to the light and be the first nation to collectively comprehend *integral spirituality!*

TEN GUIDELINES FOR ENLIGHTENMENT

By Swami Beyondananda
(a/k/a Steve Bhaerman)

1. Be a fun-damentalist. Make sure the fun always comes before the mental. Realize that life is a situation comedy that will never be cancelled. A laugh track has been provided, and the reason why we are put in the material world is to get more material. Also, have a good laughsitive twice a day to ensure regularhilarity.

2. Remember that each of us has been given a special gift just for entering the game of life. So you're already a winner!

3. The most powerful tool on the planet today is tell-a-vision That is where I tell a vision to you, and you tell a vision to me.

4. Life is like photography. You use the negative to develop.

5. As we go through life thinking heavy thoughts, thought particles can get caught between the ears, causing a condition called truth decay. So be sure to use mental floss twice a day. And when you're tempted to practice tantrum yoga, remember what we teach in Swami's Absurdiveness Training Class: Don't get even, get odd.

6. If we want world peace, we must let go of our attachments and truly live like nomads. That's where I no mad at you, and you no mad at me. That way, there surely will be no-madness on the planet. And peace begins with each of us. A little peace here, a little peace there, pretty soon all the peaces will fit together to make one big peace everywhere!

7. Great Earth changes have been predicted for the future. So if you're looking to avoid earthquakes, my advice is simple: When you find a fault, just don't dwell on it.

8. There's no need to change the world. All we have to do is toilet train the world, and we'll never have to change it again.

9. If you're looking to find the key to the Universe, I have some bad news and some good news. The bad news is: There is no key to the Universe. The good news is: It has been left unlocked.

10. Finally, everything I have written has been channeled. So if you don't like it, it's not my fault. Besides, enlightenment is not a bureaucracy. You don't have to go through channels.

Surprise! A little humor to ease the tension. Swami Beyondananda recognizes that even elevating concepts like spirituality, enlightenment, and Love can get a little heavy. He rightly feels that it is best to study these principles with a dose of humor mixed in. And he reminds us that life isn't worth living if we don't stop to smell the flowers. So let's focus for a spell on the principle of levity as it relates to Love.

Case in point: I got a dozen roses from Steve about twenty minutes ago (tomorrow is Valentine's Day). A FedEx man just delivered them, but before I realized what was happening, I got annoyed because Shadow started barking and I could hear a car coming up my gravel driveway. I had just made a bowl of soup, climbed the stairs to my office, and sat down to start narrating this final chapter. *I do not want to be disturbed! I'm about to write about Love of God, for God's sake …*

When the FedEx man left, I stood in my kitchen holding a long pink box that obviously contained roses. I thought about leaving them on the kitchen counter. *I can put them in water later – Steve won't know.* But I quickly realized how ungrateful that would be, so while my soup and my concentration started to get cold, I took ten minutes to arrange my roses in a vase (I even cut off the ends and added the white powder stuff). Then I carried the flowers upstairs with me and put them on my desk … back to work!

But then I felt guilty because I had not called Steve to thank him. *A call will delay me even further!* So I didn't call. I sat down and wrote the first paragraph of this narration. Please look again at what I wrote: *Life isn't worth living if we don't stop to smell the flowers.* Swami is right. Nothing should interfere with living life – not even a serious task like writing about Love of God. Now, I'm crying. I'm signing off to call Steve …

Okay, I'm back. You'll never guess what just happened. Before I start work each day, I pull an Angel Card. However, today I was so eager to get started that I forgot. After I called Steve, I went to the cards and asked what the theme of the narration should be for this chapter … and I pulled *Humour!* The picture on the card is an angel dressed like a clown with balloons in his hands – two red and two blue. Get it? The New Millennium, which is perfectly balanced – no buoyed – by red/female and blue/male energy. Wow!

Angel ® Cards by Joy Drake and Kathy Tyler

OUR LOVE FOR GOD:
HOW IT EXPANDS AS WE DO

By P.M.H. Atwater, L.H.D.

The hunger to be with God begins when we leave God. Have you ever heard toddlers, once verbal, chatter on and on about God and how, for sure, they will not forget God this time? Many youngsters remember their "before birth" and are determined to continue doing so. Yet, they begin to forget once other priorities fill their minds, or their hearts are punched by those who chide, "Grow up and act your age." And if their home life is abusive or overly strict, kids tend to cut God off or believe only what they are told – verbatim. We humans don't usually explore the concept of a Supreme Being or the reality of Deity until we are well beyond the limits of cultural and religious dicta, or until we feel safe enough, courageous enough, to ask questions.

The hunger to reconnect with God drives us (even when we deny it). And that hunger is Love based. Questions come: Am I just kidding myself? Maybe there really isn't a God? Can I trust what I feel? Will God Love me back? The stages between the innocence of acceptance and the maturity of expansion into higher states of understanding are many. But once we really start to seek God and search farther afield, we begin to realize that our depth of feeling, our heart's response, is all the confirmation we need.

Our desire to Love God is innate within us – literally part of our brain chemistry and structure. Quite rationally, atheists argue that our so-called "Love of God" is really just a response to cultural programming applied to this brain chemistry. However, in my work with adults and children who have experienced a near-death state, 99.9% of them return to life head over heels in Love with God – *especially the atheists*. The vast majority, as if on cue, become more loving and expressively so, exuding a compassion that seems blind to conditions, limits, or boundaries. This "unconditional Love" represents the highest and best in the human family, and it lies at the core of religious and spiritual practices designed to enable individuals to reach higher levels of bliss. Achieving this ability – to be able to Love as God does – comes about as a consequence of surviving death, of somehow cheating the "grim reaper."

The near-death phenomenon first came onto the scene in 1975, thanks to Raymond E. Moody, Jr.'s best-seller *Life After Life*. Since then, the near-death experience has become synonymous with unconditional Love and Love of God. Moreover, since 1977 – when I survived three deaths in three months, each episode a different near-death experience – I have been able to assist in this exploration. That means I wear two hats: one as an experiencer and the other as a researcher. Today, my database on adult and child near-death experiences is one of the largest in the world, and I have written nine books on my findings, some now verified in mainstream medical and clinical studies.

I want to underscore right from the start that the vast majority of near-death experiencers have positive, uplifting episodes. Experiencers talk almost non-stop about the Love they felt while on the "other side." There is nothing else quite like it, they say – a knowing of oneness and worth, of total freedom and acceptance. No demands. No stipulations. No conditions. Just Love. A boundless, infinite, all-encompassing Love, so immense that nothing can contain it. And they want to emulate, develop, and expand that Love, so that it will become a daily reality in their lives.

As one who has lived to tell the tale of my death experiences, I can explain what happens:

> As a researcher, I can assure you that any type of near-death experience can be life changing. But as an experiencer, I can positively affirm that being bathed in the Light on the other side of death is more than life changing. That Light is the very essence, the heart and soul, the all-consuming consummation of ecstatic ecstasy. It is a million Suns of compressed Love, dissolving everything unto itself, annihilating thought and cell, vaporizing humanness and history into the one great brilliance of All that is and All that ever was and All that ever will be.
>
> You know it's God. No one has to tell you. You know.
>
> You can no longer believe in God, for belief implies doubt. There is no more doubt. None. You now know God. And you know that you know, and you're never the same again.
>
> And you know who you are ... a child of God, a cell in the Greater Body, an extension of the One Force, an expression from the One Mind. No more can you forget your identify, or deny or ignore or pretend it away.
>
> There is One, and you are of the One.
>
> P.M.H. Atwater, *Beyond the Light*

Surprisingly, most children who experience near-death describe God as a loving father or grandfather type – rarely female. The younger the child, the more this is true. However, teenagers and adults who come back to life are more likely to experience God as a bright sphere of all-knowing, all-loving light. If challenged by the experiencer to reveal "itself," the God figure invariably dissolves into a burst of brilliance, "brighter than a million Suns" or "more powerful than all the bombs on Earth combined into a single blast." They also report that this figure is beyond human comprehension and unlike any other image or presence.

Eventually, the idea of gender – of Mother, Father, or It – fades. After the experience, titles most often used to depict God include: the One, Source, Deity, Isness, the Force, the Source of All Being, that which is Nameless, and other such offerings. Experiencers then claim to have a deep and abiding Love of God (or Allah, Vishnu, or whatever title is used in their particular religion). They now Love God with all their heart, soul, and mind. Most emphasize that they Love their neighbors as much or more than self. And therein hangs the challenge: *God's Love is unconditional, and what is expected from us in return is unconditional Love as well.*

There is no question that near-death experiencers become more loving – no question whatsoever. But they are not always perceived that way. In fact, many times they are perceived to be aloof, arrogant, snobbish, egotistical, or flying around on some kind of cloud unable to "land" and be normal again. Perhaps people see them this way because they are jealous of the overt enthusiasm experiencers often display, or maybe something else is involved, something far deeper and more threatening.

Consider this incident as just such an example. A woman in Bedford, Virginia, had been pronounced dead from automobile accident injuries, but she later revived. Months after she recovered, her worried family asked me for help. The woman was middle-aged, married, had several older children and a younger one, and was a professional health-care provider with yet another business on the side. After spending several hours interviewing her and her family, I noticed an all-too-familiar pattern. While she described feeling so much Love and joy that she might burst, her family shuddered. Not only did they *not* feel the Love she was describing with great animation and excitement, they thought she was hallucinating and out of touch with reality. She was gloriously happy; they were afraid. She was open, willing, and ready to change everything in her life; they wanted her to be the same person she was before she died – no changes, nothing different, just "normal." Thus, while she was utterly aglow and transformed, they were bereft.

Here is another explanation, as told by a near-death experiencer from New Britain, Connecticut:

*There is total Love and sometimes incredible sadness on the surface ...
they don't go together ... I am unable to adequately express the Love I
experienced. I have been told by some people they can feel the Love
when I am with them. That makes me very happy, because then I know
that I have shared the Love even if it was non-verbal.*

When this man spoke more about what he went through, he added, "I was
God, God was me." That kind of experience, that kind of bond with God is
beyond the comprehension of most people. How do you bring that kind of
Love and knowing back to Earth, back to everyday living, without sounding
like some kind of Messiah?

Another woman, this one from Waynesboro, Virginia, nearly collapsed in
my arms after one of my seminars, because I had stated that it was perfectly
normal for those who survive death to have difficulty personalizing Love after
such an experience. Her story was typical. She had been sent from psychologist to psychologist and had been in therapy for over a year because she could
not Love her husband and children the same way after her near-death experience. She still loved them, but in a more detached and objective way which,
to them, appeared as unloving. She cared deeply about her family, but she
now loved each family member equally and also loved them equally with
every other person she knew. Consequently, they felt that the bond of intimacy
had been broken. Her Love no longer had an object or singular focus. She was
filled with Love for them and everyone else in her life – more than ever before
– but she could not personalize it, she could not make her Love exclusive to a
select few. Sadly, her family made accusations and threats which caused her to
feel a deep, gnawing guilt. Why couldn't she Love her husband and her children as before? If she felt more loving than ever, then why couldn't they feel
it? Why couldn't they see all the incredible changes that had happened to her?

I might never have solved this strange puzzle had it not been for my oldest
daughter, Natalie. She brought it to my attention – adamantly! After my near-
death experiences, I, too, felt unusually loving. I knew I had found God, and
I was utterly devoted to sharing my experience of unconditional Love.
Natalie, though, had never heard of unconditional Love and, quite frankly,
she wasn't interested. As far as she was concerned, I had become unreachable,
and she felt abandoned. In fact, both of my daughters started to complain that
I was so detached that "nothing mattered to me anymore." Yes, I was easier
to talk with; and, yes, I was more understanding; but, no, I was no longer personal, familiar, or even lovable. I wasn't even a nice woman anymore! They
wanted Mom back, but none of us knew where to find her.

Of all the after-effects from the near-death experience, I believe this one is the most important and the most misunderstood, for Love is *the* central human emotion, and a sense of belonging is paramount to sound mental health. Therefore, perhaps we need to rethink what constitutes Love – especially unconditional Love and Love of God.

As a starting point, let us be very practical about what it means to reach the heightened states of unconditional Love and Love of God: *It means everyone is you, and you are everyone!* It also means that every woman you see is your mother, sister, aunt, and daughter; every man you meet is your father, brother, uncle, and so on. It means you cannot divide or separate people, that you have no expectations, no needs, no wants, no conditions of any sort in loving. In such a state of being, Love loses its object and becomes amorphous. Can you imagine what kind of world this would be if everyone loved like that? It could be glorious ... or it could be a disaster.

Let's be even more practical. True Love of God means no privacy, no secrets, no keys, no judgments, and no exceptions. Nothing is held back, either from God or others. You not only are vulnerable but also transparent. So, while unconditional Love may sound incredible – *and it is!* – such Love is not always sensible for all people in every situation, at least not until more of us reach this state of being.

In the meantime, perhaps the wiser choice is balance or a combination of loving skills, whereby a person can be personal and intimate with immediate family and loved ones, yet still Love others without conditions. Such a juggling act requires caution and discernment; it is exclusive to a point, yet still open, accepting, and nonjudgmental. The near-death experiencer can help set this standard of behavior by showing how one can be both objective and subjective, inclusive yet discerning with Love.

One experiencer who came to exemplify such a positive balance died in an automobile accident in 1932 while in his twenties. He revived and recovered, but he was never the same. Eventually, he married and had three sons, settling down in Parma, Idaho. He loved his wife and sons dearly, yet everyone was "family" to him. He would go out of his way to help anyone at any time – even when it meant losing his job. For example, he dared to openly defend American-born Japanese during World War II, and he dared to share his near-death experience during classroom hours as a teacher. In both cases, he was tossed out as a kook and was labeled such for years ... until he was named one of Idaho's "Most Distinguished Citizens." Only then was the wonder of his many accomplishments revealed to the world.

Obviously, people undergo similar transformations without the near-death experience, and they report similar shifts in consciousness. One may awaken to higher aspects of existence through the purity of *wanting* to know more about God. Ask any truth seeker – chances are they'll sound just like those toddlers I mentioned who chatter on and on about God. And the more personal the awakening, the stronger the conviction that what was encountered is God.

Through the ages, this kind of spirited fullness or knowingness has been termed "enlightenment" – literally a waking up to light, an illumination of light, a reunification with "the Light." There are mystical traditions that describe how one may attain such an exalted state. The pathways are numerous, yet the goal is always the same – reunion with God. When a person undergoes a major transformation of consciousness, his or her previous belief system (or lack thereof) makes no difference whatsoever. The individual is now free to walk and talk with God, without reservation or restriction.

Today, untold numbers of people are approaching enlightenment. By expanding the scope of inquiry beyond the near-death cases, researchers have discovered many other spiritual experiences that produce higher states of awareness. Generally referred to as "transformations of consciousness," these episodes include: peak experiences (spiritual highs); unitive experiences (merging into Oneness with all things); *kundalini* (normally associated with Eastern religions, when spiritual energy moves up the spine, throughout the endocrine system, then "explodes" out the top of one's head); shamanic vision quests (indigenous practices that involve moving into realms beyond the Earth plane); baptism of the Holy Spirit (the revelation held sacred in the three religions of Abraham); and sudden transformations stemming from prayer and meditation (where the power of commitment is strong enough to initiate the spiritual process).

Transformations of consciousness, regardless of how caused, change individuals in deep and profound ways. Most notably, experiencers share a similar pattern of after-effects, such as a tendency toward expressing forgiveness, unconditional Love, and true Love of God. The power unleashed by these higher states is becoming a global phenomenon. Millions of people are involved. But researchers recognize that most of these transformations are partial, that the after-effects take some getting used to, and that what seems so wondrous and desirable can be bittersweet. Balance seems to be the key. As we advance in our understanding of enlightenment, we are challenged to remember that even the most loving and forgiving have to learn how to integrate the truth of their new awareness into everyday practice.

The Creator is One, not many, say experiencers. Our Love of God – if a true Love – includes, embraces, and encircles, because God is the God of all. While we often mistakenly worship aspects of God as "mini-gods," experiencers say there is only the One. Once we awaken to this higher truth, we understand that our Love for God and God's Love for us is all encompassing.

This concept of inclusivity – of unconditional Love – is still a foreign concept to millions of people around the world. Chosen "Messengers" or "Messiahs" have revealed God in ways which appear exclusive to the needs of a given populace at a particular time and place. What has survived is religious dogma, which now is being challenged by those who are in the very act of loving God. Thus, revelation continues because Love continues. To Love God is to open one's heart beyond the boundaries of self, family, country, or religious viewpoint. To Love God is to transcend mankind's attempts to define both Love and God.

This Love of God – the core of ecstasy itself and the throne of bliss and exaltation – has been demonstrated by a parade of saints, martyrs, devotees, and even assassins, so radical in their worldview that to explain away their "selfless" acts of sacrifice or slaughter is virtually impossible. I do not believe any amount of research or psychological modeling will ever fully explain the depth of the human desire to Love God. Rightly or wrongly, whether activated by a sense of surrender or submission, we struggle to reestablish our knowingness of God by loving that which we seek – which is in fact seeking us.

As a researcher and experiencer of near-death, as a religious and spiritual practitioner, as a shaman rooted in the elemental world of mystery and magic, as a visionary who is as much at home with sky grids as with cellular molecules, and as a chaplain who hears cries of tragedy, I say this: *There is nothing that compares to a Love for God.*

Forgive me, but I must be candid. I have been married for decades and have children and grandchildren. Words are insufficient to express how much I Love my husband and my family. Even so, God is my next breath – my only breath. God is the reason I get up in the morning and the reason I go to bed at night. God is every morsel I eat, every sip of water I drink, and every smile, sneeze, tear, and heartbeat I express. Which is why I give all that I can give to God ... every day ... day after day.

To understand this type of Love – the ultimate of what a human being can feel – is to comprehend the meaning of life and the reason for our being. Words on paper cannot do this. Only the heart can. For only the heart may truly Love God.

WHERE IS GOD?

Attributed to Jalaluddin Rumi
(1207–1273)

I tried to find Him on the Christian cross,
but He was not there.

I went to the Temple of the Hindus and to the old pagodas,
but I could not find a trace of Him.

I searched on the mountains and in the valleys,
but neither in the heights nor in the depths was I able to find Him.

I went to the Ka'ba in Mecca,
but He was not there either.

I questioned the scholars and philosophers,
but He was beyond their understanding.

I then looked into my heart,
and it was there that I saw Him.

He was nowhere else to be found.

———※·◇·※———

In addition to the records left by mystics such as Rumi, we now have scientific data to help explain the enlightenment experience. P.M.H. has compiled a vast database on the subject, and her descriptions of the after-effects are fascinating. Once a person consistently models unconditional Love, he or she is often labeled "odd" or "uncaring." It is ironic, but not unprecedented.

I often have wondered about Jesus' treatment of his family. In one gospel, his family called to him from a crowd, but he turned and said, "Who are my mother and my brothers? ... Whoever does the will of God is my brother and sister and mother." (*Mark* 3:31–35). P.M.H.'s work helps explain this passage. Jesus not only passed into unconditional Love, he also merged with God. Thus, although he still Loved his family, he Loved everyone else just as much.

To those who are not ready to practice this sort of Love, it does seem odd. We Love our own children more than the ones on TV who are suffering. We see images of destitute children, but in a few minutes we forget about them. Not so for those who have passed into unconditional Love. The child on TV is their child; the war-torn village is their home; the abused millions are their family. They feel the pain of the world and set about trying to lessen it. Not surprisingly, the first time they experience this sort of Love, it rocks their world ...

LOVE, CHRIST MIND, AND THE GOD STATE

By Penny Kelly

I was thirty years old when I first encountered the Christ within, although I didn't recognize it at the time. I was helping to build the set for a community play when a friend dropped in for a visit. Deeply focused on what I was doing, yet just as engaged with my friend, I suddenly lost all sense of who and where I was. My self and my ordinary boundaries disappeared. I became everyone and everything … and that was just a taste of what would follow.

A couple of months later, a huge rumbling sound engulfed me. For a second, I thought it was the roar of jets taking off from Selfridge Air Force Base just down the street. However, the roar was coming from inside me and was accompanied by a force that traveled up the center of my body, hit my brain, and kept on going, exploding consciousness until I was floating in a limitless ocean of silent, twinkling lights … filled with indescribable Love and knowing only one thing – *I am!*

For those few amazing moments, nothing existed, except extraordinary bliss and the totality of existence. I floated there, gently, in that peaceful stillness for what seemed like an eternity, resting in the ecstasy of what it is to experience the eternal Godhead.

In the weeks and months that followed, the experience began to repeat itself without warning: at work, on the highway, in the grocery store, while vacuuming the living room. Totally ignorant about what was happening to me, I tried frantically to stop it. At the time, there was no one around to explain the phenomenon, known in Eastern traditions as a *kundalini* awakening. There was no one to tell me I had just been initiated by grace into union with God, according to Christian mysticism.

God is not something you can understand through printed words or speech. God is something you must experience to comprehend. One taste of God, however, and nothing is ever the same again. Not even a little bit. After the *kundalini* experiences began, I could no longer carry on with my life as it had been. I no longer wanted the things I once wanted. I didn't have the same interests, and I felt no obligation to maintain the same relationships. Sadly, I did not understand that the Christ within begins to awaken with that first dip into the Godhead. Worse, I was plagued by clairvoyance, clairaudience, and numerous other gifts and abilities of consciousness that left me unable to "not know" the things I now knew about people and situations. In the end, my lover left me, my career disintegrated, and I descended into a personal hell created mainly by my efforts to convince myself that life was the same as it had once been.

Although we often speak of Jesus Christ as if that were his full name, *Christ* was not Jesus' last name. Christ is the English translation for the Greek word *khristos*, which means "the anointed." It is a title given to someone who has experienced God and gone on to more fully develop the characteristics of God consciousness in the self.

The fact is that within each one of us there exists a self whose ultimate potential is to develop Christ consciousness and live that consciousness in the everyday world. In ancient days, those who touched or tasted this consciousness became prophets, yogis, or shamans who helped others progress toward their own enlightenment. These teachers often started with small groups that came together to learn the rituals and practice the discipline that would kindle such an awakening in each one. Eventually, some of these spiritual leaders assumed formal titles, and the ancient rituals became the framework of orthodox religious institutions.

Today, most religious institutions teach you to worship God, Jesus, or various prophets and saints rather than discover and develop the Christ that lives within you. The decision to develop your inner Christ is a serious commitment. It requires you to drop your belief in duality and discipline yourself to align with a thought system that allows only Oneness with *Life*. This means that you no longer believe in life *and* death; there is only Life. You no longer see good and evil; there is only good. You no longer experience joy and sorrow; there is only joy. There is no possibility of health and disease; there is only health.

To comprehend Oneness, you must discipline yourself to defer to the presence of the Christ consciousness within as if that presence were a real person living inside who knows all, is powerful, unlimited, and overflowing with Love and grace. It's like planting a seed, then carefully watering and feeding that seed, pulling out weeds, and cultivating the ground around it until there is finally a flower or fruit to harvest – the fruit being the Christ-self that emerges from inside you.

Once awakened, Christ consciousness requires ongoing attention and nurturing. It asks that you remain totally and completely in the present, with all of the life energy and Love that flows through you. You do not allow yourself to obsess about how your mother-in-law insulted you last week, or why your employee stole money from the cash register last month. Neither do you worry and fret about whether the economy might crash next year, or anticipate that you will grow old and die. To be totally present in the moment erases any past or future – it does away with time. The result is that you step into eternity.

Does this sort of belief system upset your life at first? Of course! Family, friends, and co-workers want you to be pretty much the same today as you were yesterday. Moreover, current rules of our physical reality are based on duality and contain all sorts of conflicting assumptions, expectations, and demands. When you stop living by those rules and set down rules of your own based on joy, health, abundance, and Love, chaos is likely to ensue for a while.

In the early months of nurturing Christ consciousness, the first thing I discovered was that I had nothing to talk about. Most of my prior conversations had been based on what happened in the past or might happen in the future. The rest were worried monologues about what was happening in the present. My challenge was to continue celebrating my existence while generating Love for others in the midst of chaos. I had to learn to be quiet, inside and out. Silence deepens Christ consciousness and leads you further into the God-state.

When you enter the God-state, you experience pure, complete, unmitigated, and unadulterated Life – with a capital L – and this experience is perfectly summed up in two words: *I am!* To say "I am" is to say "I exist." It is the recognition that you are alive, that you are Life itself, and that pure Life does not, and cannot, include the concept of death. Death is an illusion generated by humanity and has nothing to do with Life.

Aligning with Life requires that you give up believing in death and, instead, invest in transforming yourself. It means learning to nurture Life and generate Love at will, rather than being subject to the ups and downs of physical matter and earthly events. It means learning to manage yourself until you have "dominion over" your earthly reality – the true meaning of God's blessing in the first chapter of *Genesis*.

Love infuses Life. While in the God-state, you grasp the meaning of Love at wordless levels and later discover that no verbal description can even begin to communicate this all-encompassing Love. Only by being Love and acting it out can you express what you know ... and what you know is that Life is Love, and Love is Life. They are the same – a true Oneness that we have come to call God.

There are beings who exist permanently in the God-state. Myths and stories of this level filter down to us as "heaven," the place where angels live. Some believe heaven is a state of consciousness, but this is too simplistic.

Heaven is both a way of consciousness and the kind of reality that flows from that consciousness. When no more belief or attention goes into duality, time, physical bodies, matter, limitation, death, free will, or fear, the result is an environment characterized by Oneness, eternity, energy bodies, joy, abundance, life, Divine will, and Love.

Oneness means that you recognize the Universal Law by which every thought you think and action you perform returns to impact you. Thus, you very deliberately and consciously work to think and act in ways that will bring only vibrant life, peace of mind, joy, abundance, and Love back to you.

Eternity means there is no such thing as time, there is only now. The past and the future are illusions. What happened yesterday doesn't exist anymore, and tomorrow is not yet here. If someone hurt you last month, that event is over. The question becomes, "Why are you still thinking, feeling, or acting as if that event is happening in the present moment?"

Perhaps you've seen a bedraggled, unshaven stranger walking down the street, talking loudly and gesturing wildly to someone or something that isn't there. You rightly view this person as a little crazy and look away. Yet when you resent someone for something that happened in the past, you are doing the same thing. You are reacting to something that isn't there.

If something isn't happening right now in front of you, then it isn't something you can respond to. The only thing that makes sense is to respond to what is happening. In the heavenly worlds, you are considered insane if you continue to respond with pain or anger to something that happened last week or last year.

Once you can stay present and attentive to what is happening right now – and respond only to that – you will learn to forgive and forget. Jesus implored us to forgive, and many people struggle to do so; however, they base their forgiveness on personal preference and prejudice. This doesn't work because true forgiveness is an "across the board" decision whose larger implications are stunning, at both the personal and societal levels.

Practicing forgiveness at the personal level profoundly affects us, because letting go of the past and the future brings health and healing. Most illnesses and accidents are the result of not being present to the moment, hanging on to old thoughts, worrying about what might happen, reinforcing old pains and perceptions, or being on guard against new insults and fears. When the past and future are eliminated, the body – which is a reflection, not a source, of the mind – drops all distortion, pain, disease, sorrow, and expectation. The result is perfect health.

Forgiveness frees us from the notion that we must return to fix the errors of past lives. *Forgive yourself and the karma is neutralized!* There is no need for rebirth and another round of bruising physical reality. All too often, once in a new life, we end up caught in a whole new web of angry, conflicting illusions, and we completely forget that our original intent was to learn the thought system of the God-state, which allows us to bypass death and step into eternal Life.

Moving into Christ consciousness can be done gradually or all at once. It depends on personal style – the way some people bolt their whiskey while others sip it. In my case, it emerged spontaneously and without warning. For others, it is a slow, quiet, determined journey.

When you step into the total experience of God, there is nothing to see except light – tiny, twinkling, intelligent lights. There is nothing to hear except silence, nothing to feel except Love, and nothing to know except one, all-encompassing truth – that you *exist*, you are *Life*. As you return to ordinary awareness, you bring the gifts of an awakened consciousness, the memory of that wondrous Love, and an understanding that you are an eternal being who *is* Life.

Now you must learn to align yourself with that Life, refusing to do anything hurtful to yourself or others. You must cultivate and nurture Christ consciousness until it is active and continuously present. This requires the practice and discipline of the new way of thinking, mentioned earlier.

Often, we step in and out of Christ consciousness, unable to maintain it at first. An example of this occurred some years ago when an airliner crashed into the Potomac River. A by-stander, watching a young woman go under again and again, jumped into the icy water, swam some distance through a layer of jet fuel, and rescued her. When questioned later as to why he risked his own life for a stranger, the man said he didn't even think about the fact that he was risking his life. Instead, something deep inside – a powerful knowing that he could help the young woman – drove him into the river. He did not hesitate, nor did he contemplate failure. He simply saved her, unimpeded by fear, doubt, or worry. This is Christ consciousness in full expression.

Last year a student of mine was on a cruise in the Caribbean. He was sitting around the pool when he saw a woman slip, twist her ankle badly, and fall. Instantly, he heard a voice inside him say, "You can help her." He resisted at first, but the voice returned, even more urgently, so he went over to where she had been carried and asked permission to help. The ankle was already seriously swelling and turning colors. Following his intuition, he put both hands around her ankle and held them there for about fifteen or twenty minutes. When he removed them, the swelling had subsided and the ankle was better. The woman got up, thanked him repeatedly, and walked painlessly back to her cabin. She saw him at dinner that night and exclaimed to her companions, "There's the man who healed me!" and again thanked him profusely. When asked later how he accomplished the healing, he said, "I don't know. It wasn't me. It was something that came from inside of me, or maybe through me. It seemed to insist that I was the one to do that particular job."

He was right. The Christ within emerges unexpectedly to offer healing, inspiration, peace, and Love – whatever is needed at the moment. No planning is required. All we need do is be present and listen to what is coming from inside. Once we step into that Christ consciousness, we have the ability to transcend physical laws, heal ourselves and others, even restore the planet. If we can allow it, we will find that God is expressing Itself through us.

Each of us has a unique approach to expressing the Christ and this will depend on something that is known as *God's will*. This will is imprinted in the core of each of us and reveals itself as something we've always wanted to do. I have dozens of clients who share their dreams and their longing to do or be something that is unique to each of them. If everyone followed their heart and did what they truly loved to do, this world would be totally different – a kinder, gentler place.

Following your heart means listening to the "still, small voice within." It means choosing to do something that will bring you joy, enthusiasm, pleasure, and greater Life. When guided by this inner-knowing, your actions are imbued with power.

If you have become entangled in situations that leave you feeling responsible for others, and you never do what you would truly Love to do, you have become lost to your true self. The truth is, you are responsible for yourself *first*, and you must save yourself *first*. To do this, you must develop yourself. Once you have developed yourself, you can truly help others. Otherwise, it is a case of the blind leading the blind.

Meditation, prayer, talking with highly evolved people, or finding a teacher to work with all contribute to self-development. However, few of my own experiences of God have occurred in the midst of prayer, meditation, or classes. They have occurred mostly in the middle of full-blooded, enthusiastic, everyday living.

During a recent experience, I stepped into a body that looked like my own except that it was shining like the Sun and filled the room with a huge circle of intensely beautiful golden light. I was aware that I had shifted into a form of being that I had not experienced before. I could see the room clearly, as one sees with ordinary vision, but I simultaneously saw and knew every single molecule, atom, and particle that made up the world in which I lived.

I knew every molecule of drywall and lumber in my home as if we were longtime friends. I knew which tree every 2 x 4 in the walls and ceilings had come from, where the tree had grown, who cut it down, who milled it, as well as who sold it and shipped it. I knew every fiber in the quilt on my bed, where the cotton had been grown, when it was picked, who processed it, who wove it, and the roads it had traveled to get to my room. The same was true of everything in my cupboards, closets, and attic.

I was aware of every cell in my body and my great capacity for life and health. I was conscious of the entire Cosmos and could feel it shifting with each tiny impulse of my consciousness, and I knew that I could literally move mountains if I so desired.

We seldom realize that the Christ is within us and needs to be resurrected, thus we don't do anything to develop that capacity. When Jesus was here in physical form, people witnessed his ability to heal as well as many other miracles. They loved the miracles and teachings, but they had a difficult time with his insistence that death can be transcended. So he decided to show them this miracle as well. He allowed himself to be put to death, and approximately thirty-six hours later, he generated a body of light and returned to teach some more.

The impact of Jesus' mission has been long-lasting, even though much of what he taught has been twisted through the centuries. The lesson of Jesus' life is that there is a Christ-self in each one of us. We, too, can develop Christ consciousness and do all the things he did … and then some.

The challenge is still here, two thousand years later.

<hr />

Penny's spontaneous awakening may have caught her off guard, but her ability to reconnect with the Christ consciousness is a testament to her open nature, her zest for life, and her commitment to God. She has become a friend and mentor to me over the past few years, and I pray that I may one day attain the gifts she has received (including the *kundalini* experience!).

GOD

By Kahlil Gibran
(1883–1931)

In the ancient days, when the first quiver of speech came to my lips, I ascended the holy mountain and spoke unto God, saying, "Master, I am Thy slave. Thy hidden will is my law and I shall obey Thee for ever more."

But God made no answer ... and like a mighty tempest passed away.

And after a thousand years, I ascended the holy mountain and again spoke unto God, saying, "Creator, I am Thy creation. Out of clay hast Thou fashioned me and to Thee I owe mine all."

And God made no answer ... but like a thousand swift wings passed away.

And after a thousand years, I climbed the holy mountain and spoke unto God again, saying, "Father, I am Thy son. In pity and Love Thou hast given me birth, and through Love and worship I shall inherit Thy kingdom."

And God made no answer ... and like the mist that veils the distant hills passed away.

And after a thousand years, I climbed the sacred mountain and again spoke unto God, saying, "My God, my aim and my fulfillment, I am Thy yesterday and Thou art my tomorrow. I am Thy root in the earth and Thou art my flower in the sky, and together We grow before the face of the sun."

Then God leaned over me ... and in my ears whispered words of sweetness, and even as the sea enfolds a brook that runs into her, He enfolded me.

And when I descended to the valleys and the plains, God was there also.

———◆———

Kahlil explains the distinction between aligning yourself with Divine will and actually merging with God. In the first stanza, he merely worships God. In the immortal words of the Jerry Seinfeld show: *No soup for you!* In the second stanza, Kahlil expresses gratitude for his life: *Yes, we have no bananas.* And in the third stanza, he compares Earth plane Love with enlightenment: *Close ... but no cigar.* Not until the end, when he reaches an understanding of Oneness and the reciprocal and inter-dependent nature of the Human-Divine connection, does God respond: *When you're a Jet, you're a Jet all the way ...*

What Kahlil is saying is that *We are God.* We just haven't accepted this yet because the implications are too momentous. It would mean that we are co-creating with God, and that we are responsible for what happens next ...

GOD HAS A DREAM

By The Most Reverend Desmond Tutu

Dear Child of God, all of us are meant to be contemplatives. Frequently, we assume that this is reserved for some rare monastic life, lived by special people who alone have been called by God. But the truth of the matter is that each one of us is meant to have that space inside where we can hear God's voice. God is available to all of us. God says, "Be still and know that I am God." Each one of us wants and needs to give ourselves space for quiet. We can hear God's voice most clearly when we are quiet, uncluttered, undistracted – when we are still. Be still, be quiet, and then you will begin to see with the eyes of the heart.

One image that I have of the spiritual life is of sitting in front of a fire on a cold day. We don't have to do anything. We just have to sit in front of the fire and then gradually the qualities of the fire are transferred to us. We begin to feel the warmth. We become the attributes of the fire. It's like that with us and God. As we take time to be still and to be in God's presence, the qualities of God are transferred to us.

Far too frequently we see ourselves as "doers." We feel we must endlessly work and achieve. We have not always learned just to be receptive, to be in the presence of God, quiet, available, and letting God be God, who wants *us* to be God. We are shocked, actually, when we hear that what God wants is for us to be godlike, for us to become more and more like God. Not by doing anything, but by letting God be God in and through us.

I am deeply thankful for those moments in the early morning when I try to be quiet, to sit in the presence of the gentle and compassionate and unruffled One, to try to share in or be given some of that Divine serenity. If I do not spend a reasonable amount of time in meditation early in the morning, then I feel a physical discomfort – it is worse than having forgotten to brush my teeth! I would be completely rudderless and lost if I did not have these times with God.

People often ask about the source of my joy, and I can honestly say that it comes from my spiritual life – and specifically from these times of stillness. They are an indispensable part of my day regardless of what else I might face. I pray out loud or to myself before every meeting and before every drive in the car. I also take quiet days when I do not talk at least until supper. Once a month I take a room at a local convent and spend a day sleeping, eating, praying, and reading, and at least once a year I go on a retreat of three or more days. The importance of these retreats is hard to convey – through them I am strengthened and am able to hear what God is saying and to seek solutions to problems that seem unsolvable. You may think that as a priest I need these times of reflection but that most people who spend their lives in the market-place do not. In truth, they probably need them all the more, since the noise of the market makes it even more difficult to hear the voice of God.

I know no other way available to us besides prayer and meditation to cul-tivate a real and deeply personal relationship with God, our great Lover, in whose presence we want to luxuriate, falling into ever greater and deeper silence. This is the silence of Love, the stillness of adoration and contempla-tion – the sort of stillness that is so eloquent when it happens between two who are in Love.

We need to realize that God is much closer than we think and recognize when we have arrived in the presence of God. When you arrive in God's pres-ence, you often experience a kind of serenity and have pleasurable sensations. These are called the "consolations of God." God uses these consolations to lure us, to bribe us into wanting to be with Him. They are like sweets we use to reward children. As our relationship with God matures, we often no longer experience these sweets when we pray. God reckons that we are no longer childish nor need to be bribed in this way. Just as we give a child the food the child needs, first feeding her milk after she is born but eventually giving her more substantial fare, so God gives us more substantial fare as we mature in our spiritual life. God wants us to Love God for who He is, not for what we can get out of Him.

We arrive and yet the journey continues, as we grow ever more in our God awareness. This God awareness is shown by our God likeness and by increas-ingly becoming what we Love. People tend to look like the things they Love – which is why so many people end up looking like their dogs! But we can also look like God if we Love God and strive to be like God.

We can't have a relationship without faith. When you fall in Love, you are in a way abandoning yourself to another person whom you can't know com-pletely. Nonetheless, you commit yourself to this one person in the faith that this relationship is going to grow. Some don't, and they go wonky, but if you commit yourself only as far as the evidence carries you, you won't go very far. We are always finding that we have to act as people of faith even when we are atheists. God has a wonderful sense of humor.

Just as we must always have faith, we must always question our creeds and make sure that our beliefs bring us closer to God and to truth. Often we focus too much on concrete images of God and on overly literal readings of the *Bible*. It is a liability of many languages that they are gendered and therefore we must speak of God as either a He or a She but rarely both. There is something in the nature of God that corresponds to our maleness and our femaleness. We have tended to speak much more of the maleness, so we refer to the Fatherhood of God, which is fine but incomplete. We have missed out on the fullness that is God when we have ignored that which corresponds to our femaleness. We have hardly spoken about the Motherhood of God, and consequently we have been the poorer for this.

Reading the *Bible* can be a source of reflection and inspiration, as you listen for God's voice in your life. But you must watch how you read the *Bible* and apply it to today's world. The *Bible* is not something that came dropping from heaven, written by the hand of God. It was written by human beings, so it uses human idiom and is influenced by the context in which each story was written. People need to be very careful. Many tend to be literalists, people who believe in the verbal inerrancy of the *Bible*, who speak as if God dictated the *Bible*, when in fact God used human beings as they were, and they spoke only as they could speak at that time. There are parts of the *Bible* that have no permanent worth – that is nothing to be sorry about, it is just to say that it is the Word of God in the words of men and women.

In addition, we make ghastly mistakes if we do not ask what genre a particular piece of literature is, because if we do not know its type, then we are apt to pose inappropriate questions and will be frustrated in not getting the answers we demand and which the particular literary material was never designed to provide. When you want to bake a cake, you don't go to a geometry textbook for instructions. The *Bible* did not intend to tell the "how," but much more the "why" and "by whom" of creation. Those first chapters are much more like poetry than prose, replete with religious and not scientific truths, conveying profound truths about us, about God, and about the Universe we inhabit.

We must seek truth wherever we find it. I am a traditionalist, and yet I also sit in awe when I listen to all of the brilliant people that God has produced, whether I'm sitting at the feet of an outstanding theologian or listening to an outstanding scientist. When religious truth, scientific truth, and whatever truth come together and become part of a framework that makes sense of the

Universe, I am awestruck, and I find that truth then has a self-authenticating quality.

Jesus – both as we read about him in the *New Testament* and as we envision him as a role model for our own lives – can help Christians to know how God wants us to live. But here, too, we must be careful how we read the accounts of his life. I am foursquare in the Catholic faith that is enshrined in our prayer books, in our formularies, in the creeds. But when we say Jesus Christ ascended into heaven, you don't believe that he got into a kind of ecclesiastical lift that took him into the stratosphere. This language is being used figuratively, because the realities that are being described are not human realities, they are supranatural realities. When we speak even about the resurrection of Jesus Christ, it is not the revivification of a corpse. It is speaking about a tremendous reality: that Jesus Christ is risen, his life is real, he is accessible to me in Cape Town, as he is accessible to someone in Tokyo or New York or London or Sao Paulo or Sydney – that Jesus Christ is someone whose life makes a difference to me and to so many others two thousand years after he lived.

As we seek to know God, we also should not be beguiled by much loved dichotomies between secular and sacred, activism and contemplation. It is dangerous to pray, for an authentic spirituality is subversive of injustice. Oppressive and unjust governments should stop people from praying to God, should stop them from reading and meditating on the *Bible*, for these activities will constrain them to work for the establishment of God's kingdom of justice, of peace, of laughter, of joy, of caring, of sharing, of reconciliation, of compassion. These activities will not permit us to luxuriate in a spiritual ghetto, insulated against the harsh realities of life as most of God's children experience it.

The Spirit of God sends us into the fray, as it sent Jesus, but if we observe the sequence in his life, we will see that disengagement, waiting on God, always precedes engagement. Jesus commands his disciples to wait in Jerusalem for the gift from on high before they can embark on their mission to be his witnesses in Jerusalem and unto the ends of the Earth. Some of them were with him on the mountaintop to share in the sublime experience of the Transfiguration, and they wanted to remain there undisturbed by the clamor of the uncomprehending, demanding, maddening crowd. Surely, that is how God wanted to be worshipped and adored. But no – they did not understand yet. The Transfiguration was happening so that they could descend into the valley to help others and to share what they had seen of God. In this life, we could never remain on the mountaintop. The authenticity of the transfiguration experience is attested by how it fits us to be God's presence – healing, restoring, forgiving, reconciling, admonishing, comforting the world. It is all truly intoxicating stuff, for the God we worship and adore is the One who wants us to reflect His character so that others will know what sort of a God He is by seeing what kind of people we are. God's people must be holy because their God is holy.

Consequently, if you say you Love God, whom you have not seen, and hate your brother, whom you have, the *Bible* does not use delicate language; it does not say you are guilty of a terminological inexactitude. It says bluntly you are a liar. For he who would Love God must Love his brother also. And so the Divine judgment about out fitness for heaven will be based not on whether we went to church, whether we prayed, or did other equally important religious things. No, Jesus says it will be based on whether we fed the hungry, clothed the naked. We do this not because of our politics, but because of our religion. Blessed be God our God for being such a God. And so for us the spiritual life is utterly crucial as we work to bring God's transfiguration into our political life.

One of my favorite cartoons by Mel Calman shows God looking somewhat distraught, and God says, "I think I have lost my copy of the Divine plan." Looking at the state of the world, you might be forgiven for wondering if God ever had one. There is enough evidence that seems to justify the conclusion in another cartoon: "Create in six days and have eternity to regret it."

Countless people have suffered untold misery as a result of injustice, oppression, and exploitation. They have been brutally tortured, imprisoned, maimed, and killed as the victims of racist and repressive regimes. Thousands upon thousands have suffered the pangs of starvation, while obscene amounts have been wasted on budgets of death and destruction in the arms race. There seems to be enough evidence to cure us of the arrogant and dangerous delusion of automatic progress. Sometimes our technological expertise has seemed to top our moral capacity to use this expertise for the good of humanity. We have a capacity to feed all, and yet millions starve because we seem to lack the moral and political will to do what we know is right.

The catalogue of woe is almost endless. It is a somber picture. But it isn't the whole story, for there is a brighter side, a nobler story. Evil, injustice, oppression, disintegration will not have the last word. Surely we must agree that there is a glorious story of human achievement and liberation for the betterment of all. There is zeal for peace in a burgeoning peace movement. There is a growing concern about the environment and about our obligations to posterity. Freedom, we realize, is better than repression. Democracy is better than tightly controlled totalitarian regimes. We have had the civil rights movement, the anti-apartheid movement, the movements for women's and for children's rights, the movement for gay and lesbian rights, and the numerous movements for freedom and democracy for all people.

Our world is better because of the life and witness of Mahatma Gandhi, of Mother Teresa, of Oscar Romero, of Nelson Mandela. They are notable examples of the altruistic spirit that does things, good things, heroic things, for the sake of others, for the sake of the world, for the sake of posterity. Some may say that, by their example, they show us what the rest of us lack. But behind every Gandhi, every Mother Teresa, every Romero, every Mandela, there are millions of people who are living lives of Love and heroism. I have had the privilege to meet many of them around the world. It was the faith and the fortitude of these many that have brought the momentous achievements of the past decades.

These heroes are often poor and disenfranchised people whose nobility always amazes me. When you go into informal settlements and meet up with people in shacks who are living in such dehumanizing circumstances, you expect they would have lost their sense of personhood. What you see is the humanity, the humanness, the dignity, the capacity to laugh, the capacity to Love and to rear children in circumstances that by rights ought to make all of that impossible. It's really always such an incredible experience.

The evil that we do to one another is much easier to see than the everyday acts of goodness and generosity that we do for one another in the sweep of human history. But ultimately, this tally of history does not tell us whether God has a plan or a dream. It simply tells us to what extent we have chosen to heed God's call, to become partners with God in realizing His dream.

It is true that we are taking a long time to realize what we are really made for. We are taking a long time to realize that we are family. We are taking long to learn that no one, no nation, can exist in isolation. You are not able to quarantine yourselves off from the rest of the world. Someone who has a disease like TB or SARS in Southeast Asia can infect someone who lives in North America or Europe. He coughs and maybe he is working at an airport, and the germs slither away in the plane, and you get on the plane and you are infected.

Similarly, instability and despair in the third world lead to terrorism and instability in the first world. God says there is no way in which we can win the war against terrorism as long as there are conditions that make people desperate. It is the logic of being human. It is something we should have learned long ago and we keep not heeding – we cannot be human on our own. We can be human only together. Many Americans have begun to realize after the ghastly happenings of September 11 that we truly are bound together globally in the bundle of life.

Behind these and other political conflicts lies the question of power, of the definition and true nature of power. Jesus tried to propagate a new paradigm of power. Power and might in this paradigm are not meant for self-aggrandizement, not meant to be lorded over others. Power and might are not for throwing our weight about, disregarding any laws and conventions we may find inconvenient. Power in this new paradigm is for service – for being compassionate, for being gentle, for being caring – for being the servant of all.

We think of power as the ability to use verbs in the imperative mood and give orders. Jesus said no. It is in giving your life, in serving the weakest, the most vulnerable, that you discover true power. That's what you see with the Dalai Lama, Gandhi, King, Mother Teresa, or Mandela. All of these are people who have been extraordinary spendthrifts of themselves. Why does Nelson Mandela make people's knees turn to water? He doesn't have power in the conventional sense. He was not president of a particularly impressive country, certainly not a military power. But the world recognizes his moral power. When the world says who the great people are, they usually don't mention generals.

Yet goodness does not always prevail in the time frame of our lives. There is a wonderful Portuguese saying that God writes straight with crooked lines. God works through history to realize God's dream. God makes a proposal to each of us and hopes our response will move His dream forward. But if we don't, God does not abandon the goal, He does not abandon the dream. God adjusts God's methods to accommodate the detour, but we are going to come back onto the main road and eventually arrive at the destination. The sooner we are able to hear God's voice and to see with the eyes of the heart, the sooner God's dream of peace and harmony, of brotherly and sisterly Love, will come to pass. And the less bloodshed and suffering we will have to endure.

So how do we ensure that goodness does prevail? Who has the power to ensure that justice is done and that God's dream is realized? *We have the power.* Institutions or corporations or governments have no life of their own, despite what we typically think about bureaucracies. They are only groups of people. They are people like you and me, making choices, deciding whether to heed God's call or not, to accept God's proposal or not, to become God's partner or not.

Our decisions – personal, corporate, at play, at home, in private, and in public – make the moral fabric of our society, indeed of the world. How we interact with the people in our lives – whether we are centers of peace, oases of compassion – makes a difference. The sum total of these interactions determines nothing less than the nature of human life on our planet. Similarly, your stand for justice and right, your witness, your prayers, and your caring and concern are what change the planet – these things do not just evaporate and disappear.

We make these moral decisions – we live a life aspiring toward goodness – not because we will be punished if we are bad, or will spend eternity in hell. We do so because when we can feel God's Love for us, we want to live that Love in our lives and share that Love with others. It has often been said, "What we are is God's gift to us. What we become is our gift to God." What we become is not about status, it is about Love. Do we Love like God, as God so deeply desires? Do we become like God, as God so deeply desires us to be?

As we look forward at the evils that still await transfiguration, must we learn to be patient? Yes and no. Yes, we must have the calm assurance and patience that faith can give. But no, we must not be patient with oppression, with hunger, and with violence. We must work to bring about the time for all people to be free, to be fed, and to live in peace, because as God's partners, we help to determine the time frame in which God's plan unfolds and God's dream is realized.

Therefore, we can stand upright with our heads held high. We don't apologize for our existence. God did not make a mistake in creating us. Our God hears. Our God cares. Our God knows and our God will come down to deliver His people. Our God will come to deliver His people everywhere. When will this deliverance from oppression, from hunger, from war happen? Today? Maybe not today. Tomorrow? Maybe not tomorrow. But God will come in the fullness of time because God has a dream, and God will make His dream come true through us. For we are His partners. We are the ones He has sent to free the oppressed, to feed the hungry, and to shelter the homeless. We will turn our sadness into resolve, our despair into determination.

If you were in heaven now, you would notice the tears in God's eyes. The tears streaming down God's face as God looks on us and sees the awful things that we, God's children, are doing to each other. God cries and cries. And then you might see the smile that is breaking over God's face like sunshine through the rain, almost like a rainbow. You would see God smiling because God is looking on you and noting how deeply concerned you are. And the smile might break out into a laugh as God says, "You have vindicated Me. I had been asking Myself, 'Whatever got into Me to create that lot?' And when I see you, yes, you," God says, "you are beginning to wipe the tears from My eyes because you care. Because you care and you have come to learn that you are not your brother's or sister's keeper. You are your brother's brother and your sister's sister." And God says, "I have no one except you. Thank you for vindicating Me."

All over this magnificent world, God calls us to extend His kingdom of *shalom* – peace and wholeness – of justice, of goodness, of compassion, of caring, of sharing, of laughter, of joy, and of reconciliation. God is transfiguring the world right this very moment *through us*, because God *believes in us*, and because God *Loves us*. What can separate us from the Love of God? Nothing. Absolutely nothing. And as we share God's Love with our brothers and sisters, God's other children, there is no tyrant who can resist us, no oppression that cannot be ended, no hunger that cannot be fed, no wound that cannot be healed, no hatred that cannot be turned to Love, no dream that cannot be fulfilled.

Now I'm intimidated ... narrate after Desmond's essay? Is that even allowed? (Not the narration, but using his first name as I've done with all my other heroes.) Why couldn't this essay have run to the bottom of the page!

In God's Dream you're the hero, and we all want you to prevail! (Or maybe you like movies.) In God's Movie you're the star, and we all want a happy ending! (Or maybe you like sports.) In God's Stadium you're the quarterback, and we all want you to throw the winning pass in the Super Bowl ... touchdown! Everyone is cheering for you – and I mean *everyone* – since only your team is on the field (I know it doesn't make sense – just go with it). So because of you: WE ALL WIN THE GAME!

Actually, that's my favorite metaphor: *God Game*. The God Game depends on the moves all of us make. But in the end, we all win the game. Why? Because the God Game ends when *all of us* reach Truth, Love, and Light!

THE LAND OF HEAVEN

Caribou Inuit Thealogy

Heaven is a great land.
In that land there are many holes.
These holes we call stars.

In the land of heaven lives *Pana*, a mighty spirit.
And the *angatkut* [shamans] hold that it is a woman.
To Her pass the souls of the dead.

And sometimes when many die, there are many souls up there.
When anything is split up there, it pours out through the stars
and becomes rain or snow.

The souls of the dead are reborn in the dwellings of *Pana*
and brought down to Earth again by the Moon.
When the Moon is absent and cannot be seen in the sky,
it is because it is busy helping *Pana* by bringing souls to Earth.

Some become human beings once more;
others become animals, all manner of beasts.

And so life goes on without end.

Although a book of non-fiction, this anthology has told a story, and it is now culminating. One last step and we mount the summit.

The God Game is complex, and I am not about to proclaim a full understanding of it. However, I do know this much: The Fourth Paradigm religions are holding us back – all of us collectively – from taking that last step onto the summit … and into utopia.

Already, countless souls have made it. Individually, one by one, many have reached the top of the mountain. In fact, there's a party going on up there and we're missing it! But just like that boot camp drill where the whole platoon has to make it over the wall: *You don't get there, I don't get there, until we all get there.*

Oh, and there's one more thing I've figured out: The Fifth Spiritual Paradigm will only arrive if we balance our masculine and feminine energies. That means we need to add a word to our vocabulary. *Thealogy*: the study of the Sacred Feminine. (That's not a typo – Google it.)

EPILOGUE

Truth, Love, and Light
in the Fifth Spiritual Paradigm

Between the finite and the infinite
the missing link of Love has left a void.
Supply the link, and Earth with Heaven will join
in one continued chain of endless life.

Hell is wherever Love is not, and Heaven
is Love's location. No dogmatic creed,
no austere faith based on ignoble fear
can lead thee into realms of joy and peace.
Unless the humblest creatures on the Earth
are bettered by thy loving sympathy
think not to find a Paradise beyond.

There is no sudden entrance into Heaven.
Slow is the ascent by the path of Love.

Ella Wheeler Wilcox, *The Way*

When I founded The Oracle Institute five years ago, my friend Molly assigned me a personalized "ring" on her cell phone – the *Mission Impossible* theme song. She shared this mockery during one of our "girl nights," and my friends had a good laugh. Back then, I was able to respond good naturedly to such jokes. But today, I am wondering whether Molly is right. Will the lightworkers be able to guide us through the Great Cusp and help us build the prophesied Fifth Spiritual Paradigm ... or is it mission impossible?

The world is spinning madly right now. The Great Cusp has firmly taken hold and fear is rampant. What is so interesting about this Great Cusp is not that its effects are being globally shared – that is always the case with a millennial change – but that its impact is being globally analyzed and communicated. In the 21st Century we are all connected, so we will witness how each country and each culture handles the chaos.

I wrote in *The Truth* that when the Age of Aquarius began, sometime around 1950, big change already was in the air. During the last half of the 20th Century, we witnessed an unparalleled emergence of Truth, Love, and Light. In addition to the worldwide remapping that took place after World War II and the creation of the United Nations, within the United States, we watched the hard-won victories of the civil rights movement, the feminist movement, and the free Love or hippie movement, all of which portended the paradigm shift.

As difficult as that time period was, it represented a relatively gentle entry into the New Millennium compared to what we now face. In fact, the 2000 U.S. presidential election was our last chance to accept the challenges of the Great Cusp in a mature manner and begin to calmly correct course for the future. But it was not to be. Instead, we collectively chose to ignore reality, thereby turning the Fifth Spiritual Paradigm into a breech birth.

I called my closest cousin yesterday. She was my "third sister" during the summer, when Leslie and I would visit our grandparents. After graduating from college, she and I both took off like shots: She earned her M.B.A. and joined one of the largest trading houses on Wall Street; I earned my J.D. and joined the largest law firm in Maryland. On September 11, 2001, she would have died if she had not taken the day off work to attend a function at her daughter's school. I called her repeatedly on that fateful day and cried with joy when she finally answered the phone. Yesterday after we hung up, I cried for an entirely different reason.

You see, during an "average" year, she and her husband (also a banker) would bring home about five million dollars. Of course, they had the good sense to cash out more than two years ago. Everyone on Wall Street knew (or should have known). So when I called her yesterday, I was curious to know what she was doing with herself, since the last time we spoke both she and her husband had left Wall Street. As it turns out, she was on her way to sit for a real estate exam. Seems there's plenty of opportunity in real property, now that there's no more risky paper to push around.

It was a short phone call. I asked whether her associates feel any level of culpability for what has happened. She proceeded to lecture me on the true genesis of the financial collapse: *the greed of those who desired to live beyond their means.* I responded, "Ah yes, the greed of the masses. Surely, they are to blame." She practically hung up on me.

So today I am left wondering: How close are we to the paradigm shift if the most fortunate people on the planet are fixated on money and infatuated by power? If people still cannot discern Truth, practice Love, or accept Light, what hope is there for the utopia described in all the holy books and foretold by all indigenous wisdom cultures? In short, will we survive this breech birth?

> *A great Sign appeared in the sky: a Woman clothed with the Sun, with the Moon under her feet, and on her head a crown of twelve stars. She was with child and wailed aloud in pain as she labored to give birth.*
>
> *The Revelation to John, Chapter 12:1-2*

The apocalyptic ending to the ancient civilization of Atlantis provides a clue as to what might happen next. According to legend, Atlantis was an advanced society, but its leaders succumbed to the two cardinal sins: greed and pride. Thereafter, Atlantis became a "dystopia" and perished, just like all the man-made empires to date. Such has been the life-death-life cycle of humanity's protracted spiritual evolution.

> Then war broke out in Heaven; Michael and his angels battled against the dragon. The dragon and its angels fought back, but they did not prevail and there was no longer any place for them in Heaven.
>
> The Revelation to John, Chapter 12:7-8

Now we have another chance to manifest a utopian state. However, those who predict dystopia, those in total denial, and those who sickly and secretly crave Armageddon presently outnumber the lightworkers who are trying to build a new Atlantis. Consequently, we are witnessing another crescendo of duality – polarization of Dark and Light energies – a complex topic that the Institute will address in the final book of our foundational trilogy: The Light.

> When the dragon saw that it had been thrown down to Earth, it pursued the Woman who had given birth .... Then the dragon became angry with the Woman and went off to wage war against the rest of her offspring.
>
> The Revelation to John, Chapter 12:13-17

Despite the spectacle of the Christian version of the Apocalypse – a gory drama portrayed by all Fourth Paradigm religions – the truth is that no one is coming either to condemn or save us. We, collectively, hold that power and promise, since it is our destiny to become the "gods and goddesses" of this realm. Thus, the Fifth Spiritual Paradigm depends upon human, not Divine, intervention. Universal harmony will arrive if and when we decide we are ready.

> Then I saw a new Heaven and a new Earth. ... I also saw the holy city, a new Jerusalem, coming down out of Heaven from God .... Behold, God's dwelling is with the human race ... and there shall be no more death or mourning, wailing or pain, for the old order has passed away.
>
> The Revelation to John, Chapter 21:1-4

The lore about Atlantis and the new Jerusalem contains important lessons: It was the loss of feminine energy in the first instance and the reemergence of feminine energy in the second which doomed one utopia and will enshrine the next. I, for one, believe that we possess enough Truth, Love, and Light to manifest the Fifth Spiritual Paradigm, but we are runing out of time. A "new human" must evolve. Otherwise, we shall start all over again ...

Credits and Copyrights

Chapter One: **Love of Earth**

Prayer for Mother Earth by Joyce Pace Byrd, L.P.C. Copyright 2009 by Joyce Pace Byrd. Joyce is a licensed counselor (26 years), spiritual guide, pilgrim, and poet. Her work has appeared in various journals, including: *Journey into Wholeness; Fragile Threads;* and *The Muse.* Her current collection of poetry is entitled *Poems from the Labyrinth.* **www.JoycePaceByrd.com**

Sophia and Sustainability by Bernice Hill, Ph.D. Copyright 2009 by Bernice Hill. Bernice is a practicing therapist, senior analyst at the C.G. Jung Institute of Colorado, lecturer, essayist, and author of: *The Emergence of the Cosmic Psyche: Extraterrestrials and Subtle Energy;* and *Money and the Spiritual Warrior.* She also has written Jungian reviews of: *The Phantom of the Opera; The Cider House Rules; When the Impossible Happens;* and *The Fountain.*

Sophia by Alex Grey. Copyright 1989 by Alex Grey. Reprinted by permission of the artist.

Look Out by Wendell Berry from *Given: New Poems.* Copyright 2005 by Wendell Berry. Reprinted by permission of the author and Counterpoint, LLC. Wendell is a Professor Emeritus of Creative Writing at the University of Kentucky, Fellow of Britain's Temenos Academy, and author of more than 25 books of poetry, 16 volumes of essays, and 11 novels. He also is the recipient of numerous awards, including: the Guggenheim and Rockefeller Fellowships; the T.S. Eliot Award; the Jean Stein Award; the Thomas Merton Award; the John Hay Award; the Poets' Prize in 2000; and Kentuckian of the Year Award in 2006. His many books include: *A Place on Earth; A World Lost; Home Economics; What Are People For?; Standing on Earth; Sex, Economy, Freedom & Community; Waste Land: Meditations on a Ravaged Landscape; Citizens Dissent: Security, Morality, and Leadership in an Age of Terror; Collected Poems 1957–1982; A Timbered Choir: The Sabbath Poems; Given;* and *Window Poems.*

The Next Revolution by Bill McKibben. Copyright 2009 by Bill McKibben. Bill is a Professor of Environmental Studies at Middlebury College in Vermont, and a recipient of Guggenheim and Lyndhurst Fellowships and the Lannan Prize for non-fiction. He is a contributing journalist to *National Geographic, The New Yorker, Orion, Mother Jones, The Atlantic Monthly, Harper's,* and *Rolling Stone* magazines. He led the largest demonstration against global warming in U.S. history, and he is a best-selling author: *Fight Global Warming Now: The Handbook for Taking Action in Your Community; The Bill McKibben Reader: Pieces from an Active Life; The End of Nature; Deep Economy: The Wealth of Communities and the Durable Future; Wandering Home; Maybe One: A Personal and Environmental Argument for Single Child Families;* and *Hope, Human and Wild: True Stories of Living Lightly on the Earth.*
www.BillMcKibben.com & **www.StepItUp2007.org** & **www.350.org**

Offering Before Clearing a Field, a Kekchi Maya Invocation, undated.

Land Love by R. Bruce Hull, IV, Ph.D. Copyright 2009 by R. Bruce Hull, IV. Bruce is a Professor of Social Ecology at Virginia Polytechnic Institute and advisor to numerous community groups, including Virginia LandCare, the Model Forestry Policy Program, and Virginia's Forest Issues Working Group, all of which promote sustainable living and land use in order to respond to the pressures of urbanization and globalization. He also is the author and editor of over 100 publications, including two books: *Infinite Nature;* and *Restoring Nature: Perspectives from the Social Sciences and Humanities.* **www.fw.vt.edu/forestry/Faculty/BruceHull.html**

CHAPTER TWO: **Love of Animals**

Naked, with Skin On by Susan Chernak McElroy. Copyright 2009 by Susan Chernak McElroy. Susan is a retreat facilitator, speaker, and *New York Times* best-selling author of numerous books, including: *Why Buffalo Dance: Animal and Wilderness Meditations Through the Seasons; All My Relations; Animals as Teachers and Healers; Heart in the Wild;* and *Animals as Guides for the Soul: Stories of Life Changing Encounters.* **www.SusanChernakMcElroy.com**

My Steed, an excerpt of a poem by Imru al Quais. From *The Diwans of Abid ibn al Abras and Amir ibn al Tufail* by Charles J. Lyall, 1913.

Love Is the Answer for Unity with All Beings by Marc Bekoff, Ph.D. Copyright 2009 by Marc Bekoff. Marc is a co-founder of Ethologists for the Ethical Treatment of Animals with Jane Goodall, Fellow of the Animal Behavior Society, Professor Emeritus of Biology at the University of Colorado, Ethics Committee member at the Jane Goodall Institute, and recipient of numerous awards for his animal research and animal protection programs, including the Exemplar Award from the Animal Behavior Society and a Guggenheim Fellowship. He has published more than 200 articles, 3 encyclopedias, and 20 books, including: *The Emotional Lives of Animals; Animals Matter: A Biologist Explains Why We Should Treat Animals with Compassion and Respect; Wild Justice: The Moral Lives of Animals* (with Jessica Pierce); *The Smile of a Dolphin; The Ten Trusts: What We Must Do to Care for the Animals We Love* (with Jane Goodall); *Animal Passions and Beastly Virtues: Reflections on Redecorating Nature; Listening to Cougar;* and *The Encyclopedia of Animal Behavior.*
www.EthologicalEthics.org & **www.Literati.net/Bekoff**

Chance Encounter with a Like Soul by Jana Lee Frazier. Copyright 2008 by Jana Lee Frazier. Jana is an environmentalist, wildlife biologist and rehabilitator, former zookeeper, artist, and essayist for *The Washington Post.* Her 30 years of published work includes: *The Long Journey Back: Surviving Depression; Gifts to Cherish, Moment by Moment; A Season of Bereavement and Blessings; Dispatch from a Long-Ago October;* and *A Trap of a Different Kind.* **www.WashingtonPost.com**

The Animals Do Judge by Madeleine L'Engle from *The Irrational Season.* Copyright 1977 by Crosswicks, Ltd. Reprinted by permission of HarperCollins Publishers.

The Gift of Animals: Unconditional Love by Dawn E. Hayman. Copyright 2009 by Dawn E. Hayman. Dawn is co-founder of Spring Farm CARES in New York, a nature sanctuary, education, and healing center. She also is an animal communicator and author: *If Only They Could Talk: The Miracles at Spring Farm; A Message for Humanity* (CD); and *Stories of Animal Communication* (DVD). **www.SpringFarmCares.org**

In Search of the Sacred Heart by Brooke J. Wood. Copyright 2009 by Brooke J. Wood. Brooke is a *gnostic* teacher and the founder of the Sophia Agape Circle in Virginia. Her classes include: *Sophian Gnosticism; Christian Kabbalah*; and monthly Circle teachings. She also is a journalist and author: *Putrefaction, Devastation and Jurisprudence.* **www.Sophia-Agape-Circle.org**

CHAPTER THREE: **Love of Family**

The Law of Love by David Suzuki, Ph.D. Copyright 2009 by David Suzuki. Adapted from *The Sacred Balance: Rediscovering Our Place in Nature.* Copyright 1997, 2002, 2007 by David Suzuki. David is a Professor Emeritus of Zoology at the University of British Columbia and co-founder of the David Suzuki Foundation in Canada. Since 1979, he has hosted the CBC television program *The Nature of Things*, and he also has hosted the PBS series *The Secret of Life, A Planet for the Taking, The Sacred Balance*, and *Suzuki on Science*. He is the recipient of numerous international awards, including: Companion of the Order of Canada; UNESCO's Kalinga Prize for Science; the U.N. Environmental Programme Medal; and 22 honorary degrees. He is a leading expert and lecturer on environmental protection, an activist on global climate change, and the author of 45 books, including: *The Sacred Balance: Rediscovering Our Place in Nature; David Suzuki's Green Guide; Grassroots Rising; Tree: A Life Story; Genetics: A Beginner's Guide; Time to Change; Good News for a Change: How Everyday People are Helping the Planet; It's a Matter of Survival; From Naked Ape to Super Species; Wisdom of the Elders: Sacred Native Stories of Nature; Inventing the Future*; and *David Suzuki: The Autobiography.* **www.DavidSuzuki.org**

In the Distance I See My House by Sean R. Conroy. Copyright 2000 by Sean R. Conroy. Sean is an aspiring artist and author, and his work has been displayed at events in Virginia. He is starting his senior year of high school.

The Family Altar by Charles Alexander Eastman. From *The Soul of the Indian,* 1911.

Lakota Medicine Woman by Barbara Hand Clow from *The Mind Chronicles.* Copyright 1986, 1989, 1992, 2007 by Barbara Hand Clow. Reprinted by permission of the author and Inner Traditions, Bear & Co., www.BearandCompanyBooks.com. Barbara is a former co-publisher of Bear & Company publishing house, historian, world-renowned astrologer, lecturer, channel, and international best-selling author of numerous books, including: *The Mayan Code: Time Acceleration and Awakening the World Mind; Catastrophobia: The Truth Behind Earth Changes; The Pleiadian Agenda: A New Cosmology for the Age of Light; Liquid Light of Sex; and The Mind Chronicles: Visionary Guide into Past Lives; and Alchemy of Nine Dimensions: A New Cosmology for the Age of Light.* **www.HandClow2012.com**

Mother's Day Proclamation by Julia Ward Howe, 1870.

I Want to Tell You Something You Should Know by Nicholas Gordon, Ph.D. Copyright 2001 by Nicholas Gordon. Nick is a retired professor of English at New Jersey City University and webmaster of *Poems for Free*, a website with a collection of his books and more than 2,000 of his poems and short stories. www.PoemsForFree.com

CHAPTER FOUR: **Love of Community**

Neo-Humanism and the New Era: Excerpts of Songs and Essays by Shrii Prabhat Ranjan Sarkar. Adapted from six previously published essays:
1. "Humanity Is at the Threshold of a New Era" from *Neo-Humanism in a Nutshell: Part One.* Copyright 1987 by Ananda Marga Publications.
2. "Neohumanism Is the Ultimate Shelter" from *Liberation of Intellect: Neohumanism.* Copyright 1999 by Ananda Marga Publications.
3. "Devotional Sentiment and Neohumanism" from *Liberation of Intellect: Neohumanism.* Copyright 1999 by Ananda Marga Publications.
4. "Human Society Is One and Indivisible" from *PROUT in a Nutshell: Part Seven.* Copyright 1987 by Ananda Marga Publications.
5. "Pseudo-Humanism" from *Liberation of Intellect: Neohumanism.* Copyright 1999 by Ananda Marga Publications.
6. "Exploitation and Pseudo-Culture" from *Liberation of Intellect: Neohumanism.* Copyright 1999 by Ananda Marga Publications.

Reprinted by permission of The World Prout Assembly. www.WorldProutAssembly.org

What We Want by Ella Wheeler Wilcox. From *The Kingdom of Love and Other Poems*, edited by Gay and Hancock, 1909.

Love and Conflict: Insights from Africa on Transforming Self and Societies by Philip M. Hellmich. Copyright 2009 by Philip M. Hellmich. Philip is Director of Individual Giving at Search for Common Ground in Washington, D.C. He has 18 years of international development and peace building experience with affiliated organizations such as the Peace Corps. He also is a speaker, trainer, and author, with essays published in: *Chamalu: Shamanic Way of the Heart; Chicken Soup for the Soul series; The Power of Media: A Handbook for Peacebuilders;* and *The Washington Post.* He is featured in: *Hello Love* (DVD); and *Search for Common Mound* (DVD). www.SFCG.org

Alone by Maya Angelou from *Oh Pray My Wings Are Gonna Fit Me Well.* Copyright 1975 by Maya Angelou. Reprinted by permission of Random House, Inc. Maya is the recipient of numerous honors, including: the Presidential Medal of Arts; the Lincoln Medal; the Lifetime Achievement Award for Literature; and three Grammy awards. She also has received over 50 honorary degrees, including a lifetime appointment as a Reynolds Professor of American Studies at Wake Forest University. She has been nominated for the National Book Award, the Tony Award, and the Pulitzer Prize, and she has worked as a civil rights activist, dancer, singer, composer, actress, producer, director, playwright, lecturer, newspaper editor, and radio host for Oprah & Friends. She is a *New York Times* best-selling author of numerous works of fiction, nonfiction, children's books, and poetry, including: *I Know Why the Caged Bird Sings; Just Give Me a Cool Drink of Water 'Fore I Diiie; Oh Pray My Wings Are Gonna Fit Me Well; The Heart of a Woman; And Still I Rise; All God's Children Need Traveling Shoes; Wouldn't Take Nothing for My Journey Now; A Song Flung Up to Heaven; Even the Stars Look Lonesome; The Complete Collected Poems of Maya Angelou;* and *The Collected Autobiographies of Maya Angelou.* **www.MayaAngelou.com**

Bodhisattva Warriors in the 21st Century Community by Kenneth Porter, M.D. Copyright 2009 by Kenneth Porter. Ken is a spiritually oriented psychiatrist and psychotherapist, former President of the Association for Spirituality and Psychotherapy in New York, co-founder of the Eastern Group Psychology Training Program, and Fellow of the American Group Psychotherapy Association. He also is a Buddhist teacher at the New York Insight Meditation Center and a nationally recognized workshop leader and author: *Who We Really Are: Buddhist Approaches to Psychotherapy* (essay); *Principles of Group Therapy Technique* (essay); *Combined Individual and Group Psychotherapy* (essay); and *Heal or Die: Psychotherapists Confront Nuclear Annihilation* (co-editor).

Declaration of Cosmic Cooperation by Thomas Hansen, Ph.D. Composed in 2004. Tom is a former mathematics education researcher, and he currently works as a musician, lecturer, activist, and author. His writings include: *Trying to Remember*; and *The Declaration of Cosmic Cooperation*. And his musical compositions include: *Remembering Peace* (CD); *Take a Chance* (CD); *UFO Oil* (CD); *Promise of Peace* (CD); and *Hiding 9-11* (CD). **www.CosmicCooperation.com**

CHAPTER FIVE: **Romantic Love**

L'Amour: The Soul in Love by Brenda Schaeffer, D.Min., M.A.L.P., C.A.S. Copyright 2009 by Brenda Schaeffer. Brenda is the founder of the Healthy Relationships clinic in Minnesota, and she is a practicing licensed psychologist and a certified sex addiction specialist. She is the former host of the radio show *It's All About Love*, and she also is a spiritual teacher, speaker, and international best-selling author: *Is It Love or Is It Addiction?; Love's Way: The Union of Body, Ego, Soul and Spirit; Loving Me Loving You; Signs of Healthy Love; Signs of Addictive Love; Power Plays; Seasons of the Heart; Love or Addiction? The Power of Teen Sex and Romance;* and *Helping Yourself Out of Love Addiction.* **www.LoveAddiction.com** & **www.ItsAllABoutLove.com**

The Shyness by Sharon Olds from *The Upswept Room*. Copyright 2002 by Sharon Olds. Reprinted by permission of the author and Alfred A. Knopf, a division of Random House, Inc. Sharon is a Professor of Creative Writing at New York University and an award winning poet whose credits include: the National Book Critics Circle Award; the T.S. Eliot Prize; the Lamont Poetry Prize; and the San Francisco Poetry Center Award. Her works include: *Satan Says; The One Girl at the Boys' Party; The Dead and the Living; The Victims; The Gold Cell; The Father; The Wellspring; Blood, Tin, Straw; The Unswept Room;* and *Strike Sparks: Selected Poems.* **www.Poets.org/solds**

Anatomy of a Loving Relationship by Allyson and Alex Grey. Edited by Robin and Stephen Larson. Copyright 2009 by Allyson and Alex Grey. Allyson and Alex are the founders of the Chapel of Sacred Mirrors in New York, a sanctuary for contemplation and encouraging the creative spirit. Alex also is a mystical painter, poet, and author: *CoSM: Chapel of Sacred Mirrors; Damanhur: Chapels of Humankind; CoSM: Journal of Visionary Culture;* and *CoSM the Movie* (DVD). www.CoSM.org

Third Force by Alex Grey. Copyright 2007 by Alex Grey. Reprinted by permission of the artist.

The Invitation by Oriah from *The Invitation*. Copyright 1999 by Oriah. Published by HarperOne. All rights reserved. Reprinted by permission of the author. Oriah is a spiritual facilitator, speaker and international best-selling author and poet: *What We Ache For: Creativity and the Unfolding of Your Soul; The Invitation; The Call: Discovering Why You Are Here; The Dance: Moving to the Deep Rhythms of Your Life;* and *Embracing Fear and Finding the Courage to Live Your Life*. www.Oriah.org

Heartwork in Human Relationships by Dale L. Goldstein, LCSW. Copyright 2009 by Dale L. Goldstein. Dale is the founder of the Heartwork Institute, Inc. in Rochester, NY. He is a couples' counselor, therapist, teacher, and author: *Heartwork: How to Get What You Really, REALLY Want;* and *Embracing Stress*(CD). www.AwakenTheHeart.org

Let Me Count the Ways by Pat. Copyright 2009 by The Oracle Institute.

CHAPTER SIX: **Love of Learning**

Fun for One by Robert "Cowboy Bob" Hardison. Copyright 2009 by Robert Hardison. Bob is an ex-rodeo champ, farrier, musician, cowboy philosopher, and poet. Bob's humble beginning at an orphanage has inspired many of his poems and drives his compassion for nature and Mother Earth spirituality. His poetry has been published in several periodicals, including: *Sidelines Magazine;* and *Great Meadows Polo Club Journal*.

True Education: A Love Affair of the Heart and Mind by Chris Mercogliano. Copyright 2009 by Chris Mercogliano. Chris was the Director of the Albany Free School in New York for 35 years. He is a columnist for *Encounter* magazine, an essayist, and an author: *In Defense of Childhood: Protecting Kids' Inner Wildness; How to Grow a School: Starting and Sustaining Schools that Work; Teaching the Restless: One School's Remarkable No-Ritalin Approach to Helping Children Learn and Succeed;* and *Making It Up as We Go Along: The Story of the Albany Free School*. www.ChrisMercogliano.com

The Fellowship of Books by Edgar Guest. From *When Day is Done*, 1921.

Loving Wisdom by Margaret Starbird. Copyright 2009 by Margaret Starbird. Margaret is a leading researcher into the true history of Mary Magdalene. She is the author of numerous related works, including: *The Woman with the Alabaster Jar: Mary Magdalene and the Holy Grail; The Goddess in the Gospels: Reclaiming*

the Sacred Feminine; Mary Magdalene: Bride in Exile; Magdalene's Lost Legacy: Symbolic Numbers and Sacred Union in Christianity; The Feminine Face of Christianity; and The Tarot Trumps and The Holy Grail.
www.MargaretStarbird.net

Truth Is God by Mahatma Gandhi from *The Writings of M. K. Gandhi*. Copyright 1986 by Navajivan Trust. Adapted from three previously published works:
1.   "Truth is God" from *All Men Are Brothers*, Chapter II on Religion and Truth.
2.   *"On Satya"* from *The Collected Works of M. K. Gandhi* (Vol. 44), Letter dated July 22, 1930.
3.   "On Seeking Truth" from *The Collected Works of M. K. Gandhi* (Vol. 6), Letter dated July 6, 1940.
Reprinted by permission of the Navajivan Trust.
www.NavajivanTrust.org

Sleepwalking Through the Apocalypse by William Van Dusen Wishard. Copyright 2009 by William Van Dusen Wishard. Van is the principal in WorldTrends Research and a recognized authority on the changes reshaping the global landscape. His presentations to Congressional leaders and business executives have been televised nationally by C-SPAN and NBC's "One on One" program, and his interviews with Voice of America have been broadcast worldwide. Formerly, he served as the assistant to the Secretary and Deputy Secretary of Commerce and in four administrations. He also has worked in over 25 countries as part of a NGO team focused on conflict resolution and nation building. He has written over 50 articles in journals such as: *The Christian Science Monitor; Japan Times; The Futurist;* and the World Business Academy's *Perspectives*. His latest book is entitled: *Between Two Ages: The 21st Century and the Crisis of Meaning*.
www.WorldTrendsResearch.com

CHAPTER SEVEN: **Love of the Arts**

The Seer by Alex Grey from *Art Psalms*. Copyright 2008 by Alex Grey. Reprinted by permission of CoSM Press.

Art, Pleasure, and Love by Christopher L.C.E. Witcombe, Ph.D. Copyright 2009 by Christopher L.C.E. Witcombe. Christopher is a Professor of Art History at Sweet Briar College and creator of *Art History Resources on the Web*. He is a video producer, lecturer, and author, whose works include: *Copyright in the Renaissance: Prints and the Privilegio in Sixteenth-Century Venice and Rome; Print Publishing in Sixteenth-Century Rome: Growth and Expansion, Rivalry and Murder; The Chapel of the Courtesan and the Quarrel of the Magdalens; Gregory XIII and the Accademia di San Luca; Perception and Visual Culture; Art History in a Minute* (video series); and *What Is a Feminist?* (video).
www.Witcombe.sbc.edu

Music and The Way by Patrick Bernard. Copyright 2009 by Patrick Bernard. With poetry from *Gitanjali* by Rabindranath Tagore, 1913. Patrick is an award-winning composer and the first Canadian to climb Billboard's New Age chart. He also is a spiritual teacher, author of *Music as Yoga, Discover the Healing Power of Sound*, and producer of devotional music, including: *Archangel Miracle* (CD); *Harmonic Healing* (CD); *Bhakti Yoga Mantra* (CD); *Angelic Presence* (CD); *Shamanic Medicine* (CD); *Spa Relaxation* (CD); *Love Divine* (CD); *Sonic Feng Shui* (CD); *Spiritus* (CD); *Chakra Celebration* (CD); and O*M Spiritual Sound Vibration* (CD). www.PatrickBernard.com

An Artist's Ode to Katrina by Alice Lovelace. Copyright 2009 by Alice Lovelace. Alice is co-founder of the Southern Collective of African American Writers and the lead staff organizer for U.S. Social Forum. She also is editor of *CRUX: A Conversation in Words and Images from South Africa to South USA* and *In Motion* magazine. Her honors include: City of Atlanta Mayor's Fellowship in the Arts; Fund for Southern Communities' Torchbearers Award; Project South Voice of the Movement Award; Georgia Writers Association's Lifetime Achievement Award; and the 2007 Democratic Socialists of America Frederick Douglas-Eugene Debs Award. She also works as a performer, playwright, author, and poet: *Remembering My Birth: New and Collected Poems; The Kitchen Survival Almanac; Black Coffee; Forever; The Citizen Artist: 20 Years of Art in the Public Arena;* and selections in *Black Poetry of the 80's from the Deep South; Up Town/On the Town; Atlanta Tribune; Drumvoices Revue; Catalyst Magazine;* and *Photography Quarterly.* www.AliceLovelace.com & www.InMotionMagazine.com

Art and Shifting Spiritual Paradigms by Adelheid M. Gealt, Ph.D. Copyright 2009 by Adelheid M. Gealt. Heidi is a Professor of Art History at Indiana University, Director of the Indiana University Art Museum, and Fellow of the National Endowment of the Arts. She also has written numerous books, including: *Art of the Western World: From Ancient Greece to Post-Modernism; Domenico Tiepolo: Master Draftsman; Domenico Tiepolo: A New Testament; Looking at Art: A Visitor's Guide to Museum Collections; Painters of the Golden Age: A Biographical Dictionary of 17th Century European Painting; Italian Portrait Drawings: 1400–1800 from North American Collections;* and *Masterworks from the Indiana University Art Museum.* www.Indiana.edu/~iuam

Resurrexit by Anselm Kiefer. Copyright 1973 by Anselm Kiefer. Reprinted by permission of Gagosian Gallery on behalf of the artist.

CHAPTER EIGHT: **Love of Self**

Eight Lessons on the Art of Self Love by First Lady Elena Moreno. Copyright 2009 by Elena Moreno. Elena is a spiritual leader who was named First Lady by Chief Leonard Crow Dog of the Lakota Nation. She is a lecturer, yoga instructor, doctor of Naturopathic medicine, and business woman. She is co-founder of Circulos in Washington, D.C, a nonprofit organization dedicated to spiritual growth through education, service, and the support of indigenous ways of life. She also is the founder of *The Empowerment Series,* an educational program for personal growth and spiritual development which is taught in the United States, Mexico, and Bolivia. A mother and grandmother, Elena lives with her husband of 38 years,

Chief Oscar Moreno, in Todos Santos, a small community on the Pacific coast of Baja, California Sur in Mexico. www.ElenaMoreno.com & www.Empowerment-Series.com & www.EmpowermentWeekly.com

Ain't I a Woman? by Sojourner Truth. A speech given at the Women's Rights Convention in Akron, Ohio, 1851. Published in the *Anti-Slavery Bugle*, edited by Marcus Robinson, 1851.

Finding Your Life Mission by Henry Reed, Ph.D. Copyright 2009 by Henry Reed. Known as the "Father of the Dreamwork Movement," Henry is the founder of the Creative Spirit Studios in Mouth of Wilson, VA, where he facilitates workshops and shares his "Daily Mandala" as a blog. He also is Director of the Edgar Cayce Institute for Intuitive Studies, a Professor of Transpersonal Studies at Atlantic University, and a former Assistant Professor of Psychology at Princeton University. His writing credits include: *Dream Medicine: Learning How We Can Get Help from Our Dreams; Dream Solutions: The Dream Quest Workbook; Awakening Your Psychic Powers; Mysteries of the Mind; Channeling Your Higher Self;* and *Your Intuitive Heart.* www.HenryReed.com

Primordial Meditation: The Way of the Sacred Heart by Tau Malachi. Copyright 2009 by Tau Malachi. Tau Malachi is a Gnostic Christian Bishop and *gnostic* lineage holder in the U.S. He is the founder of Ecclesia Pistis Sophia in California, with affiliated groups in Germany, South Africa, Australia, Canada, and Hong Kong. He also is a teacher, mentor, and author: *Living Gnosis: A Practical Guide to Gnostic Christianity; Gnosis of the Cosmic Christ: A Gnostic Christian Kabbalah; Gnostic Gospel of St. Thomas: Meditations on the Mystical Teachings;* and *St. Mary Magdalene: The Gnostic Tradition of the Holy Bride.* www.Sophian.org

The Saints Teresa: From Darkness to Dawn by Laurel. Copyright 2009 by The Oracle Institute. Inspired by three works:
1. Portions of a Letter to Father Picachy (July 3, 1959) from *Mother Teresa: Come Be My Light.* Edited by Brian Kolodiejchuk. Doubleday Broadway Publishing Group, 2007.
2. Excerpts from *The Story of a Soul* by Saint Thérèse of Lisieux. Translated by Thomas N. Taylor, Oates & Washbourne, Ltd., 1912.
3. Excerpts from *The Life of Saint Teresa of Jesus* by Saint Teresa of Avila. Translated by David Lewis, Thomas Baker Publishing Company, 1904.

Sisyphus and the Sudden Lightness by Stephen Dunn from *Local Visitations.* Copyright 2003 by Stephen Dunn. Reprinted by permission of the author and W.W. Norton & Company, Inc. Stephen is a Distinguished Professor of Creative Writing at the Richard Stockton College of New Jersey and a Pulitzer Prize winning poet. His other credits include: the Academy Award for Literature; the James Wright Prize; and fellowships from the National Endowments for the Arts and the New Jersey State Council on the Arts. His books of poetry include: *Everything Else in the World; Local Visitations; Different Hours; A Circus of Needs; New and Selected Poems: 1974–1994; Landscape at the End of the Century; Loosestrife; Between Angels; Local Time; Not Dancing;* and *Work and Love.* www.StephenDunnPoet.com

CHAPTER NINE: **Love of Freedom**

Freedom from Fear by Aung San Suu Kyi, Ph.D. from *Freedom from Fear and Other Writings*. Foreword by Vaclav Havel, translated by Michael Aris. Copyright 1991, 1995 by Aung San Suu Kyi and Michael Aris. Reprinted by permission of Viking Penguin, a division of Penguin Group (USA), Inc. Daw Aung San is the recipient of numerous honors, including: the Nobel Peace Prize in 1991; the Sakharov Prize for Freedom in 1991; the Presidential Medal of Freedom in 2000; and the Congressional Gold Medal in 2008. She is the founder of the National League for Democracy in Myanmar, and their rightfully elected Prime Minister. Due to a military coup, she has been under house arrest almost continuously since 1989. She is the author of many books and articles, including: *Letters from Burma; The Voice of Hope; Freedom from Fear and Other Writings; Burma's Revolution of the Spirit: The Struggle for Democratic Freedom and Dignity; Burma and India: Some Aspects of Intellectual Life Under Colonialism;* and *Letter to Daniel: Dispatches of the Heart*. www.DASSK.com & www.Freedom-Now.org

Essay on Slavery by Robert Eisenman, Ph.D. from *The New Jerusalem*. Copyright 2007 by Robert Eisenman. Reprinted by permission of the author. Robert is a Professor Emeritus of Middle Eastern Religions and Archeology, and Director of the Institute for Judeo-Christian Origins at California State University at Long Beach. He is a Fellow at the Albright Institute of Archaeological Research in Jerusalem, an author, and a translator of *The Dead Sea Scrolls*. His numerous works include: *James the Brother of Jesus: The Key to Unlocking the Secrets of Early Christianity and the Dead Sea Scrolls; The New Testament Code: The Cup of the Lord, the Damascus Covenant, and the Blood of Christ; The Dead Sea Scrolls and the First Christians; Islamic Law in Palestine and Israel: A History of the Survival of Tanzimat and Shari'ah; The Dead Sea Scrolls Uncovered; The Facsimile Edition of the Dead Sea Scrolls* (editor); and *The New Jerusalem*. www.RobertEisenman.com

The Three Lost Books of Peace by Maxine Hong Kingston. Copyright 2009 by Maxine Hong Kingston. Adapted from *The Fifth Book of Peace*. Copyright 2003 by Maxine Hong Kingston. Reprinted by permission of the author and Alfred A. Knopf, a division of Random House, Inc. Maxine is a Professor Emeritus of English at the University of California Berkeley and the recipient of numerous honors, including the National Humanities Medal from President Bill Clinton, and the National Book Critics Award. She also is a veterans' rights and peace activist, a lecturer, and an award winning author: *The Woman Warrior: Memoirs of a Girlhood Among Ghosts; China Men; Through the Black Curtain; Tripmaster Monkey: His Fake Book; To Be the Poet; The Fifth Book of Peace;* and *Veterans of War, Veterans of Peace*.

Address to a Christian Nation by Chief Red Jacket. A speech given by the Seneca Chief in 1805. Published in *Biography and History of the Indians of North America* by Samuel G. Drake, 1848.

Remembering Freedom by Thomas Hansen, Ph.D. Copyright 2009 by Thomas Hansen. Adapted from *Trying to Remember*. Copyright 1995 by Thomas Hansen.

The Tao of Love by W. Cliff Kayser, III, M.S., SPHR, PCC. Copyright 2009 by W. Cliff Kayser, III. Cliff is the founder of Xperience, an organizational development, HR consulting, and executive coaching firm located in Washington, D.C., with retreat facilities located in West Virginia. He also is authoring a new interpretation of *The Tao* entitled: *Cliff's Notes on The Tao Te Ching: A Poetic Reinterpretation of Lao Tzu's Masterpiece.* **www.XperienceIt.com**

I Have No Relations by Mirabai. From *Hindu Mysticism* by S.N. Dasgupta, Ph.D. Open Court Publishing Co., 1927.

Liberation of the Soul by Andrew Cohen. Copyright 2009 by Andrew Cohen. Adapted from *Embracing Heaven & Earth.* Copyright 2000 by Moksha Press. Andrew is the founder of the EnlightenNext organization in Lenox, MA, and editor of *EnlightenNext* magazine. He also is a spiritual teacher, world-wide lecturer, and international author: *Living Enlightenment: A Call for Evolution Beyond Ego; Enlightenment Is a Secret; Who Am I and How Shall I Live?; In Defense of the Guru Principle; My Master Is My Self; Freedom Has No History; Autobiography of An Awakening; Embracing Heaven & Earth; An Unconditional Relationship to Life;* and *The Challenge of Enlightenment.* **www.EnlightenNext.org**

CHAPTER TEN: **Unconditional Love**

The Sputtering Buts: Bear-Hugging the Whole Enchilada by Chief Michael Hull, J.D. Copyright 2009 by Michael Hull. Mike is the founder of Grace Sanctuary in Texas and the first white man to be recognized as a Sun Dance Chief by Lakota Chief Leonard Crow Dog (spiritual leader of the American Indian Movement and Sun Dance Chief to 189 Native American tribes). Mike also is a practicing attorney and the author of: *Sun Dancing: A Spiritual Journey on the Red Road;* and *From the Ashes.* **www.GraceSanctuary.com**

The Metta Sutta: The Buddha's Teaching on Love by Karen Lang, Ph.D. Copyright 2009 by Karen Lang. Karen is Director of the Center for South Asian Studies and a Professor of Religious Studies at the University of Virginia. She also is the three-time recipient of the Sesquicentennial Award. Her writing credits include: *Aryadeva's Catuhsataka: On the Bodhisattva's Cultivation of Merit and Knowledge; Four Illusions: Candrakirti's Advice for Travelers on the Bodhisattva Path;* and *Catuhsataka: 400 Verse uber den Weg zur Erleuchtung.*

Good News for All People by Brian McLaren. Copyright 2009 by Brian McLaren. Brian is a leader of the Emerging Church Movement and recognized by *Time Magazine* as one of the 25 most influential evangelicals in America. He is the founding pastor of Cedar Ridge Community Church, co-founder of Red Letter Christians, and a lecturer, musician, and author of numerous books, including: *Finding Our Way Again; Everything Must Change: Jesus, Global Crisis, and a Revolution of Hope; The Voice of Luke; The Voice of Acts: The Dust Off Their Feet; The Church on the Other Side: Doing Ministry in the Postmodern Matrix; The Secret Message of Jesus; A Generous Orthodoxy; A New Kind of Christian; The Last Word and the Word After That; Finding Faith: A Search for What Makes Sense;* and *Church in Emerging Culture: Five Perspectives.* **www.BrianMcLaren.net**

Why Are There So Many Religions? by Barbara Talley. Copyright 2009 by Barbara Talley. Barbara is an entrepreneur, poet, speaker, and all-round dynamo. She is a member of the Bahá'i Faith, which promotes a belief in one God, one race, and one continually unfolding religion. She serves humanity by inspiring hope, promoting unity, and encouraging the search for truth. Her programs and books focus on the preciousness of human life, the importance of Love, and the obligation to embrace unity in diversity. Her writing credits include: *Miner Miracles; E-RACE: Poetry to Help Erase Race; On Track, On Fire, and On Purpose; Talley-up: The Excitement of Value Based Living;* and *Super Woman Doesn't Live Here Anymore.* www.ThePoetSpeaks.com

The Religion of Love by Barbro Karlen. Copyright 2009 by Barbro Karlen. Barbro is an internationally acclaimed poet and author. Her works include: *And the Wolves Howled: Fragments of Two Lifetimes; Man on Earth: Poems and Essays;* and *When the Storm Comes: A Moment in the Blossom Kingdom.*

A Better Tomorrow: Community Based on Unconditional Love by John Dennison, J.D. Copyright 2009 by John Dennison. John is a facilitator, speaker, and author. He also is a practicing attorney in the Florida law firm of Dennison & Dennison, P.A., and co-founder of Peace Options, a holistic firm offering counseling, written resources, classes, and networking. His writing credits include: *Whispers in the Silence: Living by the Light of Your Soul;* and *The Art of Going Your Way* (CD). www.PeaceOptions.com & www.JohnDennison.com

Gift of Love, Luminous Calling: Here I Am to Confuse Your Heart by Oberto "Falco" Airaudi. Translated by Elaine Baxendale and edited by Esperide Ananas. Copyright 2009 by Oberto Airaudi. Falco is the founder and spiritual leader of The Federation of Damanhur in Italy, an eco-society that received the United Nations sustainability award in 2005. Falco also is a world-renowned philosopher, healer, teacher, artist, and author: *The Book of Synchronicity; Tales from Damanhur; Dying to Learn; Reborn to Live; Seven Scarlet Doors; Constitution of the Federation of Damanhur; Damanhur* magazine; *Damanhur: Temples of Humankind; Damanhur: A Journey into the Temples* (DVD); *Damanhur for a Culture of Peace* (DVD); and *Bral Talej* (Divination Cards). www.Damanhur.com

O Brother! by Kabir. From *Songs of Kabir* by Rabindranath Tagore. The Macmillan Co., 1915.

CHAPTER ELEVEN: **Love of God**

Ten Guidelines to Enlightenment by Swami Beyondananda. Copyright 1996, 2009 by Steven Bhaerman. Steve is an author, comedian, performer, and co-founder of *Pathways Magazine.* His comedic work includes: *Swami for Precedent: A 7-step Plan to Heal the Body Politic and Cure Electile Dysfunction; Driving Your Own Karma: Swami Beyondananda's Tourguide to Enlightenment; Healing the Body Politic* (DVD); *Don't Squeeze the Shaman* (CD); and *Drive Your Karma: Curb Your Dogma* (CD). On the serious side, Steve is co-author with Bruce Lipton of a book entitled: *Spontaneous Evolution: Our Positive Future and a Way to Get There from Here.* www.WakeUpLaughing.com

Angel ® Cards by InnerLinks Associates. Copyright 1981 by Joy Drake and Kathy Tyler. *Humour* card reprinted by permission of InnerLinks Associates. www.InnerLinks.com

Our Love for God: How It Expands as We Do by P.M.H. Atwater, L.H.D. Copyright 2009 by P.M.H. Atwater. P.M.H. is one of the original researchers into the near-death experience. She also is an international lecturer and author of many books, including: *The Big Book of Near Death Experiences; Future Memory; Beyond the Light; Beyond the Indigo Children; The New Children and Near Death Experiences; The Complete Idiot's Guide to Near Death Experiences; Coming Back To Life; Children of the New Millennium;* and *We Live Forever: The Real Truth About Death.* www.pmhAtwater.com

Where Is God? by Jalaluddin Rumi. From *Selected Poems from the Divani Shamsi Tabriz,* edited and translated by R.A. Nicholson, 1898.

Love, Christ Mind, and the God State by Penny Kelly. Copyright 2009 by Penny Kelly. Penny is the founder of Lily Hill Farm and Learning Center in southwest Michigan. She is a Naturopathic physician with a degree from Clayton College, and she also has a degree in Humanistic Studies from Wayne State University. Penny is a spiritual teacher and author of numerous books, including: *The Evolving Human; The Elves of Lily Hill Farm; Robes: A Book of Coming Changes; From the Soil to the Stomach;* and *Consciousness and Energy.* www.PennyKelly.com

God by Kahlil Gibran. From *The Madman* by Kahlil Gibran. Knopf Publishing Co., 1918.

God Has a Dream by Archbishop Desmond Tutu. Copyright 2009 by Desmond Tutu. Adapted from *God Has a Dream: A Vision of Hope for Our Time.* Copyright 2004 by Desmond Tutu. Reprinted by permission of the author and Doubleday, a division of Random House, Inc. Archbishop Tutu is the Anglican Archbishop Emeritus of Cape Town and Primate of the Anglican Church of South Africa. He is the recipient of many honors, including: the 1984 Nobel Peace Prize; the Albert Schweitzer Prize for Humanitarianism; the Magubela Prize for Liberty; the King Hussein Prize; the Sydney Peace Prize; and the Gandhi Peace Prize. After the fall of Apartheid, Archbishop Tutu chaired the Truth and Reconciliation Commission, and he is the patron of the Desmond Tutu Peace Foundation, Desmond Tutu Educational Trust, and Tutu Foundation for Development and Relief in Southern Africa. He also is Chairperson of The Elders, a wisdom group comprised of retired world leaders. He has authored volumes of speeches, sermons, essays, and books, including: *The Rainbow People of God: The Making of a Peaceful Revolution; God Has a Dream: A Vision of Hope for Our Time; An African Prayerbook; The Essential Desmond Tutu; No Future Without Forgiveness;* and a new children's book entitled *God's Dream.* www.Tutu.org & www.TutuFoundation-USA.org & www.TheElders.org

The Land of Heaven, a Caribou Inuit Thealogy myth. From *Observations on the Intellectual Culture of the Caribou Eskimos* by Knud Rasmussen, 1930.

An Act for Establishing Religious Freedom

Authored by Thomas Jefferson in 1777
Adopted by the Virginia General Assembly in 1786

The Oracle Institute Mission Statement

As adapted from Virginia Code Section 57–1

Whereas, the Almighty hath created the mind free; and

Whereas, all attempts to influence mankind tend only to beget habits of hypocrisy and meanness and are a departure from the plan of the Holy Author of our existence who, being the Source of body, mind, and spirit, yet chose not to undermine freedom by coercions thereon; and

Whereas, the impious presumption of legislators and rulers, civil as well as ecclesiastical, who, being themselves fallible and uninspired men, have assumed dominion over the faith of others, setting up their own opinions and modes of thinking as the only true and infallible views, have established and maintained false religions over the greatest part of the world, thereby depriving mankind of comfortable liberty and spiritual freedom; and

Whereas, our civil rights have no dependence on our religious opinions any more than our opinions in physics or geometry; and

Whereas, Truth is great and will prevail if left to herself as the proper and sufficient antagonist to error and has nothing to fear from conflict unless, by human interposition, Truth is disarmed of her natural weapons - free argument and debate; errors ceasing to be dangerous when Truth is permitted freely to contradict them.

Now Therefore, The Oracle Institute is free to declare and does hereby declare:

(i)   That the purest faith is based in **Truth,** which sets us free;

(ii) That the strongest force in the Universe is **Love,** which makes us whole; and

(iii) That the guiding power of God is **Light,** which leads us toward one shared destiny.

To Wit, the Mission of The Oracle Institute shall be to serve as an Advocate for Enlightenment and a Vanguard for Spiritual Evolution.

THE ORACLE INSTITUTE

An Advocate for Enlightenment and a Vanguard for Spiritual Evolution

THE TRUTH:

The founders of The Oracle Institute are gravely concerned that the greatest crisis currently facing mankind is the resurgence of religious fundamentalism and the divisive nature of the five primary religions: Hinduism, Judaism, Buddhism, Christianity, and Islam. We believe that the time has come for humanity to shed archaic belief systems about the Supreme Being and acknowledge that the only path to God is spiritual enlightenment.

THE LOVE:

The *Saddha* process of soul growth, which is described in this work, accomplishes this goal by encouraging spiritual freedom and promoting private journeys of faith. Such an introspective path leads the soul to seek perfection and to perform compassionate acts for the benefit of others. By transforming the self and acknowledging a connection to everyone and everything, we prepare ourselves to enter a new spiritual paradigm.

THE LIGHT:

Many people are now ready to manifest the Fifth Spiritual Paradigm – the era of abundance, peace, and harmony foretold by the prophets of every religion and the elders of every indigenous culture. To that end, The Oracle Institute offers educational books, spirituality classes, and holistic products that are donated by authors and artists who wish to foster this next phase of our collective spiritual evolution.

We invite you to join us on our journey of Truth, Love, and Light

Donations may be made to:

THE ORACLE INSTITUTE
a 501(c)(3) educational charity
P.O. Box 368
Hamilton, VA 20159
www.TheOracleInstitute.org
(540)882-9252

**All donations and proceeds from our books and classes are used
to further our educational mission and to build
a sustainable spiritual community in Independence, Virginia.**